DINING WITH TERRORISTS

PHIL REES

DINING WITH TERRORISTS

MEETINGS WITH THE WORLD'S MOST WANTED MILITANTS

MACMILLAN

First published 2005 by Macmillan
an imprint of Pan Macmillan Ltd
Pan Macmillan, 20 New Wharf Road, London N1 9RR
Basingstoke and Oxford
Associated companies throughout the world
www.panmacmillan.com

ISBN 1 4050 4716 X

1 3 5 7 9 8 6 4 2

A CIP catalogue record for this book is available from
the British Library.

Typeset by SetSystems Ltd, Saffron Walden, Essex
Printed and bound in Great Britain by
Mackays of Chatham plc, Chatham, Kent

TO CARRIE

who lived through it

ACKNOWLEDGEMENTS

I would like to thank the often-unheralded local translators and researchers without whose help foreign correspondents would achieve little and this book would not have been written. Apart from those mentioned in the text, I am deeply indebted to the journalism and judgements provided by Dragan Čičič, Suzana Vasiljević, Alberto Letona, Hala El Kara, Roya Kashefi, Sanjay Sethi, Kumi Samuel, Sadia Ayata, Rollie Hudson, Christine Chameau, Men Kimseng, Chanel Khan, Israel Goldvicht, Nizar Abdul, Jane Logan, Nihiya Kawasmi and Kanthi Andayani. Several people have helped read and offer suggestions to improve the script, amongst them Michael Vatikiotis, Nicky Singh, Ivan Gonzales, Philip Luther from *Amnesty International*, as well as Dragan, Susana and Alberto. Any errors that may have slipped through are, of course, mine.

I owe gratitude to my editors at the BBC, who have encouraged and allowed me the opportunities to dine with terrorists: Fiona Stourton, John Mahoney, John Morrison, Keith Bowers, Mark Damazer and Helen Boaden, as well as George Carey from Mentorn. I also owe my thanks to the many colleagues I have worked alongside, with a special acknowledgement to the team with whom I spent four enjoyable years: Brian Barron, Eric Thirer and Fred Scott. I am grateful to Nick Dodd for finding tapes that I had lost along the years. I also want to thank my literary agent, Araminta Whitley, for backing the project and my editor at Macmillan, Natasha Martin, who showed remarkable patience as the scripts arrived well beyond their deadlines. I also must thank my partner, Cholay, for her patience, as she watched me huddled over the computer during the many evenings that we would otherwise have spent together.

Much of the content of the book is derived from off-the-record conversations, and I have spoken to many of those involved in order to ensure that they are happy that their comments are made public. On a tiny number of occasions there was hesitation and, in order not to offend, I have made the identity of these contributors more general than I would have otherwise. Another felt that remarks made some years ago would embarrass him in his present job. I have changed his name and one or two facts surrounding his identity but the substance of his argument has been recorded faithfully. I apologize to anyone I have been unable to contact and hope that they understand that they are part of this book because of the fascinating story that they had to tell.

PHIL REES *2004*

Contents

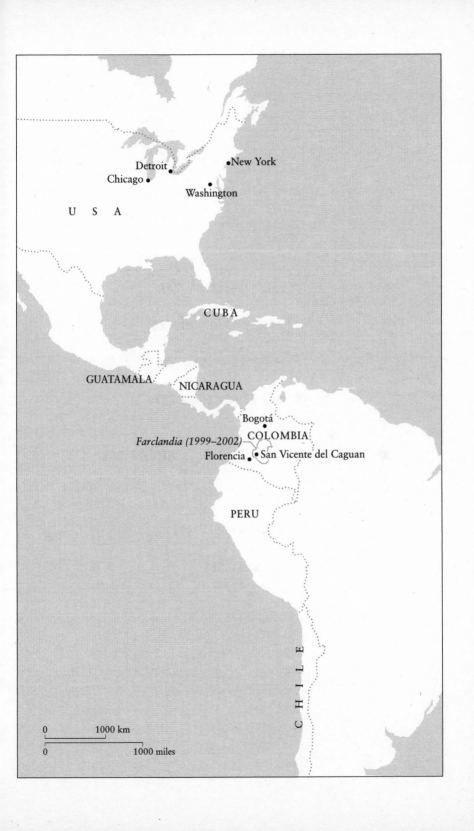

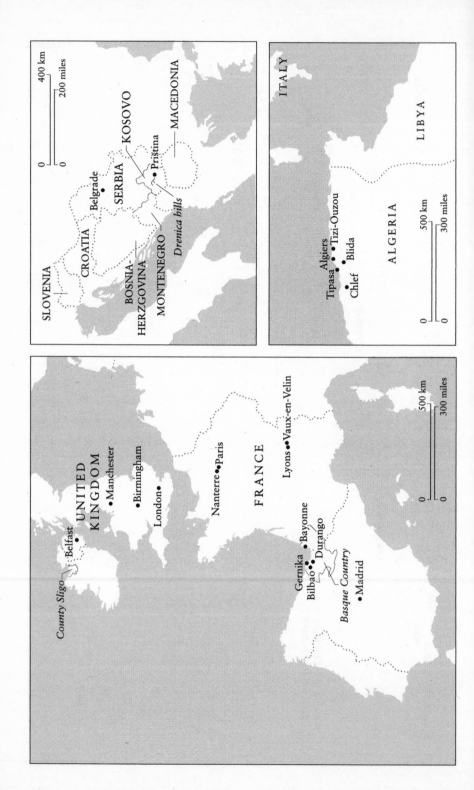

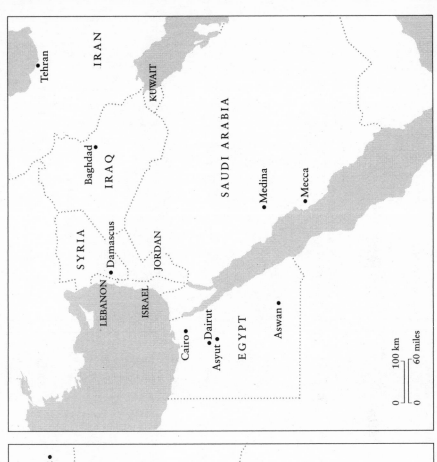

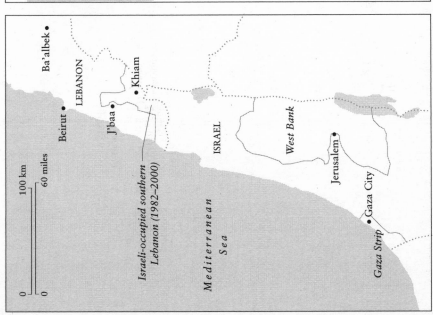

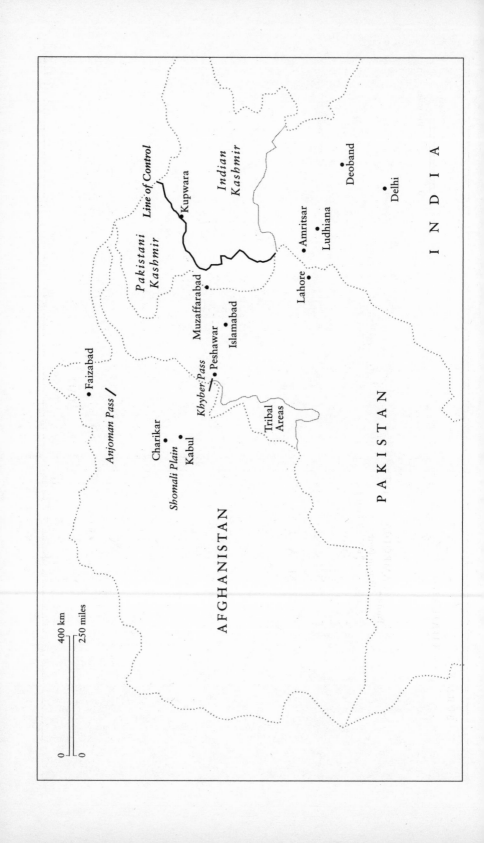

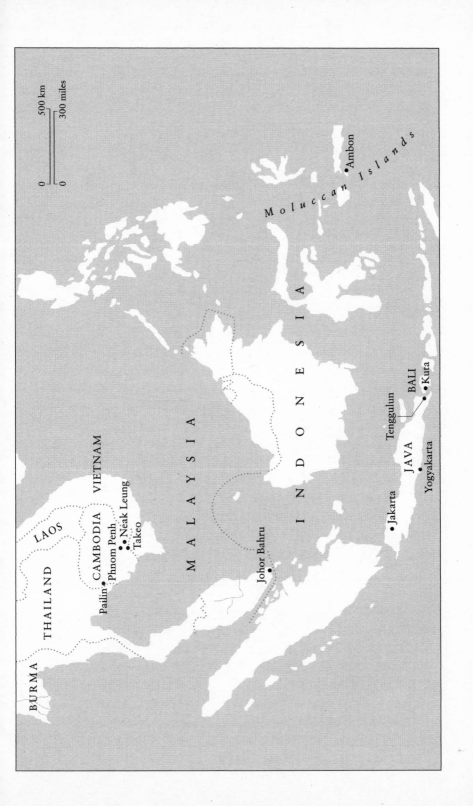

INTRODUCTION

'The war on terror is not a figure of speech.
It is an inescapable calling of our generation.'
George W. Bush, March 2003

This is the story of a personal odyssey that began a quarter of a century ago. I was visiting Ireland on the day that the Irish Republican Army had one of its boldest and bloodiest triumphs. In County Sligo, on the north-west coast of the island, Lord Mountbatten and his fourteen-year-old grandson were blown up on their boat while on holiday. Shortly afterwards, near a picturesque lough by the Irish Sea, eighteen British soldiers were killed during a well-planned and ruthless ambush. On that balmy August evening, I went to a pub in a small, unremarkable town that snuggles against the border with Northern Ireland. It was a shocking and bewildering experience. I watched men and women, young and old, as well as children, sing, dance and drink to the success of the IRA. The killers were hailed as 'brave volunteers' struggling with guns and bombs to unify Ireland. My only knowledge of the IRA was from descriptions in British newspapers. The IRA were terrorists, evil and brutal men who should be despised. I wondered how this town of friendly and otherwise normal-looking people could react in celebration to such atrocity. I set off on a detective journey that has shadowed my career like a guilty secret. I began a search for the meaning of a word. 'Terrorist'.

After my visit to Ireland, I went on to cover conflicts in the violent corners of the earth, meeting men and woman who were labelled terrorists by their foes. My journeys have taken me from Belfast to

Bilbao, from Kashmir to Cairo, from Bali to Baghdad. I have shared a bottle of rum with Marxist guerrillas in their hideaways in the jungles of Colombia. I have debated politics with gunmen over a cup of tea in Sri Lanka. During an intriguing rendezvous, I met one of the men involved in the kidnapping of Terry Waite in Lebanon. One of my most dangerous assignments was a trip to camps run by Islamic extremists in Algeria; the armed groups there had become notorious for slitting the throats of foreigners.

While I dined and drank with them, I looked in their eyes and wondered why they had turned to violence. I became fascinated by what lay behind the hoods and masks. I wanted to peer beyond the usual architecture of the news reports, the unshaven fanatics shouting hatred, the blurred videos justifying violence, the drawings by a court artist upon conviction.

On one level, everybody knows what it means to be a 'terrorist'. It is the man who plants a bomb in a crowded street; it is the masked hijacker who commandeers an airliner; it is the hostage-taker who threatens to kill his captives unless his demands are met. At its root, the type of violence often called 'terrorism' is a very old method of fighting. It's a form of rebellion by people who are stateless or feel oppressed and use non-standard military tactics against more powerful, established governments when they see no other way of resisting them. Today's military analysts describe it as 'asymmetric warfare'. It was once called guerrilla warfare in honour of Spanish fighters who used unconventional methods to attack Napoleon's forces during the Peninsular War at the start of the nineteenth century. Spanish soldiers discarded their uniforms and avoided formal confrontations with the French army. But the word 'guerrilla' is not interchangeable with 'terrorist'. If 'terrorism' simply described a technical mode of warfare, this book would not have been written.

For a word that's used so freely, it is remarkable how difficult it's been for international agencies or academics to determine accurately who is a 'terrorist'. The United Nations spent seventeen years trying to draw up a definition that its members would all accept. It failed. At one time, 'terrorism' was too hysterical a term to be included in serious commentary. It was part of the armoury of the committed, of politicians, propagandists and preachers. Most journalists, scholars and impartial witnesses accepted the adage that 'one man's terrorist is another man's freedom fighter'.

In 1980, an American newspaper, the *Christian Science Monitor*, carried an editorial under the headline: 'Terrorist' – a bomb-thrower of a word. 'Terrorist promises to be a catch-all word of the '80s,' it declared before warning: 'It is a term that bears care in its usage, not only because it provides so tempting a way to disparage an enemy but because it is one of those words (like "Fire!" in a crowded theatre) that automatically creates panic and thus clears the path for extreme acts of one's own.'

Two decades later, any residue of caution in the usage of 'terrorism' was buried in the wreckage of the World Trade Center. After September 11th, the term took on a new significance and found its way into everyday language with a meaning that was both imprecise and yet easily understood. To the Western public, terrorism became a symbol of the great challenge to its civilization.

If the twentieth century taught us anything about language, it is that words have consequences. They have the power to persuade, encourage and enrage. They provide a compass that directs a nation to war and soldiers to their death. George Orwell's dystopian novel *Nineteen Eighty-Four* exposed the link between language and political control. He also showed how the ideologies of the last century contorted words to serve their political interests. Orwell would surely recognize that in the political vocabulary of the twenty-first century, there are few words that possess the emotional power of 'terrorism'.

For nearly twenty-five years after I drank Guinness with sympathizers of the IRA in Ireland, I have tried to grab hold of the meaning of 'terrorism'; but like a fly that cannot be swatted, a generally accepted understanding has continued to elude me. I hope to indicate in the following chapters why I have never described the perpetrators of political violence as 'terrorists', despite the increasing usage of the term by politicians and commentators as well as the general public.

There are those who believe that a journey to meet men and women accused of terrorism, to shake hands, sit and eat with them, is akin to hitching a ride with the devil and becoming an apologist for the worst kind of violence known to mankind. By reporting the views of 'terrorists', one is legitimizing their violence and implying a moral equivalence between terrorism and those combating it. Rudolf Giuliani, the former Mayor of New York, declared after September 11th: 'Those who practise terrorism lose any right to have their cause understood. We're right, they're wrong. It's as simple as that.'

I take a different view; that the public should be informed about the causes of violence and decide for themselves who is right and who is wrong. Only by examining the origins of violence can one begin to deal with its causes. And of course, even those who wish to silence the voices of 'terrorists' need to define adequately what is 'terrorism'.

Within a month of the attacks on New York and Washington, I was sitting in a trench in Afghanistan during the first battle in the 'war on terror'. I watched American bombs decimate the enemy forces of the Taliban and wondered how the overwhelming military strength of the United States would be used in this conflict without boundaries. America's military superiority is now greater than that of any super-power since the Roman Empire, and the 'war on terror' generated the first national security strategy to reflect this dominance: the doctrine of pre-emptive military action.

Armed groups involved in local conflicts from every violent pocket of our planet have been listed as terrorist organizations and are now at war with the United States. How will this reconfigure our world? Will it become a safer and freer place?

During the invasion of Iraq, Brigadier General Vincent Brooks, the expressionless, hangdog face of the American military, described Saddam Hussein's regime as 'akin to global terrorism'. In his address marking the end of the invasion, President Bush declared: 'The Battle of Iraq is one victory in a war on terror that began on September 11th 2001, and still goes on.' The failure of the US administration to define 'terrorism' allowed him to equate the Iraqi regime with 'global terrorism' despite the lack of any evidence linking Saddam Hussein to al-Qa'eda. The war continued in Iraq but the coalition forces were no longer confronting a conventional army. Iraqis opposed to the American-led occupation planted bombs and kidnapped and mur-dered Westerners; the enemy had become 'terrorists' by their direct actions rather than simply their affiliations. Occasionally they were described as 'insurgents' by military spokesmen in order to differentiate rebellious Iraqis from foreign fighters, who were called 'international terrorists'. Usually, the coalition used the terms interchangeably, with no clear explanation of why one attack was described as terrorism while another was not. As Robert Fisk wryly observed in the *Independent*, 'Surely, if you could leap from being a terrorist to an insurgent, then with a little hop, skip and a jump, you could become a "freedom-fighter".'

The United States has placed 'terrorism' at the epicentre of a seismic shift that is reshaping the globe. The September 11th attacks have become the historical equivalent of the assassination of Habsburg Archduke Franz Ferdinand in 1914. On that sunny June day in Sarajevo, a young Serb called Gavrilo Princip pulled the trigger of a pistol and set in motion a chain of events that culminated in the First World War. Our international system is fissuring, as did the nine-teenth-century world order on the muddy fields of Flanders.

While the vast military power of the United States and its allies confronts an enemy called 'terror', shouldn't we at least know exactly *who is a terrorist?*

1 / A WAR ON WHAT?

'All terrorists, at the invitation of the government,
end up with drinks at the Dorchester.'
Hugh Gaitskell, former British Labour Party leader

The bar at Bush House was tucked away in a basement amid the narrow corridors and brown double doors that formed the arteries of the London home of BBC World Service. At lunchtime it filled with women in bright saris and men in traditional West African robes. I was introduced to Boris from the Russian service; he gave me a firm handshake as he ordered a vodka. Nearby, I joined colleagues who were having an impassioned discussion about the meaning of 'terrorism'. It was a debate that divided journalists at Bush House and sparked a crisis of conscience during the aftermath of September 11th.

While many media organizations seem obliged to reinvent the wheel each day, the World Service has stuck to its traditions. It has had more to lose: the high esteem and phenomenal trust that the BBC's journalism enjoys throughout the world. Bush House is an island of journalistic integrity, detached from the pressures of audience figures, advertising revenues and focus groups that have trimmed the edges of independent journalism elsewhere. Most news channels are now owned by large corporate entertainment conglomerates. Newsrooms are silver, chrome and glass with multiple television monitors lining the walls, citadels of advances in communication technology. News has become a celebration of the instant transmission of information around the world. In this often-frenzied environment, there is little appetite for debating the usage of a word.

Bush House reflected the values of a more contemplative epoch. The BBC had broadcast its first programmes for listeners abroad in 1932 on what was then called the Empire Service, which aimed to bring together the different peoples of the world under British dominion. In the Second World War, as part of the war effort, it moved into 'information'. The office of Z Organisation, a part of the British Secret Service, soon burrowed into one of Bush House's corridors. George Orwell climbed its marble steps to write a weekly political commentary designed to counter Japanese and German propaganda. It is perhaps not surprising that his successors at the World Service understand better than most the importance of political language.

It has been suggested that Orwell's wartime work for the BBC provided him with the inspiration for *Nineteen Eighty-Four*. At that time, British intelligence officers directed him to compose texts that corrected the contortions of enemy broadcasts. During the Second World War, radio broadcasting was in the service of governments, giving rise to Orwell's notion of Newspeak, the truth-denying language of Big Brother.

The BBC's reputation for fairness grew as journalists in Bush House severed day-to-day relations with their financial masters in the Foreign Office. Its stated policy of impartiality fits well with my belief that the journalist's role is to observe and record the first draft of history. Writers at Bush House are, however, asked to refer to editorial guidelines, which can be viewed on their computers. The instruction on the usage of 'terrorism' is explicit: 'We do not label people, groups or acts as terrorist . . . people's idea of what constitutes terrorism is affected by their sympathy with the aims of the group concerned and their proximity to the events described. Even though there is a dictionary definition of terrorism, there is no doubt that it is nearly always used as a political label.'

On September 11th, the BBC World Service repeatedly described the events in New York and Washington as 'acts of terrorism' or 'terrorist attacks'. It was a day that shook the world and catapulted the usually sober routine of newsgathering at Bush House into a cauldron of anger, shock and, at times, despair. There was the drama of witnessing horror, close up and live on television; the sweat and tears of the subsequent days, often working without sleep, mesmerized by accounts of anguish and heroism.

A few days later an internal memo from a newsroom editor was circulated reminding staff that 'terrorist' was a banned word unless it was in the mouth of someone else. The tone was sympathetic. 'I personally feel that the confusion and sheer scale of the destruction and the loss of innocent lives made it almost impossible not to use this word to explain what was going on,' he wrote. The memo also highlighted the problem of remaining impartial when most of the Western media was not. 'This incident seems to show the difficulties in the policy which was based on avoiding seeming to take sides. The heat of the battle was not the time to have a huge debate about the policy so I suggest we return to the status quo.'

This gentle reminder of Bush House's policy on 'terrorism' suddenly ignited outrage amongst some newsroom staff. One reporter recalled thinking that the memo was a spoof made in poor taste, a week after the world had witnessed 'terrorism as never before'. 'If my managers think that hijacking a plane and killing three thousand innocent civilians isn't terrorism, we are talking a difficult version of English,' he spat.

A middle-ranking manager, aware of the need to abide by the policy, sighed, 'You can't call the men who flew the planes into the World Trade Center freedom fighters. No one would claim that. There are no two points of view. They are terrorists and should be called terrorists.' A newsroom writer chipped in, arguing that those sentiments might apply to al-Qa'eda, but not to members of the Tamil Tigers, a militant organization that has fought for two decades for an independent Tamil homeland on the island of Sri Lanka. 'We have a Tamil-language service,' he warned. 'We regularly interview the Tamil Tigers' spokesman. How can we introduce him as a terrorist before he comes on air?'

A flurry of emails followed. One reporter, while admitting that he was physically and emotionally drained, wrote 'never in my 13 years at the BBC have I read such politically correct bollocks' as the memo from the news editor. His riposte continued: 'I hope that in the fall out from this week, the World Service can actually come into the real world'.

The manager with day-to-day responsibility for the use of 'terrorism' on the World Service had an office four floors above the bar. Mary Hockaday was the head of the news and current affairs output and was candid about the problem. 'September 11th has thrown this discussion into relief. It has made the issue a preoccupation,' she told me. 'There is no denial of the concept of terrorism. But we are uneasy about labelling groups as terrorists. There are plenty of ways of describing the aims of militant organizations and the methods they employ without being drawn into the thorny issue of who is a terrorist.' She said that the word is often used in a lazy, clichéd manner. 'It is also part of the rhetorical armoury of one president and his view of the world,' she cautioned. Mary insists that there is no categorical ban on the usage of 'terrorism' but finds very few practical occasions to recommend a journalist to use it: 'We are committed to avoid the word.'

During the coverage of a violent attack that most of the world referred to as terrorism, BBC reporters began a sinuous dance with language. Jonathan Head, the BBC's former South-East Asia Correspondent, was one of the first journalists to reach the Indonesian island of Bali after bombs slaughtered 202 revellers at a pub and nightclub in October 2002. 'I did not report Bali as a terrorist attack,' he told me in his office in Bangkok. 'I would also not call al-Qa'eda members terrorists.'

Jonathan bursts with thoughts on a topic that he has considered at some length. 'Terrorism as a concept is in the public domain and we cannot ignore that. I have attended conferences on terrorism. It is unsustainable not to use the word. So I use it in the general sense but do not refer to specific groups as terrorists.' His ideas gush at a machine-gun pace, yet he readily admits an inconsistency at the heart of his argument. 'I accept that if I report that the authorities in Indonesia are trying to prevent further terrorist attacks, it implies that the Bali bombing *was* a terrorist attack. And if one describes an attack as terrorism, its perpetrators must be terrorists. So I would be inferring [sic] that the Bali bombers were terrorists even though I would not *directly* refer to them as such.' This seems to be the compromise that most journalists now make at Bush House. They are aware that the meaning of 'terrorism' is often determined more by context than by a logical explanation.

It is not only the BBC that grapples with the usage of 'terrorist'. America's National Public Radio follows similar guidelines and its ombudsman explained why the station does not refer to Palestinian suicide bombers as terrorists.

'Sadly, nouns and adjectives are also weapons in this war. While the term "terrorist" may be accurate in many cases, it also has an extra-journalistic role in delegitimating one side and affirming the other. It is not NPR's role to do this. NPR has an obligation to provide responsible and reliable reporting by describing with accuracy and fairness events that listeners may choose to endorse or deplore as they see fit.'

The influential Reuters news agency, which has reporters in more than 150 countries and whose despatches are reprinted in papers throughout the world, sticks to a policy of avoiding the use of 'emotive words'.

'We do not use terms like "terrorist" and "freedom fighter" unless they are in a direct quote or are otherwise attributable to a third party. We do not characterize the subjects of news stories but instead report their actions, identity and background so that readers can make their own decisions based on the facts.'

After September 11th, the Reuters management faced widespread criticism in the American media for maintaining this policy. The *Washington Post* disclosed that Reuters' head of news had written an internal memo suggesting that some readers might consider the hijackers as 'freedom fighters' and he therefore stipulated that they should not be referred to as either 'freedom fighters' or 'terrorists'. The company's senior management was later forced to release a statement clarifying its position. 'Our policy is to avoid the use of emotional terms and not make value judgments concerning the facts that we attempt to report accurately and fairly.'

The American media, in contrast, appeared traumatized, bonded in empathy with the victims and in anger at the perpetrators of the attacks. CNN's website displayed a curious declaration, apparently trying to deflect criticism in America that its coverage was not muscular enough in condemning the hijackers. 'There have been false reports that CNN has not used the word "terrorist" to refer to those who attacked the World Trade Center and Pentagon. In fact, CNN has consistently and repeatedly referred to the attackers and hijackers as terrorists, and it will continue to do so.'

With the exception of CNN, the attitude of international broadcasters and agencies often collides with journalists who primarily serve a domestic audience. Most mainstream journalists in Britain and America simply bypass the question of who is a terrorist. Usually, editors assume that reporters don't need any formal directive because the appropriate usage is simply understood.

Perhaps George Orwell's celebrated essay 'Politics and the English Language' should be dusted down and read once more by another generation of writers. Orwell's primary purpose was to identify political speechwriting as a source of the abuse of language. A writer should not allow 'ready-made phrases' to crowd his mind. Writing in 1946, Orwell observed that the realities of war are 'too brutal for most people to face, and do not square with the professed aims of the political parties. Thus political language has to consist largely of euphemism, question-begging and sheer cloudy vagueness.' Hence defenceless villagers are bombed from the air and 'this is called pacification'. 'People are imprisoned for years without trial or shot in the back . . . this is called elimination of unreliable elements.'

If he were alive today, how would George Orwell identify the use of the ready-made phrase 'war on terror'? It has become shorthand in the news media and entered common dialogue to describe America's military action, without anyone defining who is a 'terrorist' and what it means to be at war with 'terror'. Would he associate it with Newspeak, whose most important aim was to provide a means of speaking that required no thought? In Newspeak, words such as *joycamp* allowed someone to talk about a forced-labour camp without thinking what the word meant. After the attacks on Manhattan and Washington, the US could have dealt with a specific question of national security and declared a 'War on al-Qa'eda'. It could have pursued the perpetrators of the carnage and punished anybody linked to them. Instead, the United States constructed its first major new military doctrine for half a century and declared a borderless, timeless 'war on terror'. Can those who speak about this conflict define exactly what the phrase means?

In the 1940s, Orwell was concerned that he was witnessing a decline in political thought because of the successful use of propaganda by governments. He observed a constantly repeating cycle: the use of euphemism by political leaders reduced the public's ability to understand political ideas; the public then began to use these euphemisms as part of political debate, without properly understanding them. 'A man may take to drink because he feels himself to be a failure and then fail all the more completely because he drinks. It is rather the same thing that is happening to the English language. It becomes ugly and inaccurate because our thoughts are foolish, but the slovenliness of our language makes it easier for us to have foolish thoughts.' Orwell insisted that the slide into Newspeak is not inevitable. 'The point is that the process is reversible. Modern English . . . is full of bad habits which spread by imitation and which can be avoided if one is willing to take the necessary trouble.'

Can we discover an understanding of 'terrorism' that allows clear thinking, or is it a truly Orwellian word, a euphemism consisting of 'question-begging and sheer cloudy vagueness'?

Part of the problem with finding a transparent and universally accepted understanding of 'terrorism' is the ability of the word to mutate its meaning like an uncontrollable virus. In recent years, it has become such a contagious word that it infects newspaper headline writers: terms such as narco-terrorism, eco-terrorism, cyber-terrorism, industrial terrorism, art terrorism and even food terrorism (the deliberate contamination of food supplies) are plastered in black ink across the front pages. What makes it so seductive, so alluring to storytellers and politicians alike? Why do people stand to attention when it's uttered, as if a giant loudspeaker rouses them from the comforting routines of everyday life? What gives it so much *power*?

One of the obvious places to start the quest for a clear definition is a dictionary. The compact edition of the *Oxford English Dictionary* offers this:

> Terrorism: *n* A system of terror. 1. Government by intimidation
> as directed and carried out by the party in power in France
> during the revolution of 1789–94; the system of 'Terror'. 2. *gen.*
> A policy intended to strike with terror those against whom it is
> adopted; the employment of methods of intimidation; the fact
> of terrorizing or the condition of being terrorized.

The first definition refers to the usage of the word when it was introduced into the English language over two centuries ago. It described the violence of the new Jacobin rulers who initiated a 'Reign of Terror', known in France simply as la Terreur. The leader of the revolution, Maximilien Robespierre, defined terror as 'nothing but justice, prompt, severe and inflexible'. The British statesman Edmund Burke subsequently rebuked 'those hell-hounds called terrorists' for their excessive use of the guillotine. Tens of thousands were decapitated until a rebellion within Robespierre's ranks led the founder of terrorism to the chop himself. The Jacobins' aim had been to instil fear in anyone who might challenge the authority of its newly formed republican government.

The core meaning of 'terrorism' as a 'system of terror' and its second, general definition suggest that a terrorist is simply someone who terrorizes. Very quickly, however, this interpretation appears far too broad for today's usage. A rapist can terrify women but is he a terrorist? Thugs can terrorize a neighbourhood but are they a band of terrorists? The atomic bombs dropped on Hiroshima and Nagasaki were primarily intended to 'terrorize' the Japanese government into an unconditional surrender. One writer has described it as 'less a military mission than a warning – the most dramatic "submit or else" in recorded history'. Does this mean the United States government and the pilot of the Enola Gay were terrorists? The bombing might be considered a war crime, but not terrorism. Rapists and thugs are not terrorists, either.

For the hundred years after the French Revolution, 'terrorism' was primarily used to refer to the activities of revolutionaries who challenged the monarchies of nineteenth-century Europe. In the royal courts, terrorists were considered an abomination, but to many of their subjects they were swashbuckling, romantic and even heroic characters. The Russian revolutionaries who assassinated Tsar Alexander II and the French anarchists who manned the Paris Commune used the word with pride. Karl Marx was amused rather than horrified to be labelled the 'Red Terrorist Doctor'. His bourgeois neighbours in North London enjoyed the fact that they could meet the 'Godfather of Terrorism' ambling on Hampstead Heath with his family on a Sunday afternoon.

By the 1930s, 'terrorism' reverted more closely to its meaning during the French Revolution, though with a highly pejorative connotation. The uniformed gangs in Germany and Italy were described in Britain as 'street terrorists'. The thugs in paramilitary black and brown shirts threatened adversaries and helped usher Hitler and Mussolini into power. Thereafter, both regimes applied a system of state-sanctioned terror to crush internal opposition. Meanwhile, in the Soviet Union, Stalin launched his 'Great Terror', resulting in the show trials that condemned hundreds of thousands to their death. Millions more were exiled or imprisoned in labour camps. One biographer described the political purges ordered by Stalin as a 'conspiracy to seize total power by terrorist action'.

In order to reflect today's more common usage, the smaller *Concise Oxford English Dictionary* ignores the 'system of terror' definition altogether and instead describes terrorism as 'the unofficial or unauthorized use of violence and intimidation in the pursuit of political aims.' Larger editions of the *Oxford English Dictionary* now provide an addendum to the traditional 'system of terror' meaning, pointing out that 'the term now usually refers to a member of a clandestine or expatriate organization aiming to coerce an established government by acts of violence against its subjects'.

The understanding of 'terrorism' as a term that applied exclusively to violence committed by non-state actors developed after the Second World War, when Britain and France, the largest colonial powers, were weakened and vulnerable. The fall of Singapore with its British naval port in 1942 was a highly symbolic event; the island was the enduring emblem of Western power in Asia and yet within a few months almost four centuries of empire had been conquered by Japan. A military analyst observed at the time that 'the white man had lost his ascendancy with the disproof of his magic.' Nationalist groups emerged throughout Asia seeking to overthrow colonial rule. British and French governments used the term to describe their adversaries in news reports and 'terrorism' became associated with movements of national liberation. In Malaya, the insurgents were simply 'CTs', communist terrorists.

The word was starting to acquire its universal stigma, especially in the media of the countries combating rebellion. Ironically, given the use of the word in the Middle East today, some of the last of the groups willing to describe themselves as terrorists were the underground Jewish militias, the Stern Gang and the Irgun Zvai Le'umi. Yitzhak Shamir, who later became Israeli Prime Minister, wrote an August 1943 article entitled 'Terror', for *Hazit*, the journal of the Stern Gang. 'We are very far from any moral hesitations when concerned with the national struggle. First and foremost, terror is for us a part of the political war appropriate for the circumstances of today.'

By the 1950s, the word had become an unequivocal term of condemnation, and Third World movements that used violence to seek the overthrow of colonial rule refused to call themselves terrorists. An alternative lexicon emerged: freedom fighters, militants, guerrillas or latterly mujahedin. 'Terrorist' became accepted as a partisan expression summed up by the often-repeated assertion that 'one man's terrorist is another man's freedom fighter'. Yasser Arafat, the Chairman of the Palestine Liberation Organization, famously declared at the

United Nations in November 1974: 'Whoever stands by a just cause and fights for the freedom and liberation of his land from the invaders, the settlers and the colonialists cannot possibly be called a terrorist.'

At this point, the dictionaries can be closed. Even the most comprehensive dictionary is unable to distinguish a violent struggle for freedom from terrorist activity. If one accepts the dictionary definition, words such as insurgent or guerrilla, which don't carry the same connotations of evil, are redundant because all insurgents or guerrillas would also be terrorists. The French Resistance, which fought the Nazis and their collaborators, would be classified as terrorists rather than heroes.

It was against this background that many news organizations became circumspect about using the word to describe groups like the PLO, the IRA and the African National Congress (ANC). Journalists recognized that using 'terrorist' to describe gunmen in insurgency movements was equivalent to being a defender of empire or apartheid. In addition, a broader pattern was emerging; the leaders of rebel movements gained power and were then described as liberators when they led their newly independent country into the United Nations. Men who were once vilified as terrorists, such as Nelson Mandela and Menachem Begin, ended their careers as winners of the Nobel Peace Prize. Former commanders of the IRA are now elected government officials in Northern Ireland.

This was my understanding of the usage of 'terrorism' when I began to follow politics as a teenager in the mid-1970s. Those condemned as terrorists by the British government at that time were the ANC and the Patriotic Front in Rhodesia, each group confronting racist regimes. A short time later, the leaders of the Patriotic Front were enjoying dinner and drinks at Lancaster House in London as guests of the British government. An agreement was thrashed out and Robert Mugabe was the victor in Zimbabwe's first popular elections. There was no longer any question of describing Mugabe as a terrorist. He'd made the seemingly standard jump from terrorist to politician after sharing a good brandy at Government House with the departing colonial ruler.

When commenting on the assassination of Lord Mountbatten by the IRA, the former Conservative MP Julian Amery contributed to the debate on language. He was willing to use 'terrorism' in its old-fashioned sense as a non-moral description of military tactics: 'I was a terrorist myself once,' he recalled, referring to his work with Britain's Special Operations Executive, whose agents were parachuted behind enemy lines during the Second World War. 'One of my duties was the recruitment of people to carry out terrorist actions against the Nazis in Yugoslavia and Albania. Terrorism is justified if there is no reasonable opportunity to redress problems by legal means. For example, terrorism is acceptable when a country is occupied, like Czechoslovakia or Afghanistan.'

☆

The crisis in Ireland clung to my ambitions as a young journalist. The repeated bomb threats and the constant flow of headlines screaming 'terrorist' became a daily backdrop to life in London. My interest was coloured by a belief that the mainstream media in Britain was not recording the conflict in a way that was either even-handed or comprehensible. I was sharing an apartment with an American friend, and during one dinner party he shocked my British guests. 'You Brits are at war in Ireland. It's your last colonial battle,' he said, silencing the English couples at the table. I had several American friends, some of Irish descent, and was very conscious that their attitude to the IRA was radically different to most of my British colleagues. In the US media, *Time* magazine regularly referred to IRA gunmen as 'volunteers', the heroic term used by the movement to describe its own members. The IRA would be called an 'outlawed' organization but never a terrorist one. The leaders of Sinn Fein, the political arm of the IRA, were often treated like heroes by the political establishments in New York and, at times, Washington. Noraid, the organization that supplied funds to the IRA, enjoyed popular support, even amongst public figures. Having grown up in the US, it seemed strange that two countries that I regarded as home, with common cultures and language, should regard the IRA in such different lights. To one nation, the IRA were volunteers in a legitimate war; to the other, they were evil terrorists who murdered the innocent.

The United States has historically shown sympathy toward 'freedom fighters' confronting colonial power. The nation itself was born from rebellion against colonial rule, and the Boston Tea Party, the revolt that sparked the War of Independence, was either an act of heroism or terrorism, depending on which side of the Atlantic you stood.

The US has had very little experience of 'terrorism' on its own territory. When it did suffer political violence, such as the race riots that followed the murder of Martin Luther King, it was never referred to as terrorism. Even the Black Panther Party, a leftist revolutionary group that was accused of murdering policemen and planting bombs, was rarely termed a terrorist organization, despite being described by the FBI as 'the greatest threat to the internal security of the country'. Instead, the Black Panther Party was equated with the real enemy, the 'Red Menace' of communism. Insurrectionist groups ranging from those inspired by 'Che' Guevara in Latin America to the Vietcong were rarely called terrorists. The communist label was enough to spark revulsion amongst most Americans and classify the group as an enemy, much as terrorist does in the twenty-first century.

During the cold war it did not suit the United States to search for a definition of 'terrorism' based on tactics or methods: involvement in insurgency movements and covert operations characterized much of its foreign policy. In the 1980s, the 'Contras', formed by the CIA in Honduras, were sent to destabilize nearby left-leaning Nicaragua, where they assassinated religious workers, teachers and elected officials. The Contras, as well as the Afghan mujahedin, described by President Reagan as 'the moral equivalent of America's founding fathers', would now conform to the US government's classification of a terrorist organization. In fact all the major powers have supported insurrectionists who used methods that their rivals would count as terrorism.

While the United States' military and security apparatus was directed toward the Soviet Union and its allies, 'terrorism' was gaining a new meaning yet again in Europe and the Middle East. Since the Second World War, the term had been primarily associated with localized nationalist uprisings. In the 1970s, it was applied to violence that crossed national boundaries. It was the birth of what George W. Bush called, three decades later, 'terrorism with a global reach'.

Following the defeat of Arab nations in the Six-Day War in 1967, Yasser Arafat believed that Palestinians needed to draw the world's attention to their cause. The PLO developed links with leftist groups in Europe and Japan. Planes were hijacked and hostages taken, and the murder of eleven Israeli athletes at the 1972 Munich Olympic Games catapulted a regional insurgency onto the international stage.

The operation by a PLO commando group called Black September to kidnap Israeli athletes became a model for a new form of guerrilla action that would be copied during following decades. Five commandos, dressed as athletes with weapons hidden in gym bags, climbed the fence surrounding the Olympic Village. Inside, they were met by three more. Just before 5 a.m., they knocked on the door of the dormitory housing Israeli athletes. The wrestling coach opened the door and, when he saw the attackers, he and a weightlifter blocked the door while six escaped through another entrance. Both men then died in a hail of bullets. The nine remaining athletes were taken hostage and the siege began.

At 9.35 a.m., Black September issued two demands: the hostages would be exchanged in return for the release of over two hundred Palestinians held in Israeli jails, as well as members of West Germany's left-wing Red Army Faction, and safe passage to an Arab nation. They threatened to kill one hostage every two hours if the demands were not met.

One deadline passed and then another, until a deal was negotiated to fly the commandos and their hostages by helicopter to a nearby airfield, where a plane would be waiting to take them to Tunisia. It was at the airfield that the West German police decided to launch a rescue attempt. The pandemonium that ensued led to the capture of three surviving Black September members but left dead all nine Israeli athletes and a policeman.

On one level, the seizure of the hostages was a complete failure because none of Black September's demands was met. Journalists reported the gruesome events on the airfield as a disastrous setback for the Palestinian cause. The killings spread horror and condemnation around the world. But contrast this with a statement by Black September released a week after the incident: 'A bomb in the White House, a mine in the Vatican, the death of Mao Zedong, an earthquake in Paris could not have echoed through the consciousness of every man in the world like the operation at Munich . . . The choice of the Olympics, from the purely propagandist point of view, was 100 per cent successful. It was like painting the name of Palestine on a mountain that can be seen from the four corners of the earth.'

During the weeks that followed, thousands of recruits joined the PLO. Eighteen months later, Yasser Arafat received warm applause when he addressed the General Assembly of the United Nations. Despite the failure of the Oslo accords, the Palestinians became closer to establishing a state than the Kurds, whose leaders decided against 'internationalizing' their cause with the blood of innocents abroad.

While the tactic alerted the world to the Palestinian question, it also brought political violence into the homes of millions of viewers. Newly available satellites began to beam live images of the hijacking of commercial airliners or hostage dramas in the Middle East to televisions in Europe and America.

The media coverage of the global reach of Palestinian violence played a critical part in the gestation of a new understanding of 'terrorism'. The word was developing a binding relationship with the media. The violence was not part of a military campaign, albeit unconventional, against an enemy. The intent of the militants was to shock and spark worldwide alarm. The violence took place because of the exposure provided by the media and its purpose was to send a message to primarily Western governments. Ted Koppel, the distinguished presenter of the American current affairs programme *ABC Nightline*, said that television and terrorism had formed a symbiotic relationship: 'Without television, terrorism becomes rather like the philosopher's hypothetical tree falling in the forest: no one hears it fall and therefore it has no reason for being.' A Palestinian observer at the United Nations commented, 'The first several hijackings aroused the consciousness of the world and awakened the media and world opinion much more, and more effectively, than twenty years of pleading at the United Nations.'

Political actions therefore become terrorism, and their perpetrators terrorists, if the intent is to send a message through the media. The California-based political scientist Brian Jenkins contributed to redefining the word in 1980. 'What sets terrorism apart from other violence is this: terrorism consists of acts carried out in a dramatic way to attract publicity and create an atmosphere of alarm that goes far beyond the actual victims. Indeed, the identity of the victims is often secondary or irrelevant to the terrorists who aim their violence at the people watching. This distinction between actual victims and a target audience is the hallmark of terrorism and separates it from other modes of armed conflict. Terrorism is theatre.'

The 1980s provided the word with yet another connotation that propelled its modern understanding, especially in the United States. During the post-war period, groups that were designated as terrorist organizations usually sought ethnic or nationalist objectives. Their ideology was scientific, often Marxist, and based upon theories of social unrest and political violence that were debated on university campuses and in theoretical journals. Terrorists might be evil and ruthless but could be understood in terms of Western political thought.

The phenomenon that was now emerging was the use of political violence to fulfil millenarian, religious demands – what later became known as 'sacred terror'. The actions were committed in the name of God and often followed a clerical edict. The violence was nearly always inspired by Islam; the roots of this militant interpretation of the faith lie in clerical writings from Egypt and Pakistan but its origin on the global stage is usually traced to the Iranian Revolution. In November 1979, after forcing the American-backed Shah into exile, a group of Islamic students seized the US Embassy in Tehran and kept more than fifty diplomats hostage for 444 days. Ayatollah Khomeini, Iran's political and spiritual leader, supported the hostage-takers and declared the United States an enemy of Islam. He ordered the release of non-white Americans, citing them as amongst people oppressed by the US government. The young men who had entered the American Embassy and held the diplomats hostage were known as radical students in most of the media until President Jimmy Carter designated the group as 'terrorists'. The crisis plagued the last year of the Carter presidency. Eight US Marines died in a failed rescue attempt. Iran released the hostages only after the presidency had passed from Carter to Ronald Reagan.

This was followed in the early and mid-1980s by the abduction of Western hostages by Hizbollah guerrillas in Lebanon. A perception became established that the West in general and the United States in particular were victims of terrorism emanating from Muslim countries. Western civilians were becoming caught in conflicts that they usually knew little about. Consumers of news increasingly began to believe that a terrorist could no longer claim to be confronting injustice in a far-off country or wear the badge of a freedom fighter. Terrorism was becoming a threat to Western society. The prevailing judgement in the West was that Hizbollah, or the Party of God, had no right to be considered a legitimate resistance fighting an occupying power. Hizbollah emerged as an influential force in Lebanese politics following the Israeli invasion in 1982 and had the financial and military backing of Iran. To Western TV viewers, its supporters looked fanatical; bearded and wild-eyed, screaming anti-American slogans and waving AK-47 assault rifles. Hizbollah fighters were soon perceived as insane due to their willingness to die for their faith. The world was outraged in 1983 when the man who drove a truck full of explosives into a US Marine barracks in Beirut smiled at the perimeter guard seconds before blowing him and 241 American servicemen to bits. President Reagan committed his second administration to fighting 'the evil scourge of terrorism'. The primary targets of US foreign policy during the 1980s, however, were not the militants themselves but the states accused of 'sponsoring terrorism'.

I visited a Hizbollah stronghold in southern Lebanon in 1993, two years after the release of two British hostages, Terry Waite and John McCarthy. The group that had held them captive were the Islamic Jihad organization, a 'special forces' unit within Hizbollah. The group apparently no longer considered Westerners as useful pawns in their political game. When Lebanon's fifteen-year civil war ended, the long-running saga of the Western hostages was also resolved. Hizbollah's attention was now directed against the border strip in the south that was occupied by Israel after its invasion.

I was told it would be a perilous journey from the port city of Sidon to the hilltop town of J'baa, where I had arranged a meeting with a regional Hizbollah commander. The town is perched amid the foothills of Mount Niha, nearly 3,000 feet above sea level. J'baa was at one time a retreat for the better-off merchants from Sidon during the numbing heat of summer. Now, however, the few visitors were usually volunteers wanting to fight for Hizbollah. It was on the front line of the war with Israel.

As we climbed up the winding road, we travelled at breakneck speed through sections visible to Israeli gunners in hilltop posts over-looking the route. Mustafa, the driver, enjoyed the run to J'baa. He had a looping moustache and had a sparkle in his eye when he put on a pair of leather driving gloves. At one time he'd been a professional saloon-car racer and his ageing BMW had a lowered suspension and racing tyres. It was a white-knuckle ride; for most of the journey I feared less the Israeli artillery than ending up over a cliff.

A yellow and green Hizbollah flag fluttered on the main street next to an oversized cut-out picture, perhaps twenty feet high, of Ayatollah Khomeini, the Iranian leader and guardian of the Shi'ite faith here. J'baa had looked fairly normal from a distance, if not picturesque. The town appeared as an orderly collection of four- and five-storey white-washed buildings snuggled together against a mountainous backdrop. What I did not see from afar were the blown-out walls and collapsed roofs and rubble on the streets. The barber's shop was only accessible by climbing over broken masonry. The roof was at an unnatural angle but the barber continued to work; at that moment he was trimming the hair of a teenaged boy. 'You've got to carry on,' he told me. 'People still need their hair cut.' Another house had a six-foot-wide hole punched in the side of a wall, caused by an Israeli shell shortly before we arrived in J'baa.

Israeli planes crisscrossed overhead all afternoon, leaving long white streaks like scars across the clear blue sky. Hizbollah had a party office in J'baa, a small building in the middle of a row of shops. Inside there were files on the shelves, leaflets and posters lying around as well as party paraphernalia; a key ring with a picture of Hizbollah's leader, headbands with slogans and a leather bookmark embossed with the distinctive party symbol, a raised fist holding aloft a Kalashnikov rifle.

The man behind the desk made a phone call and announced that I had a dinner appointment that evening with a Hizbollah commander. I had a minder assigned to me called Abbas, a sullen man in his early twenties. Perhaps it was lost in translation, but I was unable to determine whether I was to meet the military commander or the spiritual leader. He was referred to as 'Shaykh', but in Hizbollah, the men of God and the men of guns can be one and the same.

It was a moonless night and I was being led down a path from the centre of J'baa. The odd bare bulb hung in distant corners but each step forward was an act of faith. I suspected that I was being taken on a circular route in order to prevent me finding the building on the following day. Hizbollah were obsessive with secrecy and security. Our destination turned out to be a three-storey house with shards of light poking from cracks in the doors and window shutters.

I was ushered into a room with a large dining table, which stood only eighteen inches above the floor. A white plastic sheet was draped over it and a few men were scurrying about, some carrying plates of food. At least a dozen people, probably many more in a squeeze, could sit or kneel around the edge. One of the fluorescent bars above it flickered annoyingly.

Shaykh Muhammad sat, legs crossed, at the top end. His black robe fell like a small tent around his seated body. His bearded head was cocked at forty-five degrees, as if in constant contemplation, with a round white turban on top. He was a shaykh, a part of the Shi'ite clergy and apparently close to Hizbollah's ruling council. I never did discover whether he was also a military commander.

The Shaykh looked up as I entered the room and Abbas introduced me. He smiled curtly and nodded as I offered the Islamic greeting, 'Peace be upon you,' but otherwise didn't respond. After a while we started eating, a spread of meze; there was tahina, a sesame dip, and baba ghanouj, an aubergine paste with lemon and parsley. They were eaten with warm flat bread. The tomatoes and radishes in Lebanon were luscious and oversized, often dwarfing the plate. There were also some slightly oily falafel, the patties made from dried peas and vegetables. Curiously, a plate of chips was also brought in with a bottle of tomato ketchup.

Around the table were about a dozen men, in their twenties and thirties: most were unshaven with wispy tufts of facial hair; a few had long, thick beards. They seemed to be soldiers. They ate noisily while the Shaykh nibbled at this food without speaking. I tried to appear friendly by muttering that the dinner was tasty; 'Excellent,' I told him, patting my stomach. He seemed unimpressed. He was watching me carefully over the top of his old-fashioned brown-rimmed spectacles. I later discovered that every member of the Hizbollah clergy wore exactly the same glasses, or so it seemed. I couldn't work out how old Muhammad was; my initial guess put him in his early fifties because of his title and middle-aged demeanour. He was a little overweight but his beard had no hints of grey. I later learned that he was only thirty-five.

The mutton kebabs arrived next and the man sitting alongside me insisted on piling a huge mound onto my plate. I smiled and ate far too much out of politeness. Then, suddenly, with several kebabs still on my plate, Shaykh Muhammad banged a fork on the table and began reciting what I believe were verses from the Qur'ān. Then he turned to me.

He folded his spectacles and set off on a lengthy speech on English colonialism, the Balfour Declaration (which committed Britain to establishing a Jewish State in 1918) and the way that the colonial powers had carved up Muslim lands after the First World War. 'Did I know Woodrow Wilson?' he asked. I nodded. Then he pulled out a notebook and squinted at a quote from the American President on Anglo-French diplomacy after the collapse of the Ottoman Empire. 'It was a disgusting scramble for Arab lands by England and France!'

he shouted, paraphrasing Wilson. He also mentioned the role of MI6 in overthrowing the elected Iranian leader, Mohammed Mosaddeq, in 1953. England had caused a great deal of damage in this part of the world, I was told.

I listened attentively and nodded, not quite sure what I should say. I was there to negotiate access to film Hizbollah fighters in the front line and these sorts of meetings can be very tiresome, especially if one doesn't have a beer or glass of wine to ease the proceedings. After repeatedly using the Arabic word *Inglizi* to describe me, I thought I'd stop the flow by declaring that I am not English.

I was born in Wales and at three, left for the United States. In the Middle East, I never talk about my American roots and as a representative of the BBC most seem to assume that I must be English. I announced to the shaykh that I am Welsh and I also told him, in a playful manner, that Wales had been colonized by the English for almost five hundred years, much longer than the Israelis or anybody else had occupied Arab lands.

Shaykh Muhammad fell silent for a moment. Then he became rather excited. 'Do you have a Resistance?' he asked, using the term that Hizbollah used to describe themselves. I replied that some Welsh nationalists had burned down the houses of English families who owned holiday homes in Wales. Muhammad seemed pleased but hinted that that was not enough. He then asked whether there was a Welsh Republican Army modelled on the IRA. 'Not yet,' I replied. 'There should be one, though.' I was enjoying the conversation now and hoped it would help our relations over the next few days. But then Muhammad picked up my business card, which I had offered him earlier. He suddenly asked: 'Do you need any military assistance?'

He wanted names of people in Wales that he should contact. I was now trying to wiggle out from the conversation. I told him that many Welsh people would be pleased to have the support of Hizbollah and that I would look into the question and provide him with some names when I returned to Wales. I'm afraid that I never followed up the shaykh's request. But we did have a few good days' filming, and for a brief moment it seemed that Islam, anti-colonialism and nationalism could have formed a fiery international alliance in the cause of Welsh independence.

Needless to say, Shaykh Muhammad and his men did not consider themselves terrorists. 'We are fighting to expel the Israelis from the lands they occupy,' he said. One could easily argue that Hizbollah guerrillas were 'freedom fighters'. The United Nations declared in Resolution 425 that Israel 'should withdraw forthwith its forces from all Lebanese territory'. 'We are fulfilling a UN resolution, just like Bush did in Kuwait,' the Shaykh smiled, referring to President George Bush senior's expedition to expel Iraq from Kuwait to implement a UN resolution in 1991.

I suspected that the only difference between Hizbollah and earlier anti-colonialist guerrillas, aside from the fact that Islam has replaced Marxism as the rallying ideology, is that Hizbollah considered the United States as the architect of their problems. Hizbollah believed that while Israel was the occupying power, America was the controlling power. Most observers, however, especially those who reported on the Middle East without visiting the region, differed from my view. Many of the academics and writers who before hesitated to use the word, now described the beginning of a 'new terrorism'. There were no intellectuals on American campuses legitimizing the kidnapping of Western hostages. Hizbollah used tactics, such as suicide bombers, that spooked the American public and unsettled a superpower. And they worked. While a serious body of opinion in the United States believed the IRA was a traditional and acceptable insurgency organization, the religious violence that began in the early 1980s and culminated in the September 11th attacks was seen as a different kind of violence altogether.

Typical of the people holding this view was Pete King, a Republican Congressman from New York. He often heaped praise on Martin Galvin, the head of Noraid. An Irish-American, King is thick-set with large round glasses and a hearty laugh. He was prone to off-the-cuff remarks and would often give succour to the IRA; some have hinted that it was calculated to secure votes from Irish descendants living in New York.

Pete King reconciles his past support for Irish Republican movements with his present commitment to the 'war on terror' by drawing a distinction between organizations that are prepared to come forward and negotiate, even if they are also engaged in armed struggle, from those for whom negotiation is not a goal. For King, the IRA represented a form of legitimate rebellion, whereas Islamic militants such as al-Qa'eda will never negotiate with the US because they are fuelled only by religious zeal and hatred.

The Republican Party Congressman had an unusual ally in his argument; the former militant Palestinian leader Abu Abbas. US Special Forces arrested Abbas at his home in Baghdad shortly after the city was captured during the overthrow of Saddam Hussein. His arrest was touted as a 'victory in the global war on terrorism' and evidence of the former Iraqi regime's support for terror. In fact, Abu Abbas had denounced violence a decade earlier and had not been involved in any militant activities since 1990. But he was said to be the mastermind behind one act that has lived in the memory of those who watched it on television. In 1985, members of Abu Abbas' organization, the Palestinian Liberation Front, hijacked an Italian cruise liner, the *Achille Lauro*. During the stand-off, in a moment of piercing horror, one of the hijackers shot a sixty-nine-year-old wheelchair-bound passenger. Leon Klinghoffer, an American Jew, was then pushed, still in his wheelchair, from the deck of the ship into the Mediterranean.

A few years later, I visited Abu Abbas at his walled house in a prosperous suburb in southern Baghdad. Saddam Hussein had provided sanctuary when he had few places to flee after Italy sentenced him, in absentia, to five terms of life imprisonment. The First Gulf War was about to begin, and Iraqi government minders led me to his house. Bougainvillaea grew in the well-tended courtyard. We met in a room filled with books, some in English, and many on international politics. I also recall seeing Ernest Hemingway's taut classic, *For Whom the Bell Tolls*, an account of a young American volunteer who joined the International Brigade to fight Franco's fascists. Abbas was a bear of a man, with a thick handlebar moustache under his dominating nose. He was also very courteous and quiet for someone I had until then known as the murderer of a disabled pensioner. As he sipped coffee and dragged on a cigarette he said the killing of Klinghoffer was a mistake. He was in Jordan at the time and said that he had nothing to do with it. He said he'd negotiated a deal that would have saved the passengers of the *Achille Lauro* in return for safe passage for the hijackers to the PLO's headquarters in Tunis. He described the killing as a consequence of war, a military mission that went wrong. 'Innocent civilians are dying in Palestine in the intifada,' he said, referring to the Palestinian popular uprising against Israeli rule. 'I regret all unnecessary deaths.'

He asked that I call him Mohammed; his personal name was Mohammed Zaidan and Abu simply means 'father of' in Arabic as well as providing a nom de guerre. He pointed out on several occasions during our meeting that United Nations Resolution 242, calling on Israel to withdraw from the Palestinian territories it occupied in 1967, was being ignored by the outside world. Meanwhile, a coalition of dozens of nations was assembling hundreds of thousands of troops in the Saudi desert to implement a UN resolution calling on Saddam Hussein to withdraw from Kuwait. 'Why the double standards?' he asked. 'Politics,' I murmured, a little sheepishly, shrugging my shoulders. 'And politics caused the tragic death of Klinghoffer,' he retorted, lighting up another cigarette, his black eyes locked onto mine.

Abu Abbas had a powerful handshake and a quiet charisma; he seemed a man with a conscience who thought deeply about life and death. American investigators said he ordered the execution of Klinghoffer but it seemed incongruous that such a pensive man would agree to the cold-blooded murder of an invalid. But then again, political violence, whether committed by a state or by 'terrorists', often obeys a compassionless, cruel logic.

Abu Abbas later left Baghdad and went to Gaza after a general amnesty was granted as part of the Oslo peace accords. He agreed to lay down his arms and Israel allowed him safe passage. After four years working alongside the newly formed Palestinian Authority he was forced to return to Baghdad; Jewish organizations in the United States were pressuring Washington to demand that Arafat turn him over to the US authorities. For all sides, it became inconvenient for him to remain in the Palestinian territories.

Abu Abbas went back to his house in Baghdad. He lived a quiet life, mostly reading and looking after his son. Neighbours described him as a family man. He roundly condemned the attacks on the World Trade Center, arguing that they made no political sense and had taken thousands of innocent lives. He went on to construct his definition of terrorism. The essential difference between his organization and al-Qa'eda is that the *Achille Lauro* operation served 'a limited historical goal – the liberation of Palestine and the recovery of occupied lands – and not the borderless, limitless war on America and Israel declared by bin Laden.' What bin Laden does, he said definitively, 'is terrorism'. Abu Abbas died of heart failure while in US custody less than a year after his arrest. Yasser Arafat described him as a 'distinguished combatant and a martyr'.

A growing consensus, which included the likes of Abu Abbas,

believed that September 11th created a new category of terrorism. 'We are now living in a very different world,' declared the Prime Minister of Australia, as he warned of 'borderless terrorism' that could strike anyone, anywhere on the planet. A year later, eighty-eight Australians were blown up in Bali. It appeared that the violence was no longer based on comprehensible motives by a disciplined organization. The attacks were seemingly not aimed to achieve specific political change but were instead expressions of fury based on the will of God. The view had become widely held that, unlike terrorist groups of the past, there could be no negotiation with al-Qa'eda. There will be no drinks with bin Laden at the Dorchester once a compromise is reached.

According to this view, if there was a precursor to the September 11th attacks, it might be found in the Tokyo subway on a Monday morning in March 1995. At the height of the rush hour, six members of a Japanese religious sect took boxes filled with the deadly nerve agent sarin into stations. The cult members punctured the boxes with umbrellas and a thick, oily gas leaked into the air. Only twelve people died but more than five thousand were hospitalized. Subway entrances resembled medieval battlefields as injured commuters lay gasping on the ground with blood gushing from their noses or mouths.

The Aum Shinrikyo sect aimed to take over Japan and then the world before the planet experienced an apocalypse. The sect's political goals were not based on an accepted ideology and their motivation was rooted in absolutist religious belief. There was no suggestion that the Japanese government should attempt a rational dialogue with them. The subway attack also showed how easy it was for a militant organization to use weapons of mass destruction.

Six years later, the media in the West defined a new genre of 'September 11th category terrorists'. It supposed that al-Qa'eda was inspired by visions of an apocalypse similar to Aum Shinrikyo's. Al-Qa'eda communiqués spoke of Judgement Day, when Muslims will fight Jews to the death. Its only coherent political objective appeared to be the destruction of the West; there was no obvious list of demands that could become the basis of a future accommodation. The argument continued that the men of al-Qa'eda believed in a war pitting the West against the Muslim civilization that will end in Armageddon: polluted by a mistaken, literal interpretation of the Qur'ān, the 'new terrorists' are deranged and cannot be reasoned with.

I always try to avoid the conclusion that any large group of people are insane. However unpalatable it sounds, there are millions of Muslims around the world who welcomed, at least in part, the events of September 11th. I have spoken to a journalist from Jordan, a teacher from Lyon, a shopkeeper in Jakarta, who, even if they only admit it in private, have a quiet respect for what bin Laden has done. They express regret for the civilian deaths but point out that when Muslim civilians are killed there are no memorial services or candlelit vigils on Western television. Secondly, bin Laden has turned his back on his vast wealth and made an arrogant superpower tremble. There is a strong sense that the United States deserved a kicking.

Osama bin Laden has offered his own definition of 'terrorism'. In a television interview in 1998, he criticized the blanket use of the term as a publicity tool of American policy. He argued that Muslims were only involved in a defensive jihad, protecting their faith and their land. 'They rob us of our wealth and of our resources and of our oil. Our religion is under attack. They kill and murder our brothers. They compromise our honour and our dignity and dare we utter a single word of protest against the injustice, we are called terrorists.'

☆

A storm had blown across northern England. Squalls lashed the full-fronted windows of the cafe in central Manchester as I sat down for food. Swirling fists of rain punched the glass next to me. I was having lunch with an American Muslim who had voiced support for al-Qa'eda. The tempest provided a fitting backdrop as Imam Ramee Muhammed spoke of a confrontation between the Abrahamic faiths of Judaism, Christianity and Islam. 'The US is at war with Islam so Islam must fight back. You are going to see a uniting of the Muslim community worldwide,' he prophesied. 'One day, Islam is going to return to its elevated position as the leading religion in the world. America will be defeated.'

Ramee is a hugely slabbed man, his upper body locked in an upright posture by muscle and tendon. He spoke in a thoughtful, purposeful drawl that had been honed in the slums of Chicago, preaching Islam to black men and women who were trapped in America's unforgiving correctional system. As well as being an Islamic scholar, he's a former US Marine, a bodybuilder and a martial arts teacher. He wore a black djellaba, the traditional floor-length Arabic robe, and a red fez. You don't lose Ramee in a crowd.

I had first met him six years earlier at a mosque in the tumbledown
part of Chicago called Southside. With its vacant lots and smashed-up
cars, the only shops that remained open sold liquor. Locals called this
district 'Terror Town' because of the gangs that prowled its streets.
Like millions of other black Americans, Ramee turned away from a
life of crime and drugs in this decayed landscape and became a Muslim.
He discarded the name of the slave owners who shackled his ancestors
and Ron McCrae became Ramee Muhammed. He went to Syria to
learn Arabic and became versed in Qur'ānic studies. On his return, he
led prayers in a mosque that he opened on 75th Street.

Ramee spent his time in Chicago blending social work with an
aggressive attempt to introduce young people to Islam. He has helped
dozens, perhaps hundreds, of young black men overcome their life of
crime and addiction. After an incident when two children were killed
in drive-by shootings, he began a campaign to expel the gangs and
improve conditions in the neighbourhood of 75th Street. He claimed
to have cleared drug trafficking, gang intimidation and prostitution
from three blocks and has even converted former gang leaders to Islam.

He was in England on a lecture tour, encouraging Muslims to
combat drugs and prostitution in Britain's inner cities. But the invasion
of Iraq had just begun and it dominated his thoughts. He pulled the
Independent from under his arm and read from a report about a
wayward American missile that landed on a residential district of
Baghdad. 'It was an outrage, an obscenity.' He paused and glowered
at me. 'The severed hand on the metal door, the swamp of blood and
mud across the road, the human brains inside a garage, the incinerated,
skeletal remains of an Iraqi mother and her three small children in
their still-smouldering car.' He put down the newspaper and continued, as if that event led to another. 'Inside the heart of every
Muslim, Osama bin Laden is a hero. Many are too scared to say it out
loud but they feel it. When they see what is happening in Iraq, they
support anyone who stands up to America.'

Ramee accepts that civilians will die in the 'war' between Islam and
the West. He does not distinguish between the innocent who died
at the World Trade Center and the Iraqi civilians who perished during
the Anglo-American invasion. 'It is allowed in war to attack the
finances as well as the soldiers of an enemy. The World Trade Center
was a symbol of trade and commerce so it was a lawful target,' he
proclaimed. 'As a Muslim, we celebrate Osama bin Laden in the same

way that returning soldiers in America are given medals of honour for their successful kills. Nobody wants innocent people to die but it happens in war. Muslims have no recourse but to defend themselves.'

Ramee was with his driver, Shakeel, who nodded in agreement. Shakeel was born in Britain of Pakistani parents. He told me that while his father wore Western clothes, he preferred the salwar kameez, the loose pyjamas from South Asia. A white *imamah* (the style of headscarf worn by the Prophet) was wrapped around his head. 'Anybody who attacks Islam is our enemy. When a Muslim sees other Muslims attacked, it triggers something in their heart,' he added.

The three of us were having a lunch of chicken and lamb kebabs and flat bread at the Halal Cafe near Manchester's main railway station. Ramee's faith, of course, requires that he eat only halal (lawful) food.

I told Ramee that I was writing a book on the meaning of 'terrorism'. I wanted to find out how different people used the word and understood its meaning. In a heartbeat he gave his definition of the popular usage of the word, mockingly pretending to read an entry from the dictionary. ' "Terrorist. A noun," ' he said. ' "A victim of Jewish and American aggression who dares to fight back." The war on terror is a war on Islam. It's as simple as that. Look back at history. Uncle Sam is the leading terrorist.' He gave a potted history of the American nation, including the near-genocide of the native Indians and the atomic bombs dropped on Japan. He spoke calmly, without a hint of rage in his voice. I wondered whether the legacy of slavery had left a rage in his heart. 'My people, African-Americans, have been victims of terrorism. They've been taken from their land as slaves, their women raped, the men lynched. Millions of Africans died on the way to America.'

Ramee said he was under investigation and that British authorities had withheld his US passport, preventing him returning to the States during the war in Iraq. When he last checked in at Manchester airport for a domestic flight, two security guards monitored his movements until he boarded the plane.

'I know people who are called terrorists by the US government. They are good people, Muslims who have given their life to Allah,' he mused as he sipped his cola. He described the United States as the leading producer of weapons of mass destruction. 'The US terrorizes the people of Iraq. The US is a terrorist nation, taking over the world and consuming the world's resources. In Iraq, over one million babies died due to the blockade and now thousands are being slaughtered by weapons of mass destruction and the gun of the invader.' He pointed his finger at me and exclaimed: 'This is terrorism. Don't try and tell me who is the real terrorist.'

He took me to the railway station and gave me a warm bear hug. I knew that Ramee was a man with strong moral convictions. He had given hope to hundreds of hopeless kids in Chicago, selflessly doing social work in prisons and trying to improve the condition of his crime-infested neighbourhood. How could a man who cared about humanity applaud the attacks on the World Trade Center?

Ramee left me with his version of the old adage: 'Today the word "terrorist" means a Muslim fighting for his honour and dignity. If you want to call them terrorists, go ahead. To me, the men of al-Qa'eda are freedom fighters.'

2 / WAR OVER A WORD

'Washington has much to learn from Algeria on ways to fight terrorism.'
William Burns, US Assistant Secretary of State, December 2002

'Hello, we are terrorists,' declared the older, smaller man, probably the commander. There were half a dozen others in the room. Some were sitting on the floor, propped up by the wall; others lounged on a makeshift bed. A few wore olive military fatigues but none had insignia. Each was draped with an automatic rifle or shotgun. 'Aren't you worried that we're going to kill you?'

Six hours earlier, I had left the quarantined luxury of the El-Djazair Hotel in Algiers. For over a week, I had been making detailed preparations for a rendezvous with members of the Islamic Salvation Army, a guerrilla movement of several thousand men that was at war with the Algerian state.

At four thirty that morning, I opened the door of my hotel room to check that no one was watching the corridor. I put the 'Do not disturb' sign on the handle. I had already told officials at the Interior Ministry that I was unwell. Nerves and fear of the 'terrorists' had affected my health, I'd said, while feigning abdominal pains. I hoped that government minders allocated to watch over foreign journalists would assume that I was recuperating in my room for a few days.

Foreign journalists were instructed to tell the Interior Ministry when they planned to leave the hotel so that if necessary security men could accompany them. It was 'for our protection'. A year earlier, Islamist militants had issued an ultimatum to all foreigners to leave Algeria. Nearly seventy non-Algerians had been murdered. Journalists, too, had become a target of the armed groups; twenty Algerian writers and broadcasters had been killed because they refused to bend their words to please the militants.

I was travelling with my television team. Morsi was the cameraman; educated at French schools in Cairo, he was urbane and pensive. He never wasted words and was calm under pressure. Nasser was the sound recordist; he was over six feet tall and lanky, the son of a Nubian chief from Aswan in southern Egypt. He didn't talk much but he had an impish smile. A chuckle and casual wave of the hand brushed away any suggestion that he remain in the hotel. Hamid was my translator and assistant, fluent in Arabic as well as French and English. He had spent his youth in the psychedelic world of 1960s London and was now teaching English at a private school west of Algiers. The taxi driver was Malek, well toned and youthful despite his full mop of grey hair. I still don't know why he agreed to take his rusty Peugeot station wagon into guerrilla territory. He certainly didn't risk his life for the $100 a day I paid for his services. It seemed he had a genuine desire to meet his fellow countrymen who had taken up arms to fight a revolution. I warned him that he'd be charged with a serious crime if his role were discovered. Malek had no love for the Islamic militants, nor did he have any respect for the regime. 'Fuck the government,' was his curt response.

As for me, I had read the headlines in the British newspapers and it seemed that Algeria had degenerated into a medieval madhouse where the criminally insane were marauding the streets and murdering at will. 'Algeria; the New Horror Story' screamed one headline. 'Twelve Foreigners Murdered by Killers from God' announced another. 'When Death Knocks at the Door' introduced an account of a family, including a six-year-old boy and an ailing grandmother, massacred for no apparent reason.

I wanted to make sense of the seemingly senseless. I was intrigued by a people who could be both so cultured and so savage, a nation so violently torn between its French and Arabic heritage. My introduction to Algeria was as a teenager through the writings of the French humanist Albert Camus. The first place I visited when I arrived in Algiers was the beaches near Tipasa, where Camus's anti-hero killed an Arab in his existentialist novel *The Outsider*. The protagonist, Meursault, is a detached observer of life, responding to the world around him in as truthful a manner as possible. I saw in the tragic character of Meursault also a man with a noble ambition; it was akin to the role of a journalist as an impartial observer.

Meursault was also, like Camus, a French settler, a *pied-noir*, and an outsider in an Arab land. Most *pieds-noirs* denied this truth, preferring to believe that the soil of Algeria belonged to the mother country; their homeland was Algérie française.

The relationship between France and Algeria was one of extremes; of passion, hatred and ultimately savagery. The 132 years of union between the two countries was not a marriage of imperial power and colony; it was an affair of the heart, intense and, finally, deeply destructive for both nations. When one and a half million *pieds-noirs* left Algeria in 1961, in the largest single voluntary human migration of the twentieth century, it was the end of the affair. But the damage and the pain of the break-up, as well as the continued intimacy between many Algerians and France, cast a deep shadow on the present day.

In the 1990s, a new phase of Algeria's history began. History is often created in periods of turbulence and violence. On that surprisingly chilly October morning in 1994, we assembled, rather sleepily, where Malek had parked his Peugeot taxi. The car had been loaded with supplies and camera equipment the afternoon before. We had to depart at dawn in order to avoid alerting our minders from the Interior Ministry. The man assigned to watch over me stayed in a room a few doors away. He was friendly enough and keen to chat about football and girls. He joked that his name was 'Sylvester', as in Sylvester Stallone. He had the looks and build of an action star. He was in his mid-twenties, with short-cropped hair, a wide smile and remarkably white teeth: he said he was part of an anti-terrorist unit and he enjoyed mocking my 'fear' of the Islamists. It appeared as if each man in the unit had recently been told to visit a tailor and order a new suit. Sylvester had chosen a foppish pastel-blue cloth; another minder had a garish red check. They wore their suits awkwardly. The bulge from their oversized handguns broke the line of the jackets, belying their comical attempts to appear as hotel guests.

In Algeria, the government has eyes everywhere; if journalists bypassed the police and hired a taxi from the El-Djazair Hotel, the drivers were paid to file a report, listing where the journalist had gone and whom he'd seen. Malek was a taxi driver whom Hamid had known for many years. We left the hotel without being stopped. The only person in the lobby was a groggy receptionist, who was half asleep in his chair. He looked up with one tired eye and nodded a '*bonjour*'.

As dawn broke we passed through a checkpoint at the edge of Algiers, on the main road leading south towards Blida, a former colonial town on the great farming plain of the Mitidja. In the days of empire, it was a favourite destination for European visitors, with tree-lined boulevards, a reputable hotel and a restaurant that was known for its wine. Now the area was part of the 'triangle of death'. Blida was a stronghold for the militants and was where the Islamic uprising began in 1992.

The roads were quiet, strangely so, I thought, though we were not usually about so early. My greatest fear was driving into a *faux barrage* ('false checkpoint'), a roadblock set up by militants to demonstrate their authority in areas abandoned by government forces. The guerrillas checked identity papers and reportedly dragged out those they considered enemies, such as members of the security services, journalists and foreigners. The few remaining Western businessmen at the El-Djazair, mostly oilmen, spent most of their evenings swapping horror stories in the bar. A great deal of machismo, as well as alcohol, flowed. Foreign businessmen only left the hotel with an armed escort, a pickup truck full of police bristling with automatic weapons. When I first arrived, a British oil worker warned me with a grisly account of an elderly Frenchman who was pulled from his car and decapitated in front of onlookers, his head mounted on nearby railings.

It was about 7 a.m. and we had taken a short cut to travel around Blida – Hamid thought that it would be quicker and would avoid government checkpoints. We were travelling on a single-track paved road that cut across fields of grain. We saw no other traffic until we found ourselves behind a slow-moving white van. I had already commented that our battered taxi was not powerful enough to overtake. Malek quipped that the four of us with our recording equipment were weighing down his beloved car.

Ahead I noticed a blown-up bridge that had been crudely reconstructed to allow vehicles to pass. It looked like a small river crossing, surrounded by a clutch of trees and bushes, fed by the water below. Suddenly, three hooded gunmen emerged from the undergrowth and flagged down the van. They had also spotted our taxi. We had driven into a checkpoint. The masked men had no epaulettes and they'd wrapped scarves around their heads and faces. They carried AK-47 assault rifles. I didn't need reminding that I was the only non-Muslim in my team. Thoughts of the decapitated Frenchman spun around my mind.

The driver of the white van got out and walked to the back of the vehicle, accompanied by two of the gunmen. The third was eyeing our taxi. His rifle was in a horizontal position, the butt resting against his hips, his finger on the trigger. The driver opened the rear doors. It was a baker's van and he handed the gunmen an armful of bread and cakes.

Morsi, the Egyptian cameraman, was imperturbable. I screamed that we should have stayed on the main road. He stared at the three gunmen and said quietly, 'Ninjas. Get your passport.' ('Ninjas' was the term used for the government's anti-terrorist police. They hide behind ski masks or scarves in order to prevent the Islamist gunmen from discovering their identity. The name derives from the covert operatives of Japanese lore, whose craft is stealth. The regime says the masks are necessary to protect the security forces and their families from the rebels, who otherwise would kill them in their homes. The anonymity also allows the security forces to act without accountability. The violence committed by both sides had become faceless.)

The man who had been looking our way peered into the taxi. Hamid wound down his window and smiled a good morning. He and Malek were in the front seats and they handed over their identity cards. The gunman passed them back. All the time, his assault rifle was trained on us. The gunman looked at me and poked the AK-47 through the open window and lifted it as a gesture, as if to say, 'Show me your papers.' The nozzle was less than six inches from my throat. I said nothing and I slowly handed him my British passport with a very slow, deliberate motion. He studied it and compared the photo. Then, to my astonishment, he simply muttered, '*Merci*,' and returned my passport without further ado. The same happened with the crew's Egyptian documents. What did he think a group of foreigners was doing in the 'triangle of death'? He probably didn't care. He was a government gendarme hunting Islamists and trying to stay alive. We waved and drove off, as the ninjas turned their attention to breakfast. I punched the roof of the taxi in relief.

We had arranged a rendezvous at a cafe in Chlef, a city that lies about a hundred miles west of Algiers. Between Blida and Chlef, a journey of some eighty miles, there were no checkpoints and I witnessed no signs of government presence. A police station along the route was empty.

Chlef was known as Orléansville during colonial rule. It should be a thriving, bustling city, the administrative capital of a *wilaya* (province) of more than six hundred thousand people and a commercial centre. But the town seemed strangely subdued. A few of the small open-fronted shops were trading; street vendors sold snacks and soft drinks. Older men in djellabas were huddled in groups, sipping coffee. Younger men in jeans were standing at street corners, drawing on cigarettes and watching passers-by.

As we searched for the cafe, a convoy of blue police vehicles thundered through the city at high speed. The police in Algeria resemble soldiers much more than law-enforcement officers. Three armoured personnel carriers with machine-gunners on top, scouring the surroundings, were escorting two trucks carrying heavily armed policemen. This was the only physical sign of a government presence that I witnessed. The police station and municipal buildings were deserted. The security forces only moved through Chlef when they had the firepower to defend themselves.

Hamid went into the cafe and was soon spotted by our contact. I had jested that he wear a red carnation but it was agreed that he would instead carry a notebook under his arm. We were told to follow a beige car that was waiting outside and we drove into the hills surrounding Chlef. After climbing for a few miles into the northernmost folds of the Atlas Mountains, we ran into another checkpoint. I later learnt that it was not operated by the AIS (Armée Islamique du Salut, or Islamic Salvation Army), the guerrilla group with whom we had arranged the visit. The AIS had close links with Islamists I had met in Algiers and I felt I could trust them. The checkpoint belonged to a more radical, rival movement called the Groupe Islamique Armé (Armed Islamic Group). The GIA were said to be primarily responsible for the murder of foreigners. A giant of a man with a resplendent beard and a large machine gun across his waist gave us a firm salute.

We arrived in a village of about a dozen mud-built houses, a short distance from the checkpoint. That's where I met Oussama, the commander of the local unit, who introduced himself as a terrorist.

After he asked if I was worried that I was greeting my executioners, there was a brief pause. Before the question had properly sunk in, the men around him burst out laughing. I pretended to join in. I introduced myself and instead of shaking hands exchanged the Islamic salutation. I placed my right hand over my heart and said, 'Peace be upon you.' Each man stood up in turn and we exchanged the greeting, followed by an embrace and a kiss on each cheek.

Oussama did not look like a killer; he had an uncanny likeness to the late Peter Sellers, as well as a mischievous twinkle in his eyes. I was also to discover something of the Inspector Clouseau in him; he was disorganized and accident-prone. Much later, when I was about to leave, I asked why they didn't kill me. Oussama answered without a smile: 'Because our political masters told us to protect you. Otherwise our orders would have been to finish you off.'

Before my journey to the militants' camp, I'd spent six weeks in Algiers gaining the confidence of lawyers, doctors and teachers close to the leadership of the FIS (Front Islamique du Salut, or Islamic Salvation Front), the political party that was banned after it was poised to win elections in 1992. The Algerian military cancelled the second phase of the voting and took power instead. Thousands of supporters of the FIS fled to the mountains and began their violent rebellion. I'd been negotiating the possibility of filming a unit of the AIS with what was effectively their political wing, the underground network of professionals in Algiers. After a few weeks, word came back. Yes, it would be possible but there were conditions; first, the documentary would have to be balanced and, second, I would have to agree not to refer to the armed Islamic groups as 'terrorists'. I accepted the conditions without much hesitation because they concurred with my intention to allow each side in the conflict to air its views.

That evening I pondered the issue over a drink with Hamid. We were sitting on the veranda of the El-Djazair Hotel as the light of the golden hour drenched the natural amphitheatre of Algiers harbour below. The hotel was an island of calm, perched on a hillside above the city. The country's French rulers built it a century earlier as the opulent Hotel Saint-George. Its imposing white walls were interrupted by elaborate blue mosaic tiles and ornate balconies with turquoise shutters. The designs drew on the region's Moorish and Ottoman past, evoking a mood of sultans' palaces and desert adventure in the Sahara.

The doormen in their brightly coloured robes were wild and romantic, adding to a vision of the Muslim world that was much loved in the West before the growth of Islamic militancy.

In its terraced botanical garden, roses clustered beneath giant palms, euphorbia cacti and orange trees. 'You should not call them terrorists,' Hamid advised. He was a very thoughtful man and had no allegiance to the militants. In his forties, his receding hair, grey moustache and owlish glasses gave him a professorial authority. This image was only marred when I saw him dance to disco music, which he enjoyed playing loudly in the car.

Hamid had received a death threat a few months earlier, an anonymous handwritten note warning him to abide by the Islamic code 'or else . . .'. He was a very brave man and, bearing in mind the fate that was to befall him, perhaps also foolhardy. He laughed off the death threat, describing it as a prank from one of his pupils. Such threats had become a common feature of life here, he said. I liked Hamid very much, but I knew that if he joined me, his life would change forever. If his presence became known to the regime, he could be charged with breaking Algeria's vaguely worded laws 'relating to the struggle against subversion and terrorism'. 'Detainees accused of subversion or terrorism are held incommunicado for several weeks, during which time they are routinely tortured,' according to Amnesty International. He would face a trial before a 'special court', where evidence acquired under torture was admissible.

I also knew that Hamid was fully aware of the danger he was in and his decision to join me was wholly his own. He had a genuine desire to make sense of the conflict that was drowning his country in blood. He also became drawn into the adventure; a glint in his eye said, 'Let's go for it.' Perhaps there was another reason: ordinary lives were rotting with fear that was too difficult for a visitor to detect. The rhythms of everyday routine appeared to beat normally in Algiers. It was difficult to diagnose how much the war infected ordinary lives. Hamid suffered stomach problems and life at home had become strained. When the ordinary becomes intolerable, extraordinary choices then seem normal.

The threat was, of course, deadly serious, though many more threats were issued than acted upon. Hundreds of teachers had been told to introduce traditional Islamic practices in schools, including sexual segregation and dress codes. The Islamic groups issued decrees banning the teaching of French and music, and sports for girls. English was not specifically mentioned. The colonial tongue still roused resentment; it remained the language of Algeria's Westernized elite. As a result of the threats, many teachers refused to work. More than five hundred schools had been destroyed.

Hamid was a devout Muslim but he believed in a liberal interpretation of the Qur'ān that accommodated modernity. He also believed that genuine faith was an intensely personal matter. Despite his antipathy toward the values of the Islamists, Hamid still believed that an even-handed journalist should not use the term 'terrorist' to describe them. I was glad of his support.

I did wonder, however, whether I had unwittingly allowed myself to be manipulated by brutal and unscrupulous gunmen. Would the omission of the word 'terrorist' result in a documentary that would appear to side with the militants? Why did the Islamists consider it such an important requirement of my reporting? That evening in the El-Djazair Hotel, I took my first step in trying to properly define 'terrorism'. I couldn't ever recall looking up its meaning in a dictionary. I had with me in Algiers a small Longman Pocket English. 'Terrorism: n use of violence for political purposes.'

I scribbled some words in my notebook: 'One can distinguish "terrorist" violence from that committed by criminals. A "terrorist" has a cause – that is, a political agenda – that he or she is fighting for.'

If this definition were applied to America's 'war on terror', the declaration would be understood to mean a 'war on political violence'. But that seemed far too broad. Political leaders order military personnel to commit acts of violence, and they are not criminals. I stuck with this logic for a moment and realized that it soon became absurd. The 'war on terror' could be defined as 'One form of political violence confronting another form of political violence'. Clearly, the dictionary didn't tell the whole story.

The following day, I had an appointment with a man who believed he had an exact definition. Majid Djebbari was a wiry, combative retired policeman in his fifties who spent his days recording the brutality unfolding around him, counting the bodies and consoling the relatives. He ran the Association for the Victims of Terrorism, an independent and poorly funded organization that offered help to dependants whose loved ones had been murdered by the Islamic militants. I met him at his modest home on the outskirts of Blida. He wore a blue jacket that had seen better days and a shirt fraying at the collar. He had a 'salt and pepper' stubble and as we spoke, he coughed through his umpteenth cigarette. Majid may have supported the regime (it was a government official who suggested I see him) but he was not part of the regime and enjoyed none of its privileges.

Alongside him on the sofa were his daughter, Ghania, and his two-year-old granddaughter. Ghania was in her late twenties, and sat motionless for most of the afternoon. Her large brown eyes and thick mane of dark hair were framed by the sunlight as it eased through the window. She seemed lost in her thoughts. Once her daughter had left her arms, she stared into space.

Ghania's husband, Samir, was a thirty-four-year-old teacher at a police academy. He had a round, friendly face and a thick moustache. In the photographs they showed me, he was always smiling. Wearing his peaked police cap, which seemed far too small for his large face, Samir looked more like a genial ticket inspector than a hard-nosed cop. His murder was part of a routine narrative of death that had taken hold of Algeria; he died on a bus while on his way to work. What hurt the most, Ghania told me, was that he had been killed by a neighbour. A few months earlier, she'd brought groceries for the murderer. 'One day he said good morning to my husband and they shook hands,' she recalled in a soft monotone. 'Then he pulled out a gun and fired two bullets at his head.'

Majid drew from another cigarette and told me that no one could be trusted. A neighbour or a friend could turn out to be a terrorist. 'This enemy is invisible and can be everywhere. The terrorists have been brainwashed in the name of Islam, despite the fact that the Qur'ān forbids killing. The terrorists have been tricked into thinking that anyone who kills in the name of God will go to paradise. These men kill civilians and have no scruples,' he told me. 'They are terrorists.'

Majid Djebbari used 'terrorist' to primarily mean a hidden, pernicious enemy but he also seemed to hint at a definition. He would probably define a terrorist as someone who deliberately murders civilians to achieve a political goal. His son-in-law's killer would fall into that category. My notebook entry continued:

'All political violence is not terrorism. It needs to be defined by specific acts of violence, such as killing civilians. If terrorism is evil, terrorists must employ some means of violence that no end can justify.

Many organisations, such as green activists, animal rights or anti-abortion campaigners, have an agenda to achieve political change using some form of violence but they are not usually called terrorists.' (This was well before the popular press adopted phrases such as 'eco-terrorism'.)

☆

Algiers retains the unmistakable influence of its former colonial rulers. Its elegant boulevards carry an aura of Paris, despite the dilapidated edges of the grand facades. Rue Didouche Mourad, full of shops and cafes, cuts through the centre of Algiers before reaching an abrupt end at the sixteenth-century casbah. As Rue Didouche Mourad snakes south, it becomes Avenue Franklin Roosevelt, recalling the role that Algiers played as headquarters for Allied forces in the Mediterranean during the Second World War.

During the colonial era, Rue Didouche Mourad had another name. Francophone street names usually place the family name of the honoured person first, and Mourad Didouche was one of the founders of the Algerian independence movement, the National Liberation Front (FLN). He was killed during a skirmish with French soldiers at an early stage of the war. Once wanted as a terrorist, he became a national hero when the FLN forced the end of French colonial rule in July 1962.

The shifting judgements of history became more evident when I entered the offices of a lawyer on Rue Didouche Mourad. Mostefa Bouchachi was a senior *avocat*, who had rights of audience in Algeria's Supreme Court. His black courtroom robes, tipped with white ermine, hung alongside his desk. (The Algerian penal system continues to follow the code that France imposed during colonial times. Their court attire has remained mostly unchanged since the Napoleonic decree.)

Mostefa had rings of prematurely greying hair pushed back over his forehead and caring, generous eyes. Shortly after I met him, he became the lawyer representing the imprisoned leaders of the Islamic Salvation Front, Abbassi Madani and Ali Belhadj, who were arrested in 1992 for undermining state security. He spoke with a measured softness, when recounting the facts as he knew them: 'The judiciary is not independent since the anti-terrorist laws. Eighty per cent of the people are condemned with no evidence whatsoever. All the institutions of this country have collapsed.'

Mourad Didouche's successors now governed Algeria. They implemented tactics against a new insurgency that their former French rulers had used against them. They adopted the same language; their challengers become terrorists. 'Suspects are kidnapped,' explained Mostefa. 'People come to me saying my son or my father was taken a week ago. We don't know where he is. We wait two weeks, a month, two months and he is still not brought before the courts.' Often he never appears. 'It's common knowledge that people are killed by the security forces,' he said, shrugging his shoulders. Abduction had become an established tactic of the military-backed regime. A bullet-ridden body would turn up the next day and the police would report that another terrorist had been killed.

One of Mostefa's clients was introduced to me as Mrs Moussaoui, but she was too fearful to give her real name. She was the mother of six young children; her husband, Kamel, was an accountant. I met her at an empty house because she was too scared to let me visit her home. She showed me a family portrait, laughing children alongside their smiling, proud father. Kamel had a thick, curly beard and wore a flowing white Arabic robe, a dress code that some in the regime considered the telltale signs of an Islamist.

One night, the family were in bed when they heard a crowd attempting to break in through the front door. Kamel went downstairs but before he could reach the door, the police rushed in. 'My husband was standing in the hallway and his hands were up because he was sure they were policemen. Then they shot him.' The first bullet struck under his armpit, the second his heart. 'I couldn't react. I was numb,' Mrs Moussaoui said. 'Then the policeman asked, "Who is this man?" It was after they shot him that they asked his name.'

Amnesty International reported 'hundreds of civilians have been killed as an alternative to arrest or in retaliation' for attacks by armed Islamists. It documented one case where twenty people were shot dead by security forces outside their homes in Algiers. Apparently, an armed group had earlier ambushed two army vehicles in the district.

A few days later, I met Majid Djebbari again, this time in the colonial elegance of the El-Djazair Hotel. He sipped a small glass of mint tea, hunched on an ornate stool in the lounge. The more we chatted, the more I realized that he had no affection for the regime. In common with everyone else I met in Algeria, he used an enigmatic, Orwellian phrase to refer to his remote leaders: le Pouvoir, or 'the power'. 'The main culprits are the higher executives who have ruled Algeria for thirty years,' he told me. 'They have used their rule for their own personal interest or for the benefit of their friends. Some people are getting richer and richer, others are getting poorer and poorer.'

Did he understand, then, why some people had taken up arms? 'It's not by attacking the poor policeman or the poor soldier that you can solve this crisis. No one amongst le Pouvoir has been touched. Why doesn't someone do something about them?' he asked.

And I had thought that Majid was a supporter of the government. Like many decent people in Algeria, he hated the regime but also detested the intolerance of the militants. The middle ground had been eroded and he was forced to take sides. He was from a lower-middle class family whose background was in the police. I told him about Mrs Moussaoui's account of her husband's death and he shrugged his shoulders. 'The police are under a lot of pressure.'

While it seemed wholly irrelevant to Majid, I continued to push him on the definition of 'terrorism'. I asked him about reports that the Algerian air force had bombarded villages suspected to be under the control of armed groups. Of course aerial bombing is not an act of terrorism, he said, because civilians are not the primary targets. The intention is to flush out the armed fighters and destroy their infrastructure. Civilian deaths are inevitable, even though they should be minimized. Then he added, 'These villagers are probably giving refuge to the terrorists, so most are not innocent anyway.'

Majid refused to accept the possibility that his son-in-law, Samir, had taken sides in the conflict and was no longer an 'innocent' civilian either. Samir was not a policeman but neither was he a mere bystander: he played a critical part in the government's strategy to train new policemen to fight the militants. His role in the academy is probably why he was murdered. The Allies during the Second World War used the argument that some civilians were not innocent but were part of the war effort in order to justify the bombing of factories in Hamburg where workers perished. The same argument was used by NATO during the bombing of an industrial plant in Yugoslavia in 1999. Of course, no one would call the pilots who dropped the bombs terrorists, even though the number of civilians who died as a result of aerial bombing during the twentieth century far exceeded those executed by gunmen or blown up by bombs planted in public places.

I later mused that the first problem with Majid's interpretation of 'terrorism' was establishing which non-combatants were innocent and which were legitimate targets. What about the staff of government offices, such as Samir, who played an important role in the survival of a regime? The second problem was defining intent. Are civilian deaths defensible if they are known to be a predictable consequence of violence? How scrupulous does the perpetrator need to be to avoid killing civilians before he becomes a terrorist?

During my stay with the guerrillas, I met Hocine, a young chemistry graduate who had become a bomb-maker. He wore a white laboratory coat and consulted a notepad filled with lists of molecular equations. His room was stocked full of batteries, timers and detonators. I watched as he scooped an explosive powder into an empty gas canister and placed metal pellets around the rim. 'This will cause maximum damage,' he said as he showed me one of the heavy inch-long pellets. 'They're made of steel and are used in the building trade.' He demonstrated with a quick movement of his hands how, upon detonation, the small missiles would fly off at high speed and pierce any object in their path. He acted like an enthusiastic chemistry student undertaking a classroom experiment.

Shortly after I met Hocine, a bomb similar to one that he'd built killed four children in the nearby city of Mostaganem. When I mentioned this to a doctor in Algiers who backed the uprising, he said the death of the children was regrettable, but such tragedies happened in war. I was disturbed by the ease with which horror can be rationalized, especially when I saw images of the funerals on Algerian state television.

Hocine, the bomb-maker, had dark, penetrating eyes and a ski mask pulled over his face. His appearance and actions were a perfect match for the popular portrait of a 'terrorist'. But if the intentional murder of civilians is a critical component of the definition, then a bomber such as Hocine could claim the label is not for him; the explosion in Mostaganem, if it was one of his bombs, was intended to detonate as a police vehicle passed by. The death of the civilians was said to be a 'mistake', or, in American military language, collateral damage.

My quest for a satisfactory meaning of 'terrorism' often felt at best an irrelevant pastime; at worst, it was a violation of the despair and suffering of those around me. The violence seemed, at first glance, so abominable as to have no comprehensible cause; the mutilation of a baby, the execution of a whole family, the beheadings, the murder of a dozen foreigners because they happened to be Christian.

One dapper elderly Algerian who lived in Paris told me at the bar of the hotel that the violence was the work of psychopaths. 'There was no other possible explanation,' he explained over a pastis. He was small and delicately boned with a perfectly manicured moustache and twinkling eyes. He seemed to say everything with his mouth locked in a smile. After a while, it struck me that he was being rather condescending. He advised me that to analyse the butchery within a rational framework was to credit the terrorists with a reasoning they do not have. He also hinted, without saying it, that trying to determine a cause for the violence would be like searching for an excuse. He seemed to be warning me, in a most polite manner, that such a quest might cast me as a 'sympathizer'. If he told me his name I couldn't remember it. The next time I saw him he was leaving the hotel and he waived theatrically, warning me to watch out for 'the *intégristes*'.

I looked it up in my French dictionary but found no reference. Then I began to hear it used more frequently, especially by French-leaning Algerians. In the past, the word was used in Europe to describe Roman Catholics who believed that their faith should be the state religion. It was now being applied to Muslims who wanted to install governments that ruled according to sharia, or Islamic law. The usual term in English would be 'fundamentalist'; but *intégriste* carries a more fearsome connotation, suggesting an intolerant faith that poses a broader ideological threat to society. In the Anglo-Saxon world, religion is generally not seen as a force that can undermine the political system. France, on the other hand, has a long tradition of committed secularism; for many Frenchmen, as well as Algerians who have adopted their views, theocracy is, like fascism, an evil that must be rooted out.

'Has fascism been fought with words? No! You cannot combat fascism with words. You fight it with weapons,' declared Zazi Sadou, a woman in her early thirties and a prominent activist in a feminist movement that directly challenged the Islamists' vision of gender and family. Zazi had received repeated death threats and moved daily from one secure place to another. She was brave and tough-minded. She wore jeans and a purple shirt with a leopardskin pattern. 'I haven't lived at home for months.' She spoke breathlessly as she packed the black travel bag that never left her side. 'I keep my things in here. I have a change of clothes. I live badly but my concern is to live. In order to stay alive, I have to defy death every day.'

The Assembly of Democratic Women of Algeria, known by its French acronym RAFD, met secretly in safe houses and issued statements accusing the government of weakness and treachery in its war against the armed Muslims. I went to a secret meeting in the windowless basement of a small food store in downtown Algiers. About a dozen women sat around a table in the dim light. Fear was in their voices, some trembling, others shouting. They dreaded most a peace deal between the government and the Islamists. 'If tomorrow the Islamists are in power,' said one exasperated woman, 'they'll take us to a public place and cut off our heads and all of it will be legal under their sharia law.'

Zazi and her colleagues sympathized with a hard-line military faction within the regime, known as the *éradicateurs*. The shadowy grouping included the secret police and unaccountable military units accused of extrajudicial killings. Zazi took deep breaths between her sentences. 'I refuse to obey the orders of madmen,' she said as locks of her hair fell over her face. 'The only way for Algeria to come through this crisis is to fight. To confront the *intégristes*,' she said as tears of rage swelled in her eyes, 'we must wage a battle without compromise. If you put down your arms and look away, you are dead!'

When I left the gathering I felt both sympathetic and disturbed by the passion and fury that resonated around the basement. Zazi and her followers considered the Islamists as a breed apart, an inhuman mutation that had somehow landed on their doorstep. There was no answer to questions such as 'Why are they killing?' or 'What caused the crisis?' There was no point asking these questions because the Islamists were 'crazy terrorists' and 'madmen'.

My meeting with Zazi strengthened my resolve to continue with my attempt to explore the usage of 'terrorism'. I realized that unlocking its meaning was a crucial step towards understanding the causes of the brutality in Algeria. The longer I remained, the more I became aware of the complicated dynamics of the conflict. It slowly dawned on me that allegedly psychopathic behaviour was not necessarily insane at all. The war, the terror, the butchery began to fit into a grotesque but rational pattern. Many years later, the political scientist Grenville Byford aptly explained the callous rationale that I witnessed in Algeria: 'The sad fact is that the use of force for political ends, whether in the context of a declared war or otherwise, is inextricably bound up with terror. The object is not to kill every opponent but merely to do away with a sufficiently large number that those who remain fear carrying on more than they fear giving up.'*

The use of terror as a tool of combat was applied savagely and also successfully during Algeria's War of Independence, the most brutal anti-colonial struggle of the last century. It was a lesson that many Algerians learnt and did not forget.

Charles de Gaulle once said that war 'gives birth' to nations. In Algeria it was a bloody, painful delivery, littered with corpses. Nobody is sure how many died; there were too many bodies to count in repeated massacres during the eight-year confrontation. The Algerian government later claimed that over a million perished. The techniques of bloodletting seeped into the fabric of Algeria's regime and had chilling reverberations in the 1990s conflict. The first systematic attack on civilians in El-Halia in 1955, when the whole town was massacred, set the precedent.

On 20 August, four groups of fifteen to twenty men systematically slaughtered the European inhabitants in the most bloody and merciless fashion, regardless of sex or age. Throats were slit, limbs hacked off, women disembowelled, children smashed against walls. It was calculated to shock and horrify France. It did. Revenge was swift as paratroopers arrived and randomly killed Arab civilians in order to hunt out the 'terrorists'. The government claimed it killed 1,273 guerrillas in retaliation for the deaths of 71 *pied-noirs*. According to the FLN, which has given names and addresses, twelve thousand Muslims lost their lives during an orgy of bloodletting.

The same logic was unfolding four decades later in the mountains and valleys of Algeria. The Islamic guerrillas wanted to shock the regime into repressive actions that would steer public sympathy towards the rebels' cause. The parallel between the present conflict and the war of independence was made flesh in the form of Commander Ali. I'd arranged a meeting with him at the offices of a lawyer in downtown Algiers.

Ali was in his late fifties or early sixties and was wearing dark slacks and a slightly stained brown jacket over a check shirt. His cheekbones pushed through his skin, dark and leathered by the sun

---

* Grenville Byford, 'The Wrong War', *Foreign Affairs*, July/August 2002.

and wind. He wore a moustache and smoked roll-up cigarettes. He wouldn't raise a glance; he looked like hundreds of other men on the streets of Algiers.

This was his second guerrilla war. He'd fought for the FLN in the 1950s, for the same units that Mourad Didouche had led until his death. At first, Ali was taciturn; he seemed a man who preferred to speak with his deeds. He voiced a mantra that I was to hear repeatedly from the rebels; they were fighting a 'second war of independence'. The first war had expelled the French, but the leadership that replaced them adopted the values and behaviour of their former masters. Rather than look north to Paris, Algeria should find its values to the east, in Mecca.

Ali agreed that one of the aims of the guerrillas was to demonstrate their strength to villagers. Yes, they issued threats because they were the legitimate government following the Islamic Salvation Front's success in elections in 1991. And yes, they punished those who disobeyed them. 'Do you kill them?' I asked. 'If we have to,' he replied.

I recalled how, a few days earlier, Majid Djebbari from the Victims of Terrorism Association described the effect militants had on daily life in his hometown, Blida. 'People are traumatized,' he told me. 'If these terrorists give an order, it will be obeyed because they are more powerful than the government.'

While I spoke to Ali he deflected detailed questions about the violence of the guerrillas with parallel accounts of brutality from the security forces. The military had entered one village in his district and taken a dozen young men under twenty-five. They weren't seen again. The lawyer in whose office we were meeting chipped in that he had hundreds of files from mothers whose sons had 'disappeared'.

The conflict, in its most savage component, had become a war *defined* by terror. The more brutally one side behaved, the more terror it engendered and the more powerful it apparently became.

How should 'terrorism' be used in the context of such a war? I could refer to the crisis in terms of terror unleashed by the regime to combat terrorists. Or I could describe the Islamists using terror to challenge a terrorist government in Algiers. The usage would be fair, but farcical.

Early one morning, Majid Djebbari called me. He was passing the hotel: did I want to see some victims of terrorism? Within half an hour, I was standing in a mortuary facing a wall of metal boxes. Majid had wanted me to join him in order to show what 'terrorism' meant for him. He was too polite to tell me directly but his actions were now saying: 'Stop trying to define "terrorism", see the victims and you'll know what it is.'

The smell of formaldehyde was strong and the young mortuary assistant asked brusquely which ones I wanted to see. Anyone who'd been killed by terrorists, I said, assuming she understood what I meant. 'I don't know who killed them,' she shot back. 'This one had her throat slit; is that what you want?' she asked as she opened a metal casket and a woman in a neat slightly old-fashioned pink dress was pulled out. A cheap pink plastic necklace was around her neck covering an incision about four inches wide across her throat. The blood had been cleaned up, the smell disinfected, the chaotic horror of death wiped away. This method of murder is known as *l'egorgement*, a death that is intended to humiliate because the victim bleeds like an animal slaughtered for halal meat.

I tried to find out about the woman in the pink dress. What was her name? The casket was labelled FD-243. Why was she killed? How was she chosen? No one in the mortuary knew. After a few enquiries, a journalist, without callous intention, told me, 'She wasn't anybody.' She was just another victim. The woman in the pink dress wasn't relevant to the killers; she was simply the message being sent to others in her town.

One ordinary girl did, in death, become a message that terrorized millions of others and to the outside world seemed to define the insanity that had engulfed Algeria. Her family now lived in the mountainous Kabylia region, dominated by the non-Arab, Berber-speaking minority. The Berbers are the original inhabitants of Algeria and while first Roman and then Arab invaders gradually absorbed those who inhabited the plains, the Berbers of Kabylia's jagged peaks retained their culture and warlike traditions. The Berbers are Muslim but they are fiercely opposed to the militants, who they believe are trying to impose an Arab culture on their lives.

It is a region of dense forests and barren, rocky hillsides, with winding roads carved into the unforgiving terrain. We drove past Tizi-Ouzou, the urban centre of Kabylia, to a remote farm where the Bengana family had made its home. Six months earlier, the family had

fled the town of Meftah, on the southern outskirts of Algiers: it was in
the 'triangle of death', and was then a base for the Armed Islamic
Group.

'We left everything. We came here empty-handed. We abandoned
everything,' Yakout Bengana told me as she fought back tears. She
wore a paisley dress with lace edging around the neck. She was in her
late thirties and despite the extra few pounds left behind by age and
motherhood, she retained a classical beauty with sharp cheekbones
and large baleful eyes.

'When I remember that day, it is as if the bullets hit me. My
daughter arrived crying, "Mummy, Mummy, Katia has been shot,
Katia has been shot!" I said: "Is she dead?" "No," she answered, "she
is still quivering on the ground."' Yakout broke down and cried
uncontrollably.

Katia Bengana lived for less than seventeen years. Yakout handed
me a picture of her daughter in a black off-the-shoulder party dress.
She was stunningly attractive, tall and elegant, with waves of dark
curls falling down as far as her breasts. She looked a little older than
her age; perhaps that was helped by the lipstick and make-up.

Katia's father, Rashid, was pinched thin; his clothes dangled as if
they were on a hanger. His face seemed locked in thought. When I saw
him, he was tending Katia's grave. The inscription on the tombstone
was in green lettering.

> Ici repose Bengana Katia,
> nee le 20.05.1977
> decedee 28.02.1994
> A notre chere Katia
> Victime d'Integrists

Rashid recalled an ominous mood in Meftah the winter before.
'There were written warnings all over town, on the walls, outside
mosques warning that women were obliged to wear a headscarf by a
certain date – I think it was February 18th.'

On 28 February, Katia's sister Nassima was on the balcony of their
house. 'I saw Katia walking toward the house with her friend, who
was wearing a headscarf. Then I saw someone move straight towards
Katia. I didn't see his face, only the back of his head. The girl with the
headscarf was walking right next to Katia, but the gunman signalled
for her to move away. She ran and then he shot Katia three times.

'When I saw Katia falling on the ground I rushed down the street shouting, "Ambulance!" but there was no one to help as everybody fled from the scene. Neighbours and passers-by disappeared. I was left to cope alone with the situation.' Nassima held Katia's hand until a policeman arrived fifteen minutes later. 'He looked at Katia and said she was dead.'

Nassima said that Katia was adamant about refusing to wear the hijab (Islamic headscarf). 'In her school many girls covered their heads. Probably about three-quarters wore a hijab. Katia said she would obey her father if he wanted her to wear it, but never anybody else. She swore that even if she had to die, she would never wear the hijab.'

The definition of 'terrorism as theatre' applies with cruel precision to Katia's murder. It didn't matter that this particular fifteen-year-old girl was chosen; what mattered was the message it sent to other girls throughout Algeria. After Katia's death, Rashid Bengana created an association in her honour. It included friends and hundreds of sympathizers in Kabylia. Its aim was to rally support against the Islamists. 'The ideological goal is to make people understand the nature of terrorism,' he told me. 'The practical goal is to defend people from terrorism.' In the mountains of Kabylia, the Berber minority began to form armed militias to defend their villages. 'These men will fight rather than live under an Islamic government.'

Katia's death reminded me of a conversation I had while I travelled with Oussama and his band of gunmen near Chlef. It was a discussion over dinner that I dismissed at the time but three years later recalled in vivid colour.

The guerrillas were well fed; life seemed bizarrely relaxed and good-humoured. They took time over lunch. I asked whether they were concerned that government forces might spring an attack. They scoffed and carried on tucking into the food. We'd gathered for lunch in a room without furniture. A plastic mat was rolled down the centre and about twenty men sat around its edge. From a doorway leading to a room in the back, I glimpsed the gloved hand of a woman passing plates to one of the guerrillas. In the tradition of seclusion, the women are sequestered to their own quarters.

Lunch usually started with tea and a snack of flat bread dipped in yoghurt and honey. Then came the couscous; mutton stew with carrots, turnips, tomatoes and chickpeas, spiced with hot peppers and coriander. It was a freshly cooked, homemade delight. The guerrillas were proud of their couscous; it was their national dish and they said that their variety was the finest in Algeria. Oussama explained that the steamed semolina needed to be of perfect texture, dry enough to separate on the plate but moist enough to stick to the fork.

During one lengthy lunch, I chatted about news that had detonated shock and revulsion around the world a week or two earlier. Seven Italian seamen were sleeping on their ship, the *Lucina*, a small cargo vessel bringing semolina for couscous from Sardinia. They were docked near Jijel, a port between Algiers and the colonial city of Philippeville, now called Annaba.

During the night, each man had his throat sliced by 'Islamic terrorists', according to reports emanating from the Algerian media. It was in 1994, the night before the Group of Seven (G7) leaders of the world's most powerful nations met in Naples. Italy was overcome with grief; Bill Clinton joined other presidents and prime ministers in a chorus of condemnation of this latest atrocity by 'Islamic terrorists'.

'Why did you do it?' I asked. At once, about a dozen voices rose up in unison denying any involvement by the Islamists. It was the Sécurité Militaire, one said, using the popular name for the Direction des Renseignements de Securité (DRS), Algeria's internal intelligence agency. Another, the bear of a man from the GIA who was at the checkpoint when I first entered guerrilla territory, shouted, 'How could we kill them? The killers had to cross military controls. It was heavily protected. And they got away without a trace. Think about it.' They laughed as if an incident like the butchery of seven Italians was just another part of the conflict, another move in the chess game.

'They also unloaded the cargo from the ship,' said an older man who'd been listening quietly. 'Everything le Pouvoir does is to make sure that the men who control this country continue to make money. It's a mafia, that's what they are.' I didn't pursue the discussion further and dismissed the guerrillas' denial of responsibility as improbable. I did not believe that the regime was capable of such brazen violence, particularly against foreign nationals.

Three years later the *Observer* reported the account of 'Joseph', a former Algerian secret policeman who was seeking political asylum in the UK. He confirmed that the regime ordered the gruesome killings in order to spark international condemnation of the Islamists. Another defector, 'Peter', an Algerian ship's engineer, said: 'Every sailor in Algeria knows the Sécurité Militaire killed the seamen.' The seamen played the same role as Katia. They were murdered for the effect on 'the people watching'; in their case the G7 world leaders.

The definition of 'terrorism as theatre' allows a regime such as that in Algeria to be labelled 'terrorist'. I was left once again with the peculiar lexicon of terrorists fighting terrorists. The description that both sides employ terror as a tool of warfare seemed more satisfactory. In this conflict, every action seemed to have not an equal but a more ruthless reaction. In apparent retaliation for Katia's death, two veiled students were gunned down a month later while waiting for a bus. The blood of the innocent was just a message exchanged through the media from one political leadership to another, or sent to the international community.

Attracting Western support was a central objective of the Algerian regime after the military takeover in 1992 that had been encouraged by France but, initially at least, viewed with suspicion by the United States and Britain. The regime needed investment from American and British companies to tap Algeria's vast oil and gas reserves and thus had to legitimize its governance. On the one hand, the military introduced a facade of democratic reform to persuade Algerians that power was now with a civilian leadership. On the other, it chose to show the outside world that it was confronting a monstrous, diabolical enemy. The more throats that were slit, the more the Algerian military could justify its undemocratic rule.

In order to draw the outside world sympathetically into the war against the Islamists, the regime needed to control the information that left the country. It decided to close off large parts of Algeria to outsiders and prevent international journalists freely reporting the conflict. It also imposed strict controls over the Algerian media. The next stage was to repeatedly vilify its enemies as 'terrorists', mixing the noun with a merry-go-round of other repugnant terms such as 'madmen' and 'butchers'. Without independent access, the outside world would gradually begin to listen to official accounts and adopt the language.

The regime wanted to manage the Algerian media without it appearing to be controlled by the state. The man who orchestrated this was a bureaucrat with a finely trimmed moustache and a neat desk. Djamal Bouzenat was in his mid-forties and sat with a remarkably upright posture. He was a precise man who seemed to want everything to be in order. His office in the Palais du Gouvernement in Algiers was part of the Ministry of the Interior, even though his official title was media press attaché. As well as being in charge of the security forces, the Ministry of the Interior handles the government's dealings with the domestic and international media.

About a week before my journey to the mountains, I was sitting opposite Bouzenat in his moderately grand office. Around him were a small group of young men and women diligently tapping on old typewriters. The sudden sound of paper whipped from the roller signalled a completed page. One such page was handed to him. 'Where shall I place this article?' he playfully asked me. 'Which reporter shall I choose to write it?' He was feeling confident, a man who believed he held power over the truth.

Bouzenat confided in me because I had given the impression that as a Westerner I shared the government's view that radical Islam was a threat to both Algerian state power and Western civilization. I wanted to convey to the regime a confidence that I was onside and would not abscond to areas controlled by the armed groups. The Islamist militants had already killed at least twenty journalists in a gruesome campaign to pressure the newspapers to report their view. It was easy to express a fear for my life and a willingness to be guided and protected by Ministry of Interior officials. Despite the tidal wave of blood that was enveloping Algeria – three hundred people were dying each week – I believed that the government was not primarily concerned with protecting the safety of foreign journalists but controlling what they saw.

The Islamists were also keenly aware of the importance of speaking through the media. When they became frustrated by the coverage in the Algerian press, they believed they could intimidate journalists into writing more favourably about their cause. They failed and afterwards considered the Algerian media an arm of the regime. Journalists and writers became victims of their assassination squads.

For Algerian journalists, the threat from the militants was a grim daily horror. I went to the Maison de la Presse to meet Said Mekbel, the editor of *Le Matin*, one of Algeria's most popular French-language dailies.

Mekbel had a comforting, tranquil demeanour. He seemed remarkably relaxed considering that he'd received several death threats from the Islamic groups and had escaped two attempts on his life. He was a deeply respected journalist who remained fiercely independent. He did not shy from criticizing the regime: remarkably, he was as concerned about the government's pressure on his journalists as the threats they received from the militants. 'We are caught between a rock and a hard place,' he sighed.

After the murder of one of Algeria's most celebrated writers, Tahar Djaout, Mekbel formed a committee to determine the truth about his killer and the murder of other intellectuals. Djaout had been shot twice in the head as he sat in the front seat of his car. His murder typified many that followed; the police investigations were slipshod and serious doubts remained over the men who the authorities claimed were responsible. Just days after the murder a young man appeared on the television news and confessed to being the get-away driver. The security forces had killed two men during a shootout, who they claimed were the other members of the death squad. Mekbel wrote a popular column in *Le Matin* under the intriguing moniker the Rusty Nail. For him, little of the story rang true and he commented, 'The news that all the killers had been killed was like some farcical joke. One could even laugh . . . from despair.' With his trademark irony he declared that the Truth Committee was 'determined to start a new tradition . . . of unearthing the killers and those behind them.'

When my documentary *Algeria's Hidden War* was broadcast, it was watched by millions in Algeria who for the first time could listen to a wide range of views within a narrative that did not take sides. The show was transmitted on satellite television from France, which the Algerian regime is unable to control. I was true to my word. The film showed the violence and the brutality of the armed groups but did not describe them as terrorists.

The furious regime made every attempt to discredit the documentary in the media, with a strong counteroffensive. In an article in *Le Matin*, the authorities described me as 'an apprentice sorcerer' and part of a grander conspiracy. 'There is a much bigger scheme behind this venture, which is the destabilization of Algeria.' The newspaper claimed I was trying to portray Algeria 'in the grip of a savage war' when 'here we live and breathe terrorism and its terrible aftermath.' According to the lunchtime television news, 'The journalist Phil Rees has been known for many years as working as a secret agent for the CIA in Lebanon during the war, as his television reports at the time were a cover for the infiltration of Islamic factions in the area and spying on them.' The ultimate term of vilification in the Arab world, where conspiracy theories are often an established belief, is to accuse a Westerner of belonging to the CIA.

I knew that the genial and observant editor, Said Mekbel, was not responsible for the fiction that was passed off as news in *Le Matin*. On a Saturday morning, two weeks earlier, he had been at work preparing an article for Monday's paper. Aware that he was brushing with death every day, he began writing about the inability of an individual to protect himself from invisible assassins. He described the solitude of an Algerian journalist caught between the death sentence of the Islamists and the harassment of the state.

Mekbel got up from his typewriter just before noon and went to have lunch with a colleague at a pizza restaurant opposite his office. The fifty-seven-year-old journalist had sent his family to France but was unwilling to remain there himself. 'My work is in Algeria,' he told me, 'this is my home.'

On that Saturday, Mekbel's Rusty Nail painted a tragic portrait of the daily life of a journalist in Algeria. The journalist is forced to behave like a thief 'who slinks along walls to go home at night'. He warns his children not to talk about the job he does. 'This tramp who no longer knows where to spend the night, he's the one. He's the one they threaten in the privacy of a government office, the witness who must swallow what he knows, this bare and helpless citizen . . .

'This man who makes a wish not to die with his throat cut, he's the one. The body on which they sew back a severed head, he's the one. He's the one whose hands know no other skill, only his meagre writing, the one who hopes against hope, since roses grow from dung heaps.

'He's the one who leaves his house in the morning without being sure if he will make it to the office and in the evening he's the one who leaves his work unsure if he will return home.'

Said Mekbel never did return home that day. As he entered the restaurant, a regular diner who had become an acquaintance rose to greet him and shook his hand. Mekbel sat down and ordered a salad. The article that Mekbel had been working on that day was later found. 'I would like to know who will kill me,' it read. 'When will I be killed, I ask myself?'

The regular customer had eaten at the restaurant for six months in order to observe the movements of his intended victim. Just after the salad was brought to the table, he pulled out a handgun and fired twice into Said Mekbel's head.

3 / AN ENEMY CALLED 'TERROR'

'This is civilization's fight.'
President George W. Bush

A black curtain rose across the Shomali Plain, the broad valley that eased through the mountains north of Kabul, as thick palls of sand and smoke soared hundreds of feet into the air. A second later, the thuds of the explosions shook the ground beneath. The mighty B-52 bombers of the US Air Force were incinerating any who strayed into the deadly valley.

The Shomali Plain was ringed by folds of snow-capped mountains and the evening sun left a patina of luminous orange. The plain had been one of Afghanistan's few fruit baskets; at one time, two hundred thousand people farmed its fertile soil. Rows of vineyards criss-crossed though orchards growing apples, almonds and mulberries. This strategic flatland had been a battleground since the Soviet Union fought the mujahedin, or Islamic holy warriors, here in the 1980s. When the Taliban occupied it in 1999, they burnt houses and evicted villagers. To ensure that no one returned, they shovelled soil into the underground streams that irrigated the orchards, blocking their flow. The Shomali Plain had become a barren wasteland; the earth was reclaiming the decaying, mud-built houses in the empty villages.

If the dead land needed any further testament to the destructive power of man, countless tons of ordnance had poured from the skies for nearly a month, pummelling forward positions of the Taliban forces. The bombs struck their targets with ease, vaporizing makeshift defences constructed of mud and corrugated steel.

The nearest Taliban targets were just half a mile away and I had a ringside seat for the 'War on Terror'. I was peering over a sandbank atop a bunker housing men from the anti-Taliban Northern Alliance, a rebranded military partnership comprising the leftovers of the old mujahedin. The men in the trenches below had risen to their feet and stood motionless, bearded jaws hanging open with awe. Abdul Majid, the leader of this frontline band of dishevelled soldiers, suddenly leapt up and down, shrieking with childish jubilation. Howls and clapping broke out amongst his men, a few uttering the cry 'Allah u Akbar!', 'God is Great!'

It was fifty-four days since the United States had suffered the bloodiest surprise in its history. Now it was payback time. I looked up as an American fighter jet and a B-52 bomber, silver specks in the clear blue sky eight miles above, headed home to their bases.

Abdul Majid was commander of the 710th Holy Warrior (Mujahedin) Brigade. The unit was also dubbed the 'Kabul Brigade'; their mission, Majid proudly declared, was to be the first to enter the city when the Taliban was overthrown. As the mountain of dust and debris thinned, Majid peered through his Russian-made military telescope at the enemy bunkers. He gave the 'thumbs up' signal and patted me on the back. 'Very good,' he muttered.

Majid's face was lined and cracked by the dry wind and dust that scours so much of Afghanistan. He had grown up amidst the ceaseless war that began here when he was just four years old. He became a soldier at twelve, when his faction was part of the alliance of mujahedin who fought the Soviet Union. When the Soviets withdrew from Afghanistan in 1989, he fought the regime they left behind. When that government fell, he fought other factions within the mujahedin. Now he was fighting an enemy called 'terror'.

Dust had settled in his beard and in the cracks in his face. There was no opportunity to wash in the trenches. There were no supplies of water, nor was there a latrine dug into the earth. I was advised to crawl from the trench at night and squat. It was safer then, because the Taliban fighters would be less likely to spot me and open fire. The dust was also in the food, cooked on an open wood fire near the door to the bunker. It was easier to swallow large chunks, rather than chew until the sand grated my teeth.

'We will eliminate terrorism from Afghanistan,' Majid announced over a dinner of boiled meat and rice in his trench. The meat was described as 'sheep' but had an anonymous dark taste and rubbery texture. My cameraman was suffering from worms, and a grotesque image of creatures wiggling inside my intestines dominated my thoughts as I swallowed.

Majid wore an old leather biker's jacket over his salwar kameez. His hair was shoulder length and straggly. He looked like a washed-up rock star from the 60s; in fact his resemblance to Bob Dylan was so strong that we began to refer to him as 'Bob'. He also smoked marijuana after the evening meal, his only apparent diversion from the daily grind of life in the trenches. He offered us some but quickly withdrew the weed on the advice of an older man before our cameras started rolling; an army stoned on the front line was not the image the anti-Taliban forces wanted to portray.

As the sun fell, the muezzin called the Brigade of Holy Warriors to pray. A dozen men took a break from their soldiering and faced the mountains to the west, a pause that they knew would be synchronized with their enemy. For the past year, Majid's orders had been to hold his bunker and the trenches that dissected the Shomali Plain, even if his unit fought to the last man. Majid insisted that his men would gladly die for their faith.

Such grandiloquence often accompanied the drumbeat of Afghanistan's conflict, even though the tradition of martyrdom that finds such violent expression in the Middle East is eschewed here. When I asked a battery commander in the 710th Brigade called Mohammed whether the Northern Alliance would ever consider using suicide bombers, he pointed mysteriously in each direction toward the mountains. 'We are all happy to die as martyrs,' he said, with a somewhat oily smile. 'We are doing Allah's work. God willing, every man and boy will die with a happy face to defeat the terrorist Taliban.' He smiled again, broadly but without parting his lips. He repeated 'Inshallah', or 'God willing', but emphasized each syllable very slowly.

Mohammed was hugely overweight and hobbled slowly through the trenches, yet was always the first to arrive for dinner. He had two wives and fifteen children and seemed too contented with himself to treat thoughts of martyrdom seriously. Like most Afghan soldiers, he was wily enough to survive to fight another day. I remember when I travelled through the Shomali Plain with mujahedin fighters a dozen years before; one man mocked the Arab volunteers who had joined their jihad against the Soviet Union. He laughed as he described the willingness of Arabs to walk across minefields. 'Rather them than us,' he chuckled. 'They're nuts.'

After dinner, when Majid had relaxed with his joint, the official rhetoric about combating 'terror' was abandoned. The hopes he had for his life were painfully simple; to return to see his mother in Kabul and eventually to find a wife. But destiny had placed him in the bunker and he had to accept his lot. He said that he had no option but to flee when the Taliban captured Kabul because he was from the Tajik ethnic group, while the city's conquerors were overwhelmingly from the rival Pashtun community. His primary motivation for fighting was tribal loyalty rather than political principles.

At nightfall, the unit settled in to sleep in their bunker, a room about five metres square with a ceiling just high enough to be able to sit upright. While a small contingent remained on watch, the rest slept in tightly squeezed rows in the airless room. The atmosphere was stale from sweat and farts. Another factor hung in the air; a sexual desire that we felt was targeted toward our team.

During the day, I had my bottom patted more than once as I bent down. The gunmen pretended that they were removing dust. They would then snigger; one caught my eye and raised his eyebrows as if asking, 'Did you like that?' I scoffed mildly but let it pass by. Another man with eyeliner winked at me several times.

At first glance, Afghan culture promotes the virtues of simple oil-and-grease masculinity. The emphasis on unconstrained machismo is evident in the traditional portraits that Afghans favour as family heirlooms. It is almost obligatory for those posing to display their rifle and drape themselves with a bandolier and other trappings of warfare. Sometimes these props lie around the photographer's studio, even though most adult males have their own guns. The pictures are shot in black and white and the photographer paints on colour afterwards. When our team had our pictures taken as personal souvenirs, another issue arose; the photographer insisted on painting facial hair. It was not considered appropriate to be photographed without a beard, or at least a moustache. But even this apparent obsession with gender assertion is deceptive; the photographer usually paints pronounced, pouting lips, gives the cheeks a dash of rouge and adds eyeliner to twinkling eyes. While I am clutching an AK-47 assault rifle and have a painted-on moustache, the overall impression of my picture, according to friends, is that I am dressed to take part in a gay cabaret.

Homosexual love, one of the great unspoken facets of Afghani culture, is celebrated in Pashtun music, dance and poetry. Male prostitution was commonplace before the Taliban took over Afghanistan, and men lived openly with their *ashna*, or 'beloved one'. Often, a bearded, heavily armed man could be seen walking next to a fresh-faced boy of fifteen or sixteen. To an outsider, they might have appeared like father and son, but Afghans knew otherwise.

The tradition of well-to-do men acquiring *ashna*s played its part in the Taliban's remarkable rise to power. In the summer of 1994, a few months before the Taliban took control of Kandahar, two commanders confronted each other with tanks in the city's streets. It was like a duel in eighteenth-century Europe, except that the prize was a boy in his early teens and the destruction and death were incomparable.

During the Taliban's rule, the open display of fondness for young boys was curtailed. Sodomy was punishable by death and administered according to literal Islamic teaching: the guilty man was taken to the base of a huge mud and brick wall, which was pushed onto him by a tank. If he was still alive on the following day, relatives were allowed to take the crushed body away and administer to his injuries.

For the most part, the Taliban's restrictions simply kept male-on-male sexual relations behind closed doors. Our Afghan assistant, Fadlan, smiled knowingly and blushed when I asked whether homosexual liaisons were commonplace. Fadlan was in his mid-twenties, bright and mostly self-educated in a nation where only one in three can read or write. He was a good-looking man with large almond eyes and a mane of well-manicured hair. He often smelt of cologne and walked with a somewhat awkward, shuffling gait. I never discovered Fadlan's sexual orientation and, of course, it was not relevant to his excellent work as our fixer and translator. Despite his delicate manner, Fadlan dealt effectively with powerful warlords who often appeared like hairy cavemen who had replaced wooden clubs with AK-47s.

Our cameraman, Dean Johnson (known as Johno from his Royal Marines days), took the often-present sexual undercurrents a little more seriously than the rest of us. His blond hair, sparkling blue eyes and impish smile often attracted female attention elsewhere. In Afghanistan, it captured the lingering and unwanted glances of men. The most amusing incident was at a village at the front line of the war called Sarsayed, a name that celebrates the hunting skills of its men folk. The village elder was a Pashtun man in his fifties named Fareed. I was discussing the state of the war with Fareed when Fadlan began a lengthy discussion with him in Pashto.

'What's he saying?' I finally asked. Fadlan glanced at me but ignored my question. 'Come on, Fadlan, tell me what's going on,' I insisted after a further pause.

'I can't say,' Fadlan replied, looking rather embarrassed.

'Why not? You are paid to translate, not have long personal chats.'

'OK. OK,' Fadlan sighed, seemingly exasperated. 'Mr Fareed asked if Johno would like to be his son's wife for the night.'

There was a pause while this remark sank in. I looked at Johno, who was turning tomato-red. Then our producer, Frank Smith, and I burst out laughing, shocking Mr Fareed, who began to look uneasy. He soon realized that Johno would not be providing his son with a night of sexual pleasure.

This casual attitude does not suggest that vast numbers of Afghans are gay, but arises from the absolute segregation of women. Marriage is an arrangement made between families, often representing a political or financial agreement. The virtue and virginity of a woman is the central totem of family honour. Romantic, passionate sex is reserved for men, a custom similar to that in ancient Greece when sex with women was primarily to propagate.

When we slept in the trench with Abdul Majid, Johno was more frightened of a nocturnal advance from one of the Northern Alliance men than an incoming missile from the Taliban.

I wondered whether this physical bond between men helped, in part, to explain the fierce and often absolute loyalty that the men of one family, village or ethnic group have to each other. 'This trench is my home,' Majid told me, turning his head towards his fellow soldiers. 'These men are like my family, they are even closer than my own brother. Now we live in this trench together and we will defend each other's blood.'

I was awoken during the night by the sound of gunfire. I scrambled out of the bunker and climbed onto a vantage point where Majid was calling out commands into a walkie-talkie. Above, tracer fire from a 50mm gun sent spears of green light across the starry night sky. Majid had spotted Taliban pickup trucks carrying men and supplies to their forward positions on the old road to Qala-Nasrogh, twenty miles north of Kabul. He'd ordered an attack.

'Incoming,' someone shouted. Abdul Majid ducked behind the wall of the bunker; the rest of us hit the floor. The Taliban were returning fire and several rounds skimmed above our heads, aimed at artillery pieces in fortified bunkers about a hundred yards behind us. Majid seemed relaxed enough, with his radio in one hand and a cup of coffee in the other. He repeatedly ducked and then stood up as incoming and outgoing fire alternated. He resembled a crazed jack-in-the-box, silhouetted against the night sky.

Then a round from one of Majid's gunners almost hit us, striking a tree a few yards away. 'What are you doing?' Majid screeched into his radio. 'You nearly killed us. Don't shoot like that!'

'OK, OK,' the gunner replied, nonchalantly.

Majid was a victim rather than an architect of the destruction of his country. The guns he carried were forced upon him. He had a simple, straightforward manner. He was also an accomplished liar. As with other commanders and warlords that I had met in Afghanistan, lying without a hint of compunction or embarrassment came more easily than searching for truths.

An event on the battlefield revealed his casual deceit. A gun battle was taking place one afternoon and he was calling the shots from his bunker. From behind the mud wall, I peered gingerly through my binoculars; dust obscured the Taliban forward posts. It was hard to tell whether the enemy had been hit, or whether the mortars landed short of their intended target, falling onto the rock and sand of no-man's-land.

Once the battle had subsided, I asked Majid if anyone had been killed. 'I don't know,' he said. 'Let's ask them.' Surprised by his logic, I watched as he tuned into their radio frequency. The Taliban commander on the front line was called Rohani. Majid spent a few minutes speaking to him in Pashto. 'They say they have dead and wounded men,' he told me. 'They asked us to send a vehicle to help carry their dead and wounded. But we will not. They are our enemy.'

Much later, I had the tape recording of the discussion translated.

Majid: 'Are you OK, Rohani?'

Rohani: 'With God's blessing, we're fine. There's nothing to be concerned about here. Don't worry.'

Majid: 'May God bless you.'

Rohani: 'May you be well. Can we do anything for you? Give my regards to our comrades.'

Perhaps deceit is simply the way of life on the battlefields of

Afghanistan. The distinction between truth and fiction was lost on most of the Afghan warlords that I'd met, America's first allies in its battle to 'defend civilization'.

Majid's trench was only a few miles from where the BBC had set up its base camp, in an empty four-storey building in the town of Charikar. At one time Charikar was a busy suburb of Kabul. Its only economy in recent years was war, but its position on the front line gave the town an advantage over most others in Afghanistan; many of the Northern Alliance commanders were based nearby. It had a high street with clothes shops, a barber, a photographer and, nearby, a restaurant that served edible cuts of grilled meat. On Fridays, a street market selling fresh produce as well as clothes and cheap consumer items from China was heaving with women in their burkas. I even saw a traffic policeman at a roundabout. For Afghanistan, Charikar had a civilized heartbeat.

It was in Charikar that I began to understand that the bombs we had seen raining down on the Taliban were part of a much grander project than the overthrow of a regime and the capture of bin Laden. I had heard a justifiably angry George W. Bush make his speech that the world was either 'with us or with the terrorists'. The outpouring of emotion after September 11th had moved the hearts of most of the world. When the Taliban refused to hand over Osama bin Laden, a mostly sympathetic global consensus accepted the American decision to replace the regime in Kabul. But I did not realize that the conflict I was now witnessing was just the first battle in a much broader war that had begun in Afghanistan but could end anywhere, if it had an end. On 2 November, while I was in the bunker with Majid, the US State Department spokesman, Richard Boucher, made a remarkable avowal that in effect declared a new world war.

'The President has made it clear that the United States is engaged in a war against the scourge of terrorism . . . we will not rest until every terrorist group has been removed as a threat to the United States, our citizens, our interests, and our friends and allies. As the President has stated, this campaign will be a long one.'

In the shadow of the war in Afghanistan, the United States government began to construct the ideological edifice for a new military doctrine that would propel the 'war on terror'. The State Department announced that twenty-two names of 'foreign terrorist individuals, entities and groups' would be added to a list established under Executive Order 13224, signed by President Bush on 23 September. The list included the Basque independence movement, ETA; Sri Lanka's Tamil Tigers; the Kurdish separatist party, PKK; Colombia's Marxist guerrillas, the FARC; and Islamic radicals fighting for Palestinian statehood. All had their assets frozen. These twenty-two names had been on a State Department list from 1996, but none has proven (or even suggested) links to the perpetrators of the September 11th carnage. Al-Qa'eda and its myriad sister organizations were amongst the initial list of sixty-six announced a month earlier.

President Bush declared, 'Our war on terror begins with al-Qa'eda but does not end there. It will not end until every terrorist group of global reach has been found, stopped and defeated.'

The administration offered no attempt to define 'a terrorist group of global reach'. Did the Tamil Tigers, fighting for a Tamil homeland in Sri Lanka, have global reach? They had, in the past, launched operations in India and had supporters as well as financial assets outside Sri Lanka, primarily in Canada and Britain. According to this interpretation, any non-state revolutionary force had global reach if it had financial support from outside the disputed region. Two months later at the United Nations, President Bush abandoned the reference to global reach. He told the Assembly, 'We must unite in opposing all terrorists, not just some of them.'

The list continued to grow, to include hundreds of seemingly random individuals and organizations from Islamic countries, as well as Protestant paramilitary groups in Northern Ireland, leftist groups in the Philippines and movements pursuing an independent Sikh homeland in the Punjab, northern India. The United States, theoretically at least, had declared war against all militant groups. It mattered not whether they posed any threat to the United States, had widespread popular support or were primarily the victims of state repression rather than the perpetrators of violence.

The spectacle of American power crushing the Taliban from eight miles above us sparked wonderment amongst most of the world's media and even amongst the sceptics, a begrudging respect for the overwhelming dominance of its military technology. But most of us did not realize for several months the significance of what we were witnessing nor what it meant for the future of the world.

For much of Afghanistan's history, its barren, forbidding landscape has been a battleground for competing civilizations. It was here that one of the twentieth century's most influential ideologies, Soviet Communism, collapsed and a world order structured around the cold war faltered. The Soviet Union's battle with the mujahedin, who were lavishly backed by Saudi and American funds, became the last throes of a declining empire. The war drained its failed, rusty economy of its military pretensions and laid bare its inability to maintain parity with an expansionist United States. Remarkably, two decades later, a new world order was once more being forged on Afghanistan's dramatic terrain.

Half a world away from the bombing and the news headlines, an intellectual whirlwind was sweeping through America's think tanks and political circles. An emerging new creed called on the United States to use its military power without reference to the United Nations or the norms of the international community. September 11th generated a new protocol of warfare that challenged the political order that the United States had constructed alongside its partners since the 1940s.

It is, perhaps, strange that this new warrior code did not evolve immediately after the collapse of the Soviet Union. Instead, during the 1990s, the United States dilly-dallied in conflicts that had primarily humanitarian objectives, such as in Somalia or Bosnia. It marvelled at its position as the sole superpower but it had no clear military doctrine and seemed unsure how to apply its influence beyond enjoying the soaring growth of the Internet economy. That artificial moment in history came crashing down in the rubble of the Twin Towers. The US now had a defined enemy: terrorism.

The United States began to use its global influence to impose a definition of 'terrorism' on the rest of the world. Every 'freedom fighter' would now be designated a 'terrorist'. Over a hundred countries began to proscribe the same organizations. The European Union placed groups such as the FARC guerrillas on its list of 'terrorist' organizations following US diplomatic pressure. Until then, representatives from the Colombian Marxist group had often received a sympathetic hearing from some of Europe's left-leaning politicians.

Casting back, of course, to when President Reagan and Prime Minister Thatcher praised the rebellion of the armies of the mujahedin, there was no doubt in most of the Western media that the uprising was just. The facts that they wanted to establish an intolerant theocracy and that they readily murdered Russian civilians were of no consequence. According to Robert Gates, the former Director of the CIA, it did not matter who was receiving the arms so long as they were 'killing Russians'. One American Congressman from Texas visited Afghanistan and gave an emotional speech when he returned to the States. He described meeting an eleven-year-old Afghan boy who pleaded with the Americans not to allow the mujahedin to kill *all* the Russians, because the boy wanted one left for him to kill when he grew up. The anecdote was loudly applauded.

The 1979 war in Afghanistan also generated a carnival atmosphere amongst the Western media, which celebrated the mujahedin as rugged, noble warriors who time had forgotten and were now embracing the cause of freedom.

When Margaret Thatcher visited the unruly Pakistani frontier city of Peshawar, close to the border with Afghanistan, she was hosted by the local governor, General Fazle Haq. He was a dapper man, well groomed with a trimmed but ostentatious white moustache. He loved 'a good strong cup of tea at four and a gin and tonic at six'. The officer corps of the Pakistani army still clings to traditions inherited from its colonial past. In the case of Fazle Haq, his exaggerated behaviour suggested that he had graduated from the Royal Military College at Sandhurst sometime during the reign of Queen Victoria. When I met the General a few months after he hosted Margaret Thatcher, I could hardly keep him quiet. 'We got on terrifically,' he bubbled. 'She is such a jolly good lady.'

I have no idea what the British Embassy in the Pakistani capital, Islamabad, thought about Fazle Haq but I knew him by a different name: General Heroin. Journalists in Peshawar, which had become a transit point for men and material en route to the war, described to me how Fazle Haq was the mastermind behind a scheme that used Pakistani army trucks to cross the Khyber Pass carrying arms for the mujahedin in exchange for Afghani opium, a process that locals claim was overseen by the CIA.

A few years later, Fazle Haq was arrested on suspicion of conspiracy to commit murder. He was released but then shot by unknown assassins who pumped three bullets into his chest.

The mujahedin's involvement in opium cultivation was well known to Western governments but the CIA turned an 'official' blind eye. It was a 'strategic, military decision', according to an undercover

American operative that I met at their consulate in Peshawar. He said it was 'unfortunate' that some mujahedin groups were growing opium poppies but 'first and foremost we need to help them win this war'.

The guerrillas' attempts to bring down civilian aircraft were also deemed acceptable; an act of war rather than 'terrorism'. The mujahedin repeatedly tried to blow from the skies Afghan commercial airliners using the Stinger shoulder-mounted guided-missile system that had been supplied by the United States. On a flight from Delhi to Kabul, I was sitting next to a petite Afghan woman in her early thirties. Her hair was pushed back severely into a small bun. She wore Western clothes, a formal, starched white shirt and a long dark skirt. When I first said hello, she seemed startled but later we began a conversation. Her English was excellent; her name was Faruz. She had stayed in Delhi with her sister, who had apparently married a well-off Indian man. She was a teacher and had taken advantage of the May Day holiday to visit them. She did not want to talk about politics but the only remark she made was to prove prophetic. 'I am a good Muslim,' she whispered, barely audible above the aircraft noise, 'but it will be terrible if those religious men take over. Life will be even harder than it is now.'

As the plane approached Kabul, it suddenly and without warning began a sharp descent, tilting by forty-five degrees. I turned toward Faruz, who was unconcerned and smiling. 'It's to stop . . .' she paused, 'bombs.' I thought for a moment; she had confused bombs with missiles. It was a rapid fall, in a spiralling, corkscrew motion. The mujahedin-controlled areas on the rim of the city and their Stingers were capable of shooting down aircraft during a conventional descent. As a further precaution, flares were ejected from the back of the plane to divert the missile's infrared seeker from the heat of the engines.

After this eventful flight had landed, we checked into the Kabul Hotel, a large grey Soviet-style construction at Pashtunistan Square in the centre of town. A porter in an ill-fitting uniform that had not been cleaned for months growled as he gave us our room keys; it seemed that we had disturbed his sleep. In my room, my colleague Brian Barron helped to move a mattress over the window. Blast damage from flying glass is often severe and preventable.

The Kabul Hotel had been the swish hangout of the elite during the sixties and early seventies when sons and daughters of the rich held ostentatious parties in its ballroom. Marijuana was easily available in those days, I am told. Drab walls, browned by cigarette smoke as well as oversized chandeliers, made it hard to recall the days of fashionable indulgence. The Kabul Hotel was the city's finest until the Intercontinental opened in 1969. Overlooking the west of the city, it was intended as a magnet for the flourishing tourism business. Kabul was already on the hippie trail during an age when a carefree journey through Iran led to the magic of Afghanistan. By 1990, the Intercontinental had been closed; it was within easy range of mujahedin rockets. Broken glass lay in the hallway. The only clue to its past ambitions was posters for BOAC, the forerunner of British Airways, that were still on the walls. Smiling girls with beehive haircuts under hostess caps welcomed visitors to Kabul. 'Enjoy the breathtaking sites of Afghanistan', the advert pleaded.

At that time, the only situation likely to take anyone's breath away was an explosion from a mujahedin shell – their guns were poised perilously close. A spirit of doom hung in the air. The Soviet Union was about to collapse; the communist regime in Kabul clung on, but it was fighting the tsunami of history. The distant sound of shelling was a constant backdrop to conversations. One day, we were driving along the road from the Intercontinental to the deserted British Embassy when we heard an explosion. It was nearby, but we couldn't tell exactly where the shell had landed. We decided to go the Red Cross Hospital to check if there were any casualties. As we arrived, we saw the injured shuttled in by a taxi. A woman in her fifties, silenced by shock, had a foot dangling while a man tried vainly to keep it connected to the rest of her leg.

'That's an amputation,' said Peter Hanson, a young surgeon from Cambridge University who was doing his elective work in this hellish place. 'I do the best I can,' he said cheerfully, as the woman was placed on a trolley, her now almost detached foot ending up at a grotesque ninety-degree angle. Once she had been whisked away to the surgery, the buzz of flies was the only noise that remained. The patients were all silent, staring blankly as our television team passed through. The bed sheets were filthy and bloodstained. The smell of disinfectant fought with a pungent, darker odour that I couldn't identify. The wounded included a little girl without an arm. No one was sure what her name was and anyway, we couldn't stay long. I smiled at her but her face remained motionless. Whatever the legitimacy of their cause, it was hard to look at this parade of blood-soaked cripples and share

President Reagan's description of the guerrillas as 'the moral equivalent of America's founding fathers'. When the mujahedin maimed and killed in the city, the residents of Kabul considered them terrorists.

Until 1991, when the Soviet Union was dissolved, the war in Afghanistan was presented by the bulk of the Western media within the same framework that the State Department projected it: a conflict between the forces of right (freedom) and wrong (communism). The proconsul of the 'evil Empire' in Afghanistan was President Najibullah, a bear of a man with a thick moustache and a bone-crushing handshake. He was portrayed as a ruthless ogre; the epithet was convincingly supported by his record as former chief of the secret police. For seven years he headed a ruthless intelligence network modelled on the KGB, which sent hundreds of thousands to the notorious Pul-i-Charkhi prison, the 'black hole of Kabul'. It stands like a fortress, with its imposing gate and thick outer walls. Tens of thousands were taken from its dark concrete cells to a nearby firing range and dumped in large pits dug by earthmovers. Najibullah was also accused of orchestrating attacks on mujahedin training camps in Pakistan, actions that were described as 'terrorism' by Western governments.

Surprisingly, given his blackened and bloodied reputation, I rather liked 'Najib', as he was known to both friend and foe alike. We met at the Argh, the presidential palace in Pashtunistan Square, a short walk from the Kabul Hotel. We were shown into a modest dining room with a simple table and paper napkins. The President was already waiting to greet us and produced a broad, confident smile. He wore an open-necked shirt with rolled-up sleeves and appeared like an old friend offering a beer at the local pub. He had a wrestler's physique and an imposing, room-filling demeanour. When he shook my hand, I had to flex it for some moments afterwards in order to regain the blood supply. Najib's relaxed manner contrasted sharply with his obsequious translator, fluttering around in a suit and tie and hanging on his boss's every word. 'Let's eat,' Najib declared.

Najib had a hearty appetite. The soup, which was of an indistinguishable flavour, was quickly slurped down. Then a surly, stout woman in a white overalls and cap brought in lamb cutlets and overcooked chips. The scene resembled less dining with a president than lunching in an office canteen.

Najib had an ironic sense of humour and seemed to understand the futility of his fight now that the Soviets had deserted him. 'How long have I got?' he repeated my question. 'That's up to Allah,' the former communist concluded with a broad smile. He spoke of his willingness to compromise with the mujahedin and discuss sharing power. 'I am prepared to grow a beard,' he declared 'and join them in an Islamic government.' He wanted to demonstrate his commitment to the faith; Afghanistan should be 'Islamic but tolerant', he added.

It was hard to tell what he was really thinking. Perhaps his newfound piety was a theatrical ruse for visiting reporters; he did not appear like a man about to hand over Afghanistan to the muja-hedin. But nor did I see in Najib the cold-blooded secret policeman who had signed execution papers by the thousands. Maybe it was just a pretence, or perhaps he had become a little wiser. He had ample opportunity to flee to Russia or India and live in quiet retire-ment. Instead, he remained in Kabul and defied the odds, surviving for three years after the last Soviet troops had left Afghanistan. Western military analysts had long since written off his regime and few had expected him to be in power by the end of 1990. A mujahedin leader described him as 'a suspended teardrop, about to fall'. The mujahedin continued their ramshackle advance but the stalemate was only con-clusively tipped when one of his generals defected to the guerrillas in early 1992. On the night of 15 April, they entered Kabul and he fled the city. He was hoping to use a military plane to fly to India but he was captured as he approached the airport. For the next four and a half years, he lived in a strange purgatory in the United Nations' compound in Kabul, unable to leave but apparently content to read, watch satellite TV and work out at the UN gym.

The next time I recall seeing a photograph of Najib was in 1996, dangling from a post in Pashtunistan Square. His face was red and bulbous, his salwar kameez soaked in blood after he'd been disembow-elled. Rope was tied around his throat and armpits, suspending him in midair, his hands clenched in his last throes. The Taliban had arrived in Kabul and had no respect for the sanctity of the United Nations. His brother, his last security chief, was strung up beside him. Pash-tunistan Square was once a lively downtown plaza with a cooling fountain, a gathering place outside the palace of the former king. After the Taliban fled, a local man told me that the square had not been the same since the death of Najib; it was haunted by the ghost of the old secret policeman.

Once the cold war ended, the West lost interest in Afghanistan. The world had moved on; Bill Clinton was elected President and war erupted in Europe as Yugoslavia unravelled. The end of the bipolar world made it very hard to explain the importance of wars in faraway lands to a Western audience. Afghanistan became irrelevant and the leaders of the mujahedin were forgotten until 2001.

Once again, the West then imposed moral clarity onto the confusion of Afghan politics. The governing Taliban regime that had swept to power five years before was now the enemy. Within a few weeks, many of the mujahedin leaders had been transformed from a nearly defeated rebel army that controlled a distant slither of Afghanistan into a liberating force now called the Northern Alliance. The largely factional, ethnic conflict was elevated into a moral crusade against the 'evil of terrorism'.

The effective capital of this forgotten regime was a remote town in the bleak mountains of north-east Afghanistan called Faizabad. It was a jumble of flat-roofed straw-and-mud-built houses, crammed into a narrow corridor that the white waters of the Kokcha River had sliced through the mountains. The surrounding hillsides were dry and dusty, parched by two years of drought. The town merged with the brown and beige hues of the mountains.

The town's population had swelled with thousands of Tajiks fleeing Taliban-controlled Kabul. The growth had meant that another district had developed on the plateau overlooking the river valley, a windswept area where refugees congregated under metal sheeting. It was a squalid place of litter and rocks, packed with children with matted hair who lived in a fog of dust. Malnutrition was high, especially amongst children; a quarter of all infants died before they reached the age of five. Life expectancy was only about forty.

Faizabad was a timeless, isolated place with a history of stubborn resistance to outsiders. Public space was solely the domain of men; pervasive social restraints meant that the plight of women was much the same under the rule of the Northern Alliance as the Taliban.

Despite its isolation, an economy functioned; there were cafes, a flourmill and stalls selling food, clothing and arms. A grenade was sold for little more than $8. A landmine was just five. I could have purchased an AK-47 for a hundred dollars, though the bullets would be extra. My translator Fadlan warned that I was being overcharged and could haggle over the prices. I asked the shopkeeper whether he cared what I used them for. 'Up to you,' he said, laughing.

Faizabad was home to the then-recognized Afghan President, Burhanuddin Rabbani, a small-framed former professor with dancing eyes and pristine white beard that stretched almost to his middle who had replaced President Najibullah in 1992. It was intended to be a presidency that rotated amongst the seven mujahedin leaders, each term lasting four months. Nearly a decade later, Rabbani was still President, though his fiefdom had become little more than the mountain ranges surrounding Faizabad. His longevity was in part the result of his own stubborn tenacity, but also the strength of his respected military commander, Ahmed Shah Massoud, who controlled the most disciplined army and possessed the smartest military mind in the mujahedin.

Massoud was murdered on Sunday, 9 September 2001. A television team claiming to represent an Arab network in London were about to begin an interview when the man pretending to be a reporter detonated a powerful bomb strapped to his waist. His killing was probably an attempt by bin Laden to undermine the unity of the Northern Alliance and remove its most skilful commander before the United States retaliated for the September 11th attacks. The news of Massoud's death was broadcast around the world on the following day. It was the signal that nineteen al-Qa'eda members in the United States had been waiting for. On Tuesday morning they hijacked the four fateful flights.

Professor Rabbani passed me the business card of one of the suicide bombers. The name on the card was Karim Toussani, Journalist. It gave his company as IOC, with a post office box address in Maida Vale, London and a mobile phone number. He'd carried a false Belgian passport and said he was of Moroccan parentage. IOC referred to the Islamic Observation Centre, an organization run by Yasser al-Sirri, an energetic Islamic militant who was granted asylum in the UK after being sentenced to death in absentia in Egypt for attempting to assassinate the Prime Minister in 1993. On almost the same day that Rabbani passed me Toussani's business card, al-Sirri was arrested in London under Britain's new terrorism law. Amongst the charges against him was conspiracy to murder Ahmed Shah Massoud.

I had met al-Sirri several times in London. He had a particular penchant for sticky cakes and sweet pistachio desserts. For such a wiry man, he seemed to possess a huge appetite. His favourite rendezvous point was the coffee shop at the Regent's Park Hilton with its generous selection of Middle Eastern desserts. He was full of bluster and presented himself as the man at the centre of Islam's war with the West. He was also a tireless activist; his Islamic Centre published messages from Osama bin Laden and articles by Islamist ideologues, as well as raising money for Islamist charities. His 'cloak and dagger' mentality was at times comical. I never treated him too seriously and he was manipulative, but I doubt that he was responsible for Massoud's murder.

The police in Britain say the planning for Massoud's assassination started in 1999 with the theft of two Belgian passports in Strasbourg and The Hague. Two years later, the stolen passports were taken to the Pakistani High Commission in London by men claiming to be Toussani and his partner, Kacem Bakkali, to obtain journalist visas to visit Pakistan. The men arrived in Islamabad and went to the Afghan Embassy, then under the control of the Taliban. They presented the letter of introduction from al-Sirri, which described the pair as journalists for Arabic News International, a television station based in London. With the appropriate documents, the men travelled to Kabul where it's thought they picked up the bomb. They then applied to the Northern Alliance to cross into the sector that it controlled, claiming that they wanted to interview Massoud and Rabbani. Permission was granted and a week later a meeting was arranged with Massoud. Rabbani told me that the bombers had wanted to interview the two men together, but that proved impossible because of their schedules.

Yasser al-Sirri denies any involvement in Massoud's murder. 'If I had known that these men intended to kill Massoud, would I have been stupid enough to give them a letter with my signature on it? I would have covered my tracks,' al-Sirri said prior to his arrest. His centre produces videos about Islam around the world and al-Sirri claims he wrote the letter of introduction because the two killers had promised to give him access to their material. 'I had nothing to do with this plot and I never met these men in person. I only dealt with them over the phone.' I never felt that al-Sirri was discreet enough to be a serious part of al-Qa'eda. Men with much closer links with bin Laden's network would smile when his name was raised but dismiss him as a noisy pipsqueak.

A former professor of Islamic studies, Rabbani did not smile much and he was uncomfortable in the presence of foreign journalists. He squirmed under camera lights and was a poor ambassador for his cause. His answers meandered, with accounts of Qur'ānic stories and obscure events in Afghan history. He knew very little English and relied on his son, who studied at a British university, to deal with the media. The United States and Western journalists had courted Rabbani in the early 1980s, when he was glorified as a 'freedom fighter' struggling to expel the evil and godless Soviet troops. When the West turned its back, he felt betrayed and let down.

'We have been carrying the weight of defending the whole world on our shoulders,' he announced about his rivalry with the Taliban, unable to resist a dig at the United States. Rabbani began to speak as if he had been fighting a 'war on terror' long before George W. Bush joined the bandwagon. His mission was to 'liberate Afghanistan from terrorism'. The men of al-Qa'eda, or 'the Arab terrorists' as they were now described, were the committed enemies of the Northern Alliance. 'The world has now realized that we have been fighting for the security of the planet,' he immodestly concluded.

The Northern Alliance were even presenting themselves as feminists. 'We will defend the rights of women,' Rabbani announced. 'We will ensure that women's rights are protected.' At times it sounded like he was reading someone else's script by mistake. When his forces captured Kabul in 1992, the mujahedin imposed numerous restrictions on the behaviour and dress of women.

The Northern Alliance's commitment to a democratic Afghanistan also contrasted vividly with its past as a regime that was accountable to no one, when power was derived from the gun and loyalty was personal and tribal. Toward his supporters, Rabbani used the lexicon of jihad, inspiring an army of religious warriors. True, his Northern Alliance partners had severed links with bin Laden and they were less dogmatic than the Taliban regime that had replaced them. But America's new allies in the 'war on terrorism' included many of the groups whose fanatical, internecine violence had reduced eighty per cent of Kabul to rubble during the previous decade.

The sudden conversion to the cause of fighting global terrorism proved to be financially as well as politically rewarding for the Northern Alliance. At least three thousand journalists had paid $200 for visas to get to Faizabad. The flight from Dushanbe, in Tajikistan, in a rattling old Antonov propeller aircraft, was $400 each. The vehicles at Faizabad's landing strip charged $100 for the run into the town. The Northern Alliance ran a guest house and charged $30 per person for an area of floor to place a sleeping bag. All this in a nation where the average monthly income was about $50.

Most of the journalists who reached Faizabad wanted to continue to the front line north of Kabul. That involved a hazardous journey along snow-covered mountain roads that became impassable during the winter months. Local drivers quickly lined up, their eyes dilated with lucre; $2,000 for a one-way trip, they cried, with petrol on top. There was no choice of car; the only vehicles I saw in Faizabad were Toyota Hi-Luxes. If a genuine Toyota part remained in the vehicle, it was proudly displayed. 'Real Toyota,' one driver said, pointing to the engine head. 'Others, they are locally made. They are no good,' he warned.

In order to reach the front line, we had to cross the high passes of the Hindu Kush mountains; the most difficult was the Anjoman, a narrow gateway cut into the mountains at nearly fifteen thousand feet. Our first attempt failed; our two pickups were sliding on the ice, the camber pushing them toward the cliff edge that fell onto frozen rocks, hundreds of feet below. The two trucks laden with our equipment were struggling so much that we had to return to the nearest village. By the following day, we had found snow chains. It was fascinating to witness how ingenious Afghans can become if large dollar bills are offered.

For thousands of years, Afghanistan was one of the great crossroads of Asia as camel caravans and missionaries traversed the peaks of the Hindu Kush. The remote mountain passes also became the graveyard for invading armies. At some point in a conversation, most Afghans will proudly declare that their country has never been conquered. It was easy to see in the lined, weather-beaten faces of Afghan tribesmen the toughness of character that their brutish, lifeless surroundings had assigned them. We ran into families, often with young children, walking in what seemed like the middle of nowhere, in heavy snow and sub-zero temperatures.

It was mid-October and the winter snow would soon close the Anjoman Pass. Each day that bad weather delayed our journey increased the chance that we would be crossing these desolate mountains on the backs of donkeys. The thought filled me with horror. Our nerves frayed as the engines whined and screeched and the chained wheels fought for traction. Several times we broke down or were stuck in icy waters that had melted as the brief, blinding sunlight of the high mountains brought sudden warmth.

At one point, a rock-fall blocked our path on the icy cliff-edge road. Johno stood near the side of the road to capture our attempt to clear the stony avalanche. Suddenly, the edge gave way and he slipped over the precipice, clinging on by the fingertips of his left hand, his right hand holding the camera. I grabbed his hand and pulled him up. He was totally unruffled by his near-death experience; he joked that he never let his camera fall, no matter what happened to him.

When we had crossed the Anjoman Pass, we arrived in darkness at a small town called Khiaban. There was a teashop and guest house in the middle of the main street and we checked in for the night. The manager asked if we wanted food; yes, we replied, and he brought a plate of lamb kebabs and flat bread with honey and olive oil. I then asked for the bathroom. The manager looked puzzled and surprised. He pointed to the door, gesturing outside: 'The street,' he murmured. In Afghanistan, a guest house will offer a bed, laundry, tea and meals but do not expect a toilet to be included.

The next morning I decided to shave. The manager attached a small mirror to a post on the street and gradually a crowd gathered, watching closely as I applied shaving foam and grappled with a week's growth of stubble. The Taliban had banned shaving, insisting that men carried long beards, bushy enough to clasp in the fist. Having a shave in Afghanistan was a political act.

On the fifth day, we reached our destination, the front-line town of Charikar. It was there that we attached our filming team to Abdul Majid's 710th Brigade. As the days passed and the American bombing continued, it was inevitable that the pummelling of Taliban bunkers would at some point break the military stalemate that had kept Majid in his trench.

One Sunday afternoon, we were with Majid's commander on top of his mud-built fort just behind the front line. There had been heavy bombing from the B-52s overhead. Suddenly, he bellowed orders on his radio to all units in the 710th Brigade: 'By sunset, reach as far as you can walk. God willing, they cannot resist the mujahedin.' The attack on Kabul had begun.

In the nineteenth century, Afghan tribesmen declared a jihad, a war demanded by God to defend the faith, in order to repel British invaders. As Majid prepared for battle, he invoked the same language that Afghan warriors had used for generations. 'We are fighting a jihad. We have no other wish but to fight for God,' he explained. 'We will struggle against the aggressor, against anyone who attacks Islam. We want to become martyrs, to die a martyr is an honour for us.'

In the mouths of the 'terrorist' Taliban regime, the media presented religious devotion as the mantra of a brainwashed or unstable mind. When allies of the West uttered similar statements, the media tended to present their religious piety as noble and reasonable. It was puzzling that the Northern Alliance considered the Taliban as 'enemies of Islam'. The Taliban zealously and literally abided by the Qur'ān and the comments made by the Prophet in the Hadith. I tried several times, without success, to find out what they had done to 'attack' Islam, but Majid would not be drawn into a theological discussion. Nor could I see any significant differences in either side's approach to its religion.

As the Northern Alliance approached Kabul, the Taliban forces began melting into the late evening sun. Majid turned to me: 'We are going to reach Kabul.' At dawn the next morning, we rushed toward the city. The government of Afghanistan had fled overnight. On the main road into Kabul, the evidence of battle was only a few burnt-out vehicles and the bloodied bodies of half a dozen Taliban soldiers.

Some older folk clapped and gangs of children waved as the tanks of the Northern Alliance rolled in, draped in jubilant soldiers. In the shopping areas around Chicken Street, where carpets and Western goods were in abundance, a shopkeeper offered me alcohol and danced to music from a loudspeaker on the pavement. The Taliban was not much loved here. There was genuine relief that war with America was over and that Kabul had not, once more, become a battleground for competing armies.

Family reunions were heart-warming. We found Majid's old family home, where he would soon be drinking tea with aunts and uncles whom he had not seen for five years. For many who observed Kabul that day, the city's fall seemed a genuine act of liberation. But a more restrained glance suggested more solace than euphoria. Much of Kabul seemed a city numbed by war and fearful of harbouring hope.

I ventured west to the district of Afshar, where block after block of shattered housing resembled the ruins of an ancient civilization. In 1993, it was the site of repeated human butchery during fighting between a faction that adhered to the Shi'ite branch of Islam and followers of a powerful Saudi-backed mujahedin warlord, Abdul Rasul Sayyaf. Amnesty International reported that Sayyaf's forces rampaged through Afshar, murdering, raping and burning homes. Sayyaf had the active support of soldiers loyal to Professor Rabbani and Ahmad Shah Massoud. The results were horrific. One woman watched as her father was killed, his limbs amputated and fed to the dogs of one of the commanders. Another was forced to watch as her three young daughters were murdered. Sayyaf's forces were now back in Kabul, a key component of the Northern Alliance army. Abdul Majid and his 710th Brigade belonged to him.

In private, I found Abdul Rasul Sayyaf mischievous and entertaining. His Santa Claus beard, his cracker-barrel humour and the constant twinkle in his eyes belied a ruthless and probably murderous military mind. Amnesty International accused him of ordering the deaths of more than a thousand civilians, mostly during the carnage at Afshar. When I asked him about the killings he straightened his back and gave me a penetrating stare.

'Believe me, believe me, nothing like this has happened. I was there.'

'There was no massacre at Afshar?'

'Not at all, not at all.' He broke into a big smile. 'Not at all.'

'So the information from all the human rights groups is mistaken?'

'A big mistake. Who is their witness? Who is their witness?' he cheerfully asked, denying the graphic, heart-wrenching accounts of survivors. 'Not one civilian died in Afshar.'

The brutalizing of truth in Afghanistan is often as vulgar and grotesque as the shelling and murdering. After the overthrow of the Taliban, Sayyaf's forces returned to control much of the west of the city, including Afshar. His bloodied past prevented him from having a formal post in the government of President Hamid Karzai, but he retained a powerful role behind the scenes.

As I entered Kabul on its day of 'liberation', my mind travelled back a decade to an event I experienced during the similarly dubbed 'liberation' of Kuwait City at the end of the Gulf War (1990). The sound of gunfire echoed in the distance as I entered the city alongside American troops. It had rained overnight and the air was filled with smoke from burning oilfields, ignited by fleeing Iraqi soldiers. I went into the nearly deserted Hilton Hotel on Arabian Gulf Street. The hotel staff had long gone and there was no power, but I was still hoping to grab an empty room.

Cowering in a corner in near darkness were half a dozen Filipino girls who had been working as domestic maids for local Kuwaitis. I asked how they were; the Iraqis had treated them well, they said. Then suddenly, struck with fear, one of the girls grabbed my arm and pleaded that I should not allow the Kuwaitis to return. I listened as two of the girls told me that they had been raped by their Kuwaiti masters who held their passports. After listening to their harrowing accounts, I had to admit to them that I was powerless to help. Somewhat embarrassed, I simply wished them well. My job that day was to interview jubilant Kuwaitis as they returned home.

A similar mood of moral confusion emerged in Kabul as I walked through the devastation of Afshar. I noticed a woman peering from the doorway of her home. She was perhaps fifty, though the poor diet and harsh climate often makes Afghans appear older. She was not wearing the burka, and her face was showing under a headscarf. I asked if she was happy that she longer needed to abide by the Taliban's strict dress code. She shrugged. Her name was Mrs Waseeq. It didn't matter who was in charge, she said, and wearing the burka was of little consequence.

'The Taliban were OK for a while but they soon turned out like all the rest,' she answered matter-of-factly. 'I don't want those others back,' she said, referring to a leader whose name she was too scared to mention. It was clear that the years of mujahedin misrule from 1992 to 1996 had not been forgotten. 'They are all the same,' she repeated, dejected and forlorn.

I made an attempt to sympathize with her plight and wished her well. I was about to say goodbye, when, in a sudden flurry of excitement, she called out to her son, a thin young man who looked about fifteen. She pushed him towards me. 'His name is Sayed. Take him home with you,' she pleaded, 'he is a strong young man. He can help you.'

Mrs Waseeq's sullen face was now round with anticipation, her eyes widened by hope. Taken aback, I said the boy should stay to look after his mother and it was impossible to bring him into Britain. Her face narrowed in disappointment. 'There's no future here. There is nothing to live for.' Resigned, Mrs Waseeq pulled her son back and closed the door behind them. She was trapped in her world and I was powerless to liberate her.

I had to remind myself that the aim of the First Gulf War was to secure oil supplies for Western nations, not to improve human rights in Kuwait. And the aim of the war in Afghanistan was to ensure that the West became a safer place, rather than provide hope to Mrs Waseeq and her son Sayed.

Decades of war and social decay have skewed the social structure of Afghanistan; they have made military commanders into an economic class, like medieval knights of old, and eroded the power of the urban professional classes. Aseel Khan, a soft-spoken, contemplative man, was a warlord who had inherited his post after the death of his uncle in the front-line town of Sarsayed. He was a cross between a mayor, a sheriff and a mafia boss. Like the other warlords that checkerboard the map of Afghanistan, he also played a part in the wider governing of the nation. He joined the Taliban when they captured Kabul in 1996. At that time, the mujahedin were locked in murderous squabbling and he thought the Taliban might provide stability. 'People were hopeful that they would bring the killing to an end,' he recalled. 'When the Taliban came, at first I welcomed them.'

Unlike the leadership of the Northern Alliance, Khan was a Pashtun, the same ethnic group as the majority of the Taliban. After a few years, he and his soldiers switched sides and joined the Northern Alliance. The Taliban tried to entice them back. 'They kept coming to me and saying, "Forget any problems from the past, just return to us because we are friends and we are all Pashtuns." They constantly offered me large sums of American dollars.' Some of the money that the Taliban paid to warlords came from Osama bin Laden's personal wealth. It's estimated that he handed over $3 million to purchase the defections that prompted the fall of Kabul in September 1996.

Aseel Khan turned down the Taliban's approaches, despite the respect he had for the movement. Khan had no time for the newly adopted view in the Northern Alliance that the Taliban were 'terrorists'. 'They are good Muslims,' he said, 'good Muslims.' For Afghans, a terrorist is someone who, first and foremost, damages Islam; all Muslims are brothers; and a Westerner is always a non-Muslim.

The moral issues surrounding the 'war on terror' failed to gain a serious foothold in the morbid routine of Afghanistan's civil war. In the days after the death of its military commander, Ahmed Shah Massoud, Burhanuddin Rabbani desperately tried to rally the crumbling alliance around a new political reality. News of his murder spread consternation amongst the men who had relied on his dominant leadership. Rabbani spent nearly a week claiming that Massoud was still alive, despite US state briefings to the contrary. Meanwhile the Northern Alliance had a chance, politically and militarily, to return from the dead.

Professor Rabbani's otherwise lacklustre skills as a politician shone brightly in the netherworld of Afghan politics, the tribal council meetings where warlords traded power and wealth. These meetings bubbled with a dark comedy and provided a snapshot of Afghan politics. I sat outside one such gathering arranged by Rabbani inside a villa in the narrow valley of the Panjshir River. It was attended by about a dozen warlords. Nearly all drove to the villa accompanied by a pickup truck, its back spilling over with armed men often carrying grenade launchers and heavy machine guns. As each warlord entered the house, he scoured the car park, checking who had the fiercest-looking bodyguards. Occasionally one of the gunmen, dripping with bandoliers, would pause to be photographed by journalists. The men milling around outside could start a minor war by themselves. Inside, the bearded warlords earnestly discussed trade-offs and deals while sitting in a circle on the floor. Rabbani was aware that financial dealings underpin most political loyalties in Afghanistan. He commanded the respect of these men as he spoke openly about American offers of money if everybody stayed loyal to the anti-Taliban alliance. The Taliban will soon be overthrown, he told the men as they sipped tea and nibbled at flat bread with honey, biscuits and figs. Most of the time Rabbani listened, occasionally fumbling sandalwood prayer beads that dangled from his left palm. Much of the discussion was about details, but the purpose of the meeting was to maintain a power-sharing deal that would allow greater riches to flow to the assembled guests.

Rabbani was eager to tell me afterwards that he could unite Afghanistan by attracting Pashtun commanders from the south into the Northern Alliance government that he led. 'Give me the money and I'll deliver peace,' he told me as he left the tribal council, a message that he wanted the Americans to hear. Rabbani insisted that he could do much better than the CIA in attracting defectors: 'If my government was in charge of the resources, then it would be much easier to attract these commanders,' he told me confidently. 'We know how to deal with every individual and what to offer. So with even modest amounts we could bring them round.' His message was simple; the CIA was overpaying.

At the time of the war, the news media did not report the payments made to warlords, preferring instead to emphasize the success of the advanced technology of the American military. The State Department denied knowledge of any handover of money to Afghan warlords, calling it 'bizarre'. A spokesman said it was 'not something the State Department would normally do'. A year later, the veteran American reporter Bob Woodward described how a CIA operative, codenamed 'Jawbreaker', was dropped into Afghanistan in late September 2001 with an attaché case containing $3 million. At his ranch in Texas, President Bush told Woodward that he considered the cost of the operation 'a bargain'. $70m was distributed to Afghan warlords during the last three months of 2001. The fall of the key northern city of Mazar-e-Sharif, which prompted the rapid collapse of the Taliban, was only possible after the CIA bribed two opposition commanders to defect.

Abdul Rasul Sayyaf was also uncannily honest about the Afghan culture of treachery and bribes. Sitting cross-legged on a rug, we were sipping sweet *chai* with him in one of his dachas as he recounted tales of largesse and betrayal. 'Some people are easy to be bought,' he said, recollecting the Taliban's capture of Kabul in 1996. 'The Taliban had money, they bought people, that's the way it is.' He shrugged before laughing heartily. When I asked why Afghanistan's Islamic fighters changed sides so often and so brazenly, he threw me a knowing smile. 'What goes around, comes around,' he mused without further elaboration.

Sayyaf was a charismatic raconteur; he was most entertaining when his dark, mischievous humour was applied to Afghan politics. Despite his reputation as a hard-line Islamist, he could not resist poking fun at the cynical manipulation of faith that has taken hold of his country. He described how a rival commander, using funds provided by a foreign country, would typically seal a defection with a briefcase of money. 'He will say: "You are working for Islam, for jihad, for the benefit of the country. We are tired of all the infighting. Please take this money."' Sayyaf then leant back and shook with laughter before wiping tears from his eyes.

Other accounts surrounding the clunky mechanics of distributing the bribes are equally redolent of farce. According to the driver of one warlord from Kunduz, he made the long trip to the US Embassy in the Pakistani capital, Islamabad, to collect his bounty. The warlord apparently spent an hour inside and emerged carrying a large black briefcase. He then went to Peshawar on the frontier with Afghanistan and immediately called his banker. The warlord is said to have opened his briefcase and handed over $200,000 in crisp, new $100 notes. Other bankers recounted tales of at least thirty-five tribal commanders, most of them Taliban defectors, depositing $200,000 at a time. The bonanza prompted a spending spree on sports utility vehicles. Toyota Landcruisers quickly sold out and local dealers say the manufacturer had to increase its exports to Pakistan.

For centuries, Afghan leaders and warlords have looked to overseas powers to provide the funds to sustain their personal fiefdoms. The outside world has been keen to pay because of the importance of Afghanistan's location as a strategic gateway between the Middle East, India and Central Asia. It has developed a peculiar dependency in the Afghan psychology. The typical warlord will grandly proclaim, with puffed-chest machismo, that Afghanistan has never been conquered. But he would eagerly become the stooge of a foreign power so long as the price was right. The US for years has been willing to oblige.

Abdul Rasul Sayyaf is also the man who brought Osama bin Laden to Afghanistan in the 1980s. Sayyaf had studied in Saudi Arabia and speaks fluent Arabic. He received lavish funding from its royal family and bin Laden became a commander of one of his units. If there is any doubt that telling the difference between violent struggle for freedom and terrorist activity can be difficult, Sayyaf captured the confusion perfectly. When I first raised the subject of bin Laden, he praised him as an 'excellent freedom-fighter', before adding quickly, 'that was, of course, in the past'. Now he was 'on the wrong side', he paused before adding 'the side of terrorism'. He chuckled, seeming to mock the role of the Northern Alliance as the standard-bearers for the 'war on terror'.

I detected a continuing fondness for his old unit commander, despite the shifting alliances that had made him a battlefield enemy. American intelligence placed Sayyaf at a camp with bin Laden in 1996 near the Pakistan border. If these reports are correct, the gathering was a worldwide 'terrorist' jamboree. Former Afghan fighters including bin Laden's Egyptian lieutenant, Ayman Zawahri, and commanders from

Hamas in Palestine, Hizbollah in Lebanon and the GIA from Algeria. Sayyaf believed bin Laden had been misunderstood by the West, despite his role as the chief architect of the September 11th attacks. 'He is not that much of an atom bomb, such an evil man, as the Western media have made him. I know him,' he laughed heartily. 'I don't know why they have described him like that. He's a simple man, a very religious, simple man.'

As I drove away through the throat-clenching dust of the Shomali Plain and into the jagged corridors of the Panjshir Valley, I momentarily laughed out loud. The spectre of CIA operatives buying off former Taliban commanders and forging alliances with dollar bills in this barren, inhospitable terrain where little of material value can be bought was hilarious.

I never asked how Sayyaf might define a terrorist. In a cynical moment I thought about one possibility, were he to contribute to a dictionary definition: 'terrorist: *n.* a person or group that refuses to accept American dollars and challenges the United States' right to attack its territory.'

It was less funny to think that those who had previously been labelled terrorists were now allies if they accepted a suitcase of money. I have always found it hard to understand the long-term goal of purchasing loyalty from people who have a proven record of treachery. Shrewd Afghans now cite with pride the unflattering colonial proverb: 'You cannot buy an Afghan; you can only rent him for a while.'

4 / WAR AS METAPHOR

'We must pay more attention to the mechanisms of
metaphorical thought, especially because such mechanisms are
necessarily used in foreign policy deliberations, and because,
as we are witnessing, metaphors backed up by bombs can kill.'
George Lakoff, Linguistics Department,
University of California, Berkeley

Miguel was a 'terrorist', although he didn't quite know why. He wore
Wellington boots with baggy brown trousers tucked inside. His shirt
was open almost to the waist, stained by sweat from labouring under
the equatorial sun. A golden talisman of the Virgin Mary nestled on
his hirsute chest. His faith, dark complexion, moustache and warm
demeanour suggested Latin American roots. He was short and stocky;
his wife was of similar, squat frame. They had three children, all of
whom were under ten.

A superpower was at war with him and, surprisingly, he wasn't
actually aware of it. He knew that the 'gringos' were not too friendly
but then, as he put it, 'they've never liked us'. But he was blissfully
benighted about his predicament as he faced the awesome might of
the United States military on two distinct fronts. According to George
W. Bush's speeches, Miguel passed all the necessary tests to become
one of the terrorists who would be 'smoked out' from his hideaway.
Miguel was in the cross hairs of the 'war on terror' because he was
linked to what the US government calls a terrorist organization. He
was also the quarry in another war, which was initiated in 1982 and
remains the longest undeclared war in American history. The 'war on

drugs' has targeted Miguel because he is a coca farmer living in the jungles of southern Colombia.

'I worked with cattle for ten years,' he told me. 'I thought that I was going to be able to make a living with the cows, but I couldn't. After that I had to go back to the coca plants.'

Miguel's house was little more than a shack made of wood with a corrugated-steel roof that he had painted orange. His wife, Maria, made some wonderful hot chocolate from locally grown cacao beans. It was bitter, like dark chocolate, but was also rich and milky; she added nutmeg and other local herbs. It was a few days before Christmas and the walls were covered with cheap pictures of the Nativity and, incongruously, in the sauna heat of the jungle, Santa Claus and his reindeer gliding through snow. The family were devout Catholics who would not consider taking drugs themselves.

'I don't want to harm anyone, it's just a way of surviving,' he told me. 'Why do people buy it?' he asked, bemused, genuinely searching for an answer. I avoided the question. I could hardly say that it was fashionable to snort cocaine at parties and nightclubs and then expect Miguel to understand why America was at war with him. 'They don't have to buy it,' he added.

As well as herding cattle, Miguel had tried to grow yucca and plantain. But these are difficult crops to harvest successfully in this remote region of grassland and jungle, snaking brown rivers and dirt tracks. In this vast uncharted expanse, which accounts for almost half the national territory of Colombia, the lack of infrastructure means that fruits and vegetables often rot before reaching the market. 'There are no roads and it takes too long. With the coca, the planes come when it's ready,' he explained, referring to the small single-engine Cessnas that land on improvised strips in the jungle.

Miguel then led me to his plot. We trekked through dense foliage in the dark shadow of the rainforest canopy. Suddenly, a dazzling light directed us toward a clearing of perhaps two or three acres. It was surrounded by a wall of trees that stretched into the sky. Inside this unnatural enclosure were rows of neatly arranged four-foot-high coca bushes. Miguel then began to pluck the ripe tea-like leaves. For centuries, Andean peoples have chewed coca leaves for their medicinal powers to alleviate stomach pains, hunger and altitude sickness. The prized elixir is an alkaloid liquid that flows in the veins of the coca leaf which is mixed with chemicals to form cocaine.

On the edge of the plot was a small wooden hut covered with a tarpaulin roof. It was Miguel's processing 'laboratory'. Inside, large plastic sacks of cement surrounded a rusty can of petrol. An oil drum was nearby in which the coca leaves were placed. Petrol and the powdery cement were added. Miguel stood inside the drum with plastic bags over his shoes and he crushed the mixture with his feet. A dull white mushy resin was produced, which he cut into blocks. He wrapped them in plastic sheeting and they would soon be flown to the north for processing, before the cocaine made the long, adulterating route into the one-gram packets that are bagged by street dealers around the world. 'It's good business,' Miguel repeated, shrugging his shoulders apologetically.

The United States has poured billions of dollars into attempts to eradicate the coca crops by dropping poisons onto the Amazonian jungle. It has been a losing battle. Once one area is fumigated, the farmers move production elsewhere. Coca is the lifeblood of the economy of southern Colombia, as well as parts of Peru and Bolivia. When the Colombian army last tried to take control of the plantations in 1998, the coca growers, backed by the local communist guerrillas, mobilized a hundred thousand farmers in a protest that forced the army to withdraw.

It was the alliance of farmers such as Miguel with Marxist guerrillas that landed him the label of 'terrorist'. He supported, at least passively, and paid a monthly fee to the Revolutionary Armed Forces of Colombia. Known by its Spanish acronym (FARC), it is one of the last remaining communist-inspired insurgencies in South America. Colombia also has a smaller Marxist guerrilla force, the ELN (Ejercito de Liberación Nacional, or National Liberation Army), which operates in the northern jungles. Almost two-thirds of the world's coca is cultivated in areas controlled by these guerrillas. The FARC called Miguel's payments a 'tax'. It charged pilots a 'landing fee' for the use of airstrips in territory under its control. Both groups have been classified as terrorist organizations by the United States and European Union and anyone supporting or financing the movements is liable for prosecution.

Miguel wasn't ideological. The FARC were the government in this area and he had little to say about them. 'They're OK. It's good business,' he would keep saying, 'I need to care for my family.' I doubt that the CIA were targeting Miguel as an enemy terrorist even if they knew where to find him. Yet he was seemingly at the forefront of the wars that the United States is fighting, not against a nation but against abstractions. Neither the 'war on terror' nor the 'war on drugs' properly or accurately define military targets. Both wars are an abstraction; the United States and its allies cannot confront enemies simply called 'terror' or 'drugs'. Despite this, these conflicts are real wars fought with bombs, missiles, helicopters, tanks and blood.

Both metaphorical wars invite military solutions to problems with complex causes and only an idealized resolution. If the 'war on drugs' in Colombia successfully prevented any cocaine reaching the United States, that could be seen as a tangible sign of victory. But the war against the *campesino*, or peasant coca cultivator, and his guerrilla allies is just the military side of a broad campaign where the only sustainable solution lies in controlling the demand for drugs in Western countries. When one drug becomes unavailable, users have shown a wily tenacity in seeking out an alternative. Cocaine users are more likely to seek out ketamine, ecstasy or amphetamines than accept the behavioural changes that lie at the heart of any solution to this 'war'.

Similarly, the 'war on terror' has no properly defined finish line. Al-Qa'eda could be destroyed but the 'war on terror' would continue. The United States and its partners do not have a precise military objective. Instead the aim of the 'war on terror' is to engineer a change in social behaviour; the objective is to stop people becoming engaged in politically motivated violence against governments. Anywhere in the world, a group of disenchanted individuals could organize opposition to a regime in power and respond to oppression with non-standard military tactics or 'terrorism'. The US government would then add another enemy without considering the military implications of waging war against them.

While these symbolic, metaphorical wars may appear as harmless shorthand for broad policy goals, declaring war creates fundamental changes in a society. The metaphor necessarily creates an enemy, which becomes entrenched in a Biblical lexicon of right and wrong, good and evil. The language of war, with its references to heroes and sacrifices, demands duty and urgency. The culture of the society shifts toward glorifying violence. There are also many casualties of war, including the accountability of government, the freedom of the media and the legal rights of a nation's citizens.

In a prescient article penned a week before September 11th, 2001, the American pacifist writer Alan Bock argued that his country's politicians were becoming increasingly casual about applying the metaphor of war to domestic political issues from drunk driving to greenhouse gases to illiteracy. In a story entitled 'War on X: When the Metaphor Becomes Too Real', he pondered whether 'a particular social ill is really likely to yield to a military style action or whether an assault is really the way to handle a delicate social situation'. He concluded with a warning on the power of words: 'When the metaphorical use of the term war is common and seldom challenged, resistance to actual war becomes more difficult and uncommon.'

While it would not be considered acceptable to send cruise missiles into homes where wealthy partygoers are snorting lines of cocaine or black inhabitants are smoking crack, billions of dollars of US military aid are granted to the Colombian military to combat the FARC guerrillas and their *campesino* partners. The proportion of federal drug funds going to treatment was cut in half during the Reagan administration and has never recovered. But then, an anti-drugs programme that concentrates on rehabilitation and education doesn't spark the martial mentality needed to wage a 'war'.

The United States spends more today on its military than the rest of the world combined, and when a nation has by far the most powerful army in the world, it tends to see problems through a military lens. An old seer apparently once said that if all you have in your toolbox are hammers then every problem looks like a nail.

I suspect that George Orwell would consider these 'wars on metaphors' as another assault on English by sinister political scriptwriters who have injured the language with new euphemisms that conceal the meaning of war. Instead of generating images of bloodshed, loss and agony, 'war' has been transformed into a word with positive, healthy connotations. It becomes associated with a crusade to 'clean up' a dirty world. The 'war on terror' becomes a term generally meaning 'restoring world peace' and the 'war on drugs' is understood as 'creating a drug-free world'.

Miguel and his associates in the FARC can easily be described as villainous and evil by a Washington speechwriter because the 'war on terror' and the 'war on drugs' are by definition patriotic endeavours; the only requirement is to finger an intended enemy as either a terrorist or a drug producer. A 'war on a metaphor' can allow a government to begin military action on almost anyone it chooses.

The doctrine underpinning the 'war on terror' is that no country should be able to become powerful enough to attack the United States, either through conventional means or by sponsoring 'terrorism'. This allows the United States to claim the right to attack any nation or group with a pre-emptive strike. For well over a century, this de facto strategy has been applied towards the United States' neighbours in Central and South America. The 'war on drugs' was used as a cover for this policy long before the 'war on terror' was formulated.

A month after the disintegration of the Berlin Wall, the US invaded Panama in order to overthrow its leader, General Manuel Noriega. Noriega had been an American ally who had worked for the CIA but had become a liability, particularly when his drug dealing became public knowledge. The United States invoked Article 51 of the UN Charter, as it did prior to the invasion of Iraq fourteen years later. Article 51 allows force to be used only as self-defence against an armed attack. The Bush administration claimed that it was defending 'our interests and our people', arguing that the Charter entitled the United States to invade Panama to prevent 'its territory from being used as a base to smuggle drugs into the United States'. A newspaper columnist, George Will, described the invasion as 'good-neighbour policy' that showed America's 'rights and responsibilities' in the hemisphere.

US political leaders have justified inducing 'regime change' in Latin America by claiming that countries in the United States' 'backyard' can pose a serious threat to its national security. In 1954, the CIA overthrew the President of Guatemala, Jacobo Arbenz, because his democratic government included communists. In 1983, the US invaded Grenada, a small, impoverished island of around a hundred thousand people, on grounds of self-defence, although it was hard to see the left-leaning regime of Maurice Bishop and his successors as a threat to US security. On 11 September 1973, Salvador Allende, the President of Chile (the first freely elected socialist leader in the world since the beginning of the cold war), was ousted by General Augusto Pinochet with the determined backing of President Nixon, Henry Kissinger and the CIA. More than three thousand people perished in the bloody repression that followed. Pinochet's secret police set up Operation Condor in collaboration with the intelligence services of several other South American countries. It formed an international network that kidnapped and assassinated leftist political opponents. Again, the CIA knew about its murderous activities and may have assisted in them. In the 1980s, Ronald Reagan's administration covertly sold arms to Iran in order to finance an attempt by 'Contra' guerrillas to topple a socialist regime in Nicaragua which 'threatened' the US with its purchase of vintage Soviet MiG fighters.

The Contras were never considered terrorists by the mainstream media in the West, even though their actions would easily comply with today's State Department definition. In 1988, Congress provided 'Assistance for the Nicaraguan Resistance' just three days after the Contras had attacked a passenger ship, killing two civilians and wounding twenty-seven. The incident was not mentioned in the Senate debate. Once again, one man's terrorist became another man's resistance fighter. As Noam Chomsky summarized: 'The message is clear: no one has the right of self-defense against US terrorist attack. The US is a terrorist state *by right*. That is unchallengeable doctrine.'

The source of so much American angst in the region is, of course, Cuba, and its socialist leader, Fidel Castro, a loyal ally of the former Soviet Union. Castro's audacity has long enraged Americans and emboldened anti-American elements in Latin America. President Kennedy's botched overthrow at the Bay of Pigs and Castro's involvement in the 1962 missile crisis still niggle in the US government's psyche. Cuba's non-existent military threat is countered by continued sanctions and isolation, orchestrated by a powerful political lobby of Cuban émigrés based in Florida.

The State Department placed Cuba on the list of nations that sponsor terrorism partly because it provided a haven for fugitives from the Black Panther Party and other radical black-power groups from the 1970s, as well as Basque militants from ETA wanted by Spanish authorities. These are mostly ageing militants easing their way into retirement and avoiding decades-old arrest warrants. The most significant accusation, however, is that Colombia's two main guerrilla movements, the largest being the Revolutionary Armed Forces of Colombia, have 'a permanent presence on the island'.

Most armed leftist movements in the hemisphere laid down their arms after the collapse of the Soviet Union, unable to sustain rebellion without Moscow's patronage. The FARC has been able to fight on thanks to the drug trade. President Clinton's Drug Czar, General Barry McCaffrey, told me in his Washington office that the FARC earned half a billion dollars a year in drug profits that it mostly used to purchase arms.

With his upright military gait and steely stare, General McCaffrey was clear about allies and enemies. The FARC are a threat to the United States. 'Our State Department has labelled them a terrorist organization. We've got a situation where a friendly democratic government is faced by an internal threat of such serious magnitude that they have lost almost half the land area of the country. The FARC are a very well-armed, a very cunning and ruthless force that is sitting on top of the largest production of illegal drugs in North, Central or South America.' But, General, I asked, forced to interrupt his flow, why are they a threat to the United States? In a heartbeat, he continued without changing his facial expression or averting his stare, 'They are a huge threat, not only to Colombia and her neighbours, but also to the United States. The problem is neither their ideology nor their weapons but instead their threat as a drug-producing nation to the United States.' So, this is Washington's message to Miguel, the befuddled coca farmer; you are a 'terrorist threat' because large numbers of American citizens are buying your cocaine.

The 'war on drugs' is, of course, often fought with good intentions but the result is a consistent failure to significantly alter the volume of controlled drugs in Western societies. This repeated policy deficiency has made some well-respected and scholarly people conclude that a conspiracy must be taking place and that the 'war on drugs' is simply window dressing for a more sinister, secretive government agenda. I have heard many thoughtful and well-educated African-Americans say that the police brought heroin (in the late sixties) and then crack (in the early eighties) into the inner cities in order to weaken the fabric and political resolve of the black community. I heard another, more specific account of the US government's ambivalence towards 'the war on drugs' during a visit to Florida in 1992. I was lunching with a former agent from the Bureau of Alcohol, Tobacco and Firearms (ATF) at a restaurant in Coconut Grove, south of Miami. Over a dessert of key lime pie, he told me about alleged drug-dealing by persons close to the then newly elected Jamaican Prime Minister, Edward Seaga. Seaga had defeated Michael Manley, a friend of Castro, in a bloody, murderous election in 1980. Seaga was a welcome ally for the new Reagan administration. The ATF agent described how a man from the CIA had warned him, 'Lay off Seaga,' adding that the request 'comes straight from the Oval Office'. According to this evidence, just as President Reagan was launching his 'War on Drugs' and First Lady Nancy Reagan implored

American schoolchildren to 'Just Say No', the President was allowing 'one of the largest drug networks' that the ATF agent had seen to continue importing cocaine through Jamaica into the United States.

After September 11th, the metaphorical 'wars on drugs and terror' merged into a unified fight against Marxist guerrillas in Colombia. The US Attorney General, John Ashcroft, held the FARC accountable for its 'reign of terror' in Colombia and pledged to defend American citizens. 'Just as we fight terrorism in the mountains of South Asia, we will fight terrorism in our own hemisphere.' A statement by an intelligence officer to a US Senate judiciary committee in May 2003 summed up the new world order: 'Whether it is a state, such as formerly Taliban-controlled Afghanistan, or a narco-terrorist organization, such as the FARC, the nexus between drugs and terrorism is perilously evident.'

The FARC are a ruthless, often murderous army. They have killed both their own people and foreign visitors. They have kidnapped thousands of Colombians for lucrative ransoms. Despite their brutality, they did not comply with the conventional image of a terrorist; they had an eighteen-thousand-strong army and mostly engaged in combat with the Colombian armed forces or rightist militias. Before September 11th, the world's media avoided the use of 'terrorist' in chronicling Colombia's war. The lexicon of this complex, three-sided conflict had been carefully honed: the leftist armies were called guerrillas or rebels; the right-wing militias that were allied to sections of the army were called paramilitaries. Nevertheless, the FARC and ELN soon joined al-Qa'eda in a list of organizations that were defined as 'terrorists' and perceived as enemies of the West in a global conflict.

In Washington, government officials peppered their comments on Colombia with references to terrorists and the evil they commit. It was as if they were hitting me over the head with a word that, if used frequently enough, would trip off my tongue whenever I referred to the FARC. A few days later, I was skirting the Andes in a small Dash-8 jet on my way to a rendezvous with the 'terrorists', far from the manipulated habitat of news conferences and briefings. From my window seat I watched snow-capped mountains shimmering in the morning light. A carpet of cloud had sunk between the peaks. Forests grew above the clouds and I saw villages perched on the edge of mountains. The plane was heading for Florencia, the capital of Caqueta, a *departamento* of jungles and coca plantations in southern Colombia that provided sanctuary for thousands of armed rebels.

We were met by our driver, Lelo, a man who wore a permanent smile, or perhaps a smirk. He was in his early forties with well-trimmed, slightly greying hair and an obligatory moustache. While he clearly took some pride in his looks, his clothes were a mess. His shirt was open to the waist; he repeatedly hitched up baggy trousers that were lined with dirt. Lelo claimed to know the leadership of the FARC very well. 'They trust me,' he reassured us. He worked alongside his son, Lelito, or 'Little Lelo', a younger version of his father. The two men loaded our bags and Lelo gestured for me to hop into his battered mustard-yellow taxi. He looked at me with mocking concern. 'Don't worry, I can handle any problems,' he smiled.

After more than an hour's journey through lush countryside of banana trees and slender, looping palms, Lelo slowed the car down and told us to get our passports and the faxed invitation we had received from the guerrilla leadership. He then drove gingerly toward a makeshift checkpoint.

Three men and two female FARC *guerrilleras*, dressed in combat fatigues, manned the roadblock. They were guarding the entrance to a Marxist mini-state, inside the territory of Colombia. The government had formally conceded a region, twice the size of Wales, in an attempt to draw the rebels into negotiations about peace. One of the women raised a languid arm and flagged down our taxi. Lelo spoke to her through the open window in rapid-fire Spanish, mentioning the BBC. She nodded and glanced without smiling at each member of our team, who had squeezed into the back of the taxi. The *guerrillera* then shouted something at her colleagues before beckoning us from the car. 'They just want to search your bags,' Lelo reassured, his tone suggesting it was routine. A girl, who was about eighteen with long black hair held loosely in a bun, gestured that I should lift up my arms. She wore shiny golden earrings that sparkled in the evening sun and her nails were carefully manicured and painted. I watched her hands as she patted me down, checking for guns or knives, her battleworn M-16 rifle slung across her back.

The guerrillas manning the roadblock were courteous, but it was impossible to forget that a few months earlier their colleagues had executed three American civilians. One of the guerrillas yawned. Another looked, with popping eyes, at my passport. He casually gave it back, unable to tell my name from my city of birth. None of the guerrillas appeared older than twenty. It was a cursory search, more a demonstration of authority. After hiding in the jungles for nearly forty years, the FARC were keen to display their new political power.

The effective capital of 'Farclandia' was San Vicente del Caguan, a dusty market town where farmers deliver produce in ageing rusty Chevrolet pickup trucks. The *campesinos* strutted around town wearing ten-gallon hats and checked shirts opened to the waist. Cans of Aguila beer stacked up at the bars from breakfast onwards. At night, Cumbia music, a blend of jazz with Cuban salsa, was blaring from the open-fronted clubs, shaking the streets. My hotel room vibrated to the beat until 3 a.m. Tubby prostitutes languished on stools as *campesinos* played pool, exchanging glances that sometimes solidified into stares. Occasionally, a FARC soldier ambled in and checked that all was well. Patrons gave respectful, if overly obsequious, smiles to the young guerrillas as they manoeuvred through the drunks and the prostitutes.

Lelo had led us to 'the best hotel in town'. The Saman was a basic, opulence-free guest house snuggled between shops on a busy street. Sullen women sat in the hallway watching blaring soap operas on television. I was woken before 7 a.m. by passionate, hammed-up Spanish dialogue. Silence was not part of life in San Vicente.

We spent four days in San Vicente with the guerrillas. Our main aim was to gain access to one of their military camps outside of town. The BBC team included Ewa Ewart, a vastly experienced Polish-born producer of remarkable courage. The cameraman was an affable and amusing Australian, Greg Barbera. Our assistant or 'fixer' was a maestro of persuasion, an adventurous Peruvian called Guillermo. He had good contacts within the FARC, including a friendship with the daughter of the movement's military commander, Jorge Briceño Suárez. Briceño's nom de guerre is 'Mono Jojoy', which means 'blond jungle monkey'. He was a cunning, bloodthirsty field commander and was thought to be a likely future leader of the FARC. 'Mono Jojoy' modelled himself on 'Che' Guevara; he sported a black beret and was often heard quoting from Guevara's works. Unlike Guevara, he was known to enjoy civilian luxuries and was chauffeured in an expensive four-wheel-drive Toyota. From pictures I've seen, 'Mono Jojoy' resembles rather more an overweight French farmer than the dashing young 'Che'. Nevertheless, he was known to be merciless towards those who anger him and I wondered whether Guillermo was playing with fire. When I met Amparo, I could understand fully why Guillermo was prepared to risk his anger. Mono Jojoy's daughter was tall and slender, with large eyes and long flowing hair. She wore a snug-fitting uniform and carried her AK-47 with the confident swagger of a catwalk model. Guillermo's chutzpah reached new heights when he told me that she was married and that a former boyfriend had ended up in a ditch.

The FARC headquarters were an unassuming former municipal building. In the hallway, a portrait of 'Che' greeted visitors. In the media room a black-and-white portrait of Lenin, Marx and Engels hung from a rusty nail on one wall; on the other a young Fidel Castro glared at visitors. The FARC's radio station, Radio Resistance, was playing in the background, announcing news of police brutality. The next programme included uplifting martial music inviting *campesinos* to overthrow powerful landowners. When I asked the meaning of one song, a *guerrillera* with her fatigues unbuttoned enough to reveal a full cleavage told me that the rich needed to pay for their cruelty. 'In what way should they pay?' I asked. 'Money, or maybe something not so nice,' she smiled playfully and apologized as the phone rang and she carried on with her work.

The FARC continued to use the language of the cold war in its official communiqués and propaganda. It presented an inevitable clash between capitalism, 'gringo imperialism' and the exploited, landless peasants of Colombia. The movement had set up institutions faithful to the writings of Karl Marx and Friedrich Engels, Marx's loyal Mancunian friend. Next in ascending order in the FARC's pantheon of heroes was Lenin, who provided an often-crude blueprint for applying Marx's theories. Next stood Simón Bolívar, the Venezuelan general who ended Spain's rule over Colombia in 1819 and also led the liberation of Venezuela, Ecuador, Bolivia and Peru. The Argentinian guerrilla fighter, Ernesto 'Che' Guevara, stood tallest amongst the revolutionary heroes. He argued for armed struggle, based on the model of the Cuban revolution of 1959, when small and mobile bands of *campesinos* overthrew Fulgencio Batista, an ally of America, and brought socialist revolution to the doorstep of a superpower. (Fidel Castro couldn't be considered in this list, I was told, because he was still alive.)

I was shown an example of 'socialist reform' in a field outside San Vicente. A structure of roughly constructed wooden beams covered with tarpaulin had become a 'People's Court'. This judicial system had no prisons and disputes were settled between the parties under the watchful and usually persuasive gaze of a FARC judge. Commander

Ivan Rios, a moustachioed veteran jungle guerrilla, was sitting in a camouflage T-shirt behind a small wooden table, like a traditional schoolroom desk. The first case on the court list was a murder; the killer, a twenty-year-old farmer, had stabbed a man during a drunken brawl in one of San Vicente's pool bars.

The family of the accused sat on one bench facing the relatives of the murdered man. After listening for an hour, Ivan told the mothers of both men to go to nearby woods. 'I would like you to talk in private and find a solution that you are both happy with.'

The mother of the dead man wore a Mickey Mouse T-shirt over faded jeans. She rose from the bench and walked toward a similar-aged woman in a red top. Somewhat hesitantly, they shuffled down a path leading into dense jungle. From outside the court I spotted the two women, sitting on the trunk of a fallen tree, fanning themselves with a palm leaf.

Ivan turned to me and boasted that no one was sent to jail in areas under the FARC's control; prisons were a symptom of state oppression. 'We do not put human dignity behind bars and no one is condemned here,' he explained. 'We conciliate; we always look for a solution to all problems.'

The women agreed that the family of the murderer would pay $1,500 compensation to the victim's mother. The killer would be forced to leave the region until the debt was paid. It seemed idyllic and laughably naive. Yet the mother who'd lost her son told me through held-back tears that the two women had become friends; her thirst for revenge had been quenched. In the Colombian courts, the murderer would have been jailed for up to sixty years.

Ivan cheerfully ended court proceedings with the cry, 'Long live the Revolution.' When I suggested that brutal, heinous crimes couldn't be dealt with in the same style as an accidental killing, he told me that his court could only work successfully alongside 'social re-education programmes'. 'We educate the people every day through cultural campaigns. They have become more aware and that's why there are no thieves in San Vicente any more. Everything has changed because the people are provided with cultural education on a daily basis.'

Judge Rios gained a law degree from Bogotá but after working as a solicitor for a few years he embraced the jungle and the theory of revolution. He believed that Farclandia provided the laboratory where a pure form of social engineering could be nourished without the corrupting virus of capitalism. When I pressed Ivan on the need to incarcerate the truly evil, he told me that evil would soon cease in San Vicente. 'People will get on with each other better; the streets will be repaired, there'll be schools and hospital services, the *campesinos* will live in peace, the cattle numbers will go up. There will not be that kind of crime.' He seemed faithful to an old saying in the Soviet Union: the past keeps changing but the future can be predicted with certainty.

Ivan was in his late thirties but exuded a childlike enthusiasm, unblemished by doubt. Like the very religious, he smiled knowingly, as if he had privileged access to the truth. It was only some months after we left San Vicente that we discovered more about 'the people's judge'. Commander Ivan Rios had been killed. He had apparently been summarily executed by a FARC hit squad for siphoning funds for his own use and spending the money on prostitutes and rum. A man on the back of a motorcycle is said to have shot him as he walked down a busy street in Florencia. I suppose Ivan knew that if he were caught, he would never end up in jail. While the FARC may contend that prisons are immoral, the movement seems very comfortable with the death penalty.

The FARC was formed in 1964 under the leadership of Pedro Marin, now known by his nom de guerre, Manuel 'Sureshot' Marulanda. He was a respected marksman who apparently never missed a target when he trained new recruits. He remained in charge until 2004 when he finally succumbed to prostate cancer. He was then a rumpled, stooping guerrilla in his mid-seventies who had lived in the jungle for half a century and had never been to the capital, Bogotá. He had already been at war for nearly two decades when he established the FARC, with a revolutionary programme calling together all the citizens who dreamt of a Colombia for Colombians, with equality of opportunities and equitable distribution of wealth.

Marulanda's political consciousness had evolved during the 1950s, when Colombian society was torn apart by La Violencia, a long decade of brutality between supporters of the two main political parties, the Liberals and the Conservatives. A presidential candidate was murdered; shoot-outs broke out on the floor of the legislature; corpses piled up in the countryside. It became a civil war where terror was its language, with brutal killings and mutilations becoming increasingly elaborate and ghoulish. Yet neither side was considered terrorists.

La Violencia had begun amongst the urban elite and ended there.

The deal that brought an end to the violence in 1957 excluded the rural left, including 'Sureshot'. The educated elite that had earlier sponsored his rebellion betrayed him. Marulanda then carried on alone under the banner of communism, shifting the violence into its present, largely urban–rural divide that saw fifty thousand killed in the 1990s alone. The Colombian army has never since been able to crush his rebellion, permeate his jungle headquarters or suppress his influence on rural communities

When we arranged to travel to one of the FARC's military camps, deep in the jungle, Lelo said he knew the rendezvous point. It was a small restaurant in the middle of nowhere selling beer and a local speciality, banana soup. Lelito also travelled with us. It was a punishing journey from San Vicente along unmade, rutted roads. Neither taxi had effective shock absorbers and the potholes seemed to throw the cars into the air, as if they were toys dragged by an angry infant.

When we arrived at the rendezvous point we had to wait for about three hours until a large Toyota pickup truck came to meet us. Lelo and his son stayed behind and our team climbed into the back of the pickup for another two-hour journey. I was sitting alongside three *guerrilleras*. They were pretty girls; one was eighteen and called Violetta. The other two were in their early twenties. Each carried an automatic rifle and wore a military uniform. At first they looked stern and unflinching but after a short time on the bumpy, dusty road, I occasionally threw a smile and got back a girly giggle as we shared water or complained about our aching backsides.

When we arrived at the camp, it was clear that the company of some eighty guerrillas had also just turned up. I wondered whether this was their real base or whether, like a film set, some guerrillas simply turned up here to meet television cameras. Then I recalled that mobility is the 'basic tactic' of the guerrilla, as described by 'Che' Guevara in *Guerrilla Warfare*. 'His house will be the open sky', he writes, and he lists what the guerrilla must carry in his knapsack: a hammock; grease for the gun; a bottle of water; a knife, fork and plate; and soap. 'Che' accepts that personal hygiene is sometimes sacrificed for the cause; he recalled how after one march, 'our bodies gave off a peculiar and offensive odour that repelled anyone who came near. The hammocks of guerrilla fighters are known for their characteristic, individual odour.'

The fighters draped their rifles and ammunition over branches, unpacked their rucksacks and strung up their hammocks. A few began building a fire and preparing food over a basic stove. They removed branches and foliage that had hidden some stools, a table and a few wooden beds, revealing that this wasn't just random woodland. It was a column of fifty-two men and twenty-four women, a unit that guarded and were under the command of one of the men on the FARC's ruling seven-man committee. The female fighters brought out mirrors and make-up boxes and spent the hour before dinner washing their hair in a stream or painting their nails. 'Che' Guevara's guidebook was written for men; while he accepted that women can fight alongside men, he envisaged them having a different role, as teacher, nurse or messenger. 'The woman as cook can greatly improve the diet', he enthused. Thirty years later, at the FARC's Eighth Conference, a ruling declared that women should gain full control of their personal lives; women would fight alongside their male counterparts and be considered equals within the organization. It may not have meant much, but two men cooked the meal that was prepared that night, a beef stew with rice and an earthy, bitter vegetable resembling okra.

The adoption of equality within the FARC–People's Army seemed less literal than in other forces, such as the US Army. Violetta laughed when I praised her nail varnish, a purple colour with shimmering flecks of silver. When I asked her why she bothered dressing up at night in a guerrilla camp, she giggled some more. 'I want to look nice,' she said. I was to soon realize that this is not a puritanical army; the girls dress up for the night because sexual contact between the soldiers is encouraged, albeit within bounds set by unit commanders. The FARC issued guidelines on sex amongst the guerrillas entitled *Love beneath the intimacy of the mosquito netting*. It describes how 'flirting' is a mystery to no one in the guerrilla world.

A commander called Sonia described the correct procedure: 'If they want to build a relationship then they talk to the commander: "I want to have a relationship with such-and-such comrade," or the comrade says, "I want to spend the night with such-and-such," and they let them. They make sure the woman is using protection and that they don't have any STDs and they let them.' She added, 'We have mountains of condoms.'

The military leadership controls who sleeps with whom. The liaison is then announced before the group and, apparently, reported to the 'high command'. There are no marriages amongst FARC guerrillas, just 'associations'. But these 'associations' can be fiery, high-octane affairs.

The leadership is aware that the passion can dwindle, and the 'association' can be ended with a simple military command. The 'bourgeois marriage', based on sexual monogamy, is mocked as 'unrealistic' and monotonous. In Farclandia, either party can seek a separation and neither jealousy nor anger is allowed.

The commanders also accept that loving couples can have a baby. The guidebook notes: 'Stable couples can have a child if they want. They both must agree and ask for permission to have the child. It's something normal.' But 'Children become secondary in the life of the fighter' so they must be brought up by 'relatives of the couple'.

We were there to meet Raul Reyes, a senior commander and a member of the FARC's ruling council. He was a chubby, bearded and bespectacled fighter who was a schoolteacher before he joined the rebels in the late 1960s. He struggled to get out from the pickup truck that shuttled him from place to place, as his well-padded stomach seemed momentarily caught up with his M-16 and ammunition belt. A lean, wiry 'Che' Guevara, with only dried fish in his knapsack and a burning zeal in his heart, contrasted sharply with the ambling, middle-aged leadership of the FARC today. Despite his portly manner, Reyes was a hardened revolutionary. I had brought with me a bottle of Cuban rum, which I'd heard was his favourite tipple. ('Che' wrote that alcohol is prohibited for the guerrilla, but I thought it best not to bring that up.) When most of the troops had gone to bed, we opened the bottle over candlelight and discussed what had happened to Marxism after the end of the cold war.

Reyes clearly enjoyed the prospect of a political discussion over drinks – I suspect the debating chamber was more his natural habitat than the battlefield. We agreed that Marxism was as relevant now as during the period of the Soviet Union; perhaps more so, as global capitalism imposed its values on a sometimes resentful developing world. We also agreed that *Das Kapital* was a meandering, badly written book. But despite his desire to talk about theoretical Marxism, he was genuinely concerned to portray the FARC's struggle as a uniquely Colombian phenomenon, born from the injustices of its society.

'We take Marxism–Leninism as our guide for action but not as a dogma,' he said, shaking his head. While his vision involved discounting cases that broke the rhythm of his argument, Reyes was less

hemmed in by ideology than I had thought. He had earlier greeted the
CEOs from two of America's largest capitalist conglomerates and said
he would welcome their investment in the poor regions of southern
Colombia.

He lifted his finger at me and said with national pride, 'Remember
that our guerrilla struggle existed before "Che" Guevara arrived in
Cuba. In Colombia the struggle began in 1948. The Commander and
Chief of the FARC [Marulanda] was a Liberal *guerrillero* before
becoming a revolutionary.'

His analysis about Colombia's conflict today was sadly reduced to
simplistic dogma. 'The war going on in Colombia at the moment is a
violent confrontation between the state and the people,' he said
grandly. He was no longer speaking intelligently but was quoting from
the FARC's songbook. 'The revolutionary forces are fighting against
social injustice, authoritarianism, corruption, *gringo* imperialism and
the pillaging of the country's natural resources. Our aim is nothing
short of becoming the government of Colombia.'

But what about the 'war on drugs'? Surely it is wrong for the FARC
to be making money from farmers who cultivate coca and opium? He
laughed. 'The "war on drugs" is not a war against drugs trafficking, it
is a war on the Colombian people and the Colombian guerrilla
movement.' He said that the FARC did not traffic, but simply helped
local farmers who have no option but to grow coca. 'The so-called
"war on drugs" is an excuse to intervene in Colombia's domestic
affairs. We don't see any "war on drugs" in their country, which is the
main consumer of narcotics in the world.'

Reyes is probably correct when he says the FARC are not the group
chiefly responsible for processing and exporting drugs from Colombia.
Certainly, during the 1980s, criminal cartels in the cities of Cali and
Medellín had dominated the coca trade. When the cartels were broken
up, many of the coca plantations fell under the control of the various
armed groups, including the guerrillas.

I detected a smile on his face when he described the 'tax for peace'
that coca farmers are forced to pay the FARC. Perhaps he saw in the
candlelight that I couldn't resist a wry laugh, emboldened as I was by
several slugs of rum. 'We never think about the drugs trade,' he
insisted without great commitment. 'We demand a tax regardless of
whether they are drug producers or not. We tax sugar and coffee
growers, cattle-raisers, and those who farm soya and sorghum.' Of

course they do. But the tax on coca provides a golden stream of income that finances their war. Drugs finance wars in South America and Asia (in Africa, it is diamonds). Soya beans do not.

'We condemn narcotics as well,' Reyes declared before adding, somewhat surprisingly, 'The United States would have no better friend in the "war against drugs" than the FARC.' I was rather tired and didn't pursue this comment. The income from 'taxing' coca producers was a persuasive reason for the movement to forget its ideological opposition to narcotics. There was, however, at least some evidence that the FARC might, in the right circumstances, be willing to cut back its connection with coca production. Human-rights groups lean toward Reyes' view that the FARC could be persuaded to sever its links with drug traffickers if a political deal was agreed. The United Nations organized a crop-substitution programme working in zones where the FARC was, in effect, sovereign and the movement has publicly encouraged any scheme that would subsidize farmers who ended coca cultivation. Winifred Tate from the Washington Office on Latin America argues that by focusing on the guerrillas, US policy is ignoring more pivotal groups at the nucleus of Colombia's drug industry. 'Right-wing paramilitaries operating with the clear support of the Colombian military are much more deeply involved in drug trafficking than the guerrillas,' she told me. 'A counter-narcotics strategy that simply targets the FARC is destined to failure.'

While drinking rum with an urbane, humorous man who is well versed in leftist thought from Gramsci to Chomsky, it is easy to forget that he commanded a hardened, uncompromising guerrilla organization. I never asked Reyes if he had killed anyone or planted a bomb in a crowded street. When I asked about the hundreds of people that the FARC abduct and then hold for ransom, Reyes feigned indignation: 'The FARC doesn't kidnap. On the contrary, the FARC condemns kidnapping. What the FARC does is charge a tax,' he continued disingenuously. 'There are many Colombians who pay this tax without any need to pressure them, but there are others who try to evade the taxes, so we hold them until they pay.'

The callous simplicity of this argument and the cruelty it inflicts on the victims of its logic did not strike me while sipping rum with Commander Reyes. A few days later, his words would fill me with rage when I left the jungles of the south and returned to Bogotá.

I was at the studios of Colombian National Radio for a programme called *In Search of Lost Liberty*. The show allows relatives to read out letters that appeal for the safe return of kidnapped victims. They hope that those imprisoned by the FARC in their jungle hideaways can listen to news from home and tender messages from loved ones.

For a long while, Colombia's urban middle class had largely been content to ignore the war in the south. Then the guerrillas took the war to them with the constant threat of kidnapping. There are over two hundred seizures a month. Rubia was a well-dressed woman with pearl earrings and a bright red Italian-designed woollen suit. Her husband had been abducted six months earlier.

'Hello, my darling fatty,' she began. 'This has been a very difficult time but everything is going to be fine; God is always with us. We miss you very much and we just ask the Lord for this suffering to increase our mutual love. My darling baldy, I don't have much in life but I love everything I have . . .' She broke down and sobbed, tears falling on the microphone. The host was a gentle, compassionate man who, after a dignified pause, took Rubia to a nearby chair and beckoned her daughter, clasping a short written note, to the microphone. 'Hi, Dad, it's Adriana, lots and lots of kisses from my little brothers and sisters, all my love and God bless you.'

Another message was more practical but equally moving from Ingrid, whose husband had been snatched by the FARC. At first she seemed bewildered, her eyes darting around the studio. Then she then read her message like a schoolteacher scolding a pupil, or a shopper returning faulty merchandise. 'Monito, I want to tell you that it's been difficult to accept that it will soon be seven months since they took you away from us. Time goes by and we're not getting anywhere. The people who are holding you hostage aren't communicating with us, which makes it difficult to come to any agreement. Ask them to call us so that we can make some progress.'

There was very little anger; when I asked the uncle and aunt of one little boy whose mother had been kidnapped about Raul Reyes' contention that the FARC were simply demanding a tax, their replies were suitably caustic. 'It's money in exchange for someone's life. That's kidnapping,' concluded the uncle. His wife looked at me with a question mark carved on her face. 'How can you talk about bargaining for a life? You bargain for a house, for a car, but for someone's life? It's very difficult to understand that this is a business for them. For us it's torture . . .'

The FARC were categorized as a 'foreign terrorist group' by the State Department because they are accused of murdering at least a dozen US citizens over the past two decades. Raul Reyes dismissed the 'terrorist' label as cheap propaganda. He immediately responded that the United States trained 'terrorists' at the School of the Americas at Fort Benning, Georgia. Tens of thousands of soldiers and policemen from Latin America have graduated from the school, where they are taught basic warfare, counter-terrorist tactics, commando operations and so forth. 'Most Colombian officers have been to that academy,' Reyes said. 'That's where they've been turned into terrorists who torture the Colombian people. That's where they've been educated in the theory of terror in order to defend the interests of big money.'

I was interested to discover that 'Che' Guevara appeared to have a clear idea of what constituted 'terrorism'. In *Guerrilla Warfare*, as part of a chapter on the importance of blowing up bridges and disrupting communications, he rejects 'terrorism' as an effective tool of warfare, except in special circumstances.

'Sabotage has nothing to do with terrorism; terrorism and personal assaults are entirely different tactics. We sincerely believe that terrorism is of negative value, that it by no means produces the desired effects, that it can turn a people against a revolutionary movement, and that it can bring a loss of lives to its agents out of proportion to what it produces. On the other hand, attempts to take the lives of particular persons are to be made, though only in very special circumstances; this tactic should be used where it will eliminate a leader of the oppression. What ought never to be done is to employ specially trained, heroic, self-sacrificing human beings in eliminating a little assassin whose death can provoke the destruction in reprisal of all the revolutionaries employed and even more.' 'Che' seemed to define 'terrorism' as an act close to assassination and quite different to blowing up bridges. He also rejected it, not because the killing would be morally repugnant, but because it would be ineffective.

After drinking nearly half a bottle of rum I could sleep anywhere, including on a hard bed of wooden planks. I stared into the clear night sky. We were many miles from the nearest town and there was no background light to dull the universe; the stars were brighter than I had seen them anywhere in the world. As I dozed off, I listened for sounds, but both the forest and the guerrilla army were silent.

The prosperous northern suburbs of Bogotá seemed like a different country. Our hotel was near a leafy square lined with expensive shops, restaurants and nightclubs. Families strolled in the park at the centre of the square on a Sunday afternoon. It was nearly Christmas and a Santa welcomed children into his grotto. The smell of roasted coffee from one shop mingled with aromas from the *chocolatier* next door. Women in furs carried presents wrapped with red ribbon. A group of teenagers laughed at the entrance to TGI Friday restaurant. We had dinner in an excellent, chrome and glass designed French restaurant. I could easily have been in New York, London or Paris.

We ordered a bottle of champagne; we hadn't had a good meal for some time and we felt it time to celebrate two weeks' hard work with the guerrillas. Guillermo then arrived with a tall, attractive lady in a tight-fitting short skirt. As an unmarried young man who enjoys life to the full, Guillermo was often accompanied by female friends who were easy on the eye. But this time I put my hands over my face.

'I think you know Amparo,' he gestured, as the daughter of Mono Jojoy joined us at the table. I poured her a glass of champagne and asked how she was. 'Very well,' she replied. She sat down for some nouvelle cuisine amongst Colombia's most privileged, as if it was the most natural activity in the world. For a moment I was bothered that we were compromising ourselves by having the daughter of the most wanted FARC commander at dinner. Her uncle had also just executed three Americans. What would the police say if they found her with us? But very soon, as we chatted about our Christmas plans and presents for our families, I just admired, and not for the last time, Guillermo's brio. It was a very pleasant dinner and Amparo fitted in perfectly. If she caught the eye, as she did on several occasions, it was from prosperous-looking young men who were struck by her beauty. If only they had known that she was the enemy that brought fear and death into their lives.

As we left the restaurant, a group of boisterous young men were preparing to 'drag race' their matching Corvette sports cars down one side of the park. Carefree laughter was in the air. A chauffeur in a Mercedes with dark windows dropped off two girls who looked like sisters in their late teens. They were drunk and they almost fell into me before disappearing into a bar. Weren't these people scared? I thought. More than half the world's kidnappings occur in Colombia, where three thousand people every year are ransomed, sometimes for payments as high as $500,000. There were security men peppered at doorways but I didn't see many policemen. Then I realized that we were in what amounted to a 'gated' district. A truck patrolled the square, with a locked cage in the back. Inside were faces staring from behind bars; poor people, with dark complexions and broad, round faces. The undesirables, beggars or simply those who looked out of place, were simply picked up and bundled into the back of the truck and dumped elsewhere. The truck circled slowly, like a street-cleaning vehicle, sweeping up the poor.

Robert White has a playful, understated humour, especially when he talks about his country's policies in Latin America. He was the US Ambassador in El Salvador during the Ronald Reagan presidency, when America backed Salvadorian generals who suffered from what he described as 'an addiction to killing unarmed people'. In a slow, careful drawl, he speaks with authority and at times disbelief about his nation's actions. I met him in Washington after I left Bogotá. In common with nearly everyone who has had experience in Latin America or studied the region's problems, White avoided the use of 'terrorism'. 'It is singularly unhelpful to call any of the sides terrorists,' he sighed. 'Eventually you're going to have a negotiated peace here. Neither side can win militarily. The US should be pressuring the FARC to negotiate. Characterizing them as terrorists isn't likely to put them in a good mood as far as any negotiation goes.' He was pessimistic about an end to the civil war. 'It will need decades,' he added wearily. 'The primary sacrifice that's going to be required has to come from that small sector of very rich people who have controlled Colombia for many years.'

Robert White took me back to 1984, when the FARC declared a ceasefire and many of its members formed a party called the Patriotic Union in order to take part in elections. Upper-class Colombians were horrified and threatened, seeing a new country emerging on the political stage, a country they had neglected and abandoned. 'There would be no FARC today,' insisted White, 'and there would be no large revolutionary movement in Colombia, had the military and their auxiliaries not killed almost every revolutionary who laid down his gun to follow the road of parliamentary democracy. But what's worse is that there was no outcry from the business or economic elite of Colombia. It was conveniently shrugged off.'

It's now believed that right-wing death squads with links to the army killed some three thousand people who were either former guerrillas or leftist sympathizers, including two presidential candidates. The death squads, or *paramilitares*, lie on one side of a division that has prevented consensus and peace in Colombia for decades. The events of 1984 unleashed the contradictions that have been ripping Colombia apart ever since.

As our helicopter broke through the mist and approached the mountainous savannah, a company of perhaps a hundred soldiers in fatigues stood to attention surrounding a makeshift landing site. Each bore the large white lettering of the AUC, the Spanish acronym for the United Self-Defence Forces of Colombia, on their armband. Many had bandanas over their faces. We were arriving at a secret location for an interview with Colombia's most notorious and fabled paramilitary leader, Carlos Castaño. The paramilitaries equally hold to a mythology of heroic resistance. Castaño's campaign began to revenge his father's kidnap and murder by the FARC by forming one of many private armies during the 1960s and 70s.

In 1997 he brought together regional paramilitary groups under the banner of the AUC. With about seven thousand armed men, it is the largest paramilitary force and has the closest links to the Colombian government. In 2001 the US State Department added the AUC to its list of 'terrorist organizations'. Castaño was pugnacious and combative. He wore a two-day stubble and his index finger stabbed any nearby table as he spoke. Stout, with a paunch that sagged over an undersized military belt, his leadership qualities stemmed not from his physical presence but from intimidating black marble eyes. He was also breathtakingly direct about the methods the AUC used to combat the FARC. 'We are effective in fighting the guerrillas because we have methods that produce results,' he explained matter-of-factly. 'A person that commits an act that puts society at risk, even if that person is a civilian, then becomes a military target for us.'

Castaño said he received training in Israel from retired Israeli Defence Force instructors in the early 1980s. He spoke quickly but decisively with a refreshingly straightforward manner. He admitted that his organization committed atrocities and human-rights abuses. 'It is true that we use methods which are despicable.' He paused and then added, 'Yes, you are right but these are the methods the guerrillas imposed on us. I have to operate in these ways because if I didn't, no one on earth could stop the guerrillas killing us and thousands of other Colombians.'

Castaño said that he was not prepared to pay the price that peace with the guerrillas would entail. While talks were taking place between the FARC and the government, he kidnapped the brother of a top official involved in the negotiations, claiming that he had been 'too generous' in offering concessions.

There have been numerous documented cases of the army and the paramilitaries collaborating, including one in 1997 when FARC-controlled territory was ambushed while the army turned a blind eye. Castaño's men executed at least thirty people. Four were beheaded in the main square, a killing method favoured by the paramilitaries. The village elder was hung from a meat hook and then chopped into pieces. Many of the bodies were thrown into a river or dismembered. After the massacre, the town was abandoned as the remaining citizens fled.

Castaño was candid about his actions, nodding in agreement that he had ordered the killing of the civilians. 'Sure, there were some executions that took place outside of the combat zone,' he explained matter-of-factly. 'We wanted to show the guerrillas that they didn't own an independent republic. We were in guerrilla country, that's to say an area where they were all guerrillas in their hearts, so the people that we encountered were linked to the guerrillas. I am comforted by the thought that nobody who died was innocent.'

Castaño had yearned for political respectability as well as immunity for his murderous activities but attempts at collaboration failed. President Uribe regularly referred to the FARC as 'terrorists', a phrase that would have been unthinkable before September 11th. When he went to see George W. Bush, both sides repeated their common commitment to fight 'terrorism'. Beyond politicians scoring rhetorical points (or receiving billions of dollars of aid, in the case of President Uribe), it is difficult to find the advantages of designating the two non-state armies stalking the Coiombian countryside as 'terrorists'. It is unlikely to help the United States and Europe stem external financial support for the warring groups because, of course, this conflict is self-financing, primarily from the sale of narcotics to the US and Europe. Six million Americans regularly use cocaine and $60 billion a year is spent on illegal narcotics. There is no mystery as to the source of the funding for 'terrorism' in Colombia. In a peculiar irony, American citizens are providing the bulk of the funds for both sides in Colombia's war.

It has become fashionable to argue that the conflict in Colombia is

ALGERIA

1. *Above.* A unit of the Algerian Islamic Salvation Army (AIS) receiving a briefing from their commander.

2. *Below.* A roadblock manned by guerrillas from the AIS.

ALGERIA

3. *Top.* Two AIS guerrillas concealing their identity. Many fighters regularly entered towns and cities under the noses of the security forces.

4. *Centre.* The commander of the western division of the AIS, the movement's deputy emir, Aouad Abu Abdallah.

5. *Bottom.* Yakout Bengana holding a picture of her daughter, Katia, who was murdered by Islamist extremists in Mefta in the 'Triangle of Death' because she refused to wear a veil. She was a victim of 'Terrorism as Theatre'.

AFGHANISTAN

6. *Above.* An Afghan sunset on the front line, north of Kabul, 1989.

7. *Right.* A mujahedin soldier looking into Soviet-controlled Afghanistan at the Khyber Pass in 1989.

8. *Below, right.* A member of the 710th Brigade of Holy Warriors in 2001.

9. *Below.* The author disguised as a mujahedin soldier in a traditional Afghan-style photograph of a fighting male. The result is more cabaret that fearsome warrior!

© Fred Scott

AFGHANISTAN

10. *Above.* The author's cameraman, Johno, looking uncomfortable after declining an invitation from an Afghan elder in the village of Sarsayed (centre) to be his 'son's wife for the night'. Homosexual liaisons such as this are common in Afghanistan.

11. *Left.* A mujahedin faction leader, Abdul Rasul Sayyaf. He was Osama bin Laden commander when the Saudi billionaire first visited Afghanistan, in the early 1980s.

12. *Below.* The author shaving outside a 'hotel' at a small town called Khiaban in the foothills of the Anjoman Pass. Shaving had been banned under the Taliban and it was a political act that bemused the locals.

COLOMBIA

13. *Right.* Our 'fixer' in Colombia, Guillermo, on the right, and drivers Lelo and his son Lelito (crouching in the centre). Suspected FARC guerrillas later decapitated Lelo and set his yellow taxi on fire for 'knowing too much'. Lelito still works as a taxi driver.

14. *Left.* One of the FARC's senior commanders, Raul Reyes.

15. *Below, left.* A FARC guerrilla, Violetta, after putting on her nail polish.

16. *Below.* Miguel – a terrorist without realizing – is a coca farmer, here pictured in front of his tin-roofed house in the Colombian jungle.

ISRAEL

17. *Above.* Two of Israeli settler Duli Basok's children, reciting from the Torah, Zwika aged nine and Miyan aged five.

18. *Below.* Ibrahim Abu Tair, standing outside his house in the village of Aum Touba on the southern edge of Jerusalem. Part of his land was confiscated by the Israeli government in order to build an access road to the Jewish settlement Har Homa.

KOSOVO

Right. Ivan Stambolić, the former communist ~~~er of Serbia, who was later found murdered. ~~he police believe that Slobodan Milošović's wife Mira was responsible.

, *Below.* Danilo and his wife Kosara, Kosovan ~rbs who ran a restaurant in Decani which ~as ambushed. They were armed to protect ~emselves against their Albanian neighbours.

?1. *Bottom.* Sladjana and her husband Dejan ~tending an Easter mass. It was their last in ~sovo. Less than a year later the couple had ~led and an Albanian family moved into their apartment in Priština.

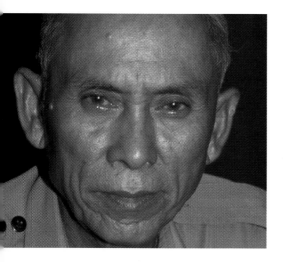

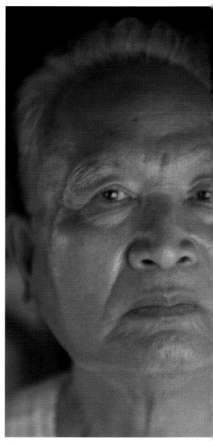

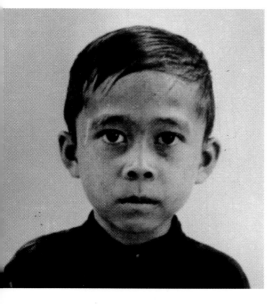

CAMBODIA

22. *Top, right.* Nuon Chea, Brother Number Two and Pol Pot's deputy, shows no remorse for the millions of Cambodians who died under his rule. (2001)

23. *Top, left.* Chum Mai, one of only seven prisoners who left Tuol Sleng alive, is still haunted by survivor's guilt.

24. *Centre, left.* An unidentified young boy, murdered at Tuol Sleng during the rule of the Khmer Rouge.

25. *Left.* A girl killed at Tuol Sleng.

now devoid of ideology or politics, presenting each side as simply a 'drugs cartel'. But this fails to place the conflict in a meaningful context. The invention of the word 'narco-terrorist' by the US government conjures an image of crazed, drug-dealing killers inculcated with Marxism and detached from the mainstream of democratic Colombia. In reality, drug production contributes more than 5 per cent of the country's GDP and roughly 30 per cent of its exports, earning around $5 billion in foreign currency. No enterprise of that magnitude can exist without the collaboration of important figures inside business, commerce, banking, government and the military. Furthermore, if the 'terrorists' are now simply interested in enriching themselves and have lost any political purpose, how can they be defined as 'terrorists'? They would be merely criminals.

The simplistic 'war on drugs' also obscures the essential difference between drug traffickers and Marxist insurgents: their different long-term objectives of economic gain and social revolution. Robert White was perplexed by the charged vocabulary. 'It's certainly curious to me that a government as sophisticated as ours describes the FARC as narco-terrorists involved in a criminal conspiracy and then concludes "This is why they fight". It makes no sense to me that a guerrilla movement that's captured 40 per cent of the national territory and has the cohesion and the structure to carry this on for many, many years can be explained away in terms of commercial illicit profits.'

Wars on metaphors such as 'drugs' forge a broad crusade but lack the ability or patience to find the source of complex problems. In Colombia, they target left-wing guerrillas and reduce the rhetoric of political debate to one simplistic vision. In Washington, the political system demands no more. If President George W. Bush managed to persuade a majority of the American people that Saddam Hussein was linked to the September 11th atrocities, then his scriptwriters can easily convince parents in marginal states such as Michigan or Ohio that substance abuse by American teenagers is caused by 'drug-producing terrorists' who happen also to be communists. There was even a hilarious attempt by one US government official to assert that FARC fighters had been trained in al-Qa'eda camps in Afghanistan. The claim was withdrawn.

The 'war on terror' will not help to solve Colombia's three-decades-old conflict or allow the outside world to understand a long-standing and tangled war whose roots lie in the legacy of Spanish colonial rule and whose solution can only be a new social and political deal for the 60 per cent of Colombians living in absolute poverty.

Death stalks Colombia like a noonday shadow; you don't often see it but it is always there. Nearly two million Colombians have fled their homes to escape the violence. Fifty thousand people have perished in the civil war during the last decade. Colombia has one of the highest per-capita murder rates in the world and political executions account for about four thousand deaths a year. Both sides have assassinated dozens of judges, mayors and other public officials, and at any moment hundreds more are trembling over their death notices. Remarkably, if a mayor is murdered another will step into his shoes.

Amparo, Mono Jojoy's daughter, was shot dead by men from Carlos Castaño's band of paramilitaries shortly after I left Colombia. The details of her killing are not clear; she was apparently in Bogotá observing and selecting victims to kidnap. It was probably her task when I met her for dinner a few months earlier. It's not known whether she was 'executed' at close range or gunned down in the street. Her book of contacts included Guillermo, our assistant and her one-time suitor. Castaño apparently let it be known that he wanted to see Guillermo. Of course, Guillermo's links to Amparo had nothing to do with ideology and when he spoke to Castaño, the paramilitary leader seemed satisfied that he need not remain on his lengthy death list. Guillermo continues to travel to Colombia and his balanced, well-honed journalism helps to bring the tragedy of this pained nation to television screens the world over.

Carlos Castaño disappeared in April 2004. There were reports that he died after members of his own paramilitary unit accused him of treachery. It was claimed that he planned to turn himself in to the US authorities and provide names and routes used by the paramilitaries for drug trafficking. Eyewitnesses said he was captured after a shootout and then 'executed' by hanging at a ranch in north-west Colombia.

Lelo, our efficient but cocky driver from San Vicente, was also murdered. It was a particularly gruesome death. He was made to kneel by his car and allowed to pray before he was decapitated. This is the traditional trademark of a killing by a paramilitary outfit. His rusty but reliable yellow taxi was then set on fire. But rumours in San Vicente apparently suggested not a paramilitary execution but a brutal killing by FARC guerrillas who were imitating their style. When government troops retook San Vicente in February 2002, there were loud whispers that the FARC leadership believed Lelo 'knew too much'.

It's said that his son Lelito has taken over his taxi business in San Vicente. Somehow, life goes on in Colombia.

5 / TERROR AS NATION-BUILDING

'I am not fighting against the Palestinians;
I am fighting against terror.'
Binyamin Ben-Eliezer, Israeli Defence Minister

'I have no future. I have no choice but to become a suicide bomber.'
As Ibrahim Abu Teir spoke, his grandchildren played at his feet and
his son nodded in agreement. Ibrahim's face was reddening with rage.
'When we see what's happening around us and what's boiling inside,
why live?'

Ibrahim has lived the recent history of Palestine; the loss of nationhood and a repeating cycle of war and defeat. He was fourteen when
the land he lived on became part of a Jewish state. He was growing
old with hatred, a hatred that he was passing on to his children and
grandchildren.

I was sitting on the patio outside his house, sipping dark, bitter
Arabian coffee. The house was on the edge of the village of Aum
Touba, on the southern fringes of 'Greater' Jerusalem. It had been an
Arab village for over two hundred years and its entire population of
three thousand had the same family name. On the hillside above,
bulldozers were carving the earth, preparing for the construction of
the Jewish settlement of Har Homa, where the Israeli government
planned to build nearly seven thousand Jewish homes to accommodate
thirty thousand Israelis. The whine of the engines pierced the conscience of the village like a dentist's drill, reinforcing its feeling of
impotence.

Ibrahim and his son, Aziz, had a portion of their land expropriated

by the Israeli government in order to build an access road to the settlement. They were discussing their plight with an elderly villager, whose
chubby hand was banging the table. 'This is torture,' he said. 'Are we
expected to sit here and do nothing while the Jews build cities on our
land?' Ibrahim added. 'Look at these children . . .' His hand stretched
out to his five young grandchildren. Before he could finish his sentence
he broke down and sobbed uncontrollably. Aziz sent his children away;
they were too young, he said, to see their grandfather in tears.

Aziz was thirty-four years old and had spent half his life in Britain.
He was an engineer with a degree from Brunel University in West
London. 'Every day they remind you with their bulldozers that they
are taking our land. The people of Aum Touba are being killed by
this.' Aziz compared the Israeli policy on settlement building to ethnic
cleansing in the former Yugoslavia. 'They push us off our land and say
we must live in this or that area. They treat us worse than animals.'

I felt sad for Ibrahim as I watched his eyes brimming with tears, his
mind lost in thought. His head was wrapped in a black-and-white-
chequered *kuffiyeh*, the Arab headscarf. The scarf was a sign of support
for the Palestine Liberation Organization (PLO), the motif of its
leader, Yasser Arafat. Wisps of blondish-white hair dropped onto his
forehead; when he was telling a story, his lively blue eyes danced like
fireflies in the night.

Ibrahim was a farmer who herded sheep and goats. I joined him on
horseback as he led his flock up the hillside that would soon become
Jewish homes. While the Israelis called the settlement Har Homa,
Palestinians referred to it as Jabal Abu Ghneim, or 'the hill for grazing',
although only a few patches of coarse grassland remained. On the
other side of the hill lay the holy city of Bethlehem.

The construction of Har Homa was the first serious tear in the
already tattered 1993 Oslo peace accords because it forced a debate
that had been postponed: the disputed status of Jerusalem, a city sacred
to the three Abrahamic faiths, and claimed as capital by both Israel
and Palestine. In the peace initiative Israel agreed to trade occupied
land for peace, but a decision on Jerusalem was delayed, both signatories hoping it would be resolved at a later date when sufficient trust
had built up.

When the United Nations voted in favour of the partition of Palestine
into an Arab and a Jewish state in 1948, Jerusalem was designated an
'international' city, but the war that ensued left Jerusalem chopped in

two. The Six-Day War (1967) brought Jerusalem under Israeli control, including this hillside. The 1993 peace deal failed to clarify the issue, and trust between the two sides never congealed; the opportunity for peace effectively died with Yitzhak Rabin, the progressive Israeli Prime Minister who was murdered in 1995 by a Jewish assassin who opposed the Oslo accords.

The Israeli Prime Minister in 1997, Benjamin Netanyahu, asserted that the Har Homa housing project was a legitimate expansion of Jerusalem, but it was twice condemned at the United Nations by all but the US, Israel and Micronesia.

In the 1990s, illegal Israeli settlements continued to grow despite international condemnation. Har Homa became the final piece in a jigsaw of projects that surrounded Jerusalem and restricted Palestinian access to the city. The settlements and the bypass roads that served them became physical barriers that dissected Palestinian communities, forming a ring outside the traditional city limits that redrew the map of Jerusalem.

Ibrahim said that the land he'd lost had been in his family for generations and produced title deeds from 1923. Postage stamps bearing the crest of King George V remained glued to the bottom. An Israeli lawyer whom Aziz had hired to contest their case in court joined us in Ibrahim's house. Daniel Seidemann was part of a large, liberal Israeli community whose voice was rarely heard at senior levels of government. Mostly secular in instinct, Jews such as Seidemann probably constituted half the population of Israel and yet were seemingly marginalized by the electoral system. Proportional representation had granted inordinate influence to tiny radical religious parties, who often ended up holding the balance of power in the Israeli Parliament, the Knesset. Daniel Seidemann told me that the Supreme Court rarely dismissed Palestinian land claims as invalid. 'Instead they usually rule that it's a political issue, they say go somewhere else to sort it out.' He offered Aziz little expectation that the building programme could be stopped. By 2001, Har Homa's first synagogue and nursery had opened. A supermarket was built a year later. The Construction and Housing Ministry offered special mortgage incentives and grants to entice Jews to move into occupied land.

The Israeli government often disguised policies involving national expansion as purely technical, legal manoeuvres underwritten by the courts. Israel has the institutions of a Western political system: democracy, an independent judiciary, a free press and safeguards for human rights. But these do not apply to the stateless Palestinians from the occupied territories. Israeli law is often administered arbitrarily, usually through bureaucratic interventions or court decisions. In most cases, policy within the Palestinian territories is considered a matter of Israeli national security. Military commanders in the West Bank and Gaza use forcible measures to control Palestinian communities and individuals, including administrative detention, torture and the destruction of property.

Israel has carefully used language that encourages a perception of legitimacy in the Western media. The activities of the stateless Palestinians who challenge the Israeli state are described as illegal because they have no institutions to validate their activities. Media reports rarely emphasize that Israel has illegally occupied these territories for over three decades and that her mere presence is a breach of international law. Instead of implying the brutality of seizure and subjugation, the phrase 'occupied territories' has become in the news media a non-moral cliché. Israeli soldiers intimidate and sometimes kill Palestinians on territory that they have no legal authority to retain and yet their actions are often reported as self-defence in response to Palestinian aggression: when a Palestinian carries a weapon he is a gunman or a militant. Israel has created a lexicon of the conflict that the Western media has mostly copied, conveying to audiences that Israel's actions are legal and justified. This extends, of course, to the use of 'terrorism' to describe the actions of Palestinians who are resisting the occupation of their territory. Israel's media pronouncements often remind me of the Declaration of Independence of the thirteen united States of America on 4 July 1776: 'We hold these truths to be self-evident, that all men are created equal, that they are endowed by their Creator with certain unalienable Rights . . .' while it was overlooked that nearly one in four of the population of the new nation were slaves who had no rights at all.

Duli Basok wore a baggy white shirt and held aloft a copy of the Tenakh, the Jewish holy text that includes scriptures from the Old Testament of the Bible. An Israeli flag fluttered in the breeze next to him. He was reading aloud verses from the book of Psalms with a dramatic poetic cadence. We were standing on the roof terrace of his house on a hillside known to Jews as the City of David. Three armed guards in sunglasses, T-shirts and jeans kept watch on us with

Israeli-made Uzi sub-machine guns across their chests. Duli's hair was cropped short, with a white-and-blue-embroidered *kippah* on his head. He had a large fluffy reddish-brown beard that hung almost to his waist, and his mouth curved into an unbroken smile.

'More than half of Scriptures were written on this hill,' he told me as he launched his hand theatrically towards the valley below. 'If we look around us, we see a famous verse from Psalms. "As the mountains surround Jerusalem, so God is protecting his people for ever."' Jews believe this hillside was the site of the biblical City of David, where the founder of the first Kingdom of Israel lived and died three thousand years ago. King David declared Jerusalem as the religious centre of Judaism by making it the everlasting home for the Ark, the sacred wooden box where Moses supposedly placed the Ten Commandments. During the following centuries, King David became a symbol of a united homeland for Jews, with his six-pointed shield its universally recognized emblem.

The City of David lies a short distance below the Muslim holy site, al-Haram ash Shareef, or the Noble Sanctuary. It is a flat expanse of some thirty-five acres that stands more than two thousand feet above sea level and dominates the surrounding districts of Jerusalem. The glistening, golden Dome of the Rock and al-Aqsa Mosque were built on the site in the seventh century, after Arab armies conquered Jerusalem. Muslims believe that the Prophet Mohammed ascended to heaven from there, leaving his footprint behind. Jews continue to call al-Haram ash Shareef the Temple Mount, a reference to the first Jewish Temple, which was constructed on the same location by King David's successor, Solomon, nearly two thousand years earlier. Jews who visit their faith's holiest site now pray below al-Haram ash Shareef at the 'Wailing Wall'.

'There are about eighty families on this small hill,' Duli told me as he scanned the large multi-floored sandstone houses built into the rock. 'Now twelve are Jewish. With God's help, by the end of the summer, there will be twenty. Within a decade, the whole City of David will be homes full of Jewish families.' Duli was speaking in 1997. By 2004, the City of David Foundation, or Elad, had bought up forty-two homes in legal transactions that were upheld by the courts. Israeli human-rights groups said that Elad was responsible for ethnic cleansing by stealth through the seizure and occupation of property. Duli may not achieve his dream of an exclusively Jewish hillside within a decade; he may have to wait a further five years. The latest projection is that all Palestinian families will have left their homes or been ejected by 2012.

Duli's wife, Osi, wanted to come to the City of David more than a decade ago. She told me that she had received a personal message directly from God, who told her to move there to wait for the Messiah, the promised king that Jews believe will unite them in one spiritual homeland. 'In the Jewish tradition we wait for the Messiah every day,' she told me as she rolled flour to make *saluf*, Jewish flat bread with tomato and crushed fenugreek seeds. 'There won't be any more wars,' she told me with a caring smile. 'Jerusalem will be the world's spiritual centre. The Temple will be for everyone, not only Jews. Muslims and Christians' – she nodded towards me – 'there will be peace between all of mankind.' Osi was referring to the belief held by orthodox Jews that a temple will be constructed or appear miraculously on the site of al-Haram ash Shareef, requiring the dismantling or destruction of the Dome of the Rock and al-Aqsa Mosque. Al-Haram ash Shareef is the third holiest site for Muslims, after Mecca and Medina, so Osi's conviction that peace would result from its demolition is difficult to agree with.

By the time Duli was thirty-four, he and Osi had five children. Every school morning, the children were picked up by a Land Rover with three guards, each carrying a short-barrelled Uzi. The Land Rover was a twenty-four-hour taxi service, taking families past Palestinian districts into the safety of the Jewish old city, half a mile away. Each Jewish home had a small security cabin on its terraced roof from where the guards provided around-the-clock protection.

Duli was unfazed about bringing up his children in the midst of such weaponry. 'We have to protect ourselves against terrorists,' he told me as he padded a bulge in his shirt. 'I have been carrying a gun for nearly seventeen years. I hope that I shall never have to use it. If I will be forced to, it will be there.' He gave a broad smile.

'Perhaps you wouldn't need a gun if you didn't throw others from their houses?' I asked.

He looked me in the eye, paused for a moment as he searched for complicity. 'This is *our* land. That is all we want. The Arabs have fourteen countries to go to. The Arabs can find friends all over the Middle East.' He squeezed his eyes tightly shut and his hands drew together in front of his chest. 'God gave this land to the Jews . . . We are very, very stubborn. No problem will deter us.'

The tension of life on this contended hillside was revealed one morning in a small incident. There was a sudden security alert when Palestinian children were spotted near the fence at the bottom of Duli's property. He was radioed by one of the guards. 'What's wrong?' Duli asked. Then he looked puzzled: 'A doghouse?' We went to the front of his roof terrace and saw a group of four children, aged between perhaps ten and fifteen, along with a slightly bedraggled, brown husky. They had a small piece of tarpaulin and a few sticks, as if to provide a shaded area for the dog, and had tied the leash to Duli's fence. Within minutes, a military-looking green armoured vehicle appeared. Three of the guards with Uzis walked down the path and told the Palestinian kids to take down their makeshift tent. Duli suddenly regained his composure and his smile snapped back into place. 'Suddenly they build a shed for the dog. Tomorrow they'll say, "Wait a minute, the dog is thirsty, he needs a tap and lighting." They'll build him a hut and all of a sudden, the doghouse can become an Arab's house! A war could break out over a doghouse.' I think Duli was deadly serious.

But the problem of the doghouse wasn't over. The Palestinian boys had brought the dog back. What happened next was surreal. Duli sent three of his boys, Alexander, who was thirteen, Biet Zion, aged eleven, and Zwika, nine, to the fence. They stared, eyeball to eyeball, and not a word was spoken. Each set of children remained motionless, maintaining their hard stares. Finally, the Israelis won the battle of nerves; the Palestinians unleashed the dog and walked away. Duli's face broke into a wide smile as he patted me on the back and swelled with pride. 'A person who feels this is his home shows strength and deters others,' he said, congratulating his kids. 'A person who feels nervous and doesn't know why he is here, he reveals weakness.'

Every international peace initiative has required that Israel halts all settlement activity but Israeli officials refuse to do so until the Palestinian leadership ends 'terrorism'. I drove to west Jerusalem, to interview the mayor of the city, Ehud Olmert. He had a cheerful face with large round glasses and receding hair. His delivery was slightly nasal and he maintained the genial smile of a salesman. 'Jerusalem is the purest expression of everything that symbolizes Jewish history, Jewish dreams, Jewish life and Jewish future. How can anyone question the right of Jews to live in any part of Jerusalem?' Olmert was one of the architects of the policy of ringing Jerusalem with illegal Jewish settlements. He became Deputy Prime Minister in Ariel Sharon's government.

'Jerusalem is one city. It will not be a capital for the Palestinians,' Mayor Olmert continued, as if it was a straightforward, incontroverti-ble fact, rather than a stumbling block preventing peace in the Middle East and beyond. 'It is not a divided city, it will never be a divided city and as such, as one united city, as such it will be the capital of Israel forever.'

The sun appears nearer in the Middle East. There is an intimacy unbroken by cloud between the sun and the soil, an oversized fireball that day after day beats the parched earth. I felt its furnace heat as I climbed a path past the churned soil that would soon be homes and schools in Har Homa. Aziz and Ibrahim were taking food to Palestin-ian protesters who had set up tents on another hillside overlooking the land being prepared for the Israeli settlement. The protest had almost fizzled out and only half a dozen remained. Ibrahim and Aziz brought them oranges, walnuts and some sweet, sticky pistachio dessert. The protesters felt let down by the Palestinian leadership, who they believed had given in too readily. 'The PLO must make it clear that either the settlement is stopped or we get out of the peace process.' The chief protester spoke without conviction, as if accepting the routine of defeat and humiliation as new settlements appeared like a spreading rash over a landscape that Palestinians still hoped would become their state. Ibrahim's anger was more visible. 'Let's go back to the way it was. We were better off under the intifada,' he shouted, referring to the uprising that ended with the Oslo peace accord in 1993. As Aziz listened to his father's voice breaking with rage, he grabbed my arm. 'If the building of settlements continues as it is, the Palestinian people will keep boiling inside and the West Bank and Gaza is going to explode.'

Aziz spoke near-perfect English. He was well educated and reason-able but also proud of his identity and culture. He was the sort of Arab whose voice was rarely heard on Western television. He was very normal. He was also very hospitable and was concerned that I should enjoy a typical Palestinian meal before I left. The first task was for me to choose a lamb for slaughter. There was a barn behind Ibrahim's house with sheep, goats and three small, very white lambs that stood barely two feet tall. Aziz dragged the lambs toward me. Their heads were tilted back. Each had alert eyes that stared at me longingly, making noises as if they were expecting food. I turned away, unwilling to choose. 'It's up to you, Aziz,' I told him. It was an act of total hypocrisy, of course, as I was quite happy to eat the succulent lamb casserole that Aziz prepared. It was seasoned with saffron, sumac (a spice made from dried berries that tastes of lemon) and garnished with pine nuts. It was delicious.

Over dinner, Aziz told me that he'd been made to feel powerless, humiliated and emasculated. He put his hands around his face and thought for a moment. 'They are going to kill the peace process and it's going to kill any hope in us living together. They can occupy our land but we will find a way to fight the occupation.' I didn't say it at the time but I should have stopped him and said: 'Aziz, are you suggesting *terrorism*?'

When Ibrahim spoke of the despair that led Palestinian suicide bombers to murder Israelis, he paused during our conversation and recalled memories from his teenage years under the British Mandate. 'The British couldn't stop the Jewish terrorists. Your people gave in to terrorists.' He glowered at me and warned: 'One cannot forget his nation or his land.'

Ibrahim was referring to the debacle surrounding Britain's with-drawal from Palestine in 1948. Israeli militants who were campaigning for a Jewish homeland had made a crude calculation in blood. Between 1936 and 1939, the Palestinians staged the 'Arab Rebellion' in order to protest against the increasing number of Jewish immigrants. During widespread rioting, nearly five thousand people died as the British rulers proved unable to maintain law and order. The rebellion made Britain realize that it had to take heed of Arab opinion. Golda Meir, Prime Minister of Israel from 1969 to 1974, summed up the logic of what happened next. 'We kept hearing the argument, "The Arabs can cause so much trouble, therefore you have to give in." In the end we decided, very well, *we'll* create trouble.'

The background to the Israeli–Palestinian crisis is long, bloody and complicated. It stems from Britain's incompetent handling of the situation after the First World War when it was allocated Palestine as part of the defeated Ottoman Empire. During the Great War, Britain's Foreign Secretary, Arthur Balfour, had made a peculiar contract with Zionists, who were campaigning for a Jewish state. Balfour declared that 'His Majesty's government views with favour the establishment in Palestine of a national home for the Jewish people'. Unsurprisingly, this 'neat solution' was the catalyst of insurrection, political violence, resistance and today's stalemate.

In 1947, Britain refused to implement the United Nations' partition plan because it felt unable to contain the violence that would erupt. So it simply left when the UN voted in favour of creating Israel from the territory of Palestine. War immediately broke out between the Israeli and Arab armies. In April 1948, Irgun commandos attacked the village of Deir Yassin. After its capture, they murdered more than two hundred Arab men, women and children. The slaughter so terrified Palestinians that three-quarters of a million fled their homes to create the refugee population whose tragedy remains central to the Middle East conflict today.

It is in the former Palestine that the competing claims of nationhood have been most conspicuous in recent decades in using violence in order to obtain a homeland. The Israeli nation was born using methods that the Palestinians espouse today, such as the indiscriminate killing of civilians. The underground Jewish militias known as the Stern Gang and the Irgun Zvai Le'umi (National Military Organization) not only ended British colonial rule in Palestine, they also established a revolutionary model that was emulated by many other militant organizations around the world.

The Second World War had a seismic effect on the growth of nationalist insurgency movements. After the war, rebellions began in Malaya, Burma, Vietnam and Indonesia. A new language was born and armed fighters were described as either 'terrorists' or 'freedom fighters', depending on who was talking. Ethno-nationalist rebellions spread throughout the world using the logic of terror to achieve their aims, such as the Kenyan Mau Mau independence movement, which terrorized white farmers into leaving the country. Many terrorists later became the rulers of their independent nations and players on the world stage. Most had some level of popular support and history has treated their violence with kindness. Indeed, both the United States and Britain at one time described Nelson Mandela as a terrorist.

Another problem arose for the colonial powers that wanted to brand all nationalist insurgents as terrorists. By sustaining and encouraging groups such as the French Resistance during the Second World War, sabotage, bombings and assassination, even of civilian collaborators, became the acts of heroes. Thus popular support for the Resistance sanctioned the use of such violence. According to this argument, the Palestinian uprising after the 1967 war should be considered legitimate because the cause of nationhood and opposition to the occupying power had the overwhelming backing of the Palestinian people.

'Whether you call it terrorism or resistance, the words have no meaning.' Ismail Abu Shanab, a leader of the Palestinian militant organization Hamas, was thoughtful and spoke English with a hint of an American drawl. 'What you have to start from is Israel occupying Palestinian land. We react to that. Then they start their oppression, killing our men, women and children and choking the life out of the Palestinian economy.' He sighed and continued without rage. 'We retaliate. If the Israeli tanks shell Palestinians, if their F-16s and Apache helicopters send missiles at us, how should we fight back? All we can do is send our children to Israel and sacrifice themselves.'

I met the Hamas leader for the first time in 1997 at his concrete home on the outskirts of Gaza city. His son opened the gate and led me to his spacious office. Abu Shanab was on the phone and he apologized, he'd be a few minutes. He put his hand over the receiver and asked, 'Do you want tea, cake?' I nodded and his son returned shortly afterwards with a china tea set and a slice of banana cake.

Ismail Abu Shanab was born in a Gaza refugee camp in 1950. He earned a master's degree in civil engineering from the University of Colorado. When he returned to Gaza, he became an engineering professor at Gaza's Islamic University and one of the founders of Hamas. He spent eight years in an Israeli jail, two in a solitary cell underground. The father of eleven children, he later became Dean of the Faculty of Applied Science at the university.

Abu Shanab explained without emotion why Hamas used suicide bombers to attack Israelis. 'During the first intifada, Palestinians began to oppose the Israeli occupation without guns. The Israelis responded by shooting demonstrators. When the settler Baruch Goldstein massacred Palestinians in Hebron, we did not have weapons to fight back. It was after that we looked at our options.' Baruch Goldstein was a Brooklyn-born Jewish radical who killed twenty-nine Muslims during their Friday prayers in February 1994. 'So a man found explosives and gave his life in an attack on Israelis. Palestinians then found that martyrdom operations were an effective weapon. They have little else.'

Abu Shanab spoke confidently and calmly. He told me that by 2002 the situation had become so desperate that he no longer cared what the West thought about Hamas' actions. He considered that the Western media reported the conflict from an Israeli perspective. 'Even sympathetic writers,' he said, 'see the Palestinian conflict in terms of the war on terror rather than the struggle of an occupied people to achieve freedom.'

Abu Shanab's books on politics and engineering mingled on his shelves with portraits of dead Hamas fighters. He had a map of the Middle East that had no mention of Israel. He also had a Qassam rocket, named after a prominent Palestinian Islamist who was killed by the British in 1935. The rocket was home-made and wildly inaccurate. 'When I see it, I know that Israelis can never be sure that we won't strike them in their beds,' he smiled broadly.

During our first meeting in 1997, hundreds of Hamas activists had been jailed by Yasser Arafat and the Palestinian Authority. The rivalry between the two groups had burst into street fighting and deaths. He told me: 'I agree with the Oslo negotiations if they lead to a Palestinian state. But I don't trust the Israelis. It will blow up again and there will be another intifada.'

When we spoke again five years later, I read out my notes and told Abu Shanab that he'd been correct. 'I am not happy about that,' he said, his voice remaining expressionless. Was he angry with Arafat? 'Absolutely not. Arafat tried to achieve peace and now he is under siege. Sharon [the Israeli Prime Minister] wants a military, not peaceful, solution to the Israeli–Palestinian problem. It's as simple as that.'

Abu Shanab reasoned that there was a moral equivalence between attacks on Israeli civilians and the harm that Israel inflicted, both economically and militarily, on Palestinian civilians. 'We respond this way [suicide bombings] because we suffer from the Israeli occupation. The Israeli military kills our people, limits our freedom and destroys our economic infrastructure. They set the rules for this war. Nobody likes killing innocent people. But the Palestinian position is one of self-defence.' He also suggested that Israeli civilians were not necessarily 'innocent' targets. 'Everyone over seventeen is recruited into the army,' he told me. 'The army occupying the West Bank is mainly made up of reservists,' he added, claiming that the distinction between soldier and civilian is blurred in Israel.

'Do you think that you can ever defeat Israel by using tactics such as suicide bombings?'

Abu Shanab thought for a moment without averting his gaze. 'A military victory is not possible. What we are doing is sending a message that we are refusing to be occupied. The only alternative we have is to surrender.' He saw the conflict in terms of a classical anti-colonial insurgency. 'The Palestinians have the greater will because we are fighting for our lives. We can outlast the Israelis.'

If the conflict is compared to the anti-colonialist insurgencies of the twentieth century, the Israelis, as an occupation force, have suffered unsustainably high casualties. During the four years after the second intifada, nearly a thousand Israelis died compared to more than three thousand Palestinians. There also appeared to be an endless stream of recruits willing to give up their lives. The materials for suicide vest bombs cost around £50. 'At some point,' Abu Shanab said with confidence, 'the Israeli public will say, "We've had enough," and they won't be able to tolerate their losses.'

The Gaza Strip is one of the strangest political entities on earth. It is a narrow stretch of land thirty miles long and five wide squeezed between the Mediterranean and the Negev Desert. During a journey to Gaza from Jerusalem, the traveller passes the empty desert landscape of southern Israel before suddenly confronting walls of barbed wire and watchtowers.

While parts of Gaza City are presentable, I was never able to clear my nose of the stench of uncollected garbage. I was once in Rafah refugee camp, on the southern tip of Gaza, during a rainstorm and watched as children danced in streams of raw effluent while playing a game. The drains were blocked but the soaked children were oblivious to the smell that was turning my stomach. Older boys stood in doorways, staring and dragging on cigarettes. Rows of square cement houses gave way to closed-up shops. Occasionally the empty space was the rubble of a destroyed house. Most of Gaza's inhabitants were descendents of refugees from the 1948 war. By the end of the century, a million people lived in this teeming, caged outpost of humanity. Gaza had no active air- or seaport and no contact with the outside world except through Israel.

During my visit in 1997, thousands of Gazan workers travelled to Israel to provide cheap labour to its factories, building sites and agricultural industry. At dawn, long lines of workers who'd risen in the middle of the night spent several hours crossing the border. They passed through a revolving steel gate and a series of metal detectors before being frisked by an Israeli soldier, while his colleagues watched with their guns trained. A similar process occurred in the evening. Those were the good times. During the intifada, the crossing was shut to the overwhelming majority of Palestinians. Twenty thousand had lost their jobs in Israel. In 2002, the average income in Gaza was under $100 a month.

Hamas is an acronym for Harakat al-Muqawama al-Islamiya (Islamic Resistance Movement), and the word means 'zeal' in Arabic. It emerged from Gaza's gritty, overpopulated slums in 1987 as an offshoot of a charitable religious organization, the Muslim Brotherhood, which provided grass-roots humanitarian aid. Hamas's official policy was to obliterate Israel and raise 'the banner of Allah over every inch of Palestine'. From my discussions with Ismail Abu Shanab, I believed that Hamas would lay down its arms if there were a fair division of the British Mandate into two sustainable nations, although Israel refused to countenance that prospect.

Under the Brotherhood's spiritual leader, the wheelchair-bound Sheikh Ahmed Yassin, the movement built up a vast network of social services to serve the needy. Sheikh Yassin had an unusual ally; in the 1980s the Israeli government secretly funded the movement in order to provide a counterweight to the secular PLO and to undermine it. Israeli donations were reported to be in the millions of dollars.

Early one morning in Gaza City I drove by a long line of perhaps fifty people. Many were elderly, some had children. It was still cool and most were wrapped in shawls. A woman in a black scarf, bowed by age and arthritis, told me free medicine was being offered at the charity shop. A rusty sign with chipped paint read al-Mujama al-Islami, or Islamic Congress. The green flag of Hamas was flapping in the morning breeze. One man with an amputated leg asked me for money and I pulled out the notes in my back pocket. I only had a wad of $100 bills and found no small change. I felt embarrassed that he'd seen so much cash and on the spur of the moment, I crumpled a $100 note and handed it to him. His eyes widened in disbelief. Since September 11th, the US has frozen donations to charities run by Hamas, claiming that the funds are financing terrorism.

Even if a Palestinian state does emerge, how can the Gaza Strip become a part of a meaningful nation? Israel can control all aspects of life there. Lumps of disjoined territory surrounded by Israel, with no functional international airport or borders, could never be considered an authentically independent nation. Self-rule in the West Bank and

Gaza would serve primarily to validate Israel's policy of managing Palestinian territory. It is difficult to see that the establishment of a Palestinian state within the present framework would do more than reinforce the essential elements of apartheid that had formerly applied in South Africa: separation, inequality and dependency.

A powerful strand in Israeli society, including many orthodox Jews and some members of Likud, the dominant party of government since 1977, believes that Palestinians have no right to a state and Israeli sovereignty should be extended to the whole of the British Mandate of Palestine. Rabbi Hagai Yekutiel believed that the Jewish Messiah will only arrive when 'Greater Israel' became a reality. 'It is our religious duty,' he told me. 'In our eternal Book of Books,' he said, holding up a battered and well-thumbed Torah, 'the land of Israel is not a narrow strip of land with funny, jagged borders, but a large state with broad, natural frontiers.' Hagai was a chirpy, amusing man. Short, with a trimmed beard, he wore a blue suit and *kippah*, rather than the long black jackets, hats and earlocks favoured by Hasidic Jews. 'In this book, it says, "I give unto the Jews the land where they have sown their seed, from the river of Egypt to the great river Euphrates."' If Hagai could draw the boundaries of Greater Israel on a map, it would include parts of Egypt as well as Iraq and Jordan. He smiled when I pointed this out. 'We will take our time to achieve it,' he replied mischievously. Hagai's perspective was only held by a minority in Israel, but it was a vocal and influential one. Any compromise that would allow Palestinian statehood was out of the question.

The first time I met Hagai was in a cafe in one of the winding alleyways of the old walled city of Jerusalem. He regularly came to pray at the nearby 'Wailing Wall'. Rows of worshippers recite from the Torah while moving their upper bodies back and forth in a bowing motion known as dovening. I respectfully assumed that was one of the highest forms of religious experience for the faithful. Hagai then made me spit out my coffee. 'When I saw the Jews praying by the Wall,' he told me, 'I thought, "This is incomprehensible, people are talking to the walls?"' Hagai believed that Jews should pray on the site of the first Jewish Temple built by King Solomon, where the Dome of the Rock and al-Aqsa Mosque now stand. 'We are stuck here in the same place by the western wall,' he complained. 'It is just a supporting wall for the Temple, which is the important thing. It's at the heart of Judaism. It's the only Holy Place and without a doubt there will be a

Temple. All Jews must believe in this. It's one of the commandments of the Torah to build the Temple today.'

Hagai took me to the offices of the Temple Institute, a movement that was making preparations for the construction of the building. The Rabbi in charge showed me ceremonial items that he planned to take to the new Temple. They included a silver-plated mug with a long handle, a copy of a vessel used during animal sacrifices; sheep's blood was collected and then poured on the foundation of the altar. There were also brass trumpets, about three feet long. 'These trumpets will accompany the service in the Temple,' Hagai informed me. 'All the ritual objects have been made, whatever is needed is ready. All of the technical issues have been more or less solved. The next stage is to build the Temple.'

Hagai caught my eye as I wondered whether he and his colleagues at the Institute either enjoyed fantasy, had gone mad or were simply very devout. He anticipated my next question. 'What will I do with the Dome of the Rock? I think that that is a minor, technical problem.' The certainty of absolute belief can remove the faithful from the real world. Hundreds of millions of Muslims would hardly regard the obliteration of their holy shrine as a trifling matter. When I suggested that constructing the Temple might lead to more than a few tricky problems, he conceded. 'I agree,' he reflected, 'we shouldn't blow up the Dome of the Rock and start a world war, I think at this moment that would be a mistake. We have to agree these things with the Arabs and I think that's possible.'

In 1990, when a group of orthodox Jews tried to carry a foundation stone for the building of a new Temple onto al-Haram ash Shareef, a fatal riot followed. Muslim leaders called on worshippers to defend the shrines. Rocks were thrown on Jews praying beneath at the Wailing Wall. The Israeli police stormed al-Haram ash Shareef: nineteen Muslims died, and several hundred were wounded.

Rabbi Hagai taught at a theological college in a Jewish settlement on the West Bank. At one of his lectures, about twenty young men sat earnestly noting his comments on archaeological evidence that apparently proved the existence of the first two Jewish Temples on the site of al-Haram ash Shareef. Hagai didn't only teach history. He advised his students to pray, not at the Wailing Wall, but inside the Muslim area on al-Haram ash Shareef, which he called the Temple Mount. Hagai's teachings overlooked one problem: under an agreement between the Israeli government and the Muslim authorities that manage al-Haram ash Shareef, it was illegal for a Jew to pray on the site. The Jewish claim to land under the third holiest shrine in the Islamic faith is the most incendiary battle for territory in the world. Israel is hardly likely to dismantle the Dome of the Rock in the near future but the religious dynamic in its society, fuelled by the core belief in Judaism that the Messiah and the Temple will one day appear, has continued to irritate and bewilder Muslims.

I followed the Rabbi as he entered al-Haram ash Shareef. As soon as he walked through the gate he was accompanied by an Israeli policeman and a Muslim official from the trust that has day-to-day responsibility for managing the religious site. Israeli law prohibits Hagai from opening his mouth to pray but doesn't stop him visiting. Suddenly Hagai's lips twitched and the policeman suspected that he was praying.

'You are praying!' accused the policeman.

'I am just saying something silently. I am not praying!' Hagai responded. Several Muslim officials surrounded him and told him to leave.

An overweight guard bundled in, pushed me out of the way and pointed at Hagai, alleging that his lips had moved. 'Did I say something that I am not allowed to say?' Hagai pleaded as if he had no idea what the fuss was about. 'Can't a person talk to himself?'

The Muslim guards grabbed him and urged the Israeli policemen, 'Take him out! Take him out!' One Muslim official was restrained by the police. The Israelis, afraid of stirring up trouble around the Dome of the Rock, expelled Hagai despite his protests.

The Muslim officials were still fuming after he had been thrown out. 'They must not be allowed to enter al-Aqsa,' one told me, shaking with fury. 'We must stand by to protect the mosque so that they don't come even one centimetre inside. Every time they come in here, it is as if they have stabbed us in the heart.'

Five years after I watched Hagai spark a minor crisis at al-Haram ash Shareef, Ariel Sharon, then the leader of Israel's opposition party, brazenly marched onto the Muslims' holy site surrounded by a phalanx of a thousand soldiers and police. The man who became Israeli Prime Minister spent forty-five minutes strolling around the grounds of al-Aqsa Mosque and Dome of the Rock. Sharon said with an absurd contortion of language that his visit was a 'peace mission'. In fact, the deliberate provocation was designed to assert Israeli sovereignty over the site. 'The Temple Mount is in our hands and will remain in our hands,' the former general declared.

Within hours of Sharon's visit, he destroyed prospects for peace and touched off the second intifada with several days of bloody rioting.

The price of his deliberate provocation was hard to overestimate. Thousands of Palestinian men and women soon became willing to kill and die in the name of their God and nationhood. A new generation of terrorists had been unleashed.

Ariel Sharon's display of power helped his Likud party win elections and propel him to become Israel's Prime Minister in 2001. While the intifada helped to deliver Sharon to power, suicide bombings allowed him to absolve Israel of responsibility for the consequences of thirty-five years of military occupation. After September 11th, Sharon reshaped Israel's conflict to dovetail with America's 'war on terror'. Palestinian militants were equated with al-Qa'eda and Yasser Arafat with Osama bin Laden. Sharon has persuaded many Western reporters to perceive the conflict within a wider struggle between Western civilization and Islamist terrorism. When Bush visited Israel on a rare foreign trip, he apparently told Sharon: 'I want you to know that Israel is not just a foreign-policy issue to me. I feel it in my heart.'

I had planned to telephone Ismail Abu Shanab to update our interview in August 2003, but when I turned on the satellite television, I saw pictures of a white car engulfed in a ball of orange flame. The passengers were burnt black, almost beyond recognition. One of the passengers had been decapitated. It was Abu Shanab.

Abu Shanab and his two bodyguards had been driving through Gaza City when the car slowed down to avoid a large rock that had been placed in the road. Suddenly, an Apache helicopter swooped low and fired at least three Hellfire missiles into the vehicle. As a crowd gathered and the body of Ismail Abu Shanab was pulled from the charred wreckage, the air was filled with screams demanding revenge against Israel.

The killing of Abu Shanab had followed an attack by a suicide bomber from Hamas. He'd boarded a bus in Jerusalem before blowing himself up along with twenty-one Israelis, including five children. 'Abu Shanab was a murderer. I hope it's a lesson for the Hamas people,' said the Israeli Deputy Prime Minister, Ehud Olmert, the former Mayor of Jerusalem. Abu Shanab's death was the 138th 'targeted killing' by the Israeli military since Ariel Sharon's visit to al-Haram ash Shareef and the beginning of the second intifada. In March 2004, the quadriplegic Hamas founder and spiritual leader, Sheik Ahmed Yassin, was killed in another deadly helicopter strike outside a Gaza City mosque. While Yassin had publicly defended suicide bombings, he had increasingly leaned toward a political compromise that recognized the right of Israel to exist within its 1967 borders. News reports showed a picture of a frail and crippled, white-bearded man, before cutting to a crumpled wheel from his chair and a large red bloodstain on the road. The most senior remaining Hamas leader, Dr Abdel Aziz Rantisi, described the assassination as an attack on Islam and called for a broadening of the conflict. 'It is now a war against Islam,' he declared. 'There is war in Iraq and Palestine. I say to the Muslim nations that they have to wake up from their sleep.' A month later, Dr Rantisi left his apartment in Gaza City and got into his car. An Apache helicopter promptly emerged from the skies and vaporized his vehicle.

The US State Department's decision to expand its list of terrorist groups to include Hamas triggered a wave of protest in Arab and Muslim countries, which considered the group as 'freedom fighters' against Israeli occupation of Arab land. Lebanon and Syria refused to confiscate Hamas' assets despite persistent requests from the United States. Lebanon's Prime Minister, Rafik Hariri, said his country had suffered greatly from terrorism but he said that Hamas' military activities were a legitimate resistance to Israel. In order to win the 'war on terror', he argued, the conflict between Israel and the Palestinians needed to be solved. In contrast, the White House spokesman, Ari Fleischer, told reporters, 'The issue is Hamas. The terrorists are Hamas.'

After September 11th, European Union foreign ministers bowed to US pressure and declared Hamas a terrorist organization and sought to blacklist every charity deemed to be affiliated to the Islamist organization. That did nothing to dent Hamas' legitimacy and popularity amongst the Palestinian people. It caused greater hardship for the deprived of Gaza and divided the world along lines defined by America's 'war on terror'.

The murder of Abu Shanab and the other Hamas leaders further raised the question of the distinction between state terrorism and individual terrorist acts. While Yasser Arafat was constantly pressed during his final years by the Western media into condemning 'terrorism', Israel committed acts that Arabs see as morally equivalent, yet US officials define them as 'self-defense'. Unlike most of the world's news organizations, the BBC has remained resolute in avoiding the use of 'terrorist' in reporting the Israeli–Palestinian conflict, despite repeated pressure from the Israeli government and accusations of anti-Semitism.

The conflict has driven Palestinian society into forging a definition of 'terrorism' that emphasizes ends rather than means. It also contrasts sharply with the usage of the word by the mainstream Western media. In a poll conducted by the Palestinian Centre for Policy and Survey Research in December 2001, 94 per cent considered Israeli military activity on the West Bank as 'terrorism', while 82 per cent refused to categorize the killing of twenty-one Israelis outside a Tel Aviv night-club in the same way. For Palestinians, 'terrorism' applied to the aggressive actions of their enemy.

It is obvious that the Palestinian perception of terror focuses on the aims of the perpetrators rather than their methods. In this case, any violent act aimed at ending Israeli occupation, regardless of the means, is not likely to be viewed as terror, while all violent acts of the Israeli occupier are seen as acts of terror. It reminded me of what Abu Shanab had told me a few months before his murder: 'terrorism' has no meaning in the conflict between Israel and Palestine.

6 / TERROR AND THE STATUS QUO

'America crosses the globe to fight against terrorism in Afghanistan . . .
whereas the struggle against terrorism in the heart of one's own country,
one's own home, is considered to be a crime.'

Slobodan Milošović, speaking at the War Crimes Tribunal
at The Hague in February 2002

The traffic was thick. It was the usual morning rush hour in Belgrade. Limousines with blackened windows jostled impatiently with
small rusty Yugos, the domestically manufactured cars based on a
1970s Fiat design. The men driving their Yugos were unshaven and
dishevelled. Unemployment was so high that most were not going to
work. But their destination was just another of the mysteries that
made Serbia into an unfathomable, detached region in the heart of
Europe.

I was planning to leave that afternoon for Kosovo, the troubled
province in southern Serbia. Before I left Belgrade, I needed to call at
Yugoslavia's Foreign Ministry in Knez Miloš Street to extend my visa.
I knew a reliable official called Rade Drobac who looked after visiting
journalists. He was a smallish, precise man with thick eyebrows who
wore threadbare suits that frayed slightly at the edges. He seemed
weary of life; always helpful but resigned to his predicament as a
powerless bureaucrat. I suspected that he had no love for Yugoslavia's
President, Slobodan Milošović. Sometimes he drew his breath deeply
and lifted his hands in the air when he needed to turn down a request.
'They wouldn't allow it,' he'd say. I didn't know whether he meant
President Milošović and his powerful wife, Mira, or a broader, faceless

clique that ran Yugoslavia and of which Rade was not a part. But he was a proud, patriotic man and carried a strong sense of injustice over the West's treatment of his country.

As I left, he told me to stay safe and watch out for the mostly Muslim Albanian 'terrorists' in Kosovo. He was being sarcastic. It was a pointed jibe at the largely close and uncritical relationship between Albanian separatists and the Western media. Rade handed over Serbian magazines, including the *Kosovo Dossier*, which listed examples of a 'policy of terror by one million Albanians from Kosovo'. It chronicled intimidation by Albanians as they 'expelled from the province thousands of their Slav neighbours.' A book, *Dialogue versus Separatism and Terrorism*, listed examples of a 'policy of terror'. In one incident 'hooded terrorists armed with machine-guns stopped an official car and introduced themselves as members of the Kosovo Liberation Army. While this was going on, a group of another ten armed terrorists were on their left-hand side'. The list included more than forty 'terrorist attacks on civilian targets'. I also had a glossy pamphlet called *Yugoslavia and Human Rights*, which had on its cover kites flying in a blue sky in the colours of the national flag. It described Yugoslavia as a 'multiethnic, multireligious and multilingual community', which guaranteed equality and human rights 'to all citizens, regardless of their nationality, race, sex, language or creed'.

The small library that I left clutching would sit comfortably with Western pronouncements regarding the 'war on terror'. Even at that time, a year before planes from the North Atlantic Treaty Organisation bombed Yugoslavia, the United States condemned what it called 'terrorist action by the so-called Kosovar Liberation Army.' The KLA's name, known in Albanian as the UCK, meant National Liberation Army. The English name of the guerrilla army was variously translated as the Liberation Army of Kosovo or Kosovar, the latter referring to the name given to Albanians who lived in the province that Serbs called 'Kosovo and Metohija'. In February 1998, Robert Gelbard, the US State Department's Special Envoy to Kosovo, declared, 'the Kosovar Liberation Army . . . is, without any question, a terrorist group.' A year later, the CIA and US Special Forces gathered intelligence and worked alongside the KLA from an operations centre in Kukes, on the Albanian border with Yugoslavia. Robert Gelbard was later forced to find a crack to wiggle through. When asked why NATO was working alongside an organization that he had recently condemned as terrorists, he pointed out that the KLA was not 'classified legally by the US government as a terrorist organization'.

It was a cruel, cutting wind that swept into the plain of Kosovo from the mountains surrounding this small province. *Kosovo* is derived from the Serbian word *kos*, which is often translated as blackbird, even though it really means a type of brown-speckled thrush. The plain, or *polje* in Serbian, forms the geographical centre of Kosovo. When the traveller drives west from the capital, Priština, there is a steady climb into the hills on the edges of the plain. As the road levels, a glance behind reveals the rugged heartland of Kosovo. Although springtime was edging into summer, there was nothing lush or verdant. It was amongst this brown, sterile landscape, including the occasional clutches of red-roofed houses, that the KLA made its journey from terrorist to freedom fighter.

The story of freedom or terror in Kosovo began much earlier than my first visit. In the minds of the Serb minority that lived there before the NATO bombs fell on Serbia, the story of freedom, occupation and terror began centuries before. It was a typically blustery day on the plain of Kosovo when I met Kosta Bulatović, a Serb patriot and poet. Bulatović was a great oak of a man, the broadness of his chest exaggerated by the stiffness of his back. His face was gnarled, honed by the wind and the pain that he appeared to suffer on behalf of his nation. The poetry he wrote was a celebration of hardship; romantic verse that described a seemingly eternal injustice that inflicts the Serbian people. The distant, watery blueness of his eyes invoked a sadness that he and other Serbs in Kosovo have carried for generations.

The side of the road was sprinkled with rubbish, white and dark objects that mingled in the wind with the dried grass and thickets. There was little sign of life on the barren landscape. There were no villages in sight, but the leftovers of life was everywhere: broken bottles, milk cartons, empty biscuit boxes. Here, amongst the garbage, were the shattered remains of a Serb cemetery. Kosta often visited and wallowed in the symbolism of the debris. He brushed away the page of an old newspaper that had clung to a tombstone, lying broken and cut in two on the damp soil. The name of the dead man was lost, the faded inscription that remained revealed only the name of his wife, Marica, written in the Cyrillic alphabet, his son Arsenije and grandson Simo. The cemetery used to claim the dead from the village of Krivovo, which was destroyed during the Second World War, probably by

Albanians. Nothing was left of Krivovo. It is a tradition in the Balkans to destroy a village in order to deny the existence of the community that had made it their home. In this county, called Glogovac, twenty-seven Serb villages had been erased from the map in the last fifty years, according to Kosta.

In the spring of 1998, Glogovac was an agricultural region where the Albanian population vastly outnumbered Serbs. A month earlier, a few miles from Krivovo, the first significant gunfight in the battle for Kosovo had broken out. Albanians made up more than 80 per cent of Kosovo as a whole and had enjoyed a large degree of self-government until Slobodan Milošović withdrew its autonomy when he became President of Serbia. After years of peaceful protest a group of Albanians decided to take up the gun to fight for independence. In January 1997, Serb forces rounded up sixty suspected members of the KLA, prompting Milošović to announce that 'terrorism in Kosovo has been cut at its roots'. Later that year, a convoy of blue armoured personnel carriers belonging to the Serbian police entered the hilly region near Glogovac called Drenica and were forced to turn back after an ambush. The police then withdrew from the Drenica hills altogether, which created a triangle that Albanians referred to as 'liberated territory'.

Two weeks after Gelbard's condemnation of the KLA, Serbian forces razed the village of Prekaz, a KLA stronghold in the Drenica hills. The paramilitary police annihilated resistance and extinguished all life as well as political opposition. More than forty died, including the very young and the very old. Tanks destroyed houses, anti-aircraft guns fired on civilians. All that remained of Prekaz was rubble, the walls of burnt-out houses and the rotting carcasses of animals. The attack triggered the uprising that finally led to the NATO bombing of Yugoslavia. That, in turn, was launched because Robert Gelbard had used a word loaded with dynamite. A member of the Yugoslav regime later told me that Milošović had understood Gelbard's categorization of the KLA as terrorists as a green light from the US to root out the movement from its bases in Drenica.

Milošović's perpetual leaning towards a policy of ethnic cleansing was born from the region's past. In the eighteenth century, a sense of national identity emerged amongst the peoples of Western Europe. In the Balkans, there were few durable geographical land boundaries and too few opportunities for the creation of nation states. In the midst of conquest and shifting alliances, the Great Powers carved frontiers that often divided communities. Those dispossessed and dispersed by war migrated to new settlements. The land they left remained contested for generations.

One ethnic group will lay claim to a narrow set of historical truths that contradicts a carefully culled version adopted by their adversary. The dead of the ghost village of Krivovo, said my Albanian colleagues, were Serbs sent to Kosovo in the 1920s to colonize the region. Serb armies had conquered Kosovo in 1912 and reclaimed it as Serbian lands after five hundred years of rule by Muslim Turks. A Vienna-based journalist called Lev Bronstein, who was later known to the world as Leon Trotsky, reported in 1912: 'The Serbs, in their national endeavour to correct data in the ethnographical statistics that are not quite favourable to them, are engaged quite simply in systematic extermination of the Muslim population.'

After the First World War, Serbia became the dominant partner in the newly established Kingdom of Serbs, Croats and Slovenes, which was later renamed Yugoslavia. Over the next twenty years, Serb families were sent to Kosovo to set up homes on land that had become, during the dying years of the Ottoman Empire, the centre of an emerging Albanian nation. During the Second World War the Nazis annexed the mineral-rich north of Kosovo, while the remainder was given to Albania, which was ruled by Mussolini's Italy. Many Kosovars sided with the Italians who united them with Albania and provided an escape from Serbian rule.

The Serbs fought alongside the British during the two world wars. It was an ever-present refrain from elderly Serbs who seemed genuinely shocked and hurt that nations such as Britain were now siding with 'Albanian collaborators'. 'We are subject to genocide, we are victims, yet we are labelled as culprits in front of the international community,' bemoaned Kosta Bulatović.

In the former Yugoslavia, many Serbs had lived and buried their dead in regions dominated by other ethnic groups. As the country unravelled, Serb nationalism fostered a mystical attachment to this land. At the graveside in Krivovo, tears swelled in Kosta's eyes. Kosta had a bellowing voice that carried across the landscape like a bushfire. There was an epic tragedy in his soliloquy to a foreign journalist. 'We have to die,' he announced. 'There's nothing else for us. We are like a lost man in the desert who is looking for a path to salvation, meandering across the sand. Are there people on this planet who will extend their hands to the Serb people and deliver us from evil? In the cradle of my state, where my ancestors came fifteen centuries ago, my offspring now have no right to live. Everything which is Serb is being cursed at and destroyed.'

Kosta defined Serb nationhood not as the land within Serbia's borders, but as the right of Serbs to the soil that entombed the bones of their brethren. 'There is no square foot in Kosovo where there hasn't been a Serb house or a Serb graveyard,' he intoned. 'The most important things are under this soil.'

Kosta evoked images of rustic harmony; of an innocent people swept aside by a faceless enemy called the 'international community'. 'You have seen the field where the village was.' He showed me a patch of grassland. 'There were houses there, barns and stables, workers, peasants.' He worked his way through the graveyard, pointing to a broken stone or a piece of hallowed turf in a dramatic pantomime before pausing to reminisce. 'That village was minding its own business; it is now gone from the map of Serbia. Is it our sin that we are defending our nation, our fatherland?'

At that time, Kosta lived in Priština, a vast concrete city built by Yugoslavia's Communist ruler, Marshal Tito (1945–80). Kosta owned an apartment in the city's vast, inchoate jumble of high-rise blocks, where Serb and Albanian lived in resentful proximity. His first recollection was being carried as a young child in his mother's arms as she fled the family home in Kosovo. It was 1942; Albanians had set fire to the Serb homes in his village. It was a childhood memory that spawned adult hatred.

After the war, the Bulatović family moved about twenty miles to Kosovo Polje, or the Field of Blackbirds, a drab, colourless settlement, where Serbs lived on the main streets and Albanians were found only on the edge of town. Many worked in the local power plant, with its towering chimneystacks forever spewing noxious black smoke over the surrounding grassland. For Serbs, Kosovo Polje retained key historical significance as the setting for the defeat by Ottoman Turks at the Battle of Kosovo (1389). The battle entered Serbian folklore as a majestic defeat and a metaphor for the hardships that Serbs believe they have endured through the centuries. For most of the next half-millennium, Serbs lived under the yoke of the victorious Ottomans. The battle gained mythical proportions through its glorification in epic verse. It was enshrined in the national consciousness and defined the patriotism of Kosta Bulatović. He was sustained by a belief that Serbs endure perpetual injustice.

Kosta regularly recited poetry celebrating these stories of past pain and glory. Playing the *gusle*, the one-stringed lute that sounds discordant to outsiders, he entertained his fellow nationalists in the local bars and clubs, blending poetry, patriotism and alcohol. It fired the souls of a lost tribe in Kosovo who survived on a denial of a demographic truth.

His favourite verses included the threatening curse attributed to the Serbian commander, Tsar Lazar, at the Battle of Kosovo.

> Whoever is a Serb, of Serbian blood,
> Whoever shares with me this heritage,
> And he comes not to fight at Kosovo,
> May he never have the progeny
> His heart desires, neither son nor daughter;
> Beneath his hand let nothing decent grow –
> Neither purple grapes nor wholesome wheat;
> Let him rust away like dripping iron
> Until his name shall be extinguished!

Kosta knew and admired the work of another Serb poet, living at that time in Sarajevo, Radovan Karadzić. He had been the inspirational leader of the murderous Bosnian Serb paramilitaries and was later indicted as a war criminal. Both men were originally from Montenegro, itself a contested mountainous crucible of Serb culture, and both wrote poetry about a romantic and fabled national history.

In 1985, Kosta became the inspiration for an idea that was soon to shape the destiny of the Balkans. He and other Serbs living in Kosovo focused their anger on a constitutional change that Tito introduced in 1974 that established a large measure of self-rule for Albanians in Kosovo. After the Second World War, Tito's newly formed Yugoslavia consisted of six republics, Slovenia, Croatia, Montenegro, Macedonia, Bosnia and Serbia. Tito harnessed the national aspirations of each republic by combining coercion with a careful balancing act. When he saw signs of an awakening of Serb nationalism in the 1960s and 70s, he concluded that Serbia had become too powerful. A new constitution effectively divided Serbia by granting self-government to two provinces within its boundaries: Vojvodina in the north had a large Hungarian minority, and Kosovo in the south had an Albanian population that was a minority within Serbia but an overwhelming majority within a newly created mini-republic of Kosovo. Increasingly, Serbs in Kosovo began to consider themselves a minority within their own country. The Albanian population was growing fast, with the highest birth rate of any ethnic group within Europe. And another demographic shift was taking place; from the mid-1960s onwards, an Albanian intelligentsia emerged in Priština, establishing a distinctive national culture and identity to Kosovo. Until then, Serbs had regarded the Albanians as poorly educated farm workers who kept to themselves.

In 1985, five years after Tito died, Kosta Bulatović gathered over two thousand signatures of dissatisfied Serbs. He described the treatment of Serbs by the Albanian majority as a form of terrorism. 'Under their authority we were under unprecedented terror. Our girls and women, even mothers and nuns, were raped. There were attacks on our property. They destroyed our monuments, ploughed over our graveyards and demolished our churches.' While some of the allegations of mistreatment were probably true, most Serbs simply felt a general disgruntlement in a region that no longer seemed like home. Serbs were leaving Kosovo, as they had for decades, mostly for economic reasons. It was a poor region with high unemployment and Albanians were offering inflated prices for their property. 'There was not a single town or village without signs announcing Serbs houses for sale,' Kosta told me bitterly.

The Communist authorities arrested Kosta and thousands of Kosovo Serbs then marched on the capital, Belgrade, to protest at his detention. The President of Serbia was Ivan Stambolić, an urbane man with penetrating blue eyes. I met him at his office in a well-heeled district, peppered with embassies, near the stadium of Red Star Belgrade, once one of Europe's top football clubs. It was a few weeks before NATO began bombing Yugoslavia, and he reflected on this incident. 'I went to Kosovo to negotiate with Bulatović's supporters. I had to cool their heads a little.' Stambolić believed that Serb nationalist intellectuals in Belgrade at the influential Academy of Sciences were manipulating Kosta and his followers. They in turn had influence in the Party, the Church and the Yugoslav army. 'The people in Kosovo were being poisoned and sent into a rage by these people. I explained some important things to them and they accepted what I said.' Kosta was released and the matter was seemingly defused. Stambolić reported to party leaders that the state of mind of Serbs in Kosovo was 'hot and full of electricity'. It was important that a nationalist did not visit there to rouse 'a passion for triumph and revenge'. It was April 1986.

Ivan Stambolić had a dignified presence. His face was lean, chiselled by age and his curly white hair was neatly brushed. He was also a proud man, haunted by the knowledge that he was responsible for the political career of Slobodan Milošović. Stambolić was Milošović's mentor and closest friend for a quarter of a century. The two men met at Belgrade University and as Stambolić rose through the ranks of the Communist Party bureaucracy, Milošović was always one step behind.

In April 1987, Stambolić sent Milošović to Kosovo Polje to calm the reignited situation. While Milošović was addressing the meeting inside a hall in Kosovo Polje, Kosta and his supporters provoked a confrontation with the police, who were under the control of the ethnically Albanian, Kosovo government. The Serb crowd outside began throwing stones at the police. Slavko Ćuruvija was a journalist covering the meeting. 'The secret service people went in saying, "Mr President, if you don't go out and speak to these people outside, there'll be blood on the streets." Milošović was really shaking.' Ćuruvija was a tall, suave man, lightly bearded and bespectacled, epitomizing elegance and intellect. As a young man and aspiring journalist, he had a career as an intelligence analyst for the Yugoslav secret police. He later became editor of the *Dnevni Telegraf*, at one time Serbia's most popular tabloid. 'One old man with a yellowy-white moustache was crying and saying, "Mr President, they are beating us, they're beating us."' Milošović was pushed up the stairs and onto a balcony, above an angry, jeering crowd of ten thousand or more Serbs. 'When he appeared he was "small Slobo". He was pale, shaking and uncertain,' Ćuruvija recounted. 'He appeared in the window and said, "No one should dare beat you," and that was the moment that he became "Great Slobo". Slobo means freedom, Slobodan is man of freedom.'

Kosta Bulatović instantly knew the importance of those six words. 'There and then, he publicly promised that the terror would stop. We were overwhelmed with joy.' Ivan Stambolić believed that while the words may have been uttered spontaneously, senior people in the party as well as the intelligence and security services had wanted Milošović to come to power on a nationalist agenda. 'There were political games that I did not see at the time,' he told me as he rubbed his eyes. Shortly after his trip to Kosovo, Milošović orchestrated a classic 'party coup' at a communist conference and ousted his old friend. 'I was betrayed. It hit me in the head like a stone,' Stambolić told me quietly. 'I learnt a hard lesson. In politics, it is dangerous to be overconfident.' Milošović had become a conundrum that continued to confound and bemuse his former mentor. 'He was a good servant but as the master of evil, as a war leader, I know nothing of this Milošović.'

In 1990, Milošović passed a new constitution imposing Serb rule in Kosovo. Milošović ordered the Serb-dominated Yugoslav army into Priština, and deployed police forces against protesting Albanians. Educated Albanians lost their jobs, schools changed their curricula and the Albanian language was removed from official communiqués.

Kosovo's majority reacted by setting up a parallel civil society alongside the official, Serb-controlled state institutions with its own government, health care and education system.

The Dardania district of Priština was a colourless maze of concrete apartment blocks and walkways. The local school was named after Lenin when Yugoslavia was communist. Now it had two names and two head teachers. In 1993, the Serb headmaster, Bogi Gogić, built a wall that divided the school. Bearded and beady-eyed, Gogić embodied a narrow, intoxicating vision of patriotism. The wall was painted cream on the Serb side and decorated with portraits of Serbian artists and writers. 'Why was it built?' he repeated my question as if it was naive to enquire. 'Have a look at the decorations in the corridor. Their part was once decorated too, but they ruined everything. We do our best to keep our part of the school tidy, not like a pigsty.' He appealed to my common sense, as if repeating universally accepted truths. 'The standard of hygiene is much better here. Hygiene affects behaviour. You can visit the Albanian part and you'll see no decorations, no flowers, only dirt and untidiness.'

Such broad-stroke racism, which has been purged from public debate in the West, remained a feature of everyday conversation in the Balkans. The lid had remained tightly shut on the boiling pot of nationalism amongst the constituents of Yugoslavia for nearly half a century. It was unable to evolve and mature alongside nationalism in Western Europe and, when the lid flew off, it released a sewer-gas bubble. Bogi Gogić's view was that in Serbia, the Serbs should be able to do what they wanted. 'We couldn't put pictures of Serbian writers into the classrooms,' he complained, 'because if we did the Albanian pupils would destroy it. Albanians wanted to introduce their national symbols in classrooms and they wrote "Kosovo Republic" on the wall. Such behaviour was unacceptable for us. Real friendship is impossible with them.'

The Albanian head teacher, Sedat Ramadani, appeared worldlier and better travelled than his Serb counterpart. Elegantly dressed with an easy, relaxed manner, he could barely subdue a smile as he stood by the floor-to-ceiling partition. 'To say that he built the wall because Albanian pupils are dirty or not well disciplined does not stand. It was divided purely for political reasons. The Serbs took over the biggest part of the building, 60 per cent for around 500 pupils, and left 40 per cent for 2,200 Albanian pupils. The curriculum imposed on us by the Serbian Education Ministry tried to assimilate Albanians. It didn't recognize our language or our culture. So we taught our own curriculum. We have created a new generation of young Albanians: the generation of the "Republic"'.

On either side of the wall, different versions of history were being taught. Sedat Ramadani began his history class by asking about the subject of his last lesson. A girl of about fifteen with frizzy hair raised her hand immediately. 'We learnt about the division of Albanian lands, and the struggle for national unification . . .' On the other side, Bogi Gogić taught his pupils the Serb version of truth. 'The Muslim Turks demolished a lot of the monasteries and churches. Now you can only see the remains of these monasteries. They show what our enemies did to our culture and religion. We must remember the past to know how to behave in the future.' Prejudice took root early in Priština.

At a casual glance, life in Priština appeared normal, but everywhere there was an invisible wall that marked the ethnic divide. Albanians ate in Albanian restaurants and Serbs in theirs. Often the restaurants served the same meal under different names. A high-cholesterol favourite of both sides was a steak that was rolled up, filled with cheese and deep-fried. Serbs knew it as a Karadjordjević Šnicla, after the royal dynasty established by the nineteenth-century Serb patriot Karadjordje or Black George. In a nearby Albanian restaurant, the same dish was served up as a Skenderbeg, after the fifteenth-century Catholic warrior who challenged the Ottoman Empire and founded the first Albanian nation.

In Dardania's drab and decrepit housing estates, I befriended two families whose children attended the local school. The balconies of their apartments overlooked each other but the families had never spoken. Both wives worked at the same hospital but in segregated areas.

Zeqir Metaj was in his forties and also taught on the Albanian side of the Lenin school. He was lugubrious and someone for whom the phrase mild-mannered might have been invented, but protest had infused the routine of daily existence. On most days, in Priština's main street, there was a silent, peaceful protest against Serb rule that Zeqir Metaj and his family attended. By 1998, patience was at breaking point. 'It is impossible for Albanians to live within a Serbian state,' Zeqir told me. 'The time has come for Albanians to take their independence. If it means war, it will be war.' He spoke of war as casually as asking his wife, Haneef, to bring more tea and biscuits. 'We are mentally ready for war and massacres,' she told me with a calm assurance, 'every minute, we expect war to start.'

Their eldest daughter, Ardita, studied law. She had long curly hair and was engaged to be married 'after the war'. She had grown up with apartheid. 'There are Serbs in our building,' she told me when I asked about them, 'but it's just as if they don't exist at all. There are no conflicts, no insults, but also no greetings.'

Dejan and his wife Sladjana were Serbs who lived opposite the Metaj family. They had no contact and little affection for their Albanian neighbours. Sladjana was tall and thinly framed, with high cheekbones and short black hair. She worked as a nurse in the hospital where Haneef was a doctor. She told me that Albanians would rather die than be treated in Serb-run clinics. 'They do not bring their kids to hospital. Often, a pregnant woman will die in childbirth. One Albanian woman less, it's all the same to them,' she added flippantly. Sladjana believed that women only had one role in the Albanian community. 'Women must have as many kids as possible because their aim is to be more numerous in Kosovo.'

Dejan was less interested in politics or prejudice. He had experienced emotional difficulties as a child growing up in Kosovo's bizarre, looking-glass world. The couple had a six-year-old son and Dejan was concerned for his future. 'It's quite possible that he will not develop properly. It's a great burden for the children and many will have emotional problems. But I don't know what the solution is.' He dragged on a cigarette and seemed resigned to his fate. He always wore a faded jean jacket and had a goatee beard. He seemed happiest with his friends in the bars, dousing his pain with alcohol. Sladjana was a very kind person to us but continued her bitter rant. 'If they are not served in a shop, they become aggressive, they begin to swear and shout. That is the culture, their culture is different, the way they dine, the way they eat. They eat with their fingers and they don't pay attention to personal hygiene. One can still see things that show they have only recently become civilized. We have an eye department. A major problem with Albanians is a disease they get as a result of infection from their hands . . . I mean they do not use toilet paper. After defecating, it all remains on their nails and on their hands. It gets into their eyes and mouth, etc. All Muslims do that in all the Muslim countries . . .'

Sladjana chain-smoked and nervously picked at her nails. Her bigotry was born from fear; Serbs were vastly outnumbered by Albanians, who showed them little sympathy. It was remarkable how secure and confident Albanians felt compared to their Serb neighbours. It was as if Albanians knew that time was on their side and Serbs knew that it was running out.

I joined Sladjana and Dejan for dinner in their flat. She cooked grilled meat known as a *cevapi* in a warmed bread bun or *lepinja*, with salami, cheese and sour peppers. The couple were not active Serb nationalists and had little time for Milošović. 'But he's the best we've got,' Dejan added wearily. Milošović had built his political career by fostering prejudice. His most potent tool was television news broadcasts beamed from Belgrade. For Dejan and Sladjana, they were their main source of information. Belgrade TV used often crude but clever propaganda techniques developed under communism. Before dinner, we watched a report showing about a dozen men holding machine guns and running through a clearing in a forest. It purported to show 'terrorists from the Kosovo Liberation Army', although I doubted the authenticity of the film. 'Nobody can support the rights of terrorists to take away part of your country,' Dejan told me. 'The whole world must agree with us. If terrorists tried to make Florida independent, would Washington do nothing?'

Serbs will often remind a Westerner about their Slavic souls, an internal space where the visitor experiences broad, quixotic flights of emotion concerning life, nationhood and love. It was both an asset and a burden that Serbs had to bear, I was told, sharing it only with their Orthodox Christian kinsmen from Russia. The West with its work ethic and humdrum mechanized lifestyle had lost its soul to the crude demands of market capitalism. The Slavic soul was brought to life in poetry and song, as well as copious quantities of alcohol. Drink tended to bring out the cult of suffering amongst Serbs in Kosovo. A few years earlier, I had witnessed a hundred and fifty thousand Serbs leaving their homes in the Krajina region of Croatia; old men and women travelled on the back of tractors, taking only the possessions they could carry. It was a pitiful human exodus but celebrated in Kosovo's bars as a noble act of suffering. A year after I visited, a hundred thousand Serbs fled Kosovo in another great migration.

I often found myself offered *rakija*, a clear fruit brandy and the Serb national drink, in the morning. My cameraman and long-time friend Fred Scott quipped that he had donated his liver to make our documentary, such was the extent of social drinking amongst the Serbs in Kosovo. Units of the Serb police, tall and threatening in their military-style flak jackets, would descend on our hotel at breakfast and down several bottles of Niksic beer before their day's work. At times, it seemed as if we were witnessing the last days of Rome. Fred and I joined Sladjana and Dejan at a party at a bar opposite the layered arches of a Byzantine-style monastery at Gracanica. The packed bar shook to 'turbo-folk' music, a combination of Arab melodies and throbbing techno beats, which became the anthems of the Serb nation-alist movement during the wars in Bosnia and Croatia. As a sign of friendship and loyalty, Kosovo Serbs take their drink in one hand and cross arms with another person. Both must then empty their glass. After several such friendly greetings, a blur can descend on proceed-ings. Many of the drinkers raised their hands in the three-fingered salute, representing the Holy Trinity of the Orthodox Church as well as the Serb national revival. Most of the policemen casually discarded their AK-47s on the floor and danced. On one occasion, I watched a grenade slowly roll off the nearby table. Dejan drove me back, barely able to talk, let alone drive. I remember his comment at some point that night: 'Why not have fun – who knows what tomorrow will bring?'

There was a contrasting mood in Albanian homes, a confidence that they would soon triumph. When I joined Zeqir Metaj and his family for dinner, the Albanian television news focused on the violence committed by the Serb paramilitary police.

I asked Zeqir's twenty-year-old daughter, Ardita, whether she would accept any deal that allowed Serbian sovereignty to remain over

Kosovo. 'No, absolutely not,' she replied. 'We want independence.'
Her fiancé added: 'We are an independent country. We are under
occupation. If war breaks out, I would join the KLA.' Ardita interrupted, 'As an Albanian of Kosovo it is my obligation and honour to
do whatever is necessary for the solution of the question of Kosovo
even if it is necessary to die. Why not? Girls of my age have died for
Kosovo.' Haneef nodded in agreement and smiled. 'It would be a
matter of great pride if my husband, my children or myself died for
freedom.'

After six years of peaceful protest, it became clear that ethnic
Albanians were losing patience with their Serb masters. When Yugoslavia dissolved in bloodshed in the early 1990s, Kosovo's leadership
under the French-educated intellectual Ibrahim Rugova retained a
remarkable civility. The peaceful nature of the rebellion in Kosovo
lulled the outside world into believing that dialogue could resolve the
contradictions of Kosovo. Professor Fehmi Agani was Rugova's deputy
in the Democratic League of Kosovo, the leading Albanian political
party. I met him in its headquarters, a wooden hut in the middle of a
busy bus station in Priština. He looked like a professor, with shock-
white hair and a well-pressed suit. 'War would hurt Albanian civilians
very badly,' he told me as he considered the increasing prospect of
violence. Did he support the KLA? 'The problem will not be resolved
through the KLA,' he said 'they are the mirror of Milošović.' 'So
you've had no contact with the KLA?' I asked, surprised. 'None at all,'
he replied. I had suspected that the political leadership of the Democratic League of Kosovo was coordinating attacks with the militants.
At the time I was sceptical whether he had told me the whole truth,
but it later emerged that he had. 'We have always said that we want a
peaceful settlement,' he told me, 'but we cannot control the anger of
all our people.' As we shook hands and I left his meagre office, it
seemed that the quickening pace of the violence was marginalizing this
kindly intellectual.

The Kosovo Liberation Army emerged in the untamed hills surrounding Priština, as angry farmers received arms and support from
Albanians living outside Kosovo. One of the first serious attacks
credited to the group was in April 1996, when a gunman sprayed
automatic gunfire into a restaurant in Decani. Serbs who had been
resettled from Croatia were known to use the restaurant. Three died in
the attack.

The owners of the restaurant, Danilo and his wife Kosara, were in their late sixties. They were serving lunch when Danilo saw a man kick open the door and start firing with a machine gun. 'For a second, I stood facing him. When I realized I wasn't wounded, I fell down and crawled into the kitchen.' In a theatrical display, Danilo showed me how he dodged the bullets and scampered behind a brick wall and into the kitchen. The gunman continued shooting into the far corner, killing two diners and a young waitress. 'She had brought water to a man over there,' Danilo pointed. 'Then she turned around and started spinning as the bullets struck her.'

Danilo and Kosara lived in a town where only one in a hundred was a Serb. The couple had a son who lived in Switzerland but otherwise had little contact with the world outside the walls of their restaurant. Perhaps it was justified, but the couple displayed a profound sense of paranoia. 'I have a Kalashnikov,' Danilo told me. 'It will be him or me. We are on guard throughout the night. It's my turn before midnight and my wife afterwards. We sleep very little, we suffer a lot.' All the windows to their flat above the restaurant were boarded. 'Any Albanian can be a terrorist,' she concluded, peering at passersby. 'There is lots of hatred. If only they could, they would kill us all in an instant.' As evening fell, Danilo sat in his chair at the top of the stairs leading up from the restaurant, an AK-47 across his lap, a spare magazine and 150 extra bullets on the table next to him.

My initial reaction was that tragedy, insecurity and isolation had infected their minds. Then I remembered that they had witnessed bloodshed from which they were lucky to escape. They also had nowhere to go. Danilo responded angrily when I suggested they leave such a wretched existence. 'How would you feel if you had to run from everything you own in order to sleep in a field? My ancestors built this house. Should I just hand it over to a bunch of terrorists? I say by God, I won't go anywhere else, this is my home and my land.'

A short walk from Danilo's restaurant was the office of the Albanian Council for the Defence of Human Rights. It was long name for the work of mostly one man. Musa Berisha was a former poet who had spent much of his time in 1998 recording the names of victims of Serb violence on an old typewriter. He also sent reports to news agencies in Albania by satellite phone. He had unkempt light-brown hair and a three-day stubble, and wore an ill-fitting suit. 'The KLA are not terrorists. Our people get killed and we are accused of terrorism?'

he asked in mock surprise. 'The KLA are defending us from terrorism. We are occupied, the KLA are involved in a liberation struggle.'

I had tried on several occasions to meet members of the KLA but the movement was at that stage mostly unwilling to be filmed. There had been only a few, fleeting photographs of men in military fatigues, with the letters UCK. The problems had arisen following the American remarks that that the KLA was a terrorist organization. The Albanians knew that the West's sympathies depended on them appearing as victims of Serb aggression. Images of military training and armed Albanian fighters on the BBC would not help their cause.

The KLA had a further problem. The US State Department refused to contemplate an independent Kosovo because traditional diplomatic thinking believed that severing Kosovo from Serbia would trigger a much wider Balkans conflict. The argument ran like this. Nearly half of the Albanians lived outside the borders of Albania. If war broke out in Kosovo, ethnic Albanians in Macedonia would join the conflict and fight alongside their compatriots in Kosovo. Western countries believed Macedonia was the key to stability in the southern Balkans. If Macedonia's ethnic Albanians joined forces with those in Kosovo, Macedonia would fall apart, dragging the region into a series of territorial disputes. The scenario speculated that Bulgaria, which has historical claims on Macedonia, would annex the remainder of the country. Greece, which had never recognized an independent Macedonia, would move troops to secure its northern border. With chaos in Macedonia, Turkey would challenge Greek interference and pursue other territorial claims against Greece. A major regional conflict could erupt. The KLA therefore had to provoke the Serb forces without appearing to be the aggressors.

Our final attempt to meet a KLA commander was in the village of Izbica, some thirty miles north-west of Priština, deep in the Drenica hills. The village is not marked on most maps of Kosovo. Although only a few hours' drive from Priština, it was a world away from the political landscape inhabited by the parallel government of the 'Republic of Kosovo'. The villagers were as steeped in tribal codes of kinship, blood and honour as characters in a Shakespeare play. Old men wore the white conical hat known as the *qeleshe*. Women dressed in white headscarves and flowing trousers called *shallvare*. Each village contained an extended family, or clan, to whom loyalty was absolute.

Vengeance killing was a duty if the pride or standing of the clan was damaged. Feuding was a routine of life.

During my first visit to Izbica, I stayed with a family in a large brick house. In the evening, the men of the clan sat around a red carpet and drank tea in a plain room without furniture. Most wore grease-stained jackets and carried several days' stubble. Many had shotguns. They spoke of defending their village and shooting any Serb who tried to enter. It would have been a short step for these men to transform themselves from an informal militia into a unit of the KLA. They all said they would fight if called to; in fact, several said they were *already* at war. I sensed that the significance of the KLA was as much a revolutionary calling as a real armed rebellion. If I'd brought a dozen khaki uniforms and a few AK-47s, I think I could have created a KLA squadron over dinner.

Our evening meal began with a sharp, salty white cheese and flat bread, similar in texture to an Indian nan but without the spices. There was also a watery beef stew. About 90 per cent of Kosovars were from a Muslim tradition and while the majority rarely adhered strictly to their faith, there was no alcohol to lighten that evening's discussion. Everyone in Izbica spoke openly about the KLA but when I asked where they were, they smiled as if they were ghosts that had slipped into the forest. On my next trip, I was taken to see a doctor who ran a clinic in a village near Izbica. Dr Zain seemed a thoughtful, hard-working man who bore the area's troubles on his shoulders. 'We are very short of supplies,' he complained. I realized later that he was an informal medical officer for the KLA. The drugs and bandages were being gathered to supply an army preparing for war.

We spent another night in the Drenica hills. There was the constant backdrop of gunfire as Serb paramilitaries fired into the forests and KLA snipers shot back. After lengthy negotiations, our translator, Safet, a young Kosovar who was over six feet tall, finally led us to a uniformed commander. Abedin Rexha was on the KLA General Staff, the movement's central command. He was not in a good mood when he saw us. He drove up briskly in his jeep. We tried to explain that we had spent days trying to cooperate with the KLA. Commander Rexha was a smallish, thin man with an overly upright gait. One of his hands was fumbling the leather covering on his holster. His body language was worrying and the situation soon spun out of control.

Safet shouted at Commander Rexha as tears fell down his face. The commander was red with rage; he waved his hand in a violent motion and suddenly jumped into his jeep and slammed the door. He screeched the tyres as he reversed out, slid across the road and smashed into a hay-bale carrier behind a tractor. The furious soldier then accelerated away without apologizing to the farmer. The villagers stood in silence, unsure whether to laugh at Rexha's theatrical display. Safet wiped his tears and said quietly, 'He ordered us to leave Drenica. He accused us of being spies. We must go.' We drove back to our hotel in Priština in silence.

I had to give up my ambition to spend time with formal members of the KLA. The movement was so concerned with its image abroad that relations with the Western media, who were overwhelmingly favourable towards its cause, were fraught and tense. Their primary concern was to wage an insurgency against Serb forces and yet present themselves as a disciplined, national army rather than a terrorist organization.

If the crisis in Kosovo had erupted after September 11th, the United States would have listed the KLA as a foreign terrorist organization, confiscated its funds and sought to arrest those who were raising money for the group in Europe. The new doctrine widened the definition of a terrorist organization to include all insurgencies that threatened existing nation states even though many were born from legitimate concerns about self-determination and human rights. The policies instigated by George W. Bush have legitimized the right of an existing nation state to suppress internal challenges to its authority, however much a rebellion may be justified by United Nations' charters on human rights and religious freedoms. Does this mean that no new nations will be created through war or violence? What would the US have done if Yugoslavia had unravelled a decade later?

The American lawyer Alan Dershowitz takes this argument a stage further in his book *Why Terrorism Works*. He writes that terrorism has been rewarded in the past, and after September 11th its perpetrators anywhere in the world should never again be accepted as political leaders of the future. In other words, there will never be another Nelson Mandela. Dershowitz envisages a variation on the World Court where those accused of terrorism are brought before the judge and condemned. As so often with such arguments, it trips up on the definition of 'terrorism'; it presumes that a universally accepted formula exists, which can categorize a list of political activities as terrorist and 'illegal'. It also assumes that a global consensus will support and police this protocol. If 'terrorism' is defined by specific actions, then international law can apply to methods used by certain militant organizations. International agreements already prohibit hijacking aircraft, taking hostages and transporting nuclear materials. Together, these comprise a piecemeal approach to outlawing actions that are often attributed to terrorists. But such a list includes only a small percentage of the violent acts instigated by non-state militants and most of these protocols apply to international situations rather than the battlefield of a domestic insurgency. If the car bombing of a civilian target was deemed an illegal 'terrorist' act in international law, what would be the status of a missile attack from a helicopter on a car carrying civilians?

Those who look to a World Court or the United Nations to become the global police and judiciary should talk to Slobodan Milošović. He would immediately respond that not everyone is equal before international law. Russian soldiers in Chechnya or Chinese public-security officers in Tibet are unlikely to face a World Court and most certainly an American political leader will never become liable for his actions. But the leader of a small nation such as Yugoslavia can easily be rounded up and thrown in jail. After all, not all UN resolutions are the same. The resolutions that call for Israel to withdraw from the territories that it 'occupied' during the Six-Day War in 1967 have no prospect of being enforced. Do the Palestinians have the right to resort to violence because the UN is unable to apply international law? As a defence against the charge of terrorism in a 'World Court', Islamic guerrillas in the Palestinian territories could argue that they are only using violence in order to *establish* the rule of law.

In Kosovo, Milošović's behaviour played into the hands of the KLA. At an international conference in Rambouillet, France, the KLA agreed to a peace deal drafted by the major powers. Milošović was portrayed as a tyrant who rejected peace. A spokesman for the KLA told the world's media that the international community was obliged to 'intervene against this fascist and barbaric regime'. The Americans had been forced to backtrack several months earlier and now agreed that the KLA was not a terrorist organization, arguing that it had the broad support of the Albanian population of Kosovo. They might have offered this definition of a terrorist: 'Terrorist: *n* a member of a militant organization that engages in violent action to achieve a political goal *without* the support of a majority of the population.'

Ćuruvija had his own definition of 'terrorism'. 'The KLA are, of course, terrorists,' he told me, 'just like the IRA was in Northern Ireland or the Kurdish PKK in Turkey.' The main difference for Ćuruvija was the effective use of public relations by the Albanian side. 'The key for modern warfare, whether you are a state or a terrorist, is to make your war popular in the West. The Albanians have done that.' I enjoyed Ćuruvija's casual cynicism. His indictment of Milošović, which was sweeping, was based on incompetence and failure; above all, he was a marketing disaster for his nation. 'He didn't understand how to play to the West,' he told me, smiling. 'The Serb police kill the KLA and the KLA kill the Serb police, and the world should say the KLA are terrorists but instead they say it the other way round.' For Ćuruvija, that was poor news management.

NATO's propaganda claimed it was defending Albanians from the wrath of Milošović to prevent another 'Bosnia'. Bosnia, however, was a mirror image of Kosovo. In Bosnia, one ethnic group, the Serbs, had tried to break away from an ethnically mixed state and create a 'Greater Serbia'. The KLA's aim was to carve an ethnically pure 'Greater Albania' from Serbia and Macedonia. The only difference between these two separatist, if not terrorist, groups was that the West detested the Bosnian Serbs while the KLA had gained its sympathy.

The result of the NATO bombing of the remnants of Yugoslavia was the effective partition of Serbia. Kosovo will inevitability become either an independent nation or part of an Albanian federation. With the ashes of defeat in their nostrils, over a hundred thousand Serbs fled the region that had been their home for generations. Kosta Bulatović fled to Montenegro with only the possessions he could put in his car. Dejan and Sladjana also left their apartment, though I never discovered where they went. When we returned after the war, most of their furniture remained but Albanians were living in their flat.

During the bombing Professor Fehmi Agani, the well-dressed deputy leader of the Democratic League of Kosovo, left Priština with his wife and son by train for Macedonia. His body was found on a roadside en route with three bullet holes in his head.

The men who I stayed with in Izbica also suffered from the Serb security services. A group of about two hundred armed men in civilian clothes, thought to be Serb paramilitaries, entered Izbica as the bombing took place. Women and children were sent from the village. Most of the remaining men were lined up in four rows in a field and shot. The very old were ordered to dig shallow graves for 148 bodies. Dr Zain was amongst the dead.

The KLA commander who accused us of being spies, Abedin Rexha, survived the bombing and the war against the Serb forces. He was killed a year later during an argument with another KLA officer. It was said to be the result of an angry feud between rival clans.

Ten days into the war, Belgrade state television read an open attack on Slavko Ćuruvija, calling him a 'traitor' and accusing him of supporting the NATO bombing of Yugoslavia. A week later Ćuruvija's brains were shot out by two men wearing black masks who had waited for his return. The Interior Ministry said afterwards that it was 'intensively looking for the terrorists who carried out this attack'. Needless to say, no arrests were made.

The roll call of the dead from my work in Yugoslavia included the former Communist leader of Serbia, Ivan Stambolić. He disappeared in the summer of 2000 while jogging in a Belgrade park. A witness said they saw a man being bundled into a van. Three years later, his body was discovered in a pit on a mountain in northern Serbia. He had been shot twice. The police said they wanted to question Slobodan Milošović and his influential wife, Mira, concerning the murder.

7 / STATE TERROR

*'The thought that the state has lost its mind
and is punishing so many innocent people is intolerable.
And so the evidence has to be internally denied.'*
Arthur Miller

Men and women ambled towards their destinations looking straight ahead. A few rode on bicycles that looked oversized against their small frames; others rode tricycle rickshaws, scouring the streets for clients. The only vehicles on the dusty, rutted roads were Russian-built military jeeps. In the centre of the city, the yellow, once-grand buildings from the French colonial era lay mostly deserted, their stucco faded and cracking. A rusty, peeling sign above an empty shop with a frontage of smashed glass suggested it had once been a Renault showroom. It seemed that I had reached some abandoned, distant outpost of humanity and had discovered relics from a former civilization.

I had travelled for about eight hours to reach Phnom Penh on unmade, pitted roads, with potholes as large as kitchen sinks. The journey began in Ho Chi Minh City, where Highway One, Vietnam's main north–south artery, looped westwards toward Cambodia. The choppy, lurching ride could have mixed a Martini for James Bond. The constant jarring loosened screws on electrical equipment and shook my body with the power of a high-voltage current. The only way to make the day-long journey bearable was to let my head bobble and my limbs dangle freely. I looked like an unhinged puppet. I saw a crowded bus with dozens seated on the roof and others clinging to its side approach us and then topple into a ditch after failing to deal with a huge hole in the road. There were probably fatalities and certainly dozens seriously injured but our driver, from the Vietnamese Foreign Ministry, refused to stop and offer assistance. He shrugged his large shoulders as if to say that Highway One was a giant monster that regularly consumed those who dared traverse its clay-red surface. The driver's sizable body worked its way around each pothole, his stubby hands twisting and turning the steering wheel in a ceaseless, nimble pantomime.

The Cambodian countryside was marked by towering sugar palms with spherical clusters of leaves that were balanced on top like lollipops on long sticks. It was the rainy season and by late afternoon black monsoon clouds rolled into the empty sky. For a short while, the sun threw a magical light onto emerald rice fields that glowed against the dark backdrop of the approaching clouds. Pochentong airport had been closed since 1975, when the last American evacuation flights left Phnom Penh as the communist Khmer Rouge advanced on the city. More than a dozen years later the carcasses of rusty, burnt-out planes still littered the airfield and bomb craters prevented planes landing. In order to reach the Cambodian capital, I had to use ferries that shuttled vehicles across rivers bursting with the monsoon rains. I crossed the mighty Mekong at Neak Leung, where American bombs had killed scores of villagers. No one knows for sure how many were blown up by the eight-engine B-52 Stratofortress planes that secretly 'carpet-bombed' the Cambodian countryside in 1969 and 1973. My best guess is well over a hundred thousand civilians. The bombing was intended to destroy the Ho Chi Minh Trail, a route through Laos and Cambodia used by the North Vietnamese Army to supply Vietcong guerrillas who were fighting American troops in South Vietnam. In 1993, during elections organized by the United Nations, I flew low in a helicopter along the eastern border with Vietnam and saw an undulating terrain that at one time had been flat. The 750lb bombs had reshaped the land, erasing scores of villages from the map of Cambodia.

It was nearly a decade since the Khmer Rouge had been driven from Phnom Penh, but time had not exorcised the legacy of their rule. If 'terrorism' is defined as an act that instils fear in a civilian population in order to achieve a political goal, then the Khmer Rouge were possibly the most successful and brutal terrorist organization of the twentieth century. The systematic and deliberate terror that Cambodians sustained from their own leaders between 1975 and 1979 was unparalleled in modern history. It cast a giant, bloody shadow over the latter half of the twentieth century.

My translator, Chhay Song Heng, was a kind man in his thirties who survived because he had tricked the Khmer Rouge into believing that he didn't understand English. Guards used to test him by suddenly asking a question in English and watching for a response; Chhay pretended not to understand. The Khmer Rouge executed all 'class enemies', which included teachers, doctors and lawyers. Those who wore glasses or spoke a foreign language were also categorized as an enemy. Alongside other members of the educated elite who survived, he suffered from guilt. He was barely five feet tall and his dignity had been crushed. Survival required giving absolute loyalty and total power to a regime that despised him. Chhay was traumatized by his four years in a commune as a rice farmer. He would break down and sob if one of our team raised their voice.

On a side road in the south of Phnom Penh, among overgrown banana palms, there was a rundown three-storey building. Its white paint was peeling and most of the brown shutters were closed. It was a former secondary school, called Tuol Svay Prey High, or 'School on the Hill of the Wild Mango'. There was also a primary school on the grounds, called Tuol Sleng, which means the 'Hill of the Poison Tree'. It is the latter name that was used to describe the site after the Khmer Rouge took over. They had turned the school into a secret prison, codenamed Security Office 21, or S-21. It was created as an interrogation centre and more than sixteen thousand people were executed there. Only seven prisoners left S-21 alive. Each victim was forced, under torture, to write a final testimony shortly before their execution. The archives of S-21 were a library of terror. Everyone was photographed and logged. There were thousands of black-and-white pictures; faces staring at the camera with a number pinned on their chest. Many were children. One photograph is of a girl, perhaps twelve years old, her eyes widened by fear, almost popping from her face. There were young and old, women with babies, some beaten and bloodied. The images screamed, silently. The photographs and confessions were voices from the killing fields, evidence of a grotesque killing machine that was designed by paranoid leaders to purge foreign spies from the ranks of the movement.

My producer, Frank Smith, and I tracked down one of the men who guarded and executed prisoners at S-21. Him Huy was now a farmer with a few cows and chickens, which were kept underneath his traditional-style house that was raised on stilts. Believing that he'll never face trial, he has admitted killing two thousand people.

Every evening, Him Huy would load a batch of prisoners from S-21 and take them to a killing field, a short drive away. 'We pushed them onto the trucks,' he said in a hollow monotone. 'I wrote down the names of the prisoners and sent them one after another to the killing place. The prisoners were blindfolded and handcuffed when they were walked there. We told them that we were taking them somewhere else.

'When they reached the pit, we told the prisoners to sit down and then they were hit with a cart axle from behind. Then their throats were cut before their handcuffs were removed and they were kicked into the pit.' Each day, in a dulling routine, Him Huy would bludgeon prisoners with a cart axle. His eyes glazed over and his delivery was mechanical. 'It varied, sometimes there were fifteen people, at other times as many as forty a night. Prisoners were killed one after another.'

Each prisoner was numbered by the warden of S-21, a skeletal man known as Duch. He wanted to give the leadership a detailed record of the enemies within. The names of anyone known to the prisoner were extracted under torture. Confessions led to more arrests. Arrests led to more confessions.

Him Huy described the tactics. 'They would arrest and kill the entire families of alleged traitors. No one was spared. They would arrest the wives, husbands and children, and even brothers, sisters and other relatives. After arresting the mothers, soldiers would take the children away. They were killed in the same way as the adults. The children were also blindfolded and their hands were tied behind their backs.'

Prisoner number 320 was a healthy-looking girl who was almost smiling in her photo. Beside her was a naked baby, barely six months old. The horror of the image is knowing what happened next. Him Huy flinched only once during our interview, when I asked what happened to the baby. 'The babies were killed as well. They weren't spared.' He paused and looked at the ground. 'I was only obeying orders,' he told me. 'If I didn't kill, I'd be killed.'

It was the tyrant Josef Stalin who supposedly said that one death was a tragedy while a million deaths was just a statistic. For me, the story of one death would speak volumes about the searing pain that still lacerated Cambodian society a quarter of a century after the slaughter. Chum Mai was a small, frail man in his sixties. He had worked for the Khmer Rouge as a mechanic. During our discussion, I asked what had happened to his wife. He broke down. No comforting could stop him.

Khmer Rouge soldiers in the dead of night arrested him and his wife at gunpoint. In the darkness, they were separated. He then heard gunshots and his wife's screams. He jumped into a nearby ditch and crawled away. He soon realized that his wife had been shot dead. He was torn up by guilt; a man broken by the thought that he had fled and left his wife to face her executioner alone.

I met Chum Mai in a restaurant in Phnom Penh. By then, it had been two decades since the Khmer Rouge had fled and Phnom Penh had sprung back to life with shops, restaurants and tourists, mostly en route to Asia's greatest ruins at the temple complex at Angkor. More than half the population of Cambodia had been born after the overthrow of the Khmer Rouge. But the ghosts of the Khmer Rouge continued to haunt the generation that survived. Chum's small, fragile frame shook with emotion when he spoke.

The Khmer Rouge took his children and he never discovered whether they were alive or dead. After his arrest, he was taken to an interrogator in S-21. 'He asked me, "You, the traitor, when did you join the CIA and when did you join the KGB? And how many of you are there?" I said, "I don't know, I don't know." Then he said, "If you refuse to confess, I will beat you to death, you mother-fucker! You must tell the truth. Then I won't kill you. If not, I must kill you!" But how could I confess when I didn't know what the CIA or KGB were? So, he kept beating me; the first day, the second day, the third day and the fourth day.'

Chum was speaking slowly, looking through me, his eyes fixed on some place a quarter of a century before. 'Then he took out a pair of pliers to twist and pull out my toenails while my leg was shackled. When I still refused to confess anything, he twisted and pulled out the toenails of my other foot. Finally, he electrocuted me till I fainted. When I came round, he asked me again to confess. I didn't know what to say, so I just confessed to anything so that he wouldn't beat me.'

Chum Mai wrote in his confession that he was working for the CIA and had recruited dozens of agents in Cambodia. It was all a fiction. But he also gave the names of sixty-eight acquaintances, innocent men and women, who would soon be arrested, tortured and murdered. 'I realized that I was guilty of implicating other people and I beg that God forgive me if anybody else was tortured like I was. People who had been arrested and killed previously had implicated me. And I implicated others, so did other people. It was just like rear waves pushing the front waves forward. People would die one after another, after another after another.'

Many of the survivors suffered from guilt. They lived because they lied, stole food from friends or gave their loyalty to the Khmer Rouge. The level of terror imposed a psychology of dependence upon a generation.

'I worked very hard for them. I didn't dare to break even a saw. But they still jailed me and tortured me.' Chum began to cry. For most Cambodians, the memory of this period was a shameful one of submission and fear. Men and women were unable to protect their own families. When he spoke about his wife, Chum wailed uncontrollably. I have interviewed dozens of people who have broken down and cried as they recalled their pain but no one was as mentally lacerated as Chum. His howls of anguish were unstoppable. 'Please, seek justice for me,' he pleaded, holding his hands out as if I could provide salvation. 'I appeal to the world, please find justice for me. I am still suffering.'

Khmer Rouge was the French colloquial name used by outsiders to describe the Communist Party of Kampuchea, a more faithful transliteration of the Khmer-language name for Cambodia. The guerrilla movement prospered during the chaos following the US bombing of Cambodia during the Vietnam War. The leader, King Norodom Sihanouk, was overthrown in a coup engineered by the CIA in 1970. The regime that the US installed under General Lon Nol was intended to assist the American war effort in Vietnam but it became corrupt and militarily ineffective. Meanwhile the Khmer Rouge recruited uneducated youngsters who were told to give up family ties and obey only the party. It instilled in children, often as young as twelve years old, a belief that violence was a virtue. The movement was led by a group of former exchange students who had studied at the Sorbonne in Paris in the 1950s and 60s. Saloth Sar, who later called himself Pol Pot or Brother Number One, became the party's General Secretary. He and his followers combined Western ideas from Marx, Lenin and Jean-Paul Sartre with a naive, literal simplicity. Political theory was followed to its logical conclusion, even if the consequences were absurd or brutal. Pol Pot spent five months in China in 1965 and Mao Zedong's Cultural Revolution added the final ingredient to the Khmer Rouge's strategy: a belief that society could be instantly transformed. Young people were considered blank pages on which a revolution could be inscribed. The movement followed Mao's dictum, 'A clean sheet of paper has no blotches'. The result was that small children were turned into killers of their own parents.

On 17 April 1975, the Khmer Rouge overthrew Lon Nol's unprincipled regime and captured Phnom Penh, before implementing one of the most radical social experiments of the twentieth century. The Khmer Rouge's ideology defined the urban population as 'parasites' who lived off the 'surplus labour' of peasant farmers. Cambodia closed its borders and forced its people to work in labour communes. All Cambodia's cities were emptied. No one could own property and marriages were arranged by the Party. Religion was also banned.

Heng Liang Hor was a softly spoken monk in his fifties when I met him at a newly refurbished monastery in Phnom Penh. In the 1990s, after twenty years of neglect, Buddhism was reborn in Cambodia. The pagodas, with roofs curling upwards at their edges, were repainted in bright colours and ornate patterns. Destroyed icons of the Buddha had been restored. Monsoon rains crashed against the roof of the monastery as Heng recalled the day the communists, wearing baggy black pyjamas, entered Phnom Penh. 'At about nine o'clock in the morning, they told everybody to leave. They said it would only be for three days and then they'd allow us back. Whoever refused to do so would be shot and killed. Those who were in hospital, including those who were being drip-fed, had to remove the drip and leave. Those who could not walk had to be carried out by their relatives, if they had any, or else they would be left behind and killed.' Heng drew breath and he cooled himself with a fan made from braided jute. 'Then they said that all Buddhist monks had sided with the enemy. So, all monks must disrobe or be beaten to death.' In order to survive, Heng spent nearly four years denying his faith and repeating a new mantra to his communist masters; that Buddhism had 'cheated the people for two and a half thousand years'.

Genocide became official state policy. According to a census by the Cambodian Genocide Project, between 1.7 million and 2.2 million people died, out of a population of 8 million. Between half and one million were intentionally murdered. Another million starved to death or perished from overwork in the communes the Khmer Rouge imposed at gunpoint throughout the country.

In the 1970s, the US State Department held a schematic view that the Khmer Rouge were simply another communist guerrilla movement whose existence justified the military doctrine known as the 'Domino theory'. It was a theory of containment, which supposed that if one nation fell to the general enemy called 'communism', neighbouring nations would fall as well, like dominos. I spent a month travelling through Cambodia in 1992 with the author William Shawcross, whose seminal book, *Sideshow: Kissinger, Nixon and the Destruction of Cambodia*, revealed the extent of the secret bombing campaign ordered by the US President and his Secretary of State. William told me that the State Department disregarded evidence of the Khmer Rouge's intense ethnic hatred for the North Vietnamese. In the 'Domino theory', other nations had no history or culture; they were simply dominos in a row, to be knocked down or propped up by the communists or the 'free world'. William was convinced that the motivation for the madness of the Khmer Rouge was rooted in Cambodia's geography and history. 'Since the thirteenth century, Cambodia's power has been in decline,' he told me. 'At that time, the Khmer people were the dominant warrior race in South-East Asia. For the next six centuries, Cambodia's central drama became that of a small nation dominated by two neighbouring countries, Vietnam and Thailand. Both countries have invaded its soil and exploited its people.' The Khmer Rouge was primarily a chauvinistic movement; its literal version of communism was, in the minds of its leaders, the means to re-establish a great and pure Khmer race.

Racial minorities in Cambodia, such as the Cham people, were executed, alongside anyone with Vietnamese lineage. Villagers in the administrative region the Khmer Rouge called the 'Eastern Zone', along the border separating the two countries, were routinely executed because they had 'Vietnamese minds in Cambodian bodies'. On Cambodia's western border, numerous attacks were launched by Khmer Rouge soldiers on Thai villages in 1977.

It was on the border with Vietnam that the Khmer Rouge incursions onto foreign soil led to their downfall and the first war ever fought between two communist regimes. Pol Pot wrongly believed that Cambodia faced an imminent attack from the new communist rulers of a united Vietnam. During the previous decades, the Vietnamese had sponsored the Cambodian communist movement. Pol Pot and his Brother Number Two, Noun Chea, became paranoid, believing that members of their own movement were Vietnamese agents. This led to wave after wave of internal purges and executions of cadres, as well as border skirmishes with Vietnamese troops. Despite public gestures of friendship between the leadership of the two nations, Khmer Rouge forces repeatedly made sorties into Vietnam, burning villages and murdering civilians. It remains puzzling why the Khmer Rouge insisted on sparking a suicidal war with an enemy whose army was ten times larger and much better equipped. Phnom Penh Radio broadcast that victory against the Vietnamese was achievable despite the numerical disadvantages. All that the Khmer Rouge soldiers needed to do, it reported matter-of-factly, was kill thirty Vietnamese for every one dead Cambodian.

In December 1978, the Vietnamese, whose responses until then had been cautious and defensive, finally decided to invade Cambodia. The attack began on Christmas Day, using thirteen divisions and a hundred and fifty thousand men. On 7 January they entered Phnom Penh, and the Khmer Rouge's leadership, with half its army destroyed, fled to the jungles in the north and west of Cambodia. The Vietnamese installed a regime that consisted mostly of defected Khmer Rouge commanders. The Foreign Minister of the new regime was Hun Sen, who later dominated Cambodian politics as its long-standing Prime Minister.

The West condemned the Vietnamese invasion and refused to recognize the new regime, depriving the shattered nation of desperately needed aid and assistance. The Khmer Rouge formed an alliance with two non-communist factions and were still considered by the United Nations as the legitimate government of Cambodia. With the financial and military support of the West and China, the Khmer Rouge continued to wage an insurrection against the Vietnamese-backed regime. Vietnamese troops remained in Cambodia for over a decade but became victims of a similar type of guerrilla war that they had used to defeat the United States. Fifty thousand Vietnamese troops died, many from malaria. In the midst of the cold war, the West was happy to allow the Khmer Rouge to sap the strength of the Soviet-backed Vietnamese forces.

The absurdity of the West's support for the alliance that included the Khmer Rouge struck me during a visit to Paris in 1988 to interview Khieu Samphan, the ceremonial Head of State of the Pol Pot regime and Brother Number Five. The former guerrilla fighter wrote a doctoral thesis in economics at the Sorbonne in 1959, which advocated the evacuation of cities as part of a programme for economic growth. He argued that the 'mass transfer' of the urban population was needed to stimulate food production. It was also necessary to encourage 'self-conscious, autonomous development', which meant closing Cambodia's borders; otherwise the country would be exploited as it was by the French colonialists. Apparently, his professors lavished praise on the thesis.

I met Khieu at his office in the wealthy 16th arrondissement. He was a precise, neat man and wore a suit and tie. He gave me his card.

KHIEU SAMPHAN
Vice President of Democratic Kampuchea in Charge of Foreign Affairs

'I am the Vice President of Democratic Kampuchea,' Khieu told me as we sat down, as if he registered surprise on my face. 'We must fight to liberate our country from the illegal Vietnamese occupation and the puppet government they have installed.' His ritzy office was provided by the United Nations; it officially belonged to the Kampuchean delegation to UNESCO. The regime still held Cambodia's seat at the UN General Assembly and the continued recognition of 'Democratic Kampuchea' allowed the Khmer Rouge to retain access to international resources. Khieu's secretary, Poc Yanine, wore a bun pulled back tightly, an expensive-looking jacket and skirt and a constant smile. She brought us coffee in bone-china cups and a selection of biscuits on an ornate tray.

What about the killing fields? 'What killing fields?' Khieu asked with a smile. 'Have you seen the film? Ah,' he said smugly. 'That story is propaganda from the Vietnamese.' But what about the mass graves? 'How do you know who killed those people and whose bones they are?' he asked. My meeting with Khieu Samphan was the first of a series of meetings with Khmer Rouge leaders, each of which was surreal and freakish, like opening a series of matrushka dolls and finding nothing inside.

During the period that Khieu Samphan commuted on Air France flights between Paris and Bangkok, and then crossed the Thai border into the Khmer Rouge camps, the movement employed classical guerrilla tactics in their war against the government in Phnom Penh.

Typically, they attacked Vietnamese supply convoys and then retreated back into their jungle bases. Trains were also targets; carriages would either be sprayed with bullets or the train would be forced to stop and the passengers executed. In 1989, I travelled on a train journey to Takeo, a city fifty miles south of Phnom Penh, whose surroundings were a Khmer Rouge stronghold. The train was a hand-welded fortress on rails. In front of the engine, an empty flatbed carriage was intended to detonate mines on the track. Another flat carriage had a 50mm gun mounted behind a housing resembling a tank turret the size of a phone booth. The driver's compartment had been sealed up with bullet-proof metal with only a small letterbox opening to see ahead. Each passenger compartment had a machine-gunner in a sandbag emplacement on the roof. There was no buffet car. Attacks on civilians travelling on trains were apparently considered by the outside world as a legitimate part of a liberation war against an occupying force.

The ending of the cold war paved the way for a peace conference and an end to the international isolation of the regime that governed all but small pockets of Cambodia. All the factions involved, including the Khmer Rouge, signed a peace settlement in October 1991 that proposed elections under the supervision of the United Nations. It involved twenty thousand UN troops and officials in the most ambitious operation of its kind. Cambodia rejoined the world after two decades of isolation and war. Businessmen from Singapore and Hong Kong arrived seeking investment opportunities. UN peacekeepers from around the world had $100 a day spending money; restaurants, shops and hotels opened. Prostitutes poured into Phnom Penh from Vietnam and the Cambodian countryside. A whole street was built for brothels bearing signs that offered sex for $10.

On one occasion, I drove through the night to arrive at dawn in what is now Le Royal, the finest hotel in Phnom Penh. Before Cambodia's collapse into darkness, King Sihanouk regularly held banquets in its dining rooms and Charles de Gaulle stayed there during a four-day visit to Cambodia in 1966. When I arrived in 1991 it was called the Sameki and had been allowed to decay for two decades. An old Bakelite phone stood by the bed but didn't work. The freestanding bath, tall ceilings and ornate coving were signs of an opulent, distant past. I'd stayed in the Sameki during earlier trips and on this occasion the hotel seemed little different. Following my gruelling journey from Thailand, I slept for much of the day. At about five o'clock, I woke up as the hotel shook to the sound of the hit single, 'I'm Too Sexy (for my shirt)', by Right Said Fred. I went downstairs and to see what was going on and found that the hotel lobby had been turned into a discothèque. In a scene that made me wonder if I was still dreaming, about twenty girls wearing chiffon baby-doll dresses in pink, light blue and yellow stood by a makeshift bar and ran toward me as if I was a pop star. 'Please dance with me,' they shouted, grabbing at my arms. It was then I knew that Cambodia's isolation was over.

The Khmer Rouge soon realized that Cambodia's incumbent Prime Minister, Hun Sen, who was backed by Vietnam, would maintain control of the security services and hold the levers of power, whatever the result of an election. They withdrew their cooperation and once more retreated into isolation. King Sihanouk's son, Prince Norodom Ranariddh, won the vote but lacked the political guile of Hun Sen, who refused to accept the electoral verdict; a power-share deal was hastily agreed to prevent a renewal of civil war. In 1997, Hun Sen staged a coup that secured his position as Cambodia's 'strongman' and cast Ranariddh into the political wilderness.

After the UN organized elections the Khmer Rouge lost international patronage. They maintained their guerrilla war against the regime in Phnom Penh by mining gems and logging. In 1994, the Khmer Rouge attacked a train near Takeo and captured three tourists from Australia, France and Britain. The men, all in their twenties, were held hostage for three months. Their bodies were discovered, bound and bludgeoned to death, after government soldiers overran a Khmer Rouge were. The attack on the train was then considered an act of terrorism by the West and not part of a liberation struggle. The Khmer Rouge were branded a terrorist organization by the United States in 1995 and its leaders condemned as terrorists.

By now, the movement had become weakened; in 1996, Hun Sen persuaded Brother Number Three, Ieng Sary, the former Foreign Minister, to defect in return for an amnesty. A large section of the Khmer Rouge army simply changed uniforms. I interviewed Ieng Sary shortly after his defection in Pailin, a gem-dealing town near the border with Thailand. He was tall for a Cambodian and wore glasses. He was dressed in a well-pressed safari suit. I met him at Pailin's main primary school, where he called himself Lok Ta, 'grandpa', and addressed the pupils as *khmuoy khmuoy*, 'nephews and nieces'. 'Don't fight with each other,' he urged the children. 'Don't litter the place.

Put it properly in a bin and keep your school tidy. Work hard and help your parents look after younger brothers and sisters.' My first thought was this man was a very caring mass murderer.

The 'killing fields' were nothing to do with him, of course, because he was the Foreign Minister. He was in Beijing when Phnom Penh fell and only arrived back a few days later. 'The minute I set foot on national soil I couldn't find anybody, they were all gone,' he recalled with apparent amazement. 'I asked Pol Pot, "Where is everyone?" He said they had to leave the city, otherwise they'd be killed.' Ieng Sary's mock-puzzlement was hilarious and also sickening.

Ieng Sary had been Pol Pot's friend for almost half a century and they studied in France together. He told me that Pol Pot enjoyed *The History of the Communist Party of the Soviet Union*, by Stalin, which he kept by his side and often reread. When Ieng Sary returned from Paris in 1957, the two were communist militants in Phnom Penh before entering the jungle together in 1963. When the Khmer Rouge took power, Ieng Sary said Pol Pot refused to listen to him. ' "Get on with your work," he told me, "you have your assignment." I was always reconciliatory and did what I was told.' Ieng Sary gave a vulpine performance, posing as old and forgetful, while carefully rescripting his past associations with the one man the world could never forgive.

'How could you miss over a million dead bodies?' I asked. 'And you were Brother Number Three and a permanent member of the powerful Standing Committee of the Communist Party of Kampuchea alongside Pol Pot?'

'Ah,' he explained, 'you must understand. It's different in a democratic regime. In a dictatorship we don't get information. For instance, if they were going to kill someone, we were only told that they were going to be re-educated or "to work in the fields". It was difficult to get a clear indication of what was going on in the country in spite of being a member of the Standing Committee. I was not aware of what was happening.'

He said he was Brother Number Five, not Three. 'Khieu Samphan was the third member,' he told me. He'd been demoted. Did he have any regrets? 'Yes, I regret the fact that I never knew what was going on.' And how did he think he'll be remembered? 'I think I'll be remembered as a man who loved peace, unity and national reconciliation. This is the image of myself that I will leave to the younger generation.'

Several former Khmer Rouge leaders continued to live in peaceful retirement in Pailin. Once a Khmer Rouge stronghold, in 1997 it raised the flag of a unified Cambodia. Former Khmer Rouge commanders still controlled the city but gave their loyalty to Hun Sen. In a dusty side street, opposite Ieng Sary's home, was the house of the former head of state, Khieu Samphan. He portrayed himself as having been a figurehead, restricted to a leadership compound during the Khmer Rouge regime. He, too, said he knew nothing of atrocities, which he claimed were committed by Pol Pot alone. He later wrote his memoirs, which became a bestseller among his former victims.

In April 1998, Pol Pot died, aged seventy-three, in suspicious circumstances in the jungles of northern Cambodia. He had been betrayed and arrested, and possibly murdered by his small remaining band of followers. Photographs of his body showed a frail man, whose grey hair had been blackened for the funeral ceremony. He was dressed in a blue shirt and navy trousers. To the end, Pol Pot showed no regret for or even recognition of the suffering he had caused. 'Everything I did, I did for my country,' he declared a few months before his death. 'Look at me, am I a savage person?' he asked the American reporter, Nate Thayer, in the only interview he granted for nearly two decades. He continued to believe that the Vietnamese had planned to invade and destroy Cambodia. 'My conscience is clear. Without our struggle there would be no Cambodia today.' Pol Pot's cremation site, in a jungle clearing on a mountainside north of the Angkor temples, is as bizarre and bewildering as his life. Amongst his ashes were beer cans and cigarette ends, as well as the toilet that he used during his final days. The government planned to turn it into a tourist attraction.

In 1999, the Khmer Rouge finally disbanded and the US State Department removed the movement from its list of foreign terrorist organizations. For four years, the leaders of the Khmer Rouge were wanted terrorists but no one was very interested in arresting them. Only two former Khmer Rouge officials were detained by the regime: Ta Mok, a one-legged regional commander nicknamed the Butcher, and Duch, the warden of the notorious S-21 prison.

In the latter decades of the twentieth century, extrajudicial killings by a state were not usually considered acts of terrorism. It remained more comfortable to define a terrorist as a man or woman without uniform and without a state. Most commentators did not describe Khmer Rouge leaders as terrorists while they governed Cambodia because of a distinction in meaning that Bruce Hoffman observed in the 1970s: 'state-sanctioned acts of *internal* political violence directed mostly against domestic populations are generally termed "terror" in order to distinguish that phenomenon from "terrorism", which is understood to be committed by non-state entities.'*

Right-wing military dictatorships in Latin America were often described in the news media as using death squads to impose terror on their own citizens, while Palestinian groups were said to be engaged in terrorism. The 'war on terror' has, however, overridden this distinction. The Bush administration repeatedly referred to the 'terrorist' regime of Saddam Hussein and admonished Iraq for committing 'acts of terrorism' against its own people. The flip side has also entered accepted usage. 'Terror' has become the weapon of non-state entities, such as al-Qa'eda.

On September 11th, 2001, I returned to Pailin. When I watched the hijacked planes bring down the World Trade Center on satellite television, I had just completed an interview with a man who had brought terror into every nerve and sinew of eight million people. He had also been involved in the killing of hundreds of thousands of civilians, dwarfing Osama bin Laden as the architect of mass murder, and yet was not termed a terrorist. Noun Chea was Brother Number Two, Deputy General Secretary of the Communist Party and Pol Pot's loyal deputy for nearly three decades.

I met Nuon Chea in a traditional wooden house on stilts that he lived in with his wife and grandchildren near the border with Thailand. He offered me water, a slice of jackfruit and some bananas, plucked from trees on land surrounding his modest home. Nuon Chea believed that he had acted in the interests of his nation despite the annihilation of nearly a quarter of the population. Did he terrorize the population? No, he said he only wanted to discover and eliminate traitors who were trying to destroy his nation. He was frail, but alert. His mind remained sharp. He seemed keen to see me: 'I want to show my people that I am a good man,' he declared without irony.

While he could have been accused of terrorism for sanctioning the

---

* *Inside Terrorism*, 1998.

guerrilla movement's attacks on the Phnom Penh regime following the elections organized by the UN, he was much more commonly accused of genocide and war crimes for his role in government. But even here, political language has a tendency to fail when it uses judgemental words to categorize violence. When I asked Noun Chea about the charges against him, he response was artful. 'I don't understand how I could be guilty of either war crimes or genocide,' he said, feigning bemusement. 'Please explain to me: What are war crimes? War crimes mean that we've waged war against another country. We haven't. And genocide? We never had any reason to wipe out our own race. Those I am accused of killing were Cambodian, just like me.'

He punctuated his answers with a smug, self-satisfying chuckle. It didn't matter that the questions were about mass murder, torture or the annihilation of nearly a quarter of the Cambodian nation. They still brought a smile to his lips and a chortle or two. 'Good humour is in my nature,' he told me. He then taunted those who wanted to bring him to justice. 'If they have evidence to convict me, then that's fine by me. I am now seventy-six, how long can they imprison me? If they jail me for twenty years, then I will be ninety-six.' Another wheezy, nasal laugh.

Nuon Chea was Pol Pot's chief ideologue and in charge of 're-education' during the government of the Khmer Rouge. 'We purified their minds,' he told me, referring to the daily propaganda lessons that everyone was forced to attend at gunpoint. 'Firstly, we educated them in lessons and secondly by sending them to work in the fields.' Nuon Chea still believed that mankind could be treated as a scientific experiment; turning Cambodia into a gigantic labour camp was the right policy for the time. 'We used collectivization to build up our economy. We nurtured the idea that people should love working in order to build up the country.' He then made a remarkable assertion: 'Doing agricultural work gave people enough food to eat.'

'But at least a million people died of malnutrition or overwork,' I pointed out, barely able to prevent the interview collapsing into a ghoulish, burlesque comedy. 'Were you not aware of that? You were, after all, the second most powerful man in Cambodia at the time.'

'I know that some people died of starvation but that was beyond our capacity to solve.' He leant toward me, as if to offer a genuine glance into his soul. 'We tried our best but it was out of the control of our Party. How many people died, no one knows. Some say 1.7 million, but they don't have statistics, they just say it.' He laughed again.

'There are mass graves around Cambodia, killing fields, who are in those graves?' I asked him.

He raised a finger and nodded. 'That's a good question. I do not know who they are because the situation was very chaotic. During the war, we didn't know how many were killed. There could have been people who died of starvation, but how many, we don't know.'

He did make an admission: a professional oversight that he was responsible for. 'I was not responsible for *ordering* anything, but I have a moral responsibility; I am sorry that I wasn't close enough to the work.' He moved closer as if to confide a secret. 'You see, Pol Pot was the Party Secretary. I was just Deputy Secretary and sometimes I had no influence. You must understand how the Standing Committee of the Communist Party worked.' He laughed and I had to laugh with him. The whole interview was absurd; a game played on the graves of millions.

Nuon Chea added that through his endeavours in the Communist Party he had sacrificed his own life for the betterment of the Cambodian people: 'We dared to give up our lives to protect our nation. Otherwise our nation would have disappeared and our people would have encountered hardship.'

The Governor of S-21, under arrest in Phnom Penh, has apparently said that Nuon Chea took direct control over the execution site towards the end of 1978, and gave him instructions on how to deal with new prisoners: 'Don't bother to interrogate them, just kill them.' Noun Chea looked baffled when I put that to him. 'I am not cruel. I never gave such an answer, because I have the heart of a creator, not a destroyer,' he mused.

He displayed no remorse. He even boasted that his conscience was clear. 'I have never stayed awake at night or shed any tears. I am just an ordinary person. When my parents died I was also sorry. When my people died I am sorry too.'

Nuon Chea had reason to be confident when I saw him. While Slobodan Milošović had been taken to the dock amid fanfare at The Hague, the United Nations and the Cambodian government had been bickering for nearly a decade over the make-up and control of a war-crimes tribunal that could bring him and his accomplices to court.

It took a quarter of a century for the United Nations to even consider bringing the Khmer Rouge leaders to account. They were treated as statesmen at peace accords in Paris in 1991. For a decade after the killing fields were discovered, the UN recognized the Khmer Rouge as part of the legitimate government of Cambodia. China armed it throughout the 1980s, despite full knowledge of the mass killing. The outside world had ample opportunity to arrest Pol Pot, Nuon Chea and their accomplices in the past. At one time the Royal Thai Police, with the full knowledge of Western governments, escorted Pol Pot, wearing Hawaiian shirt and sunglasses, to the beaches of Thailand's southern coast. The Thais guarded and controlled Pol Pot's movements until his death. Why? Pol Pot was useful as a stick to threaten the Cambodian government, which was backed by its regional rival Vietnam. The West's global rival, the Soviet Union, in turn, had backed Vietnam.

Several powers, including China and the United States, could be embarrassed by a war-crimes tribunal that re-examined Cambodia's past. It would raise many more allegations than the guilt of a few senior leaders of the Khmer Rouge. Nuon Chea would claim that while many died of starvation during his rule, the most culpable murderer was the then US Secretary of State, Henry Kissinger, who ordered the secret bombing of Cambodia, killing perhaps hundreds of thousands of civilians.

The problems that have hampered attempts to bring Pol Pot's henchmen to justice represented the first serious setback to the process of establishing ad hoc tribunals, which began in the former Yugoslavia and continued in Rwanda and Sierra Leone. Despite the approval by the Cambodian Parliament of a proposal in 2004 to establish a tribunal, Noun Chea and his former colleagues continued their peaceful retirement. While all sides maintained the ritual of preparing for a tribunal, I suspect that most secretly wished that the increasingly fragile Khmer Rouge leadership would simply pass away of natural causes.

The debacle in Cambodia revealed an obvious problem; ad hoc tribunals only apply selective justice. In the 1990s, however, it all seemed very different. The tribunals appeared as part of a formidable trend toward a system of international justice in which despots and tyrants would no longer shelter behind sovereign impunity. In addition, national courts began applying universal jurisdiction, as in the case of the former Chilean President, Augusto Pinochet, when a Spanish judge sought his extradition for crimes against Spanish citizens in Chile.

The momentum towards a universal law found expression in the setting up of an International Criminal Court (ICC). In 1998, the world's governments gathered in Rome to adopt the treaty creating global jurisdiction over war crimes, crimes against humanity and genocide. One prominent government has refused to sign the Rome Statute: the United States. In order to wage its 'war on terror', the Bush administration has done everything possible to obstruct the workings of the ICC. The American Servicemembers' Protection Act 2001 forbids Americans from cooperating with the court and authorizes the President to "use all means necessary and appropriate to bring about the release from captivity' of US personnel or other parties held by the ICC against their will. The US suspended aid to dozens of countries that had not signed deals to grant American soldiers immunity from prosecution for war crimes. Washington has concluded bilateral agreements with nearly a hundred nations to secure exemption for US troops and other personnel.

The 'war on terror' has changed the international legal landscape and legitimized the use of military tribunals to pursue justice, rather than international, civilian courts. There is now a 'world' army, led by America, fighting against evil, rather than a global policeman fighting for justice.

From their origins in Nuremberg, ad hoc tribunals have been accused of applying 'victor's justice', a charge that Slobodan Milošović made about his trial at The Hague. However strong that argument may be, another is incontestable: while the legal proceedings might be impartial, these courts apply justice only when it suits the political needs of the major powers, usually the United States. In 1995, Milošović was presented as a world statesman and peacemaker at Dayton, Ohio, during the signing of the accord that ended the wars in Bosnia and Croatia. Yet the indictments that will probably convict him refer to atrocities that occurred prior to Dayton and of which Western nations were fully aware. At the time, he was considered politically useful by the same governments that later encouraged his prosecution.

Perhaps the 1990s will appear as an anomaly, a moment after the cold war when foreign policy flirted with morality. After September 11th, the United States reverted to its former logic, dividing the world into those who are with America and the 'axis of evil' opposing it. As the sole military superpower, America can impose a definition of 'terrorism' or 'war crime' upon the world.

Nuon Chea shares Milošović's opinion that war-crimes tribunals represent 'victor's justice'. He has kept faith with a Marxist analysis of power structures: 'When they win, they are in power and they define right and wrong their way. That's life.' He would also contend that the definition of a terrorist lies in the hands of the powerful rather than the righteous. Perhaps there is more truth in what Noun Chea is saying than we should be comfortable with.

8 / TERROR AND DEMOCRACY

'Terrorism is not defeated with wars.'
José Luis Rodríguez Zapatero,
Prime Minister of Spain, March 2004

It was a custom in the Basque town of Durango, in northern Spain, to share a drink with friends before lunch on a Sunday afternoon. Several would enjoy a shot of the sweet dark red local liqueur, *patxaran*, made from anisette and sloe berries. Amongst the drinkers one summer's day was Jesús Maria Pedrosa, a councillor from Spain's governing Popular Party. His wife, Carmen, was at home preparing lunch for the family, which included their two grown-up daughters, Ainhoa and Estibaliz. 'He went to Mass at eleven o'clock, then he used to go for a little walk and perhaps call in at the *batzoki* on his way home.' A *batzoki* is a uniquely Basque institution; a social club and bar run by the largest party in the region, where people meet to informally chat about politics and local concerns.

Pedrosa was a jovial man who enjoyed political banter. He also enjoyed his food; he had a well-rounded physique and jowls that shook when he laughed. He was known around Durango simply as 'Jesús Mari'. 'He usually came home around one thirty.' It was just after one o'clock when he began his walk home, along one of Durango's busiest streets. Along the route, graffiti on the walls of a shop declared support for ETA, the militant Basque independence movement: *Gora ETA!* (Long live ETA!) it screamed. That afternoon, two ETA commandos were following Jesús Mari. A car pulled up beside him. A man leapt out, walked up to him and fired a single fatal shot into the back of his head.

'I was listening to the radio when the programme, a sports programme, was interrupted by a news flash,' Carmen Pedrosa told me
four months after her husband's death. 'The radio announcer said that
a Popular Party councillor had been murdered in Fray Juan de Zumár-
raga. I knew it was him even before they gave his name. I knew from
the details and the time. It must have been about 1.20 p.m.' Carmen
recalled that morning as if it was still a dream. Her words were slow
and deliberate. 'I rang my elder daughter and said, "Come home,
because I think it's Dad." My younger daughter came in from outside,
she saw that I was upset and I had to sit down because my legs were
trembling. It was then that we heard his name on the radio. That's
how we found out.'

Jesús Maria Pedrosa was the 773rd victim of ETA's violent campaign for an independent Basque nation. As a councillor he was
considered a target simply because he belonged to the party of the
Spanish government. Shortly after Carmen heard her husband's death
announced on the radio, the phone rang. It was ETA. 'We had three
calls, one after the other,' she told me. 'They said, "The bastard is
already dead", or "Now he's faced the squad." They said the same
thing each time.' Carmen had not been able to come to terms with his
death and still needed regular psychiatric counselling. She was haunted
by one thought in particular. 'I'm sure that the person who pointed
the finger at my husband is from here, someone I know. I don't know
who, but I'm sure they are from Durango.'

Durango is at the geographical heart of the Spanish Basque
Country. It lies amongst rolling hills, jagged rocks and forests, a little
over half an hour's drive from the port city of Bilbao. Founded by
the King of Navarre in the thirteenth century, Durango was heavily
bombed in the Spanish Civil War (1936–39), along with the nearby
town of Gernika, by units from Hitler's Condor Legion. The horror
was captured by Picasso in his dramatic *Guernica*.

Unlike Wales or Scotland, the Basque Country does not exist on
an international map. It is a region inland from the Bay of Biscay that
includes the south-western tip of France and the north-western corner
of Spain. Over two million people in Spain and a quarter of a million
in France regard themselves as Basque. They are probably the oldest
surviving European race and their language is distinct from all other
tongues. ETA is the Basque-language acronym for Euzkadi ta Azkatasuna, or Basque Homeland and Freedom. The movement was formed

in 1959 by students opposed to the Spanish dictator, General Franco. They opted to meet Franco's repression of Basque language and culture with armed struggle. ETA's first high-profile killing was in 1973, blowing up the car of Franco's Prime Minister and heir to his dictatorship, Admiral Luis Carrero Blanco. When Franco died two years later, Spain moved towards democracy and Europe. The Basque Country was granted significant autonomy and some ETA members put down their guns. Another faction continued with its demand for the right to choose full independence.

In Durango, one in four voters chose a party that sympathized with ETA. Of its twenty-one council seats, the Madrid-based Popular Party and the Socialists had a combined total of seven councillors; this roughly reflected the proportion of the region's voters who considered their nationality as Spanish. Carmen Pedrosa told me that she was Spanish, but also thought of herself as Basque in the sense of having a regional identity such as being from Yorkshire or Texas. Basque nationalist parties won the other two-thirds of the seats and their supporters believed that they are solely Basque and want independence from Spain and France. The majority voted for the Basque Nationalist Party, the most powerful political force in the region. It believed that independence should be achieved through peaceful and democratic means. The remaining five councillors belonged to a party called Batasuna, meaning 'Unity', which supported ETA's independence policies. Its members were not involved in violence, although it 'understood' the need for an armed struggle. Their relationship was similar to that in Northern Ireland between Sinn Fein and the Irish Republican Army. There was little doubt in my mind that some members of Batasuna had links with the gunmen but the organization had the structure and policies of a political party.

The chair where Jesús Maria Pedrosa once sat remained empty when I visited the council chamber after his murder. The other councillors from the Popular Party had round-the-clock armed protection. Pedrosa had refused to take a bodyguard; he said it would have interfered too much with his life. Juanjo Gaztañazatorre had been a close friend; he and Pedrosa had represented the Popular Party on Durango council for thirteen years. 'Those ETA scum, those murderers always go straight for their target,' he told me, shaking with anger. 'Seeing his body on the street was terrible, unimaginable. I know the risk we run, but I never imagined they'd kill Pedrosa.'

Juanjo had two bodyguards assigned to him whenever he left the house. His car was changed every day, and the chassis was checked for bombs before each trip. His weekend cottage had already been fire-bombed by ETA. After Pedrosa's death, the police found a number of documents in a flat used by ETA bomb-makers. One was a list with Juanjo's name on it. There were press photographs, details of his address, telephone numbers and so on. It was understandable that he never seemed relaxed; he stole quick, jerky glances and at times looked like a nervous wreck. A few years earlier, effigies of the two Popular Party councillors were discovered hanging from trees in the town. Inside a makeshift noose, their names were written on the faces. Underneath, the accusation 'You are not innocent!' Another poster campaign followed: *Asesino!* (Murderer!) it shouted over pictures of Juanjo and Pedrosa. The accusations referred to the use of death squads by a former government in Madrid during a secret campaign to assassinate suspected ETA commandos. Every week, supporters of Batasuna marched through Durango. 'They pass in front of my house,' Juanjo told me bitterly, 'and they chant, "Gaztañazatorre, murderer, Gaztañazatorre, jailor", when I haven't killed or imprisoned anyone. My life is one of constant uncertainty, imagining that an attack is around the corner. It's living without living, if you know what I mean. It's frightening, horrible.'

Every month, Juanjo attended a council meeting and his seat was next to those allocated to Batasuna. He neither spoke to them nor acknowledged their presence. 'I know for sure they agree with murder. It isn't very pleasant sitting next to someone who, in a way, is responsible for the death of my friend, Pedrosa.' While the council discussed routine matters such as planning permissions or road works, the question of national identity was never far from the agenda. Batasuna councillors conducted town-hall business in Basque while Juanjo spoke only Spanish. They were neighbours in one small town but each insisted they lived in a different country.

Jabi Arbeo was the senior councillor for Batasuna. 'I had a good relationship with Pedrosa on a personal level,' he told me, 'but on a political level, his views were not just against my views, but against my very identity.' Jabi (pronounced *Haby*) was in his early forties but dressed younger; he had spiky hair and an earring. I discovered that this was the common, grungy uniform of most Batasuna activists. Jabi refused to condemn ETA, believing that a political deadlock had made murder necessary. 'What can be achieved by denouncing and blaming? Nothing. The Popular Party makes political capital from public condemnations. We think that the key to the conflict must be found.' The Spanish government repeatedly refused to enter into any dialogue that addressed the underlying issue of sovereignty. It also maintained that it is unthinkable for a democratic regime to negotiate with men of violence. Jabi regarded that as sufficient justification for ETA to wage an armed struggle.

'Why is Juanjo Gaztañazatorre a legitimate target of ETA?' I asked. 'Well, I am not an ETA member. I'm not the one who defines the targets of the organization. You should ask ETA,' came the disingenuous response. 'I am just a politician that works in Durango. I don't know what their strategy is or why they decide things. Who knows?'

Once Jabi lost his guise, part of a tradition of secrecy and deceit that Batasuna members adopted in order to stay out of jail, he proved himself to be an eloquent and thoughtful politician. Would he describe ETA members as terrorists? Of course not, he told me, they are *gudariak*, a Basque word used to describe soldiers who defended their homeland from invaders during past centuries. 'The question is what it means to be a terrorist,' he explained. 'For instance, Arafat was a terrorist until a few years ago. Now he is not a terrorist any more, but a high-ranking political leader and all the politicians talk to him. The question of who is a terrorist depends on who writes the history books. In Spain, during Franco's times, it was very well defined who were the good guys and who were the bad guys. And what's the truth now? We find it is just the opposite. Franco was the bad guy.' Jabi was comfortable with this debate. 'From a historical point of view, there have been armed movements in many places. There was an armed movement in the United States during the reign of George III. They fought against the British. And we could question their legitimacy, because none of them was a native of the United States. In the end they achieved independence. Surely, the secretaries and historians of George III didn't see the matter in the same way? George III probably said that they were terrorists. Over time, that view of them as terrorists is lost.'

Two months before I visited Durango, two ETA commandos from the town died when a bomb exploded prematurely as they were carrying it toward their target. They were in their early twenties. The ETA bomb-makers used to be regulars at a bar that was only a short

walk from Carmen Pedrosa's home. It was a social club run by
Batasuna, known as an *herriko taberna*, or 'popular bar'. Outside,
poster-size pictures of the dead ETA bombers, Urko and Aranba, were
draped from windows. Inside, stickers supporting the armed organization were plastered on walls and above the bar was a wood carving
of ETA's symbol: a snake, which represents cunning, wrapped around
an axe, the symbol of strength. Photographs of ETA prisoners from
Durango hung on the walls.

Jabi introduced me to Ana, Urko's long-time partner. She was in
her early twenties and spoke good English. She was shaking as she lit
one cigarette after another. 'Urko was a normal boy, very caring. He
was a hero.' Tears welled up in her eyes as she showed me pictures of
the happy times they had together. The rest of Spain call him a
terrorist, I said, and he died while trying to plant a bomb. 'He was not
a terrorist. He was a freedom fighter. He was a soldier who died while
fighting for his country,' Ana went on angrily. 'What right have the
Spanish got to be here, to tell me I'm Spanish when I'm not? They are
to blame for his death. They are to blame for Pedrosa's death. Both
sides are suffering while the Spanish government will not try to find a
solution to the problem here.'

While it is true that Spanish democracy is vibrant and healthy,
Madrid refuses to even contemplate a referendum on the future status
of the Basque Country. And while Spain, as well as France, refuses to
discuss independence, the logic of an armed struggle finds support
amongst the committed.

Urko and Aranba were driving along a street in Bilbao late at night
when their car was vaporized by the power of the explosion. No one I
spoke to knew where they were planning to plant the bomb. When
Jabi heard the news, he took Urko's mother to identify the remains.
'Physically, I started to cry,' he told me. 'On a psychological level, I
thought: "Why?" And you think "Why?" many times, and the answer
comes on its own: because there is a conflict. Here, the existence of
a country is denied, the existence of a nation, and from that denial a
conflict arises.'

The bar was full of young people, mostly under thirty. The air was
thick with marijuana smoke. The bar reflected a wider mood of
defiance in Basque society, a subculture that had captured and politicized the region's youth. The Basque regional government had won
significant local powers in democratic Spain, including running the

education system. Basque was a dead language under Franco's suppression; now a generation had grown up speaking Basque as their mother tongue.

Amongst the drinkers were two young students from the university in nearby Bilbao. Ainhoa and her friend Nekane were part of the Haika, or Rise Up, movement, which sympathized with the actions of ETA. They were quiet, pretty girls; on most of Europe's campuses, I doubted whether they would have become involved in political rebellion. It was different in the Basque Country. 'We are involved in a fight to break the links that we have with the Spanish state. Why do I have a Spanish identity card, saying that I am Spanish, if I'm not?' said nineteen-year-old Ainhoa. The Haika movement was motivated by a fear that the Basque nation could become forgotten unless the outside world is made to listen. 'If we don't fight, some day they will bring about the end of our country,' Nekane said deliberately. She believed that murder and bombing can be morally acceptable if they are part of a campaign to end what she saw as a greater injustice. 'There is also killing and suffering on our side as a result of what's happening. The Basque Country is suffering because they are trying to destroy it. It's not just personal suffering, but the suppression of the language and a general repression, which is getting worse and worse.'

I found little evidence of any repression of Basque culture, language or identity, despite the Spanish government's often clunky efforts to combat ETA. It felt more like the remarkable resurrection of a national identity. The problem was the rising pace of expectations. It was no longer a question of Basques demanding more regional power or a greater emphasis on their culture. Thousands of young people had grown up believing they were Basque and no longer understood why they carried a Spanish passport. I left the *herriko taberna* and walked back to my car, passing the flat where I had met Carmen Pedrosa. In less than five minutes, I had walked from one world to another and even crossed national boundaries.

I later travelled with Nekane and Ainhoa to one of the weekend camps that Haika organized, combining a strong political message with entertainment. Several thousand congregated in Bayonne in France, though for them it was simply the north Basque Country. Rebellion was deeply rooted in youth culture here and it was part of the strategy of Haika to provoke confrontations with the police. By early afternoon, Haika members were throwing rocks at the riot police.

They had 'taken over' a few narrow streets near the river and erected barricades. The police responded with tear gas and there were dozens of arrests. Confrontation was routine for Haika members, a duty to challenge the authority of states they do not recognize. It is not a coincidence that at anti-globalization rallies in Europe, the Basque flag is a regular sight.

The highlight of the weekend camp was a rock concert. The main act was a band that fused heavy metal and punk, featuring songs such as 'Let's Fight until Victory'. The lead singer, wearing a T-shirt emblazoned with a print of 'Che' Guevara, screamed, 'I was born in the middle of a battle, rage and fury were my parents.' The audience joined with the chorus: 'Let's fight courageously night and day, let's fight fiercely our enemies.' As the drummer pounded the beat, the crowd shouted, 'ETA! ETA! ETA!' in time. The Spanish government accused Haika of being a recruiting ground for ETA commandos. They were probably right. Most of the young people at the camp understood why some young men and women joined the militants. 'Since they were born there has been a conflict and if they have that willingness to fight, they will know what to do. It's an individual choice,' Nekane said.

Jabi Arbeo has watched this new generation emerge, from whose ranks men and women in their late teens and early twenties have decided to join ETA. 'The young people themselves are the ones who decide to enter the armed struggle. They do it at a very young age. And if they take up arms, there is no room for regrets,' he said, shrugging his shoulders as if it was inevitable. 'It could be anyone's son or daughter.'

It was impossible in my mind to equate the death of Jesús Maria Pedrosa, killed by a stranger, with that of Urko, a man who was carrying a bomb when he perished. Yet it was also impossible not to recognize a political dynamic that the governments of Spain, France and indeed the rest of Europe refused to acknowledge. By dismissing men like Urko as terrorists the cause of a crisis that produced people prepared to kill and to die for their nationhood was simply never understood by the rest of Spain.

ETA had been included in the US State Department's list of foreign terrorist groups since 1996, but after Prime Minister José Maria Aznar committed Spanish troops to the Anglo-American alliance that invaded Iraq, he had an important favour to ask President Bush. In March

2003, Spain's Supreme Court banned Batasuna in response to a government request, ruling that the party was an extension of ETA. It was the first time since the death of Franco that a political party had been banned in Spain. The Interior Minister declared that Spain had 'eradicated ETA's political party from our democracy to the benefit of the freedom of many and the human rights of all Spaniards.' Two months later, George W. Bush added Batasuna to the list of terrorist groups, announcing that the United States had 'taken steps to cut off financing for the Batasuna organization . . . We believe that the people of Spain, like everywhere, have a right to live free from terror.' A month after that, the European Union followed. Batasuna attempted to reincarnate itself using different names, such as Herritarren Zerrenda (People's List coalition), but the Spanish courts repeatedly outlawed the newly formed movements even though the People's List was legitimate in France.

There is a commonly held belief that a movement has a legitimate right to take up arms if a regime deprives it of basic human rights. No such claim can exist in a modern democracy. In Europe, for example, there are sufficient ways to redress grievances and bloodshed can never again be justified: the argument runs that political violence cannot be accepted in a country that has a democratic government, and those who bomb and kill cannot be called 'freedom fighters'.

Jabi Arbeo didn't accept that argument. I met him for lunch at a restaurant in the mountains overlooking Durango. He hadn't yet been labelled a terrorist by the Bush administration or the European Union but he saw it coming. 'What's in a name?' he joked. 'It's the idea that matters and they can't make the thoughts in your head illegal.' When Batasuna was listed as a terrorist organization, he and his former colleagues continued holding meetings under different names.

The passion that Basques hold for their culture and identity is matched only by their love of food. The Mendi Goikoa restaurant, roughly meaning 'The Mountain Above', was Jabi's favourite. It was set on the slopes of Mount Amboto, one the tallest peaks in the region. The building was renovated from an eighteenth-century country house to recreate the romanticized rural life of the old Basque Country. 'I would like to ask a question,' Jabi said. 'What is a nation? What do you need to be a nation? A language, a culture, your own history. We've got that! What do the Lithuanian people have that we don't? Or the Czechs? We've got everything!' I had already had dinner with several Batasuna members and I discovered that eating traditional Basque food was a necessary ritual of acceptance. Few visitors were despised as much as foreign journalists who scoffed at traditional Basque dishes in favour of healthier nouvelle cuisine. I was heartily praised by one Batasuna leader for enjoying a large plate of squid, cooked in its own – uniquely Basque – black ink. The squid was stuffed with its own tentacles and dressed in a pitch-black sauce. Traditional recipes thickened the sauce with animal's blood but, on this occasion, I asked as few questions as possible. It had a pleasantly musky flavour, which was helped when I washed it down with several shots of *patxaran* liquor. At the mountain lodge, Jabi insisted on ordering a traditional rustic dish and, when he suggested grilled beef, it sounded fine. When the food arrived, blood oozed from the meat as if it still had a pulse. It was tasty and tender but seemed at times too literal a backdrop for our discussion concerning political violence in a democracy. In Jabi's view, the argument depended upon where the democratic boundary was drawn. 'Democracy is defined in Spain by the Spanish Constitution,' he told me. 'If you don't accept the Spanish Constitution you are not democratic. But in the Basque Country, there is a clear lack of democracy. The majority would vote for independence and we are being deprived that democratic right.'

It was a nineteenth-century Governor of Massachusetts, Elbridge Gerry, who has given his name to a practice that undermines democracy. He is said to have drawn up a district map of the United States. A cartoonist then satirized the shape of one electoral region by adding a head, wings and claws and declaring, 'That will do for a salamander.' Another retorted, 'Gerrymander.' A word was born that refers to a practice of manipulating electoral districts unfairly in order to secure disproportionate representation. I first came across the word, not in the US, but in a small town in Ireland.

Cootehill was established as a Georgian colonial settlement long before a mostly arbitrary border was slung along the edge of town separating the sovereign nations of the United Kingdom and the Republic of Ireland. Cootehill nestled amidst the rolling Drumlin hills of County Cavan, a part of the Irish Republic despite being within the historical province of Ulster. It was an elderly man in the town who dismissed the border as a work of 'gerrymandering to please the Planters'.

At the time, I was barely out of my teens and I needed more

explanation. The partition of Ireland had its roots in a plan devised by the Prime Minister, Lloyd George, in 1920. It was intended as a compromise to resolve the multiplying political problems that were brewing in Ireland following the Easter Rising in 1916. Lloyd George conceded a measure of Home Rule to the twenty-six counties that later made up the Republic of Ireland, and imposed another status on the six counties that became Northern Ireland. It was intended to placate the pro-British Protestants in the north who vehemently opposed an independent Ireland with a Catholic majority.

The Protestant population in Northern Ireland frequently referred to their province as Ulster, but that had nine counties, including the now separated Cavan, Donegal and Monaghan. The line that divided north from south was drawn in order to create a contiguous region that included the majority of Ireland's Protestants. In consequence, Northern Irish Catholics were destined to become a permanent minority and their campaign for civil rights and an end to discrimination led to the rebirth of the Irish Republican Army in 1969 and three decades of political violence.

The old man who dismissed the border as a shoddy piece of gerrymandering was called Fergus. As a child he had witnessed a decade of violence from 1916 that set Irishman against Irishman. He blamed the strife on English colonists who confiscated Irish land and established the Ulster Plantation in the seventeenth century. It encouraged waves of Protestant Scottish and English settlers to make Ireland their home while committing their loyalty to the English and Scottish crown. 'It's the Planters' fault,' he sighed.

Main Street in Cootehill seemed to lead nowhere. But it was the focal point for the evening. I was sitting in a cavernous pub that stretched back into the smoke as far as the eye was able to see. A row of young girls were dancing the jig; old men in flat caps and reddened faces smiled with a jumble of teeth, many of them missing. It reinforced every stereotypical image I had of Ireland. In 1979, Cootehill was poor compared to its neighbour a few miles across the border. The pub's stove was coal-fired. The young men wore shabby jackets that were too big.

It was obligatory for the visitor to drink Guinness. The atmosphere was fiercely Republican. I was from 'across the water', but my Welsh roots meant I was, at least, not the hated English. It was still light as the summer sunshine clung long into the evenings. The bartop TV was turned on and the music suddenly died. The landlord shouted that everyone should listen to the news. The headlines from Irish television from Dublin were sombre; eighteen British soldiers had died in an ambush at Narrow Water, near Warren Point. Lord Mountbatten, the Queen's cousin, was also dead, murdered by the IRA. Mountbatten had been on holiday at his castle in County Sligo. He took his fourteen-year-old grandson and a local teenaged boy onto his boat. All three died in an explosion.

After watching the report in silence, the bar erupted in loud cheering. Fergus next to me clinked my glass and with a broad smile took a huge gulp, spilling stout over his chin. The Provisional IRA had used, for the first time, remotely controlled bombs which were detonated by a radio frequency from across the border. The British army had been lured into an elaborate trap. A huge bomb, almost a thousand pounds in weight, had been hidden behind hay bales on the side of the road.

As the army convoy passed by, the IRA detonated the bomb and gunmen opened fire from an overlooking hilltop across the border. When the first bomb went off, six soldiers died immediately. During the next half-hour, army Land Rovers arrived at the scene, as the shooting continued from the Irish Republic with the British army returning fire. The soldiers who survived the first bomb had taken up a position behind a nearby wall. The trap was set; behind the wall another bomb was hidden. As a helicopter took off with injured soldiers the second bomb exploded, killing a dozen more.

In Cootehill, the television had been switched off and a nationalist ballad was blaring, distortedly, through overworked speakers. The song was dedicated to James Connolly, a leader of the Easter Rising executed by a British firing squad.

> God's curse on you, England, you cruel-hearted monster,
> Your deeds would shame all the devils in Hell,
> There were no flowers blooming but the Shamrock is growing
> On the grave of James Connolly, the Irish rebel.

Fergus was in his seventies, at least, and was now drinking whiskey. He leaned over and asked where I was from. 'Wales,' I said. 'Ah,' he said, 'you never fought the English as you should have done. They've colonized your mind.' He then gave a lecture on Irish history, through whiskey breath and the simple logic that alcohol can make so seductive. 'Irish independence began with the Phoenix Park murders in 1882, when the new British Viceroy and his under-secretary were killed by volunteers armed with long amputating knives,' he chuckled, passing his hand over their imaginary sharp edges. The 'volunteer' assassins in Phoenix Park played a part in persuading Gladstone's government that British rule in Ireland was untenable.

By this time, a group of young men at the bar started their own song; the lyrics were handed out by a girl with a round, jolly face who gave a small song sheet into my hand. I found the crumpled paper amongst my belongings a quarter of a century later.

> Go home, British soldiers, go on home
> Have you got no fucking homes of your own?
> For eight hundred years we've fought you without fear
> And we will fight you for eight hundred more.
> So fuck your Union Jack, we want our country back
> We want to see old Ireland free once more.

'James Connolly, Michael Collins,' continued Fergus, 'these are the heroes of Ireland.' In the autumn of 1920, Michael Collins, with his band of 'Twelve Apostles', assassinated fourteen British officers. The British resolve was finally broken and a truce was soon arranged. Negotiations led to the formation of the Irish Republic in 1922. If Fergus had told me his definition of a terrorist, it might be this: 'Terrorist: *n* Name given to persons who use violence against political foes but who fail to achieve political change, preventing them becoming national heroes or leaders of revolutionary governments.'

Two days later I went to Warren Point. The road ran parallel to Carlingford Lough, a green monument scooped and moulded by a giant hand from the Irish Sea. It would have been a popular tourist destination if it hadn't cast its shadow over what was then one of the most dangerous borders in the world. The road was closed at Narrow Water. A policeman from the Royal Ulster Constabulary, with an automatic rifle over his bullet-proof vest, gestured that I must turn around. Death was still being cleared up and the unpredictable judgement of history awaited.

A few years later, I joined the BBC in Northern Ireland. My rookie enthusiasm soon became mired in disappointment. The news reporters whom I worked alongside in Belfast were meticulous and fair but there was a substantial dose of self-censorship. There was an acute awareness of a red line that should not be crossed and if there were any doubts, editorial advice from management was sought. It was a culture that didn't exist for BBC journalists covering the rest of the world. News reporting in Northern Ireland was formulaic: the narrative concentrated on the human hardship followed by routine condemnation from political leaders who opposed the IRA. The script was one-dimensional, and it was not acceptable to place the violence within a political context. The violence appeared to have no history and no background.

After a few months I was glad to leave Belfast. The news agenda did not provide an opportunity to understand why the IRA existed. In the 1980s, in the midst of the most complex and burdensome domestic problem facing the UK, television journalism was mostly unable to investigate or reflect upon the crisis. The British government's policy was to try to decouple the IRA from its support base by treating its members as criminals rather than political militants. The mantra of terrorism had replaced any attempt to solve the conflict. The government used this strategy to justify censorship, arguing that the IRA and the other paramilitary groups depended for survival on what Mrs Thatcher called 'the oxygen of publicity'. Journalists were repeatedly reminded they could spill blood if they reported the views of the republican movement, which were dismissed as simply 'terrorist propaganda'.

Margaret Thatcher unleashed her fury at the BBC with metronomic regularity. It was not motivated simply by her dislike of the IRA; she was also driven by an ideological opposition to public-service broadcasting. Events in Northern Ireland became a convenient instrument for her systematic assault on the BBC. She received help from newspaper proprietors like Rupert Murdoch, who knew that weakening the BBC would enhance the prospects for his satellite-television channels. She proved a suffocating opponent. As journalists were liable to criminal prosecution for any contact with militants, the BBC's hands were tied. In whatever country it is invoked, anti-terrorist legislation stifles public debate concerning the source of a conflict and denies information to the audience most closely affected by the violence.

My next trip to Belfast was in March 1988. I had just returned to London from Sri Lanka, where I'd covered a violent uprising by angry nationalist students. A bomb, hidden in the tyre of a bicycle, had exploded near me at a political rally, killing one man and injuring several others. My ears were still ringing from the noise of the blast. Meanwhile, on the streets of Gibraltar, three unarmed members of an IRA active-service unit had been shot dead by SAS operatives. It was a brazen, extrajudicial execution that sparked outrage in the republican population of Northern Ireland. The IRA team were accused of planning to bomb British targets on the colony. Eyewitnesses said the IRA commandos made gestures of surrender but were shot anyway. The reaction of the British public was mostly agreeable and some newspapers were even jubilant, despite widespread international criticism of the murders.

The funerals of the three IRA members were held at the Milltown Cemetery in Catholic-dominated west Belfast. I went to the cemetery with my BBC colleague Gavin Esler, along with Danny Morrison, then the media director for Sinn Fein. Gavin and I had been speaking to Morrison at the Sinn Fein office and he offered us a lift to the cemetery in his car. We'd planned to interview him after the funerals so we intended to return in his car. I didn't pay much attention to our logistics until much later when we urgently needed a ride back to our car and he had vanished. The driver, who told us to meet him at an agreed place, was not around either; he'd been killed. I later learnt that he wasn't just a chauffeur. He was a member of the IRA and was given a full 'military' funeral, his coffin draped in an Irish flag, flanked with a cortège of masked guerrillas.

When we discussed the killings in Gibraltar with Morrison before the funerals, he was surprisingly low-key. He didn't want to define the incident as 'state terrorism'. He preferred to describe the shootings as part of a 'war', where each side took its losses. 'This time the IRA failed. Next time it might succeed,' he told me. The IRA described its members as volunteer combatants involved in a war with Britain. In its view, the events in Gibraltar simply made bare the real nature of the conflict between the Irish Republican Army and the British government; and during a war, soldiers inevitably die. Morrison was in a philosophical, reflective mood on that day. Always jovial, the balding activist seemed to enjoy a coffee with journalists. The killings in Gibraltar appeared to take the conflict to a new level. 'I'm tired of hearing about the democratic wishes of the people of Northern Ireland,' he said dismissively. 'It's the democratic wishes of the people of the whole of Ireland that matters.' He believed Northern Ireland was a fictitious nation created by gerrymandering. Democracy had been denied the people of Ireland as a whole, he said, and that had legitimized the armed struggle.

Margaret Thatcher was outraged by the very thought of considering the IRA as soldiers fighting for the end of British rule in Northern Ireland. For two decades, the Provisional IRA tried to gain 'political status' for its inmates, which would categorize them as prisoners of war. In 1981, ten IRA prisoners died while on hunger strike during a failed protest to gain that status. The British government repeatedly rejected the notion of a 'war on terror' in Ireland. The phrase would have been repugnant to Mrs Thatcher, who insisted that Britain was fighting terrorists, not a war against the IRA.

Before 2001, most governments facing internal insurrection used 'terrorism' instead of 'war' in order to deprive their foes of legitimacy. But when the CIA, using a missile fired by an unmanned aircraft, killed six suspected members of al-Qa'eda in Yemen in April 2002, it was described by the Pentagon as a legitimate act of war rather than an extrajudicial killing. A spokesman in Washington said it was a 'precision operation' rather than an act of state terrorism. The Pentagon explained its view that the world had become a battlefield and that al-Qa'eda operatives should be treated as enemy combatants. According to that logic, however, Osama bin Laden should be considered a war criminal rather than a terrorist.

At the Milltown Cemetery, I was standing by the graveside as one of the coffins was about to be lowered. It was the eve of St Patrick's Day and about five thousand mourners had gathered to pay their respects to the IRA trio. Each coffin was draped with the Irish flag and a solitary black beret. I saw the tall, bearded figure of Gerry Adams, the Sinn Fein President, approach the graves. Then I heard a loud explosion and fell to the ground. There was another blast and then gunfire. I lay on the ground for a few seconds and then gingerly looked up, crouching behind a gravestone. The firing had become more distant and I looked down a hill and saw a squat man with long hair running away, firing a pistol at a group of enraged mourners who were chasing him. They eventually caught up and kicked him before the police arrived. It was one of the most theatrical incidents of the conflict in Northern Ireland and it made the gunman, Michael Stone, into one of the best-known personal symbols of Protestant paramilitary violence. After his arrest, Stone apparently asked the police: 'How many of the bastards did I kill?' He killed three people and left more than fifty wounded. The succession of funerals ended that week with the execution of two British soldiers, stripped naked and shot by the IRA in a yard in west Belfast. They had inadvertently driven into the funeral procession of the chauffeur who a few days earlier had driven me to the Milltown Cemetery.

Later that year, after nearly a decade of browbeating the media over its reporting of Ireland, the Thatcher government introduced one of the most serious restrictions on freedom of expression since the Second World War. Without a debate in Parliament, the Home Secretary announced that supporters of militant groups would be banned from speaking on television or radio. Anti-terrorist legislation and self-censorship had already meant that the gunmen were no longer interviewed. This legislation was directed against anyone who argued in favour of armed struggle to achieve a united Ireland and the withdrawal of British troops, but its definitions were blurred and the act was clumsily drawn up. The government shied from a complete ban on statements by IRA sympathizers in print because it could have triggered a more sustained revolt over press freedom. Newspapers were mostly loyal to the government anyway and the target of the legislation was television. The new law allowed people from the IRA's political wing, Sinn Fein, to be quoted in reported speech. Pictures of the person speaking could be shown so long as the spoken words were voiced by someone else or shown in subtitles.

The law also resulted in an unforeseen consequence: it brought humour and farce into the coverage of the troubles. I remember being in a BBC office when an editor was putting together a news package. He was a great mimic and was working on the accent of Gerry Adams. Adams' voice was cut and the editor began to read his words, synchronized with his lips. We all folded up in laughter when it was replayed; it sounded just like Adams and it circumvented the ban. In the end, the editor moved his voice so that the viewer clearly saw that it wasn't Adams speaking. Very soon, out-of-work actors were earning £200 for voicing Sinn Fein spokesmen's words on television. Adams made great propaganda capital out of it; when he was told that his voice was to be dubbed by the actor Stephen Rea in a documentary, he replied, 'Great. His voice is much better than mine.'

The reaction abroad wasn't funny. The *New York Times* was astonished by the ban: 'Britain's good name as mother of parliaments and seedbed of political freedom is an asset more precious than the crown jewels,' it reported. When I was in Sri Lanka I was reminded of the restrictions by a grumpy, overweight and lazy press officer at the Government Information Department. She asked why I should be allowed to interview members of a terrorist group in Sri Lanka when my own government prevented me doing it in the UK.

My experience in Belfast made me aware of the need to meet participants from all sides of a conflict in order to report fairly and intelligently. While that seems an obvious prelude to balanced journalism, its implications can be colossal. When I arranged meetings with militant organizations outside the UK, I would often be committing a serious offence under that country's anti-terrorist laws and facing a possible long prison sentence. My strategy was to return to London long before the authorities discovered what I had done. I also calculated that while the journalist's trade provides no formal badge of protection, in most cases, the authorities would choose to expel me from their country rather than detain me and trigger a diplomatic incident.

In September 1994, the ban on interviewing supporters of paramilitary groups in Ireland was revoked after the IRA announced a ceasefire. The British government finally recognized what the IRA had been saying all along; that the violence in Northern Ireland had political causes and needed a political solution. The British army could have slain the entire IRA leadership in one afternoon, if it had thought the problem was really one of 'mindless terrorism' by a small band of criminals. Martin McGuinness served on the IRA Army Council and lived openly within sniper range of the main police barracks in Derry. Instead, an MI6 officer, Michael Oatley, met him and, through their talks, a political solution was reached that addressed the causes of the violence. It was a dialogue that successive governments for three decades had prevented the media placing before the British public. IRA 'terrorists' such as McGuinness became politicians and men convicted for some of the movement's most bloodthirsty actions were freed. The man who murdered Lord Mountbatten and his grandson was released from jail in 1998 under a general amnesty. Michael Stone, the Protestant graveyard killer, was also freed.

The Good Friday Agreement in 1998 meant that the IRA never suffered the financial strangulation that America's 'war on terror' has inflicted on insurgency groups after September 11th. If the conflict in Ireland had continued after 2001, George W. Bush might have placed

Sinn Fein on the State Department's list of 'foreign terrorist organizations'. Anti-terrorist legislation would have certainly choked the essential flow of funds from the United States to the IRA.

In the Basque Country, the September 11th attacks and al-Qa'eda's campaign against Western targets had a significant effect on the armed conflict. The eight-year governance of Prime Minister José Maria Aznar, which began in 1996, was based on a platform of implacable opposition to ETA. Aznar was a small man, with a longish, 1970s-style haircut and a moustache, which often gave him the appearance of a waiter. His right-wing Popular Party leaned toward the heritage of a centralized Castilian Spain. He survived an attack by ETA in 1995 and committed his government to crush the militant group. 'Only the total defeat of terror will bring victory,' he declared. 'This party totally rejects any pact and any negotiation.' Aznar had garnered considerable political support in Spain for his committed 'good versus evil' battle against ETA and used much of the terminology of the 'war on terror' before 2001. He emerged from relative international obscurity to stand next to Bush and Blair on the eve of the invasion of Iraq, and Spain, with Britain, became a pillar of the pro-American group of nations in Western Europe. Bush declared: 'José Maria is a man of principle and a man of courage. Under his leadership, Spain has been a strong partner in the war against terror ... he believes in freedom, freedom for all.'

The black body bags were lined up at Atocha Station and a man in a yellow fluorescent vest counted a row of about forty. He stopped, turned around and walked the same path again. His finger mechanically pointed at each corpse in turn as he recalculated the grim total. A few hours earlier, at 7.39 on a Thursday morning in March 2004, three bombs had exploded at the station in Madrid at the busiest time of day. The carriages were packed tight with commuters. Blood, twisted steel, severed heads, arms and legs were sent hurtling in all directions. The bombs at Atocha were the first of ten explosions on four trains in the city during fifteen minutes of mass murder. Most of the bombs were concealed in backpacks and detonated by mobile phones. One passenger staggered from the train and, still in shock, spoke to journalists at the station: 'I saw a baby torn to bits in front of my eyes,' she announced slowly. Another said the platform had been turned into a 'field of body parts'. The attacks left more than 190 people dead and nearly two thousand injured. It was the most lethal attack on European soil since the Second World War, if one sets aside the killing during the wars in the former Yugoslavia. The bombings also sent shock waves through the political landscape in Madrid as well as the Basque Country.

The Spanish government immediately blamed ETA. Prime Minister José Maria Aznar announced to the Spanish public and world leaders within hours of the carnage that ETA had carried out the attacks, and Spanish diplomats pushed a hastily drafted resolution blaming ETA through the UN Security Council. Spain was due to hold a general election three days later and Aznar was ahead in opinion polls, despite his unpopular support for the American-led invasion of Iraq. The world's media descended on Madrid. The Foreign Minister, Ana Palacio, telephoned her British counterpart, Jack Straw, to say that ETA was responsible. At the same time, the Spanish Foreign Ministry was sending instructions to its embassies, saying diplomats should 'confirm ETA's responsibility for these brutal attacks'.

The Spanish government's strategy was reflected in an interview that Ana Palacio gave to the BBC's *Newsnight* programme. The presenter, Jeremy Paxman, asked: 'Open democracies are always vulnerable, aren't they. Your government has talked about taking stronger measures against terrorists. Realistically, are there any stronger measures you can take?' Palacio's response revealed her assessment of the power of political language. 'May I suggest one measure which is quite easy. Just call them terrorists. We're appalled when we watch TV and the Western media refers to ETA as a Basque separatist organization. Can you imagine us referring to al-Qa'eda as a religious organization? It's just crazy. It is an inconsistency because ETA is on the terrorist list of the EU and the United States of America.'

The government's crude attempts to use the tragedy to gain political favour emerged over the following two days. A few hours after the attacks, the police discovered an abandoned van containing detonators and a cassette tape of verses from the Qur'ān. Arnaldo Otegi, the head of Batasuna, took the highly unusual step of condemning the bombings, saying that they were carried out by 'the Arab resistance'. By Thursday night, an Arabic newspaper in London had received a claim of responsibility on behalf of al-Qa'eda. The Spanish government, however, continued to insist ETA was the main suspect. On Saturday night, only hours before polling stations opened the following morning, three Moroccans and two Indians were arrested and videotape was found from al-Qa'eda claiming responsibility for the attacks. Thousands of Spaniards responded by protesting on the streets, denouncing the Popular Party for attempting to mislead them. Their anger helped to bring the Socialist Party back to power for the first time in eight years.

Despite its innocence of the Madrid bombings, ETA may prove to be one of their casualties. They traumatized Spain and created intolerance for political violence, whether committed by the Spanish military during the invasion of Iraq or Basque nationalists in pursuit of independence. ETA had already been weakened by a string of arrests and the Madrid bombing pushed it deeper into isolation. Arnaldo Otegi said afterwards that the events had 'provoked reflection within the ranks of ETA'.

Jabi Arbeo, the former Batasuna councillor in Durango, admitted that September 11th and March 11th had weakened the groups that supported armed struggle in the Basque Country. 'Several dozen Batasuna militants were charged on dubious grounds,' he told me. 'At one stage we thought of going underground. It was a difficult time for everyone in our movement.' After Batasuna was banned, its councillors in Durango contested the next election using a front organization, Mugarra, the name of a local mountain. While that succeeded in sidestepping the legal ban, the Mugarra Party won only three seats, instead of the five won by Batasuna in the previous election. The *herriko taberna* remained open, but the law prevented political meetings taking place in the rooms above the bar.

A sustainable peace was only achieved in Northern Ireland when the British government accepted that the cause of the violence was political and that a solution must also be political. The Aznar government had refused to negotiate with ETA and defined the Basque problem as a 'war on terror'; there was only one solution, a military victory. The incoming Socialist Prime Minister signalled a change of mood. The regional leader from the Basque Nationalist Party, Juan José Ibarretxe, made an announcement that suggested genuine optimism. From the horror of one tragedy was born hope for another. 'Madrid's new approach accepts that you can't fight terrorism with wars,' he said, 'but only by examining and resolving the underlying causes.'

9 / THE ORIGINS OF GLOBAL TERRORISM

'Islamic militancy has emerged as perhaps the single gravest
threat to the NATO alliance and to Western security.'
Willy Claes, NATO Secretary-General, 1995

As I sat on rocks on Beirut's Mediterranean coastline, it was difficult
to imagine that for nearly two decades the city had been the staging
post for a developing form of political violence that respected no
borders. In 1970, the leaders of West Germany's Red Army Faction,
Andreas Baader and Ulrike Meinhof, passed through en route to
training camps run by the Palestine Liberation Organization (PLO).
They returned to Europe to instigate and inspire leftist political violence throughout the world. A year later, the PLO, the organization
credited with the inauguration of 'international terrorism', moved its
base to Beirut. After it was expelled a decade later, Hizbollah, the
Shi'ite militia formed in 1982 and trained by Iranian Revolutionary
Guards, set up its headquarters in the south of the city. The leadership
in Iran wanted not only to transform their country, but to export their
revolution worldwide. The victims of political violence were now
found anywhere on earth. 'Terrorism' had a global reach.

During the civil war (1975–90), Lebanon had become a kaleido-
scope of bloodletting– a hundred and seventy thousand dead, three
hundred thousand wounded and eight hundred thousand homeless.
One in five Lebanese had fled abroad. The country had become a
political maelstrom, torn asunder by its neighbours while also committing a form of national hara-kiri. It was in this lawless terrain that
new approaches to non-state political violence were formulated, made

possible by the technological advances in satellite communications and air travel.

Near the Green Line that divided the city between its Christian and Muslim communities, every property was bullet-ridden. On building after building, row upon row, it was hard to find a piece of the elegant yellow-brown brickwork that was not pockmarked. People lived without glass in their windows, running water or electricity. Once-elegant balconies on Rue Damascus were now draped with washing lines, and ragged clothes fluttered in the breeze. Men sat on street corners in armchairs and sofas that once belonged to luxurious parlours. The only evidence that I witnessed of Beirut's re-emergence from the ravages of war was a newly opened shop on the ground floor of a corner block. The top two storeys were abandoned as if the building was a relic from the Roman era. The floor beneath had been tastefully refurbished with large windows and halogen lighting; bullet holes surrounding the glass had been made good with matching shades of filler. It was shop selling Louis Vuitton suitcases and accessories.

I first met Khalil in the upstairs office of a small radical newspaper to which he contributed an occasional article. He wore a light khaki jacket that seemed like military surplus. He was of slight build but sinewy and strong, with a kind oval face.

Khalil had been a fighter in the PLO during the 1970s and now worked alongside Hizbollah as an informal military adviser. He was a Palestinian who was born and grew up in southern Lebanon. He did not consider himself Lebanese: 'I am Palestinian and Palestine is my home,' he said. His father fled to Lebanon as a teenager when Israel was carved from Palestine in 1948. 'My father had to leave or else he would have been killed in his own home.'

More than a generation later, history repeated itself when, in 1982, Khalil was himself displaced from his home by the Israelis. He was brought up in Khiam, a town in southern Lebanon where his father had met his mother in the early 1950s. 'At first my parents lived in a refugee camp,' he recalled. 'Then my father built a house with his own hands.' He lifted his hands, hard as coal and brawny. In the 1970s, Khalil became involved in PLO operations against Israel's northern border. Then the enemy from the south struck back with a blow of such ferocity that Khalil fled his home and the Israeli military settled in his village for nearly two decades. They used the old French-mandate fort near his house as a jail and imprisoned many of his neighbours. Khalil told me haunting stories about Khiam prison: the removal of nails, electric wires on penises. He said he was unable to return to his family home. 'What can I do but fight these people?' he asked.

Khalil had been both participant in and witness to the complicated, multi-factional civil war that had left Lebanon in ruins and had ground to a halt three years earlier. His eyes smiled when we talked about politics; he often showed fury over the actions of Israel but it was not the sort of anger that gnawed away at his soul. 'Why should the Palestinians suffer for the sake for the Jews?' he asked in a tone that was inquisitive rather than angry. 'The British gave in to Jewish terrorism. They ran from the Jews. We were too weak. We were meek and quiet. It was only after the hijackings and Munich that anyone gave us any respect. Then you said we were the terrorists. So who made us into terrorists?'

Khalil looked back as if the 1970s were a 'golden age' for the Palestinians, a resurrection of national confidence after the humiliation of the 1967 war. He also felt that in those days the Palestinian cause was married to other global concerns, such as the fight to end apartheid in South Africa. As a teenager he was inspired by communist literature that a family friend had given him. He joined Fatah, Yasser Arafat's PLO faction, and was chosen to attend a Soviet military training school in Sevastopol. He also trained in Cuba and Vietnam; outside Hanoi he was taught urban-warfare skills at an artificial town made to resemble a city in the Middle East. He was a truly 'global' fighter for the freedom of the oppressed, according to the Soviets, or a 'terrorist' in the eyes of the West.

As Bruce Hoffman notes in *Inside Terrorism*, the PLO had welcomed militants from around the world to their guerrilla camps in Jordan 'for training, indoctrination and the general building of trans-national revolutionary bridges'. It was a milestone in the history of insurgency: probably the first time that one militant organization had trained another.

Hoffman continues: 'The PLO as a terrorist organisation is arguably unique in history. Not only was it the first truly "international" terrorist organisation, it also consistently embraced a far more inter-nationalist orientation than most other terrorist groups. Some accounts suggest that by the early 1980s at least forty different groups – from

Asia, Africa, North America, Europe and the Middle East – had been trained by the PLO at its camps in Jordan, Lebanon and the Yemen among other places.'

The struggle for Palestinian statehood became unique for another important reason: it brought together militants driven to political violence by three different though sometimes overlapping motives, nationalism, leftist anti-imperialism and political Islam. The lack of a single ideological purpose has caused rifts and long periods of infighting, but the broad movement has nevertheless been able to embrace these often conflicting revolutionary strands.

As the political impact of communism waned in the 1980s, some of the PLO's most revolutionary ambitions were grafted onto a radical, politicized model of Islam. For some Palestinians, following the Iranian Revolution in 1979, Islam emerged as an anti-imperialist 'liberation theology'. Palestinian Islamic Jihad modelled itself on the Lebanese Shi'ite movement, Hizbollah.

Khalil had grafted Islam onto communism as an ideology of rebellion. He left Fatah and the PLO in 1982, when Yasser Arafat fled the Israelis and sailed to an ignominious exile in Tunis. 'He's a coward,' he said. 'He should have stood and fought like a man. He has no pride. He is a dog.' Khalil became visibly angry when he talked about Arafat. When he spoke about Israel, he used the language of political debate, developing his argument and justifying the use of violence. When he spoke about Arafat, it was venomous and personal.

Khalil said he had become a communist because he wanted to fight for a fairer world. When he thought the PLO had capitulated, he joined hands with Hizbollah. He was not fired by Islamic fervour to join the movement; the two glasses of vodka in front of us were testimony to that. He did it because Hizbollah seemed to be the only movement that was confronting Israel effectively. It was his beliefs in communism rather than the Qur'ān that fuelled his anger. Now he fought under the banner of Islam, but his motives remained the same: injustice, the poor and the Palestinians. The enemy remained Israel.

We were drinking vodka, lots of it, in a basement bar in a dingy hotel in Rue de Lyon, one of the old French-mandate streets in the Hamra district. I had wanted to go to the Commodore Hotel but it was closed for repairs. Every building in Beirut has stories to tell but the Commodore is more loquacious than most. During the civil war, its bar became a celebrated watering hole for journalists. The News

Bar offered sanctuary from the street battles, and this strange oasis was off-limits for the feuding militias, whose leaders often held press conferences there. It was also said that the Commodore's manager paid $10,000 a month in protection money. On one occasion, apparently, as the fighting advanced perilously close to the hotel, the manager went out and persuaded the gunmen to lay down their arms. 'Why are you fighting?' he said. 'Come in and have a drink.'

Khalil recalled the day the war finally entered the Commodore. It was in 1987, and he was part of the room-to-room fighting that left the floor of the News Bar stained with blood. 'We found militiamen hiding in the rooms,' he told me. 'Someone was firing grenades at the hotel. It was chaos.'

Khalil told me that Yasser Arafat used to be a regular visitor to the Commodore Hotel. Once more, he spat his name. 'He betrayed the Palestinian people,' he fumed. It was 1994, and Arafat had recently signed the Oslo accords. 'He is a puppet of the Israelis,' he added. 'Oslo will never work.'

It was almost 2.00 a.m. and everyone else had left. The barman asked if we needed anything else, suggesting that it was time to leave. We decided to have a nightcap in my room in the newly rebuilt Riviera Hotel on the avenue de Paris, part of the winding corniche that hugs the Mediterranean. The sound of the sea striking the rocky coves provided a musical backdrop to pictures I had seen of old Beirut. It was once an alluring destination for wealthy Europeans when luxury boats bobbed in the marinas and roulette wheels were spinning in casinos throughout the city. As we drove past the ruins of the old US Marine headquarters, where 241 servicemen were killed in a suicide bombing, the city seemed more like the remains from an archaeological dig than a Monte Carlo manqué.

I had a bottle of duty-free vodka and I filled a couple of cheap hotel glasses. Khalil developed a taste for vodka while in Soviet military camps on the Black Sea. As the evening turned to morning, he asked me an astounding question. 'Do you know about the operation of a Stinger missile?' I said no, but advised that he should look up Stinger missiles in *Jane's Intelligence Review*, the military analysis magazine. We both laughed, fuelled by the alcohol, but I do recall that he implied that Hizbollah had got hold of some of the missile systems, but were unable to operate them. He mentioned something about the satellite-positioning system, which he said needed to be activated before the missile could be fired. In the 1980s, hundreds of Stinger missile systems were given to mujahedin guerrillas in Afghanistan to shoot down Soviet helicopters and low-flying planes. When the Soviets left, the weapons were sent to Islamic groups elsewhere; there were reports that CIA operatives were scouring the Middle East, offering $5,000 for the return of each launcher.

I called a taxi and Khalil stumbled into the hallway of the hotel, mimicking the firing of a SAM-7 missile from his shoulder. Pshshshsh, whewwww, pughghghg. BANG! He slumped onto the back seat of the cab, dreaming, perhaps, of surface-to-air missile systems. When I asked him about the Stingers a few days later, he seemed embarrassed and denied any recollection of our conversation.

The Central Intelligence Agency called it 'Blowback'; the explosive boomerang that they threw by fomenting an international jihad against the Soviet Union in Afghanistan. The Stingers were only one legacy of the poisonous fallout: the real 'blowback' was to be the revival of an idea, jihad, or holy war, which had mostly lain dormant since the tenth century.

'Blowback' was first used by the CIA to describe the unintended consequences of covert activities in Iran in 1954. The Agency warned of the possible repercussions of the coup d'état it had engineered to overthrow the elected government of Mohammed Mossadeq a year earlier. The joint operation with MI6 was undertaken in order to preserve the revenue Britain was receiving from Iran's oil reserves. The Iranian regime took twenty-five years to unravel, but the 'blowback' was seismic when it occurred; the creation of an Islamic Republic in 1979 that became an implacable enemy of the United States and inspired Muslims the world over to confront the West.

It is often the case that the origin of non-state political violence, when traced back, is the United States. Even hijacking, the pioneering symbol of 'international terrorism', was probably instigated, as a political tool, by the CIA. The agency is said to have secretly encouraged Cubans to hijack planes and force the pilots to fly to Florida, thus discrediting Castro and depleting his aviation fleet. In response, the Cuban regime encouraged sympathetic revolutionaries to take over domestic US flights and demand that the pilots fly to Havana. The Palestinians later contacted Castro and received advice and training on the most efficient methods of commandeering an airliner.

The Soviet Union invaded Afghanistan in the year that the Shah fled Iran, two events that redefined the world for generations to come. A year later, Ronald Reagan was elected as the fortieth President of the United States. The US intelligence community informed him that the Soviet Union could be seriously weakened by a protracted war in Afghanistan. The President gave his unqualified support to a policy that allowed the CIA to gather billions of dollars' worth of arms and ammunition and send them to mujahedin fighters in Afghanistan to establish an international pan-Islamic army.

The capital city of the international jihadist or 'holy warrior' movement was the dusty lawless Pakistani town of Peshawar, which was packed with spooks from the CIA, Saudi Arabia and Pakistan's Inter-Services Intelligence Agency. They were attempting to manage the chaotic and feuding mujahedin groups that had set up their headquarters in the town. As the money poured in, mujahedin commanders bought glistening new Toyota Landcruisers that carried no licence plates and prowled the streets like wild animals stalking their quarry. They shared the roads with noisy three-wheeled rickshaws, donkey-drawn carts and injured fighters hobbling on crutches. The wounded were left to disappear in the dust and fumes of the four-wheel-drive behemoths, which were often steered by a group of three or four men, packed into the front seats. Each would-be driver battled with the steering wheel as the Landcruisers bounced along the rutted roads, sometimes dumping a passenger or two who had clung on to the roof or the swinging doors that rarely closed. Each fighter was bearded and dressed in salwar kameez. Armed with a shiny new automatic rifle and gusto for war, they often raised their guns and screamed 'God is Great!' to passing journalists or aid workers.

Chowk Yadgar was a heaving thoroughfare on this Friday in the summer of 1990, especially before and after prayers. Behind the square was Peshawar's seventeenth-century mosque, named after the city's Mogul governor, Mahabat Khan. To enter the mosque, I had to pass stalls selling food and fabric and squeeze into an alleyway between shop windows laden with gold jewellery. Two white minarets soared above a courtyard that was thronged with worshippers. Some were washing in the ablution pond, others laying down their prayer mats. I was there to meet the leader of one of the mujahedin parties. Yunis Khalis was one of the 'Peshawar Seven', the alliance of mujahedin faction leaders who had set up an interim 'Afghan government' in Peshawar. Khalis was the oldest of the 'Seven' and was best known by outsiders for his flaming red beard. I was hoping that his men would take me to the front line of the fighting inside Afghanistan.

When I met Khalis he was polite and quickly approved a trip across the border, as well as an on-camera interview when I returned. In general, however, a mood of mayhem surrounded the mujahedin; it characterized their war and, in victory, cemented their failure to attain peace. It had another important effect; it made Western observers underestimate the power of jihad. These warriors wanted to expel the Soviet invaders and that's where journalistic enquiry ended. I certainly did not consider what they wanted to create in Afghanistan; this was not part of the narrative of the coverage of the war. Most of the journalists considered the mujahedin as heroic but shambolic. The *muj*, as we called them, were treated as amiable primitives. It was rather like discovering a lost tribe in the Amazon: they had quaint, if not bizarre customs, but were respected for their fighting skills and exaggerated hospitality. Their religious fervour was the source of endless, heretical humour. In the end, however, they were the 'good guys' on *our* side. They were, without dispute amongst the mainstream media, 'freedom fighters'.

Unknown to me during my visits in the late 1980s, one of the men with whom Yunis Khalis had worked closely was a tall Saudi with high cheekbones and a quiet, resolute manner. By the time I had met Khalis, he had already built a close friendship with Osama bin Laden. Later on, when the Taliban ruled Afghanistan, the two men became neighbours.

Against this backdrop, the Afghan war was fought over a decade that witnessed a revolution in global communications, not least in the growth of relatively inexpensive air travel. The would-be *mujahed* from Egypt or Indonesia, inspired by video footage of the Afghan War, required only a Pakistani tourist visa and an air ticket to reach Peshawar. From there, given the right connections, the jihad was only a few hours' drive away.

During the early 1980s, bin Laden made several visits to Afghanistan and supplied the mujahedin with arms, as well as tractors and drilling equipment to cut roads and tunnels through the mountains. Soon he became involved in combat with units under the command of Abdul Rasul Sayyaf, the Arabic-speaking scholar with close links to Saudi Arabia.

Aside from the effort of explaining the complex background, there was another reason for the collective failure of journalism to spot the timebomb ticking in Afghanistan. The only evidence that most reporters had of anti-Western Islamic militancy was in Iran and Lebanon, and these were Shi'ites. The tame 'Sunni majority' were perceived to be allied to Western interests, under the guiding hand of the powerful pro-American leadership of Saudi Arabia. Bin Laden's activities were not secret; in fact, he was well known to many in Peshawar and local shopkeepers joked that he was financing a 'University of Jihad'. Saudi intelligence welcomed his efforts: 'He was a model. We wanted more of him,' recalled Prince Turki al-Faisal, the man who headed the desert kingdom's intelligence service. In the collective viewpoint of Western journalism, a wealthy Saudi funding the war was little more than a 'colour story', which aroused little interest amongst news editors. He was, after all, 'one of us'.

Bin Laden became a resident of Peshawar in 1984 when he opened a guest house for foreign mujahedin, designed to be a first point of call and staging post before they left for training camps inside Afghanistan. It coincided with the setting up of Maktab al-Khadimat, or 'Office of Services', which was run by Sheikh Abdullah Azzam, a Palestinian religious scholar, whose name at the time would have meant nothing to me had it not been for a comment made by a wise local newspaper journalist, Rahimullah Yusufzai. Rahimullah is a quiet, understated man who was then the Peshawar correspondent for the *Muslim*. 'It's very interesting what's going on there,' he said from his office in the bustling Saddar Road, which leads from old Peshawar to the 'cantonment' district around the former British military camp. 'They have money pouring in from the Arab states and many dedicated fighters.' He suggested I pop in and take a look.

I had a free morning and arranged to meet some of the 'Afghan Arabs'. The note in my diary said I was to meet 'Mahmud'. I was taken to a building, a large two-storey house on the road toward the university. The metal gates at the entrance were open and I asked a man reading a newspaper if I could see Mahmud. The man didn't speak much English and shook his head before carrying on reading. In one room, a man with glasses looked at me bemused. 'Who's Mahmud?' he asked. I said I didn't know but I wanted to speak to someone about the group's activities. He waved his hand and told me to wait outside in a corridor. In another room, a man was screaming down an old Bakelite phone. Another entered carrying several boxes. Three or four fighters sat on the floor, half-asleep. Eventually, a young man with a bright, clean salwar kameez said hello and gave me a handful of leaflets. Most were in Arabic, with fuzzy pictures of jubilant mujahedin fighters and the corpses of either Russian or Afghan army soldiers. 'What do they say?' I asked. 'I don't know,' the boy replied, 'I don't read Arabic.' I enquired who was in charge and showed some impatience; 'I'm from the BBC,' I declared in a loud voice. It usually carried weight in Pakistan, where the BBC's Pashtun-language service has several million regular listeners. 'Everyone doing jihad. Everyone very busy,' the boy smiled, displaying a mouthful of perfect white teeth.

I wish I had paid more heed to the always sagacious words of Rahimullah. While I considered the Office of Afghan-Arabs an inconsequential sideshow, it was actually the hub for the nascent al-Qa'eda. The Office's publications were distributed to mosques throughout the Arab world and then translated and forwarded to Malaysia, Indonesia and elsewhere. They called on Muslims all over the globe to fulfil their religious duty to support their fellow believers in Afghanistan. Abdullah Azzam was a visionary as well as a firebrand; one of the leaflets published that year declared: 'After Afghanistan, nothing is impossible for us any more. There are no superpowers. What matters is the willpower that springs from our religious belief.'

The Office of Services attracted thousands of fighters and created a formal international recruiting network. It also organized accommodation in Peshawar that was known as Bait al-Ansar, 'Houses for the Devoted Followers'. Along with official Saudi charities, the main benefactor was Azzam's friend and prodigy, Osama bin Laden. The Sheikh had been a professor at Malik Abdul Aziz University in Jeddah in the early 1980s. One of his students who'd paid great interest in his lectures was the gaunt, lanky scion of the wealthy bin Laden family.

By 1988, bin Laden's commitment to the war had escalated sharply. He had built at least six military camps inside Afghanistan and later, as the number of recruits mushroomed, he set up training camps on the outskirts of Peshawar. The largest was called al-Ma'asadat, 'the Lion's Den'. It was a major impetus in the development of the international brigades; by 1989, many volunteers from outside Afghanistan were fighting in company-sized units of 80–100 men. Most of these units were fighting in the south-east fronts around Jalalabad and Gardez and were often better armed than their Afghan comrades.

The stories about bin Laden's piety and largesse spread amongst the mujahedin ranks and he became known as the 'Good Samaritan'. It was said that he visited Peshawar hospitals and gave nuts and chocolate bars to the wounded, and often sent money to the man's family.

Although Peshawar was brimming with international journalists, a fervent debate amongst the leadership of the foreign brigades went unrecorded. From later accounts, it seemed that Azzam and bin Laden had a falling-out over tactics. The Saudi millionaire had met and befriended an Egyptian surgeon named Ayman Zawahri, who'd become the leader of the Jihad movement in his native Egypt. It appeared that bin Laden was drawn to Islamic radicals who wanted to escalate the jihad to include arming and training militants who would then return home to fight against their own governments. Zawahri was particularly concerned to build up links with militants in Egypt and saw the potential to expand this strategy to radical Muslim groups around the world. Abdullah Azzam was sceptical; he adamantly opposed the undertaking of a global jihad before the creation of an Islamic state in Afghanistan and he disapproved of the murder of moderate Muslim leaders. It seems that Zawahri eventually persuaded bin Laden to follow a different route. The surgeon, who was brought up in a well-off suburb of Cairo by a respected family of doctors, later became bin Laden's deputy in al-Qa'eda.

One morning in late November 1989, Sheikh Abdullah Azzam was driving towards a mosque in Peshawar to deliver a sermon during Jumma, the midday Friday prayers. He was travelling with his two boys, Mohammed and Ibrahim, as well as the son of a friend. As the car approached the mosque on a rutted road, a 20 kg bomb, hidden in a pothole, was detonated by remote control. The explosion was so powerful that it was heard across the city. All four passengers died immediately. Metal fragments from the car hurtled down the street, injuring passers-by. Body parts were found up to a hundred yards from the carnage; the legs of one of Azzam's sons were found hanging from an overhead electricity cable.

Mystery still surrounds Sheikh Azzam's death. Most Pakistanis believe the CIA was responsible. The weakness in this accusation is that nothing the CIA was doing at that time, the month that the Berlin wall collapsed, suggested that they believed the Sheikh's activities were any threat to the American national interest. The claim is further diminished by the vocal chorus that routinely blames the agency for the scores of unsolved political murders that plague Pakistan. After Sheikh Azzam's assassination, Osama bin Laden became the unchallenged leader of the Muslim international brigades. It was commented that he had most to gain from Azzam's demise.

A few months later, I visited the sprawling concrete edifice of the American Consulate in Peshawar, the headquarters of the CIA's last great cold-war battle. I had a briefing but it was dull; the staff regularly spoke to journalists and their comments were well rehearsed. Despite an agreement by Moscow to withdraw its forces from Afghanistan, I was told that the US would continue funding the mujahedin while the Russians still gave money to the regime of President Najibullah. Even after the Soviet troops had left their garrisons and had crossed the ancient Oxus River into Uzbekistan on their way home in February 1989, the Americans still had an appetite for war.

If I had any doubts when I left the Consulate, I had none after a few beers in the American Club, the only drinking den in Peshawar. It was a regular hangout for foreigners; the legion of aid workers, diplomats, journalists, and, of course, spies who badly needed a break from the extremities of faith, war and death that they witnessed in the city. It was the nearest I have seen to an alcoholic version of a desert oasis. One could buy a cold bottle of beer and shoot at the dartboard, listen to Bruce Springsteen and the Eagles or choose from a menu that included T-bone steak and chicken wings.

On one occasion in 1990 I was drinking beer next to a man with long straggling black hair, a flowing beard and brown salwar kameez with a waistcoat over the top. All that was missing from the 'official' *muj* outfit was the circular woollen cap, the *kolas*. That, I discovered later, was on a chair by his side. He was gorging on a gigantic plate of barbecued spare ribs; it looked as if he had ordered half a roasted pig. Naturally, a true mujahedin would not be eating meat deemed *haram*, or unlawful, by the Qur'ān. Nor would he be sipping a can of Bud.

When I meet suspected undercover or 'non-official-cover' officers, it seems inappropriate to ask the obvious question: Are you from the CIA? Instead I stuck to more genial 'bar chat'.

'Where are you from?'

'Dallas, Texas,' he said proudly and loudly.

'Have you been, um, "inside"?' 'Inside' was the phrase used for entering Afghanistan with the mujahedin.

He nodded. 'Just got out.'

'How are things over there?' I asked, trying to be chummy. He gave the impression that he was more interested in his spare ribs than talking to me. 'There's just one problem with Afghanistan,' he blurted between mouthfuls. I could have instantly listed dozens of problems with Afghanistan but I kept quiet.

'The problem with Afghanistan is simple. There's not enough war,' declared the man from Texas. 'We need to escalate fighting and expedite mujahedin capabilities in impacting war.'

Often when I speak to US military personnel, their language is so definitive and categorical, even when I don't fully understand their jargon, that I feel like a bumbling Hugh Grant character, fumbling for words.

'Are you helping them out then, personally I mean, yourself?'

'You bet. Those are my orders.' He was wiping the barbecue sauce from his beard and preparing to leave when I asked if he wanted another beer. He declined my offer. 'I gotta go. Got work to do, plenty of it.' I assumed his work meant dealing out 'more war' to a nation that already had thousands dead and four million made homeless by the fighting.

The journey from Peshawar to Kabul, under the Khyber Gate and through the gorges of the pass, is breathtaking. The winding British-built road is flanked with machine-gun posts of Pakistan's legendary Khyber Rifles regiment. This was Britain's colonial frontier, a region of narrow chasms and harsh moonlike terrain surrounded by snow-capped mountains. The folklore tells of proud Pashtun tribesmen with a firm handclasp and penetrating stare. They were resplendent, handsome men of honour, with bullet-studded bandoliers across their chests and pistol at their sides.

The reality is somewhat different. Along hundreds of miles of lawless borderland lies a feudal territory called the Federally Administered Tribal Areas. It's like an American Indian 'reservation' that technically remains within Pakistan but lies outside the remit of its laws. The British tried to conquer the Pashtun tribes who inhabited this land but failed, leaving them to police themselves. When the British left the subcontinent in 1947, the Pakistani government found the Pashtun in rebellious mood and they were forced to continue the arrangement; its police and soldiers rarely enter without permission from the local tribal leader.

Most people in the Tribal Areas say they are Pashtun first, then either Pakistani or Afghan. Few accept the border between Pakistan and Afghanistan, which was an arbitrary creation of a British diplomat, Sir Mortimer Durand, in 1893 and which effectively cut the Pashtun population in two.

The town of Landi Kotal, once dubbed the most lawless town in Asia, nestled in the throat of the Khyber Pass; it was a truck stop and watering hole for travellers before the descent to the Afghan border posts at Tor Kham. During the 1980s, it was a mujahedin staging post and there were several dozen Russian tanks parked at Tor Kham, which regularly shelled the hills around Landi Kotal. The bazaar at Millad Chowk had a breezy, relaxed mood despite the proximity of war. A child no more than twelve carried a tall stick festooned with balloons of, amongst other things, pink rabbits, Dalmatian dogs and, curiously, a blow-up Santa Claus. He also carried a well-used AK-47 assault rifle and his webbing was bulging with magazines. Another child, perhaps no more than eight, offered me soft drinks. He too had an AK-47. As I glanced around, I realized that every male of walking age was armed.

One of our escorts from the Khyber Rifles said his sons started carrying guns when they were eight or nine. 'It's part of being a man,' he said without irony. 'It's the first sound they hear as a baby,' he added, referring to the use of celebratory gunfire at births and weddings.

The Landi Kotal Bazaar was busy; mujahedin mixed with older men and women covered from head to toe in the burka. Most boys in the Tribal Areas have traditionally chosen one of two career paths, fighting or smuggling. The economy, with scarcely any industry or agriculture, revolved around a smuggling arrangement born after the Afghan Transit Trade Agreement was signed in 1950. Containers were allowed to be loaded off ships, typically at Karachi, and driven by truck directly into Afghanistan, escaping Pakistan's crippling import duties. Tribal leaders then arranged for trucks to be unpacked in areas under their control or just over the border. The goods were then smuggled back into Pakistan, often over remote mountain passes on horseback or donkey cart.

The Tribal Areas adhere to a lifestyle similar to that imposed in Afghanistan by the Taliban. They abide by a civil code known as Pashtunwali; it provides a set of obligations regulating honour, hospitality and revenge. Pashtunwali draws much from Islam but its interpretation of Islamic law arises from centuries of tribal customs.

The central tenets of Pashtunwali begin with 'z' in the Pashto language, *zan*, *zar* and *zamin*; women, gold and land. A man is told that his pride and honour depend on gaining the three 'z's. If he loses his wealth or his women are dishonoured, he becomes an outcast.

Many families live in large mud-built houses on hillsides that resemble castles. The 'family' is essentially a clan of perhaps a hundred people that also becomes a fighting unit to safeguard property or resolve a feud. These fortress homes often have turrets and thick walls that can resist gunfire.

The Tribal Areas are also awash with stories of revenge killings or *bandal*, blood feuds that can continue for generations. The Pashtun of these territories are known to dislike foreigners and possess a temper without a fuse. It was these thoughts that filled my head as I waited for the vehicle to take our team across the border into Afghanistan with men from the mujahedin faction headed by Yunis Khalis. We'd left Dean's Hotel, a colonial resting place where Churchill and Kipling had stayed, and been dropped off at a petrol station near the outskirts of Peshawar at 5 a.m. We were left with half a dozen boxes and a tripod in the dark. It was surprisingly cold.

I handed the cameraman, Nick, and his soundman, a quiet cockney named Paul, their long shirts, baggy pants and round hats. We were being taken across the border out of sight of Pakistani border patrols. Foreigners were not allowed to enter Afghanistan and we had been told to disguise ourselves as locals or mujahedin. Our Afghani translator, Jalal, knew Khalis's men. He'd brought a light coat but had not told us that we might need warmer clothes. I shivered. It took an hour for our transport to arrive. It was a large six-wheeled truck that had been converted into a bus by covering a crudely nailed together wooden structure with a plastic canopy. Wooden benches lined either side and ammunition boxes slid around the central section. It only had one working headlight. We needed help to get into the back; Nick the cameraman winced, wishing that he was still in London.

We were unable to cross at the Khyber Pass because the border security there was more thorough. We headed south towards Darra before turning west, skirting around the border village of Terri Mangal. We reached an unmade road and started climbing. The moonlight drew the outline of a small collection of huts. A few men jumped aboard. One fighter sat on the cab and another squeezed next to me without speaking and sat half-perched on my leg in the crush.

Dawn was a spectacular sight. The sunlight was instantly warming and I saw for the first time the faces of the men around me. Some returned our smiles, but most just stared blankly. Many of them had been back to their homes and were returning to the front line. Suddenly the truck screeched to a halt. In a hurry, the men jumped down, and began to pray at the roadside. A few had prayer mats, but *pattus*, the cloaks worn over salwar kameez, were used by most. The *pattu* is a very durable item; a blanket at night, a dust sheet by day, it protects from the sun and is also used as a towel and napkin during mealtimes.

I was still concerned about being spotted by the Khyber Rifles patrolling the border. When prayers had finished I asked how far we were from the frontier with Afghanistan. 'Here, Afghanistan!' one man laughed as he pointed to the ground. Apparently we'd already crossed and I'd been unaware of the border. The mood of the men had now changed from sullen to excitable. I almost detected a gusto for war. One man looked down the barrel of his gun and pretended to shoot; one hand went flat, suggesting that his target had been fatally struck. It was followed by a booming, body-shaking laugh.

There were half a dozen mujahedin on foot and horseback on the road ahead. The driver stopped and a discussion followed. 'What's happening?' I asked Jalal. 'The driver's asking directions,' he replied sleepily. 'What,' I said alarmed, 'doesn't he know where he's going?' Jalal pondered for a moment: 'I think the fighting moves from place to place.' I was becoming edgy. Suddenly, there was a loud crack, followed by a slithering, whiplash sound from the rocks just behind us. Everyone ducked and the driver momentarily braked. One fighter then smiled, indicating with a whistle and a thumb movement that it was outgoing rockets. They were being fired by a squadron of mujahedin nearby. I asked Jalal again where we were going. 'Can we stop with those guys?' I asked. 'Not Khalis,' someone said.

We were heading west along the border and would end up south of Jalalabad, a city which had been under siege since the last Soviet troops had left, a year earlier. The truck was heaving and spitting; the gradients were becoming steeper and steeper, the crunching of the gears louder and louder. A large plume of oily smoke spewed from the exhaust; as if fatigued, the truck ground to a halt. '*Harakat! Harakat!*' shouted one man. 'Let's go!'

Above us, the stony peaks loomed like skyscrapers. Nick and Paul looked horrified but, in resignation, lifted what they could of our equipment and began the long march along a path through the rocks. The Afghan fighters have a tenacity and strength in their wiry frames that I have found impossible to understand. They moved like ants, tirelessly and without complaint; some carried ammunition, others boxes of food. We were puffing at the back, no doubt delaying their progress.

After about two hours we reached a small elevated plain; there were shrubs and clutches of poplars sprinkled amongst the angular stony red and grey landscape. The air was still and clear; it was peaceful and my earlier restive mood had been replaced by wonder at my unearthly surroundings.

We stopped at a collection of houses that looked uninhabited. A few young boys came to greet us and Jalal told me that lunch had been prepared. The mud-walled buildings were a honeycomb of bullet holes; mangled doors hung from broken hinges. It was hard to tell what had decayed and what had been destroyed in battle.

The young boys brought water in a thermos pot and we washed our hands. One man laid out his green woollen *pattu* on the floor to create a dining area. Another pulled out a Qur'ān from a knapsack.

Lunch was chicken and rice; a gentle breeze had carried dust and sand over the drumsticks and other, less well-defined parts. A large bowl of rice was placed in the middle of the *pattu* and everyone made little balls with their hands before scooping it into their mouths. The men had begun to enjoy our company and, when they saw that we were hungry, starting throwing chicken legs at us, unconcerned that most fell on the ground. The dusty soil provided a coating rather like breadcrumbs. Dust was a part of life here; to fight it was to enter an unwinnable battle.

Amongst the men at the destroyed village was Commander Noor ul-Haq, a quiet, wiry man with a long nose and feline features. He had a constant smile and looked surprisingly young to be in charge of what I was told was a company of about a hundred men. Commander Noor was planning another assault on Jalalabad. 'The city is about ten miles away, behind there,' he told me as he pointed to a mountain. 'God willing, the Maulvi will be marching on the city by the next full moon.' The honorific title 'Maulvi', which is given to religious scholars, referred to his crimson-bearded faction leader, Yunis Khalis.

The battle for Jalalabad proved to be a very costly assault; up to ten thousand people, mostly civilians, were killed in rocket attacks.

The Afghan air force had strafed these mountains with their helicopter gunships and ageing but effective MiG-21 fighters. 'We've lost many *shaheed*,' Commander Noor said quietly. After a pause, his gait stiffened and he declared: 'Twenty martyrs. Allah chose twenty of my men to deliver to paradise.' I looked at the commander with a sympathetic sorrowful expression but now he was smiling. 'Twenty!' he repeated, with satisfaction. 'We were fortunate that we could please Allah.' A few men muttered, 'God is Great,' and waved a fist in the air. Suddenly, bad news had been transformed into good, but I didn't feel it appropriate to offer congratulations.

We put our television equipment on horseback and travelled another mile or so. The commander led us to a ridge that overlooked the plain leading to Jalalabad. There was a burnt-out tank in the field below. Shimmering in the heat haze, over a mile away, I saw the gun barrels of a dozen or more Soviet-built tanks elevated in our direction. In the distance, there was the constant rumble of artillery. It echoed in the hillsides around us but it was hard to determine where it was coming from. It was a quiet day, Noor ul-Haq said. I tentatively asked if any of his gun emplacements would be firing today. He gave the reply I hated to hear.

'If you want.'

'No, I don't want you to fire for us,' I stressed. 'But if you are going to fire, I'd like to film it.'

Commander Noor muttered into his radio. 'Follow me,' he beckoned. We found four fighters in a small trench behind a rocky ridge. All of a sudden, a man with a large machine gun fired toward the Russian positions. We filmed it. Another man started loading his shoulder-mounted rocket-propelled-grenade launcher. A sharp crash like a firecracker erupted in my eardrum, leaving a dull echo and partial deafness for several minutes. The backdraft blew us all into a whirl-wind of smoke and dust. As the dust settled and the guerrillas once more saw the camera lens, they screamed a jubilant, '*Allah u Akbar!*' They were terrific pictures.

The images did not record authentic combat. It bothered me, but probably not enough. I needed a few 'action' pictures and the images reflected accurately what went on in this haphazard, mountainous shoot-out. In truth, I believe these men had seen Western television teams before and they knew what we wanted. Perhaps, however, it would have been more honest to place the word 'Reconstruction' under the images.

I interviewed Yunis Khalis on the following day and his answers were uninspiring and long-winded, with repeated quotes from religious texts. Every answer was reduced to 'God's will'. He seemed uncomfortable in front of the camera and he spoke with little passion or charisma. He wasn't 'good TV', as we'd say.

I did not spend much time trying to work out what made a man like Khalis tick. What drove him and what drove thousands of others to follow him into battle? I presented him as a devout Muslim and left it at that. The 'key' questions were political, it seemed, and the collective journalistic consensus was uncomfortable exploring personal religion. In doing so, it missed both the obvious and the central issue that was occurring around us; the revival of jihad, an idea that was until then largely subdued within the majority Sunni faith. Now, senior religious scholars were prepared to back their faith with the gun.

Yunis Khalis was the first to spark the Islamic revival amongst Afghan exiles in Pakistan in the 1970s based on Deobandism, a creed that evolved in South Asia and is usually described in the West as a form of fundamentalism. Deobandism is more accurately a strand of Salafism, a broad movement that has appeared in various forms during the past century. It describes those who follow the *salaf* or *al-salaf al-saalih*, the 'pious forefathers'. In traditional Islamic scholarship, the word refers to the Prophet Mohammed's contemporary followers, known as his 'Companions', and the next two generations of Muslims. In other words, a Salfi is an early Muslim who had access, it is believed, to a purer interpretation of the revelation of the Qur'ān and therefore understood its message more clearly. Osama bin Laden considers himself a Salafist. As an ideology, Salafism does not necessarily involve political violence. It does, however, tend to view the world through a divided, Manichean prism; during the past centuries of European and American domination of Muslim lands, the West is viewed as the primary source of impurity that darkens and besmirches the true message from God. Khalis inspired his mujahedin to fight the Soviets with his Salafist beliefs, and remained close to the Taliban while it governed from Kabul and gave shelter to several senior officers when they fled after 2001. The Taliban owed much to his teachings.

How could Khalis inspire an idea that was so potent it would soon be considered the primary threat to Western security? Those of us who segregated politics from faith could never understand the power possessed by an elderly, rather dull man who was an expert on formal logic. It was the firebrands, the loose-talkers and performers who attracted my attention. In fact, Khalis' quiet temperament and apparent devotion to his faith rather than politics that won him sympathy amongst Western diplomats and politicians. Indeed, he was also well liked because he seemed more pragmatic than many of his fellow faction leaders. He was certainly less egotistical; he announced that he was fighting for jihad in order to liberate Afghanistan rather than to become one of its rulers. As his colleagues bickered and then fought over Kabul, Khalis vainly tried to achieve unity but then gave up, saying that he wanted no part in the bloody struggle for power.

In late 2003, Yunis Khalis issued a fatwa, or religious order, describing the US and its allies as 'crusaders'. He called for jihad against all foreign forces in Afghanistan. 'Muslims all over the world are required to fight the invading infidels and refrain from befriending or assisting them,' he maintained. 'Islam does not allow friendship with infidels whose brutal armies have attacked Islamic countries.' He urged Muslims worldwide to realize the gravity of the threat to their religion. 'The US invasion of Afghanistan is unjustified and unprincipled and is no less than the Soviet aggression against our homeland,' he proclaimed.

At eighty-four, Yunis Khalis went into hiding in the mountains and caves surrounding Jalalabad. Perhaps he fled to the same gorges and peaks where, long after the fall of the Taliban, supporters of al-Qa'eda were hiding from Western troops. Perhaps he found sanctum alongside Osama bin Laden and his protégé, Mullah Omar, the former Taliban leader. Perhaps the now elderly scholar is a little confused; his fatwa against the Soviet invasion was used by the CIA to forge an army of holy warriors and 'freedom fighters'. A generation later, a similar fatwa was described by the US government as an incitement to 'terrorism'.

10 / THE SOURCE OF THE FURY

'Today the Muslims . . . are compelled to be subservient to
non-Muslims and are ruled by unbelievers. Our lands have been
trampled over, and our honour and dignity violated.'
Hasan al-Banna, *On Jihad*

It was about eight o'clock on a cool December evening in the bustling
narrow alleyways of Imbaba, the slum city on the outskirts of Cairo.
Bare bulbs hung from makeshift stalls, throwing bursts of light on
the passing faces. For some women, only their eyes peered from the
darkness of their niqab, the black shawl that also veils the face. A
throng of humanity moved like a river through the dark and dusty
lanes. The stench of urine alternated with the smells of cooking. The
buzz of flies cut through the babble. Rubbish was strewn across any
spare space. Children were knee deep in it as they played or scavenged.

Sermons by a blind cleric, Sheikh Abdel Rahman, screeched from
cassette machines on stalls selling tapes and Islamic literature. The
Sheikh was wanted by the Egyptian police and had fled to New York.
He was later convicted in the United States for his involvement in the
bombing of the World Trade Center in 1993 that killed six but failed
to topple the giant skyscrapers.

I couldn't make out many of the living spaces; I saw small kerosene
lamps in black holes in a huge mud wall on one side. No one knows
how many people live in Imbaba – 'Too many' was the only answer I
was offered. At one point I felt nauseous after I suddenly drew breath
and almost retched. There were no municipal services here; no running
water, no sewerage, no street lighting. Imbaba was a receptacle for the

dispossessed of Cairo, adjacent to yet detached from the nearby city. It was also a haven for supporters of the radical 'Islamic Association', the Gama'a Islamiyah. Several hundred Egyptian mujahedin had returned from Afghanistan and found refuge in Imbaba. Buoyed with their military training and strict Islamic teachings from Peshawar, they told their stories of jihad and heroism to students from the nearby University of Cairo. The proud fighters described how faith backed by guns and bombs defeated a superpower. The stories summoned admiration from disempowered young men who felt trapped by the lack of opportunities offered by Egypt. A few weeks earlier, the leader of the Gama'a Islamiyah had declared the breezeblock shantytown the 'Republic of Imbaba', an independent enclave within Egypt that abided by Islamic law. 'We are not only a state within a state. We have become a state itself,' he brazenly announced. It was a catchy, provocative phrase that was quoted throughout the world.

For the past few months, groups of bearded young men from the Gama'a Islamiyah, wearing white robes and crocheted skullcaps, had prowled the alleys 'promoting virtue' and 'attacking vice'. Video stores with posters of scantily clad women were burnt; hairdressers were told to place curtains over their windows. Women were warned not to leave home without covering their hair and neck. Wedding parties were raided to check that belly dancers were not in attendance. Regular street gatherings condemned the failure of the Egyptian government to introduce Islamic law. I saw one sign pasted on a wall that celebrated the killing of the former President, Anwar Sadat, in 1981. 'You will be next,' it threatened Mubarak, accusing him of not being a true Muslim.

Suddenly, in the darkness, a gunshot rang out. Then another and another. It was in the distance but the crowd around me congealed into a stampede. As I emerged from the alley into a clearing, an armoured personnel carrier was parked across the road, shining a blinding light into the crowd. Policemen pointed rifles, fitted with long bayonets, toward the crowd. I was in the midst of a raid by twelve thousand paramilitaries, some firing into the night sky, others trampling underfoot whoever stumbled in their path. That month, the Gama'a Islamiyah were flushed out of Imbaba; five thousand mostly young men were arrested and dozens were killed. The armoured personnel carrier remained at the gates of Imbaba's working-class district for nearly two months.

The events in Imbaba on that winter's night marked a new phase in the battle over the role of Islam in the Egyptian state. It was part of a long-standing, pernicious confrontation, which would later supply the beating heart for the 'war on the West', the flip side of the 'war on terror'. Today's divided world, delineated, as George W. Bush announced, by those who are either 'with us' or 'with the terrorists', has its origins in the struggle for the soul of Egypt. The century-old conflict began as a debate amongst intellectuals but it spread through mosques and universities onto the fields of southern Egypt and the alleys of Imbaba. The struggle had also become a very personal, visceral encounter between President Mubarak and his country's Islamist militants. In this theatre of hatred, the first act had been played out a decade earlier.

On 6 October 1981, President Sadat was assassinated during a military parade. Vice-President Hosni Mubarak assumed the mantle of power, and immediately declared a state of emergency, which has never been lifted. Thousands were rounded up and an uprising in Asyut, in Upper Egypt, was quashed by army paratroopers. An Amnesty International report, published a decade after Mubarak assumed power, is simply entitled *Ten Years of Torture*. It also notes that 'Waves of political arrests, which take place periodically, frequently include people rounded up arbitrarily, detained and tortured, who have no political affiliations and no association with opposition activities.'

Mubarak survived his own assassination attempt in 1995. Since then, he has behaved as if someone was out to get him – and he is right to do so. His personal struggle against militant Islam is a battle that his predecessors had fought and whose origins are in the combustible contradictions within the modern Egyptian state.

A few days after he 'cleaned out' Imbaba, we filmed President Mubarak at a press conference. The former fighter pilot and air force general was squat and strong; his body language was pugilistic and defiant. 'When someone wants to kill me, should I welcome him with open arms? If I did nothing you would say that I had lost my mind. If I did nothing, you'd say, "Is he afraid?"' He scoffed at the international media, which he believed had failed to understand the threat of militant Islam and too often reported violations of human rights committed by his regime. 'If I did nothing, there would be no law,' he lectured.

Mubarak was not someone who appreciated criticism; he won

99.96 per cent of the ballot in a presidential election in 1999, so he may believe he is a near perfect ruler. It ranks him slightly less popular than Saddam Hussein during his last venture to the polls in Iraq, where he managed a perfect 100 per cent. An Arab tyrant can never rely on such outstanding manipulation. (The most dramatic success of a dictator who dabbled with democracy was in Syria in 1953. The Interior Minister announced that President Adib Shishakli had swept to victory with 104 per cent of the popular vote. The rather embarrassed President sacked his obsequious minister for exaggerating his support, admitting that his vote was only 99.7 per cent.)

I stood atop the ancient minaret at the Mosque of Ibn Tulun and gazed at the teeming city of Cairo. Shimmering in the haze of the midday sun were rows of square blocks, cluttered and piled upon each other, the only specks of colour being lines of laundry suspended from windows. The landscape of the old city is flat, pierced only by the rising spikes of minarets. These 'thousand minarets' have placed Islam at everyone's front door. This particularly intense religiosity has been described by Hasan Hanafi, a philosophy professor from Cairo University, as the 'fundamental axis of Egyptian life'.

Five of the minarets belong to al-Azhar Mosque and University, the oldest seat of Islamic learning in the world. It was here that a rebellious theologian named Ahmad Ibn Taymiyyah came in the early fourteenth century. He was a respected though controversial jurist from Damascus, but also a firebrand who was quite willing to challenge and upset those in authority. He was described as having broad shoulders, long hair and a short temper. Apparently, when he saw backgammon players in the street, he would kick over their boards in disgust at their frivolity.

I first encountered Ibn Taymiyyah's name in a flat near Lyon, when a Muslim of Moroccan background scribbled it on my notepad. At the time I felt little need to understand legal judgements from medieval Islamic scholarship. The most remarkable thing about Brother Ibrahim, as he was introduced to me, was his fierce attacks on the Shi'ite population of Iran. 'They should be burnt at the stake,' he fumed. I was not sure whether he was applying the traditional Catholic punishment for heresy so that I could understand his point more effectively or whether he was simply confused. Brother Ibrahim wore a white burnous, a traditional Moroccan robe, and had a beard trimmed in a perfect square. He had a full face and carried a little excess weight, but nevertheless cut a dramatic figure on a gloomy night in a rundown housing block in France. It seemed as though he had travelled through time and carried with him the words of an obscure medieval philosopher. The only connection with modernity was the Jaffa Cake biscuits that he gobbled, two or three at a time. I had not come to meet Ibrahim; it was not his flat but he dominated the conversation. Before I left, he printed, in ornate lettering, 'Ibn Taïmia' in my notebook (another transliteration of his Arabic name). I jotted 'v. important' next to it, mainly to please Ibrahim, who was watching everything I wrote.

A year later I spotted that Ibn Taymiyyah was also one of Osama bin Laden's favourite writers: the al-Qa'eda leader quoted him liberally in his 1996 'Declaration of War Against the Americans'. I began to investigate the man who, until then, I had associated with the strange Brother Ibrahim and his passion for Jaffa Cakes. I discovered that the medieval iconoclast had combined Sunni Islam with a revolutionary zeal. He turned his back on wealth and chose a life of piety. He appealed directly to the 'masses', bypassing the religious establishment, and was considered a popular hero by the downtrodden of Damascus. He was reactionary and revolutionary at the same time, a sort of 'Protestant' Muslim, an Islamic version of Martin Luther, the German theologian who instigated the Reformation by attacking papal abuses and corruption by Church officials.

Ibn Taymiyyah's crucial importance in underwriting the rise of militant Islam in the twentieth century lies, however, in a doctrinal matter that at first glance appears cryptic and arcane. It hinges upon a fatwa that he issued regarding a declaration of war at the turn of the fourteenth century. Egypt was then governed by a dynasty of Mameluke Turks who were wary of a Mongol army under Genghis Khan's grandson that had swept into Baghdad and conquered present-day Iran and Iraq. The Mameluke Sultan asked Ibn Taymiyyah to issue a fatwa to sanction his proposed war against the Mongols. But there was a thorny problem: the Mongol leaders had converted to Islam, and accepted religious wisdom prohibited a jihad against fellow Muslims. Without the rallying power of a call to jihad, the Sultan wouldn't be able to muster enough men with an appetite to fight. In 1299 many of his soldiers apparently deserted a battlefield when they belatedly discovered that their enemy were Muslims.

Ibn Taymiyyah set to work at al-Azhar University to untie this knot. To the great pleasure of the Sultan, he emerged jubilant. He discovered that the Mongols were lax in applying the strict codes of Islamic law; the call to prayer was not heard at their camps and they governed according to traditional Mongol customs rather than sharia. He issued a fatwa, declaring that although the Mongols professed to be Muslims, they did not follow all the prescriptions of the religion. Therefore they were no different to infidels against whom jihad had to be waged.

Ibn Taymiyyah's verdict established a series of precedents. Most importantly, it allowed Muslims to declare fellow believers 'apostates' if their adherence was considered wanting. This in turn made it permissible to wage war against Muslim rulers who did not apply the sharia. While this may appear as no more than an act of political opportunism to provide religious 'cover' for the Sultan, it left an explosive legacy in Islamic jurisprudence. Until then, Islamic scholars were unwilling to declare another Muslim an apostate or *takfir* because the implications were so serious. It is treated as the gravest accusation that can be made against a believer and the punishment for *takfir* is death.

Militant Islam was born in the struggle between Muslim radicals and their rulers in the Arab world. It began in Egypt, where revolutionary violence was legitimized by a ruling made seven hundred years earlier. The assassins of Anwar Sadat cited Ibn Taymiyyah to justify his murder, arguing that they were fulfilling God's will.

Ahmad Ibn Taymiyyah died in prison in 1328; popular folklore suggested that he perished of a broken heart because his prison guards would not allow him to write. They had taken away his pen after many of his scripts had been smuggled from the jail and distributed to his followers. A mosque in south London was named in his honour; the Masjid Ibn Taymiyyah is a converted Victorian house on a side street behind Brixton station. Amongst its worshippers were the 'shoe bomber' Richard Reid, who attempted to blow up an American Airlines 747 airliner en route from Paris, and Zacarias Moussaoui, a French citizen who was arrested in the United States on conspiracy charges related to the September 11th attacks.

I travelled across Cairo towards the labyrinth of souks in Khan el Khalili, Cairo's ancient bazaar district. The bazaar is near al-Azhar, in the chaotic heart of old Cairo. The mosque became the epicentre of Sunni scholarship and has the largest collection of Islamic manuscripts in the world. Fading oriental rugs with ornate red patterns lined the floor of the passage leading to the Great Court. It was busy with men and women who had just completed midday prayers. On the walls above the courtyard, stucco ornaments carried Qur'ānic inscriptions in Kufic, the ancient Arabic calligraphy. Dozens of students were squatting in groups, some reading aloud from the Qur'ān, some listening to a professor. In one corner, a group of boys from Malaysia, perhaps twelve years old, were reciting verses. I spoke to an older student from Pakistan who squeezed the Qur'ān against his chest, his finger marking the page he was memorizing. An Indonesian man was eating a kebab near the Soup Gate at the rear of the mosque, where food used to be passed to students while they worked.

I had arranged an appointment with an Islamic scholar and was greeted by a precise man in a grey suit and tie, with a neatly trimmed moustache. Dr Mahmoud Mazrou looked like the manager of a small district bank. We'd had to submit questions beforehand and been told that we could only discuss religious and not political matters. The questions I wanted to ask were, of course, political, concerning the threat of militant Islam to the Egyptian state, but I wanted to avoid a debate over the questions. I thought that we could always throw in a few 'spontaneous' questions that emerged during the discussion.

'Everything that we do, including our social life, our economy and our politics, is determined by Islam,' he declared when we sat down. 'Al-Azhar ensures that Islam guides every aspect of our lives.' Did he say politics? So does that mean Islam provides a higher authority than the laws of the land or the edicts of President Mubarak? 'A Muslim is a Muslim every moment of the day. Islam has an answer to every question on our life,' he told me. Then he added, 'But the President is a good Muslim. There is no conflict.'

The relationship between religion and the state is by far the most important debate within modern Islam. It is the central, explosive issue that has fissured Egypt's intelligentsia since they encountered Western ideas in the nineteenth century. It remains unresolved within the make-up of the Egyptian state.

Westerners tend to think an 'Islamic State', where the mosque and government are linked, is medieval and backward, and associate it with images of fanatical leaders, veiled women, thieves with severed hands and, of course, 'terrorism'. It is often argued that Islamic lands never enjoyed a Renaissance, an intellectual rebirth that fostered doctrines on civil society and human rights. It is often forgotten that the union of Church and state within Christian Europe took centuries of war to dismantle, and to this day the British monarch remains 'by God's Ordinance' the 'Supreme Governor of the Church of England'. Elsewhere, the issue of a secular state almost tore France asunder in 1905 and brought civil war to Mexico in the 1920s, while powerful lobby groups in the United States still fight to bring God more openly into the political process. The problem is that an equivalent debate within the Muslim world has been stifled, either by the colonial powers or by autocratic leaders.

The prestige and power of the Muslim world was in rapid decline in the late nineteenth century. European nations were colonizing its soil. Conquered Muslim societies suffered from disorientation, political decay, economic dislocation and intellectual despair. The military dominance of an industrially advanced Europe was eroding Muslim prestige and confidence. The long-standing equilibrium between the Crusaders and Muslim warriors had disappeared. Islam was convulsing before the onward march of Christian-led modernization, which was unravelling a thousand years of Islamic expansion.

The threat to the autonomy of Muslim lands sparked a new current of thought, known as the 'Islamic Revival'. The instigator of this revival and the symbol of Islam's response to the encroachment of the West was Jamal al-Din, who adopted the name al-Afghani, or 'the Afghan'. He spent nearly a decade in Cairo in the 1870s lecturing at al-Azhar. He challenged ten centuries of orthodox thinking in the Islamic establishment. He demanded the right of Muslims to a new interpretation of the Qur'ān and the Sunna without regard to the dulling weight of failed institutions and centuries of judgements from clergy who had no understanding of modern science. He believed in allowing a new, independent interpretation of the faith that would revitalize Islam. However, to ensure that Muslims did not veer from the essentials of their religion, this new interpretation could only be achieved by returning to the beliefs of the Salafi and only then applying them to the modern era. He called on Muslims to acquire the skills of modern technology but to do it within the framework of the authentic Islam that was practised at the time of the prophet. He rejected the commonly held view that Muslims had to accept a Western culture and lifestyle in order to modernize.

The idea of returning to the Salafi began as an engine of internal reform. As the twentieth century developed, Muslim society continued to experience humiliation and defeat at the hands of the West. The descendants of al-Afghani applied the fundamentals of the faith to the modern situation and concluded that Western influences were undermining the core values of the faith. For a series of Islamic thinkers, Western values became increasingly difficult to graft onto Islam. It appeared to them that the West was trying to crush Muslim civilization by invading its lands and manipulating its governments; it seemed that the Western and Islamic worlds were unable to coexist. They finally concluded that Islam was on a path toward either extinction or confrontation with the West.

The mantle of Salafism was carried on by the journalist Rashid Rida, who edited an influential magazine, *al-Manar* ('the Minaret'), which he published in Cairo from 1897 until his death in 1935. Rida was devastated by Turkey's nationalist revolution under Mustafa Kemal, who was later known as Atatürk. He proclaimed Turkey a secular republic on the ashes of the Ottoman Empire. The sharia courts were abolished, education was no longer controlled by clerics and the mosque and state were separated. Atatürk adopted Western law and political processes and replaced the Arabic script with Latin characters. He flaunted European clothes and ordered his people to abandon the fez, veil and headscarf. Perhaps most importantly for Rida, he abolished the role of the caliph, the leader of the Islamic community who can give spiritual as well as political direction to Muslims worldwide. *Al-Manar*'s sense of crisis could not be understated: 'All Muslims will remain in a state of sin until they select another caliph and pledge allegiance to him. The sin will wreak havoc upon them in this world, not to mention the punishment of God that awaits them on the Day of Judgement.'

Rida's ideas were also instrumental in the formation of the first organized movement that tried to rectify the weakening power of Islamic civilization. Rida became a mentor for a young man called Hasan al-Banna, who grew up reading *al-Manar*. The two men regularly debated editorials in the journal, and at his death, Rida placed his hope for an Islamic revival in al-Ikhwan al-Muslimeen, the Muslim Brotherhood, which Hasan al-Banna had founded in 1928.

The Muslim Brotherhood was the first modern movement to hold an Islamic agenda and behave like a political party. The twenty-two-year-old Hasan al-Banna was disturbed when he saw the luxury of the British colonists compared to the squalor suffered by Egyptian labourers. Began as a welfare association, the organization took the opportunity to spread a Salafist message. The Suez Canal Company even assisted al-Banna, helping to provide funds for the first Muslim Brotherhood mosque in 1930. Al-Banna was usually seen in a dapper suit and tie and was impeccably courteous to the British. To them he appeared a devout and harmless 'do-gooder' rather than a quiet revolutionary.

Al-Banna believed that faith is all-encompassing. Islam is 'religion and state, book and sword and a way of life', he declared. As well as its spiritual role, the Brotherhood was 'a political organization, an athletic group, a cultural-educational union, an economic company and a social idea.' The success of the movement was phenomenal; within fifteen years, it had some five hundred branches and half a million members.

I was first struck by the deep social tentacles of the Muslim Brotherhood following an earthquake that devastated the poor Saiyida Zeinab district in Cairo in 1992. Over five hundred people were killed and thousands were made homeless and the political after-effects were felt for months. Mubarak's bureaucratic government was painfully slow to react to the crisis, while the Brotherhood 'distributed food and blankets and gave us lots of help. They gave us everything', as I was told. 'The government gave us nothing.' A man, perched on a log, had broken his leg in the earthquake. 'What government?' he scoffed. 'Look around,' he said, waving his cigarette in an arc. 'If it wasn't for the Brothers we'd all be dead.'

Dr Essam El-Erian was one of the doctors responsible for assisting the victims. He was a senior member of Egypt's doctors' union, the powerful national medical syndicate. Members of the Muslim Brotherhood held sway over several such associations, including the professional unions representing engineers and lawyers. I met Dr El-Erian in the Talbia district of Giza, just across the Nile from central Cairo. He was a consultant haematologist at a large Cairo hospital but also worked benevolently in a community clinic operated by an Islamic association linked to the Brotherhood. The clinic was in a dusty corner block, next to a tumbledown structure in the middle of el-Talbia.

'People do not believe in the government's health-care system,' Dr El-Erian told me. 'They don't think they can get decent treatment there.' Dr El-Erian had a small trimmed moustache and caring, round

face. He was worried about speaking too openly; he had appeared on
the BBC several times after the earthquake and the regime had signalled
that it was angry. After all, he belonged to a banned organization. The
Muslim Brotherhood was officially outlawed in 1954, when the newly
independent regime of President Gamel Abdel Nasser dumped the
organization that had helped him gain power in a coup. Nevertheless,
it was easy to see how the illegal Muslim Brotherhood maintained its
popularity in the face of government incompetence and repression.

Essam El-Erian had already spent a year in jail and knew that any
knock on the door could be from the *muhabarat*, the extensive
network of secret policemen. 'When we took the tents to the earthquake victims, we just wanted to help the poor. It wasn't just the
Muslim Brotherhood; it was organized by the Humanitarian Relief
Committee from the doctors' syndicate,' he added, attempting to
deflect the government's anger at the movement's achievement. But
the Muslim Brotherhood dominated the relief effort? 'Well, yes,' he
replied, with a modest smile. 'Our Brothers worked very hard.'

As we turned on the camera lights, he declared: 'Corruption is
everywhere. The most important thing in Egypt today is to be against
corruption.' In his white coat and bedside manner, Dr El-Erian was a
convincing political messenger. 'Corruption is now going to collapse
the whole system of their government.' It was a brave categorical
assertion; most Egyptians believe that government workers siphon
money into their own pockets and offer favourable contracts to
members of their own families. I began to understand why the insecure,
sometimes paranoid Egyptian, government feared a young doctor who
was working to improve the conditions of the less fortunate. He paid
the price a few years later.

El-Talbia was a charmless collection of hastily built breezeblock
apartments but not a desperately poor area; the Pyramids' Road, with
its relentless rows of tourist shops, marked its northern boundary.
Fifty years ago the region was farmland but Egypt's burgeoning
population was pushed into districts such as this. To the west, the
pyramids were two unearthly colossi that dominated the skyline.

The following day I met one of El-Erian's patients, Umm Ahmed,
to talk more about her life and the role of the Muslim Brotherhood in
the community. She was only in her late thirties but she stooped and
limped as she walked. With a cream cardigan over her blue floor-
length djellaba she took me to the market where she hunts for bargains

and leftovers. Purple posters with a white image of a mosque were plastered on several walls, with the message *al-Islam huwa al-hall*, 'Islam is the solution'.

Umm Ahmed was willing to show us the squalor surrounding her home because her anger was boiling over. Residents had repeatedly complained to local politicians but were told to keep quiet. The view from her balcony was of a sea of garbage and raw sewage, stretching hundreds of yards on either side. The apartment buildings were never connected to the city's drainage system and streams of effluent flowed from each block into the central pool. Discarded plastic bags and tyres bobbed in this open sewer that had doubled up as a dumping ground. Ducks swam amongst the detritus and sheep and dogs scavenged for food. The smell forced me to breathe through my mouth. 'We are fed up with complaining,' she moaned. 'The government says it plans a sewerage project some time. But until then we have to wait our turn. Until then, what can we do?'

Umm Ahmed wished to 'thank' the Muslim Brotherhood. 'They are big-hearted people,' she told me. She stopped by a butcher's stall. Her usual choice was the offal; she picked up a few pieces of shapeless meat, long and stringy, and asked the price. The butcher then picked up a long dark red piece of meat, wrapped it in an old newspaper and gave it to her for free. I asked him if he was a member of the Muslim Brotherhood and his answer was typically enigmatic. 'We are all Muslims,' he said. 'We are all brothers.' I never asked Umm Ahmed whether she thought the Muslim Brotherhood were 'terrorists'; she would not have understood and it would have appeared a stupid question.

I later met a close confidant of President Mubarak who was in charge of the State Information Service. Nabil Osman was suave, well dressed in an expensive suit and, like many in the higher echelons of the regime, somewhat over-manicured. He greeted me like an old friend. I asked him about the peculiar legal status of the Muslim Brotherhood.

'Why ban the Brotherhood?' I asked.

'We have to be tough on terrorism. You cannot have a dialogue with terrorists and the Muslim Brotherhood are known to be helping the terrorists.'

Despite a lack of evidence and the Brotherhood's publicly expressed commitment to pursue its goals without violence, the regime tends to include all Islamists in the category of 'terrorists'. Did he have proof of links with the Gama'a Islamiyah? He smiled, as if to say 'of course', without actually saying it. 'They are all the same. They have the same intentions and propagate the same ideas.'

Shortly after I left Cairo in 1993, the regime began a systematic attempt to restrict the Brotherhood's influence in the professional syndicates and dismantle its power base in civil society. The group was repeatedly linked to 'terrorism' in government briefings. Hints were made that the Brotherhood's charity work was a public charade for financing terrorism. President Mubarak was becoming increasingly agitated about his 'enemies', real or imagined, as he watched the neighbouring regime in Algeria become locked in a vicious confrontation with Islamists.

In the south, he was already fighting an insurgency led by the Gama'a Islamiyah. In 1994, he signalled that he wanted to curtail the Islamist challenge on a cultural and intellectual level. The regime had long been indifferent to the plight of the people in Upper Egypt and poor districts of Cairo but the Muslim Brotherhood had encroached into areas that were too close to home. It had gained the sympathy and respect of Egypt's professional classes and was said to be active in several government departments, especially the Ministry of Education. While the regime fought its 'war on terror' with the Gama'a Islamiyah with a clumsy viciousness, it was unsure how to fight the battle of ideas with an erudite younger generation of Muslim Brothers such as Essam El-Erian. In the end, the regime responded the only way it understood – with a clumsy viciousness.

The regime mustered its emergency 'anti-terrorist' powers and began a widespread crackdown on the Brotherhood. Dozens of its leaders were detained. Essam El-Erian's wife answered a knock on the door while the doctor was asleep. Three soldiers carrying automatic weapons flanked by two plainclothes members of Mabahith Amn al-Dawla, the General Directorate of State Security Investigations (SSI), stood before her. She woke him up as the men searched the house. He was told to pack a suitcase and then he prayed. 'I kissed my wife and children goodbye and I did not return for five years.' Dr El-Erian spoke without bitterness. 'It was an unfortunate experience.'

El-Erian left prison even more committed to the Islamist path. In jail, he'd enrolled in al-Azhar's Faculty of Islamic law and completed a degree in sharia. 'I am more convinced than ever that Islam should be the general road for the nation,' he declared. He immediately resumed his activities in the doctors' syndicate and the Muslim Brotherhood. When he was later asked whether he had any contact with the armed groups, he replied with a grin, 'Only in prison.'

Dr El-Erian was concerned that since September 11th the term 'terrorism' had been used much more widely to defend the use of emergency powers against Islamists. Such tactics were at one time confined to authoritarian regimes such as Egypt, he told me. He also believed there had been a very big change in the understanding of the word: 'In the West, "terrorist" now usually means an "Islamic freedom fighter".' He drew a sharp distinction between al-Qa'eda and 'resistance' fighters in Palestine or Iraq. 'Since September 11th,' he went on, ' "terrorist" has been used to describe those who resist invasion and occupation. People without freedom always have a right to fight for their freedom and are not "terrorists".'

Dr El-Erian was deeply critical of bin Laden and condemned the September 11th attacks as 'without any excuse'. The Muslim Brotherhood, along with other Islamist groups, signed a common declaration. 'We express our deepest sympathies and sorrow,' it read. 'We condemn, in the strongest terms, the incidents, which are against all human and Islamic norms.' The other signatories included the Emir of the Jamaat-i-Islami in Pakistan and Sheikh Yassin, the founder of Hamas who was murdered by the Israelis. Dr El-Erian blamed the Bush administration for using 'terrorism' as a blanket term of condemnation without any precise meaning. 'Americans say they are against terrorism and against the people who are supporting terrorists, without defining what is terrorism or who are terrorists. All the opponents of the American administration are classified as terrorists.'

'How would you define "terrorism"?' I asked.

'There is no definition of "terrorism". The United Nations can't agree on one. The United States doesn't *want* a real, agreed definition. It just wants to use the word to accuse anyone it doesn't like of being evil.'

When the Brotherhood declared its wish to create an Islamic state, albeit without violence and within a consensual framework, Western liberalism believed that, like fascism and racism, such ideas *as ideas* are incompatible with basic constitutional freedoms. When George W. Bush spoke of bringing democracy to the Middle East, he believed he was creating an 'end of history' ideal which would benefit the people of the region. An Islamist will maintain that only a state based on sharia, where the mosque and government are one, will truly benefit a Muslim nation.

President Hosni Mubarak is well aware that he is not simply fighting armed guerrillas bearing AK-47s. He is fighting the idea of Salafism, which was born in the waning years of the nineteenth century but has been kept alive by the Muslim Brotherhood despite half a century of state persecution.

The defining moment for the identity of the Muslim Brotherhood was the formation of Israel in 1948. During the subsequent Arab war against the Zionists, thousands of Brotherhood volunteers left Egypt to confront what had become to be seen as a Jewish enemy in Palestine. Encouraged by al-Banna, the Brotherhood used selected sections of the holy texts to declare that it was a Muslim's *duty* to take up arms to defend the faith against those who were attacking and occupying Muslim lands.

The gun had been introduced into a large and growing segment of the Salafist movement and the amassing of arms to fight the war in Palestine effectively legitimized the formation of armed and trained units of the Muslim Brotherhood. A bridge had been crossed in the methods used in the Islamic Revival that had started under al-Afghani more than half a century before. 'Israel will exist and will continue to exist until Islam will obliterate it,' declared al-Banna. He made the West an explicit enemy; it was, after all, Western nations that had colonized Islamic land and encroached on its culture. In the past, jihad was generally reserved for battles against infidels or unbelievers, rather than the People of the Book, the Qur'ānic term for Christians and Jews. But al-Banna maintained that Christians and Jews were now the primary enemy, quoting the Prophet during a discussion with a mother who'd lost her son in battle. Mohammed is believed to have told her: 'Your son has the reward of two martyrs.' She asked: 'Why?' He said: 'Because he was killed by the People of the Book.'

A videotaped message claiming responsibility for the Madrid train bombings of March 2004 declared, 'You love life and we love death.' The message was beamed around the world and was treated in the Western media as the utterance of madmen. The tape declared that the attacks were 'a response to the crimes that you have caused in the world, and specifically in Iraq and Afghanistan.' Al-Banna wrote a similar message in response to the disgrace and humiliation felt by

Muslims following the annexation of parts of Palestine and the continued Western control of Arab land. 'Degradation and dishonour are
the results of the love of this world and the fear of death,' he wrote.
'Therefore prepare for jihad and be the lovers of death. Life itself shall
come searching after you.'

But how would al-Banna define 'terrorism'? He would clearly
support guerrilla warfare to fight an invader, in the case of, for
example, the American-led occupation of Iraq. 'Its people are obliged
to repel them with all their force. If fighting is possible then fighting
becomes an obligation,' he declared. But he would probably condemn
the indiscriminate murder in the Madrid commuter trains. 'It is forbidden to slay women, children and old people, to kill the wounded . . .
and the peaceful who offer no resistance.' He said that 'Allah instructs
the Muslims to act with the utmost mercy'.

Hasan al-Banna's imprint on the modern Islamic revival, which
became referred to as 'political Islam', is hard to overstate. The
movement spread throughout the Arab nations and beyond to Pakistan
and Kashmir. It was at the forefront of the jihad in Afghanistan, where
Sheikh Abdullah Azzam was a Brother. In the Palestinian territories,
Sheikh Yassin founded Hamas as an extension of the Muslim Brotherhood in Gaza. Within Egypt, the Brotherhood, like a fly that couldn't
be swatted, continued to irritate the secular state that Nasser created.

Another member of the Muslim Brotherhood, Sayyid Qutb, became
the 'chief ideologist' of modern Salafism, and the role model of a
devout Muslim who, following the edict of Ibn Taymiyyah, challenged
his unbelieving rulers. Most young Muslims I have met in the West
have read Qutb and discussion groups regularly debate, if not endorse,
his views. Brother Ibrahim, the biscuit-eating Frenchman of Moroccan
descent, described Qutb as his 'hero': 'Everything about the world
becomes clear once you read Qutb,' he told me.

In the 1930s, Qutb was a bureaucrat in Egypt's Ministry of
Education who, like most of his middle-class contemporaries, wanted
to learn more about the West. The shy, prim young man, often pictured
wearing a suit and tie, was sent to the United States in 1948 to observe
the American schooling system. The experience shocked him. He saw
a soulless, material world where men were beasts and women sexual
temptresses. 'No one is more distant than the Americans from spiritu-
ality and piety,' he wrote.

He found America to be an unsophisticated society. He was repelled by its tolerance of racism and offended by a common prejudice against Arabs, who were considered dirty and ignorant. He found American attitudes feral, including the females' overt sexual awareness and the male obsession with sport.

'This primitiveness can be seen in the spectacle of the fans as they follow a game of football . . . or watch boxing matches or bloody, monstrous wrestling matches . . . This spectacle leaves no room for doubt as to the primitiveness of the feelings of those who are enamoured with muscular strength and desire it . . . The American girl is well acquainted with her body's seductive capacity. She knows it lies in the face, and in expressive eyes, and thirsty lips, the round breasts, the full buttocks, and in the shapely thighs, sleek legs – and she shows all this and does not hide it.'

Qutb is often described as the 'Che' Guevara of Islamist militancy; the two men were contemporaries and became icons for a generation of revolutionaries, but Qutb was more akin to Lenin in his thinking and strategy. Qutb was the first Islamist to think in terms of Western political models of insurrection. One of his followers wrote: 'The groundwork for the French Revolution was laid by Rousseau, Voltaire and Montesquieu; the Communist Revolution realized plans set by Marx, Engels and Lenin. The same holds true for us' with Sayyid Qutb. While it is clothed in Islamic rather than Marxist idiom, Qutb believed in the historical inevitability of his vision. 'The period of the Western system has come to an end,' he announced. 'At this crucial and bewildering juncture, the turn of Islam and the Muslim community has arrived – the turn of Islam.'

Qutb speaks in a language of 'universal freedoms' that could be confused with George W. Bush's self-righteous role in imposing freedom and democracy on Iraq. Qutb, too, shares an 'end of history' utopian vision. His mission is to liberate the world from despotic rulers and bring dignity and justice to all: 'This religion is really a universal declaration of the freedom of man from servitude to other men,' he wrote. He used Islamic reasoning to construct a world neatly divided into two, between pure Islam and savagery, between right and wrong, between God and Satan. 'Islam knows only two kinds of societies, the Islamic and the *jahili* [barbaric, pre-Islam].'

In 1965 he published his seminal book, *Mallem Fittareek* ('Milestones'), which led to his arrest. He was accused of planning to assassinate Nasser and of conspiracy against the Egyptian state. He was tried and sentenced to death by a military court. There were appeals from throughout the Muslim world to spare his life. Nasser ignored numerous formal objections from Muslim countries and sent him to the gallows in August 1966. Brother Ibrahim, the young man I met in a flat in Lyon, later told me 'a well-known fact'; apparently, as he was hanged, a smile broke out on Sayyid Qutb's face. He had entered the gates of paradise.

11 / IN THE NAME OF THE OPPRESSED

'Americans are the great Satan, the wounded snake.'
Ayatollah Khomeini

'We begin tonight's class with a Kalashnikov,' announced a man with an uncanny resemblance to Rowan Atkinson. He stood behind a wooden table at the head of the mosque. Unassembled parts from AK-47 assault rifles covered the table. A bald man in combat fatigues, whose fumbling, fussy manner suggested that he was not a soldier, continued the lesson. 'The Kalashnikov has many versions of which we have three here tonight; a Kalashnikov with a wooden stock, a rubber stock and, yes, a folding stock.' About a dozen boys, some as young as twelve, wearing desert camouflage uniforms, listened attentively. These were members of the Niruyeh Moghavemat Bassij-e Mostaz'afan, the Mobilized Resistance Force of the Oppressed (Bassij), a volunteer militia that was set up in 1980 during Iran's blood-strewn eight-year war with neighbouring Iraq.

I was at the Shahabadi Mosque in the backstreets of a well-off district in north Tehran. The mosque was a large flat-roofed building, the size of a school gymnasium. The outside brickwork was festooned with colourful lights to mark the birth of Ali, the son-in-law of the prophet who was also the foundational figure in the Shi'a branch of Islam. Before the mosque became a training base, there was a celebration. Men were singing and clapping and the air held an intense passion. A rich baritone voice brought tears to the eyes of one old man as he listened and shared the agony of Ali's persecution by other Muslim rulers. The mullah, the generic name for clergy in Farsi, wore a white swirling turban and brown woollen gown. He chatted and laughed with the faithful as tea and biscuits were brought on trays. Intricate blue and white tiles decorated the walls and brightly coloured sheeting was draped from the ceiling. Such relaxed festivities and religious drama are rarely seen in mosques that follow the orthodox, or Sunni strand of Islam.

The Shi'ite faith emerged from a religious schism that divided the Islamic world from its very beginnings. When the Prophet Muhammed died in 632, he left no details concerning his successor. Shi'ites believe that Ali was his chosen successor, while the Sunnis maintain that Mohammed's father-in-law Abu Bakr was the chosen Caliph. The celebration of the martyrdom of Hosein, the prophet's grandson, by the Shi'a Ali (Partisans of Ali) represents the first universally acknowledged instance of separate religious practice. Devout Shi'a men mark the day known as Ashura by a ritual self-flagellation. They beat their backs with leather whips, which are often studded with sharp metal tips, until they bleed. They believe that only physical pain can reflect the suffering of the Muslim world when Hosein died and the lineage of Ali lost its fight to lead the Muslims.

From its conception, the Shi'a faith was a rebellious, breakaway faction. While the faithful cannot challenge the rule of an imam, because he is appointed by Allah and is therefore sinless, they have greater scope than followers of orthodox Islam to reform their lives and challenge their secular rulers. It is thus no surprise that it was a Shi'a revolution in Iran in 1979 that changed the political face of the globe and redefined the Islamic world's vision of the West. It gave Muslims a belief that they could overturn values which they had succumbed to. Indeed, the revolution may prove to be the most significant event in Islamic history for the last five centuries. The leader, Ayatollah Ruhollah Khomeini, had translated Sayyid Qutb into Farsi during his fourteen years of enforced exile and returned to define America as the enemy of Islam. He put Qutb's face on one of the first postage stamps of the new Islamic Republic. During the overthrow of the Shah, he fostered the belief that the power of people could overcome raw military might. It was during the revolution and its associated war with Iraq that the first 'suicide fighter' was seen, a battlefield tactic that allowed a weaker power to challenge an enemy with superior military capabilities. It was also the first time the Western mind formulated an image of an 'Islamic terrorist'.

It began when President Carter criticized news reports that described the men who took over the US Embassy in Tehran as students. They are terrorists, he said. The pictures of zealous men with beards and headbands and women covered in a black chador seemed to Americans to represent people infected by an alien drug. The willingness of Shi'a radicals to seek martyrdom, which was eagerly chronicled by Western journalists in Lebanon, astounded and bewildered the American and European public. There appeared a group of people who apparently loved death.

Ayatollah Khomeini's remarkable achievement was to unite both religious and secular into a revolutionary uprising to overthrow the Western-supported dictator. Mohammed Reza Pahlavi had been the Shah of Iran since 1941, apart for a brief period in 1953 when the democratically elected Prime Minister Mohammed Mosaddeq took power. But Mosaddeq's decision to nationalize Britain's oil interests triggered his overthrow, an event orchestrated by the CIA and MI6. The Shah was returned to power and became a reliable ally of the West. He governed a country that was seething with discontent, especially after oil prices fell in 1975. Iran's secret police, SAVAK, silenced debate and stopped the evolution of democratic institutions. But this repression and discontent fuelled the revolutionists amongst the clergy.

The grip that Islamists held on the revolution was secured by the unusual crossover between Marxism and revolutionary Shi'ism. Discontent was festering equally amongst radical students, the influential merchants associated with the bazaar and the rural poor who had found themselves sidelined into the overcrowded slums of Tehran. Iranian socialists searched for an Islamic theory of revolution, in the way that 'Che' Guevara had grafted Marxism onto the peasant revolt in South America. The writer who fused the ideas most successfully was Ali Shariati, who proposed a new social order based on the principles of egalitarian justice. He argued that Shi'ism was essentially a creed of rebellion that included social justice, humanism and freedom from oppression.

Dr Shariati's sudden death in London in 1977 began rumours that he might have been killed by SAVAK. He had already succeeded in converting a generation of school and university students in Iran to his blend of Islamic radicalism. The leftist revolutionary forces joined hands with liberals and clerics under the leadership of Khomeini.

In January 1978, a week after President Carter was in Tehran praising the Shah as a great statesman beloved of his people, the government-controlled press printed an article attacking Khomeini as a traitor and foreign agent. Khomeini, who was at the time in Iraq, brought his supporters onto the streets in a protest which marked the beginning of the end for Mohammad Reza Shah. It displayed the power that Khomeini possessed to conjure popular rebellion with a symbolic wave of his hand.

On 16 January 1979, the Shah fled after he lost the confidence of his government and the security services. Two weeks later, Ayatollah Khomeini became the absolute ruler of Iran. Hundreds of thousands lined the streets in celebration when he returned. He had allowed each group within the revolutionary alliance to believe that he supported their dreams; it was a belief that was only crushed when the purges began in the aftermath of his triumph.

The revolution soon began to devour its children as Khomeini outmanoeuvred and ambushed the secular liberals and socialists who had endorsed his leadership. While his pre-revolution rhetoric had skirted religious issues, once ensconced in power he showed his true goal: a strict theocracy with a system of control based in mosques that ran parallel to official constitutional reforms.

In the summer of 1979, Khomeini established an 'Assembly of Experts', consisting of clergy and Islamic intellectuals, to draft a constitution for the Islamic Republic. When leftists challenged the power of the Assembly, he responded by encouraging five hundred 'students' to invade the US Embassy and hold its staff hostage, using the pretext that the Shah was receiving medical treatment in the United States and should be handed over for trial. The engineering of a crisis allowed him to continue his bloody purges, which soon eradicated the Islamist left.

It was the religious militia, the Revolutionary Guards (Pasdarans), that ensured that the clergy achieved near absolute power in Iran. The Revolutionary Guards were presented in the Western media as a group of zealous thugs who terrorized right-minded people and operated outside the rule of law. They usually appeared screaming religious slogans at television cameras while waving their guns aloft and burning American flags. To the devout, the Pasdarans were committed foot soldiers who guarded the revolution against meddling foreign forces and their accessories inside Iran. The Pasdarans symbolized the unstoppable power of popular mobilization, an idea that the Iranian Revolution had inherited from its French counterpart two centuries earlier.

The Mobilized Resistance Force of the Oppressed was set up as a division of the Islamic Revolutionary Guards Corps, the formal title for the Pasdarans. Iran had around four hundred thousand *bassijis* when I visited the unit based at the Shahabadi Mosque in 1996. The Shahabadi mosque had recently been renamed in honour of its previous head mullah, who died fighting in the war with Iraq. Despite being in his sixties, he apparently insisted on going to the front line, where he was hit by shrapnel. The Shahabadi name carried great respect in Iran because his father, Ayatollah Muhammad Ali Shahabadi, taught the young Khomeini at the religious centre of Qom. Mosques had been the staging posts of the resistance to the Shah and they retained their military role as 'guardians' of the revolution decades later. 'The mosques are arteries that carry Islamic orders from our Leader to every part of society,' the head cleric, Hojjatoleslam Sattari, told me. The burly, good-natured mullah seemed surprised when I asked whether armed men should be training in a house of God. 'They are a child of Islam,' he told me. 'The *bassij* represents the masses and obviously its home will be the mosque.'

'When this is in the middle,' the Rowan Atkinson lookalike pointed to a small lever, 'the weapon is ready to fire single shots and when it's down it will fire bursts.' When the lecture ended, the young *bassijis* were given the chance to hold the weapons. Some of the guns were armed. 'If you want to know whether the thirty bullets are loaded or not, you can look through this hole and you can see how full it is.' The commander passed the loaded rifle to one of the youngest boys. I sat alongside twin brothers who seemed the most experienced of the squadron-sized unit. Mehdi and Hamed were twenty and had been in the *bassij* since childhood. They had well-groomed hair and neatly trimmed beards. They displayed a composure and serenity usually associated with much older men.

'Islam is a religion of equality,' Mehdi told me. 'It takes from those who have more and gives to those less fortunate. If you go and see Imam Khomeini's home close up, you'd be deeply moved by its poverty and austerity. The house is very basic, just the bare minimum.'

Mehdi was still speaking of the dispossessed in the language of Ali Sheriati but it was more ritual than real. While the 1979 revolution claimed to liberate Iranians from 'exploitation and imperialist domination', the clerical elite formed an alliance with religious bazaar merchants and industrialists to block attempts by radicals to redistribute wealth and land ownership. A coalition of conservatives and 'reformed' populists has governed Iran for more than two decades, maintaining a stuttering, semi-capitalist economy that's awash with corruption.

After a discussion, Mehdi admitted that the economy was not at the heart of the revolution. 'Ayatollah Khomeini was our supreme spiritual leader. We carried out his orders. After his death, we followed the orders of his successor, Ayatollah Ali Khamenei.' The *bassij* are taught to obey the will of God, not the orders of politicians. They are the foot soldiers of the clergy and owe no loyalty to the president or parliament.

An official statement issued in 2000 gave a glowing portrait of the militia. 'The Bassij Resistance Force is equipped with the most modern and up-to-date weapons and is undergoing the most advanced training. It is making such achievements that if the enemy finds out it will tremble and have a heart attack.'

I asked Mehdi's brother, Hamed, who the *bassij* regarded as their enemy. 'Anybody who opposes the revolution,' he replied as he released the breechblock in an AK-47. 'We are here to protect the revolution.'

The daily duty of the *bassij* was to act as a moral police. 'Our main task is cultural work,' Hamed announced. 'A cultural invasion is the only thing that can defeat a nation. They target the youth and believe that the revolution's root can be killed by this cultural invasion. But it won't be.' Mehdi continued, 'We fight alcohol abuse and look for satellite dishes. We also check the distribution of videos given to video clubs. When people see the presence of *bassijis* in society they tend to do less wrong.'

After their military drill and lesson, it was approaching 11.00 p.m. The mosque was near the prosperous Farminiyeh district, where many of Iran's wealthy secular middle classes lived. 'Rowan' ordered his *bassijis* to set up a checkpoint at a nearby road. The group collected a set of stop signs and marched outside. 'The goal of the *bassij* is the protection of virtue and prevention of vice,' Mehdi told me, using a Qur'ānic phrase to describe the moral police. 'We caution sisters who do not observe the Islamic hijab fully.'

Gender politics was placed at the centre of the revolutionary struggle when Khomeini called for the re-veiling of women less than a month after the Shah's downfall. It became a public emblem of the purification of society from Western culture, and women's dress managed more than any other subject to infuriate and outrage Islamists and Westerners alike. I've always found it surprising that a piece of cloth over a women's head can carry such explosive emotions. Every society has its dress code. If a woman were to walk topless across Times Square in New York, she would be arrested and told to dress appropriately. In the 1920s the father of the last Shah believed that if Iran was to develop its economy, it must modernize along European lines. In a direct assault on Islamic tradition, the Shah declared it illegal for women to wear a veil. He deliberately paraded his wife with her hair uncovered and wearing European clothing. Women wearing the hijab in public were arrested. Thus when Khomeini came to power, his first 'revolutionary action' was to reverse this law.

At the checkpoint, the *bassijis* pointed torches and peered into cars, checking identity cards and searching for women whose headscarves were not drawn forward. Some secular-leaning Iranian girls enjoyed allowing their scarves to slip back, revealing a curl of hair that would fall across their forehead. Such behaviour was considered improper. Mehdi cautioned one woman in a pink scarf and red lipstick. 'We'd have no problems if people like you just covered your head,' he scolded. She smiled and adjusted her scarf. Even though Mehdi and his band of *bassijis* wielded assault rifles and appeared threatening, most of the women reacted with a dismissive shrug. The general lack of fear amongst the secular middle class was one of the peculiarities of post-revolutionary Iran. While Khomeini's clerical elite acted with a bloodthirsty ruthlessness to purge fellow revolutionaries, they allowed much of Iran's middle class to retain its wealth and property and, behind closed doors, secular lifestyle.

'In houses, parties, gatherings, people wear Western clothes. Maybe a short skirt, nylon stockings, high heels and so on.' Maryam was a fashion designer in her forties and found the clothing restrictions almost laughable. 'I've had problems wearing sunglasses,' she told me. 'Many times these boys stopped my car and asked, "Why are you wearing sunglasses?" I said it was sunny. They said, "Take them off, they are Western. You're not allowed to wear them."' Maryam's friends were artists and writers, and at dinner in her house I could have been anywhere in the West. The guests wore European clothes and a good quality French red wine was served with the casserole. Maryam showed me how much hair can be revealed. 'You don't have to wear a scarf like this.' She pulled the scarf tightly around her neck and over her forehead. 'You can wear it like this,' she said as she loosened the scarf and drew it back, revealing over an inch of hair and a fringe that fell over her face. 'A little bit of hair shows and nobody tells us anything,' she smiled and jocularly threw a seductive kiss in my direction.

It was peculiar that the Islamization of Iran often appeared to be measured by the amount of hair a woman could display above her forehead. The hijab was the focal point of the regime's propaganda and the primary vehicle for imposing its moral and political authority. Yet Iranian women have consistently been challenging this dress code, and in doing so undermining the general authority of the Islamic state. I was staggered by the brazen attitude of well-off women and girls towards the *bassij*. My friend Jay had a party and two girls arrived in their full black chadors but once inside cast them off to reveal miniskirts and see-through blouses that would have raised eyebrows on a Paris catwalk. Marijuana was smoked and Scotch swilled back without a care. Another girl laughed that during summer, all she wore under her chador were stockings and suspender belt. This was the other Iran that the authorities tolerated as long as it remained hidden. I stayed in the Vanak district of Tehran at the house of a friend's friend. He was a wonderful host and to my surprise he returned from one shopping trip to the bazaar with a packet of bacon and six-pack of lager. 'I thought these were illegal,' I said voicing concern that I should not be seen drinking or eating pork in Iran. 'You can get anything you want in the bazaar,' he joked. 'It's just like buying pornography in London. It's under the counter.'

For the first-time visitor to Iran, the country does not conform to its popular image. With its wide tree-lined boulevards, Tehran is not the dark, brooding city portrayed in the Western media. There is also a surprising level of political debate. Unlike in most of its Arab neighbours, fear of the regime does not run so deeply as to prevent criticism and discussion. I attended an underground political meeting in a house in north Tehran organized by a sixty-year-old dentist and university lecturer, Dr Habibollah Peyman. About thirty students from Tehran University sat in a large room in the basement of his house and listened attentively to his critique of the regime. An unassuming man of slight frame, he was imprisoned for five years by the Shah and his students were later active in the overthrow of the monarchy. Now he was instructing a new generation to fight for greater freedom. 'Fifteen years of silence has been imposed on our society. We have faced suppression and seen our country strangled. It may be that with the force of a gun, they can make you do something but they cannot force you to think in their way.' It was a powerful oration which voiced a level of dissent that would never be heard in Saddam's Iraq, Egypt, Libya or Syria. Dr Peyman was a devout Muslim who believed the clerical establishment had betrayed the revolution. He favoured the ideas of Dr Ali Shariati and believed that a progressive Islamic government could break the short circuit that has prevented Muslim regimes relating freely to the outside world.

Despite sweeping victories in every significant election between 1997 and 2003, the reformers were unable to repeal repressive policies favoured by the conservative clerical leadership. The country's constitution had created a body called the Council of Guardians, which was charged with examining all legislation passed by parliament, the Majlis, to determine whether it conformed to Islamic principles. The Council can also vet candidates standing for parliament if they are considered insufficiently committed to the Islamic Revolution. During this period, the Council of Guardians repeatedly blocked bills passed by the reform-leaning parliament. Iran's courts, another institution under clerical control, restricted independent political activity through a series of high-profile trials. Amongst those arrested in 2001 was Dr Peyman. He was tried behind closed doors and was only released after paying a fine equivalent to several hundred thousand US dollars. He spent more than a year in detention, much of it in solitary confinement. Students at Tehran University continued to protest against the regime and, in July 1999, sparked the biggest demonstrations Iran has seen since 1979. In 2003, more than four thousand students were rounded up by plainclothes police. A report by *Human Rights Watch* traced a downward trend for political freedoms in Iran to 2000, when reformers swept into parliament with promises to ease the grip of the clerics on daily life and clean up a corrupt economy. The reformists' victory provoked reprisals from hardliners. In the 2004 parliamentary elections, the Council of Guardians disqualified over two thousand reform-minded candidates, ensuring a conservative victory in what was, in effect, a constitutional coup.

Another central mechanism used by the conservative clergy to control dissent is an organization called Ansar-e Hezbollah, which literally means Companions of the Party of God. Its members are *bassijis* and its role is part vigilante, part police, part mob. The Iranian revolution brought the mob onto the streets and Islamic hardliners believed the mob can be used to apply pressure on those who step out of line. Ansar-e Hezbollah was responsible for breaking up political meetings and student demonstrations. A student died in the 1999 demonstrations as *bassijis* attacked them with sticks and clubs. The head of this shadowy group within the *bassij* was Allah Karam. I traced him to a boys' school in Tehran where he was lecturing to pupils who were about ten years old. Under portraits of *bassijis* who had died in the war with Iraq, as well as the ubiquitous image of the stern-faced Khomeini, Allah Karam sat in the strange beam of a red spotlight. The bearded middle-aged Karam wore the white scarf of 'martyrdom' carried by all *bassijis*.

When I reread notes of the lecture, it struck me, perversely, how similar his language was to that later adopted by the right wing neo-conservatives in America. He spoke of a Fourth World War between Islam and the West and repeatedly quoted the theories of the Harvard University professor Samuel Huntingdon, from his 1993 tract *The Clash of Civilizations*. 'Huntingdon says that Islam and Confucius from the East and Christianity and Judaism from the West are the objective forces facing each other. In other words, he is predicting a war of civilizations.' The boys, sitting cross-legged on the floor, listened attentively. He spoke of American aircraft carriers in the Persian Gulf and warned that the first line of attack is through a 'cultural invasion'. 'Today, nearly 220 satellites are bombarding us with propaganda and it is here that the Imams said we are facing a cultural massacre. The culture that he wants to massacre is the culture of martyrdom.'

The next two-thirds of the lecture encouraged the boys to adopt a death wish. He told the story of a thirteen-year-old *bassiji* boy, Hosein Fahmideh, who was fighting at the front line during the war with Iraq. 'What did he do when he ran out of ammunition? He tied a few grenades around his waist and used the vacuum that each grenade creates and threw himself under an enemy tank.' Hosein destroyed the tank but Allah Karam's account was not simply to mark this boy soldier's selfless heroism. He went on to make a macabre cost-benefit comparison. 'The tank and the training that the Iraqi personnel had received amounted to, say, a million dollars. Hosein Fahmideh carried ammunition that wasn't worth more than ten dollars. A ratio of 1:100,000. And he was thirteen and killed four Iraqis who were twenty-five years old. That's $4 \times 25 = 100$. 100 compared to 13 is a ratio of 1:8. That's equivalent to one person opposing eight people. The expansion of this thinking is what the world is presented with today.'

Allah Karam and the Shi'ite martyrdom culture effectively refined the suicide bomber into a necessary tool of combat for Islamic nations confronted by the military superiority of the West. 'It is the culture of Salah Ghondour, a Palestinian women who ties explosives around herself and enters one of those enemy buses in Jerusalem and blows herself up. You see, boys, this is the culture of martyrdom that the world is scared of. The world is frightened of this culture. Otherwise the unquestioned superiority of the American forces in the Persian Gulf will hold no limits.'

The boys were enthralled by his tales of heroism and death. There was no chattering and barely the sound of movement. In the ghostly red light, Allah Karam's gentle delivery seemed like a voice from beyond the grave. 'The culture of the *bassij* is the culture of martyrdom. It is the culture that Imam Khomeini gave for us to fight the West. It is here that the face of victory will appear like blood on a sword.'

The *bassij* was formed to dispatch volunteers of all ages for the war with Iraq. It provided the 'human waves' of troops who crossed battlefields on suicidal missions into enemy fire. Youths from poor families were recruited to fulfil a religious duty; it resulted in badly trained and equipped soldiers being sent against Iraqi machine-gunners. The appalling butchery revived the tradition of martyrdom embodied in the Ashura ritual and the sacrificial death of Hosein. *Bassijis* wrote their last testament in letters to their families that asserted a longing for death and used the most detailed language of the Shi'ite suicide wish.

An appetite for death is difficult for a non-believer to understand at the best of times but to hear a mother willing her son to commit suicide was jaw-dropping. I had dinner with Mehdi and Hamid's parents at their large home in the north of Tehran. Their father was a merchant from the bazaar, the social class that had benefited most from the revolution. They offered me dates, kebabs and oranges for dessert, washed down with fresh cherry juice. The twins' brother Mohammed became a 'martyr' when he was sixteen. 'Mohammed told me that he was tired,' their mother told me. 'All his friends had been martyred and he asked me to pray for him to be granted this tremendous blessing.' She held her chador tightly around her neck as she spoke. 'Mohammed used to say that martyrdom is the ultimate blessing and that not everyone can be so lucky as to achieve it. So, every day I prayed to God that his wish would be granted and I waited.' She gave me a tight-lipped smile. 'Then he sent a letter saying that the moment we had prayed for had arrived.'

Nothing summed up the notion that 'Islamic terrorism' is a form of unfathomable madness better than the use of suicide killers. Apart from the ritual Shi'ite association of Hosein with sacrifice, suicide has no tradition in Islam. Even within Shi'ism, the marking of Hosein's 'martyrdom' was usually a passive wailing and self-flagellation rather than an outpouring of aggression. Moreover, studies of those prepared to die for a cause contradicted the common perception of a 'terrorist fanatic'. A study published by *Science* in 2003 discovered that suicide bombers are not mentally ill and tend to be wealthier and better educated than others of their age. The survey revealed a series of misconceptions held in the West and recycled in the Western media. The popular view that suicide bombers opted for 'paradise' out of despair was wrong. Suicide bombers generally do not behave out of self-interest but a belief that they must sacrifice themselves for a rationally held cause. They are not impoverished misfits but soldiers fighting a tactical conflict.

A Princeton University study of Palestinian suicide attackers from the 1980s to 2003 discovered that only 13 per cent came from poor backgrounds, compared with 32 per cent of the general population. In addition, more than half the suicide bombers had tertiary education, compared with just 15 per cent of the Palestinian population. Similar results were gleaned from a study into Hizbollah militants in Lebanon.

The modern era of suicide attacks began in 1983 with the truck bombing on the US Embassy in Beirut, which killed sixty-three people. It was then that Iran's role in developing suicide attacks drew worldwide attention.

'We supported our Hizbollah brothers in Lebanon,' Mehdi told me. 'Some of our *bassijis* went to Lebanon to defend Islam from the Israeli terrorists. The Israelis killed thousands of Muslims. We had to help our brothers when the Israelis were slaughtering our women and children.' His twin brother Hamed stepped in. 'The Israelis are terrorists. Did you know that?' he asked me as a genuine question. 'They are brutal killers with no respect for human life.'

Mehdi and Hamed were speaking five years before the September 11th tragedy but were referring to another September day, more than a decade earlier, that shook the Muslim world. It was the Israeli invasion of Lebanon, which began on 5 September 1982. More than fifteen thousand Lebanese and Palestinians, mostly civilians, died in ceaseless bombing of Lebanese towns and cities that went on for over a week. It was five times the death toll from the attacks on America in 2001. The operation was often described using the language of the Israeli government. Its goal was to expel Yasser Arafat and the PLO from Lebanon and was committed in the name of 'fighting terrorism'. The US Secretary of State, Alexander Haig, approved the invasion and while the United States appealed for 'restraint', the call was made in a manner that Israel could ignore. Washington did not show a hardened resolve to 'smoke out' those responsible for the killings. On 16 September, a Christian militia that was backed by Israel began three days of rape and murder in Palestinian refugee camps. Over a thousand were killed while Israeli forces looked on. It was the first story that I worked on, and in the reports that I saw, there were no memorial services for the innocent dead of Lebanon or stirring speeches about evil killers or mass murder.

The legacy of the invasion was the Israeli occupation of southern Lebanon, which more than any other event spawned the modern vision of an Islamic terrorist. The revolutionary leaders in Tehran decided to respond to what they considered a new occupation of Muslim lands and formed Hizbollah from the large Shi'a population in Lebanon. They were determined to build a bridgehead for the creed of Ayatollah Khomeini, and in doing so exported the culture of martyrdom. Formed by radical Shi'ites, Hizbollah's heartland was the isolated and strategically placed town of Ba'albek, near Lebanon's border with Syria. It was at one time a tourist destination where the spectacular remains of Roman temples honouring Jupiter and Bacchus stand like outstretched fingers against snow-capped mountains. In the 1980s it became a Hizbollah stronghold and Lebanon had long ceased to attract visitors. Hizbollah declared it as the capital of the Islamic Republic of Lebanon. Posters of 'martyrs' and larger-than-life cut-outs of Ayatollah

Khomeini lined the streets and screamed their revolutionary message. At a roundabout outside the town, a captured Israeli tank stood as a war trophy. *Bassijis* from Iran were praying at the mosque when I was there and I was told to leave. The presence of Iranians was a sensitive matter that wasn't to be publicized.

Sara wore a gold scarf and a long, dark-brown gown. She was twenty-eight and had three children. She lived in a well-proportioned brick house on the edge of Ba'albek. 'Hizbollah built this house for me,' she told me proudly. The living room had an expensive-looking carpet: it too had been provided by Hizbollah. 'God will love our family because of my husband's sacrifice,' she told me with a smile. 'Hizbollah loves the family of a martyr. They pay for everything.' The Martyrs' Foundation was a charity financed by Iran that supported the families of dead Hizbollah soldiers. I was unable to work out what Sara really thought about her husband's suicide mission. Hizbollah had sent a minder who watched over me while I spoke to her. She offered gushing gratitude for the movement's generosity but seemed bemused that her husband wrote a letter saying that he wanted death rather than to stay with his family. I left her feeling that it was the dour minder from Hizbollah speaking, rather than her. 'I hope to meet Westerners,' she told me, 'to tell them the truth. They think Hizbollah are terrorists, but if people knew the truth, then everybody including Westerners would love them.'

The West began to view 'terrorism' as an enemy that originated in Iran and was fanning out through Lebanon. Saddam Hussein's Iraq was then an ally and was quietly supported by the West following its invasion of Iran. The US defined a threat as emanating from 'state-sponsored terrorism' and Iran, Syria and Libya were listed as nations that supported terrorism. The United States failed to distinguish one Muslim group from the next and the only common factor that brought the three nations together was their desire to confront Israeli aggression and challenge America's power in the region.

The aftermath of the Israeli invasion and the continued lawlessness prompted the West to send an international force of American, French and Italian troops to Lebanon to oversee the removal of Israeli, Syrian and Palestinian forces from Beirut. The regime in Tehran viewed this as a further encroachment of the West onto Muslim land and in October 1983, Hizbollah launched a spate of suicide attacks that ultimately drove the Western powers out of Lebanon. For Hizbollah, this signalled the ability of the suicide bomber to inflict defeat on much more powerful nations. 'Terrorism' had become a military tactic that reasserted the power of Islamic countries after years of decline. Spreading the Iranian Revolution abroad also realigned some groups within the Palestinian struggle for nationhood; Israel was no longer the sole enemy. The chief villain was Israel's backer, the United States.

Jerusalem Day in southern Beirut was one of the central events on the Hizbollah calendar. It resembled the May Day celebrations in the former Soviet Union, but instead of tanks, rows of men wearing black uniforms and ski masks marched to the sound of a brass band. They carried the yellow and green flags of Hizbollah displaying an AK-47 held aloft and shouted, 'Death to Israel! Death to America!' The parade was also intended to show Hizbollah's role as an all-encompassing Islamic movement. Tractors celebrating the role of farmers in feeding the people, fire engines and ambulances joined the army that declared its dream of martyrdom. Crowds lined the streets and stood on the rundown apartment blocks to get a better view. Hizbollah youth groups, in uniforms that resembled the scouts', carried banners of dead soldiers and portraits of the Iranian Ayatollahs, Khomeini and his successor Ali Khamanei. Hizbollah's General Secretary, Hasan Nasrallah, told the crowd that the festivities celebrated the cause of oppressed people everywhere. 'We live in a world full of bullying, which is led by the Great Satan, the United States of America.'

I visited one of Hizbollah's offices in a dusty backstreet in southern Beirut, where the group had a makeshift press office run by a round man in his forties called Abu Houran. It had been three years since the release of the last Western hostages. Abu Houran sat in a wooden chair playing with his prayer beads while he listened to my requests. I wanted an interview with Nasrallah and access to the Hizbollah fighters on the front line of their war with Israel in southern Lebanon. After Israel's invasion in 1982, it retreated from Beirut but maintained control of a section of southern Lebanon for nearly two decades. I was in southern Beirut for another reason, which I could not tell Abu Houran. I had reason to believe that I could obtain an interview with one of the men who had guarded the British hostages Terry Waite and John McCarthy. Hizbollah officially denied that it was involved in the kidnapping of Westerners but I knew that, under Iranian direction, a section of the movement was responsible. Once again, Iran had discovered a tactic of warfare that could intimidate and possibly defeat a superpower. The hostage-taking set a precedent that thrilled the radicals in Iran. As the American forces discovered two decades later in Iraq, kidnapping and suicide attacks are simple, cheap tools of combat that a superior military can find difficult to counter.

I was with the reporter Stephen Sackur. We were told by an intermediary to wait in an abandoned building. The former kidnapper did not want any local people to be with us and we were instructed not to reveal the location of our rendezvous. Stephen pondered whether we were walking into a trap; the bureau chief at the Reuters news agency wanted to film us making a statement in case we were later kidnapped. That was very thoughtful, I told him sarcastically. Stephen joked darkly that we should have brought a radio with us, so we'd be able to listen to the BBC, as Terry Waite had done to pass his hours of captivity. For six years the secrecy surrounding the hostage-takers was total and Western intelligence services had failed to penetrate the militant groups operating in Lebanon. Finally, our intermediary guided in another man with scarves concealing his face. He was surprisingly nervous but said he wanted to explain why he was involved in the hostage-taking. 'I do not feel guilty because the two we were holding [Waite and McCarthy] as well as the four others all returned home alive. We have many people in Israeli jails and many are dying there. Nobody asks about them.' He became agitated that a Western life seemed more valuable than a Muslim one. He also claimed that he'd treated Terry Waite humanely. 'At the beginning he was very scared but his situation got better because of the way we treated him. We used to offer him everything, including newspapers. He was held with another person, John McCarthy. After they adapted to captivity, they felt their life was normal.' His message was a common mantra from the Middle East: Israel and America kill many more civilians than Islamic militants but because the militants respond using the only military tactic available to them, they are condemned as evil terrorists.

Later, we interviewed Sheikh Hasan Nasrallah, the leader of Hizbollah. Nasrallah was a thoughtful and softly spoken man. The leader of the organization presented in much of the Western media as the world's most brutal terrorist group was friendly, chatty and well informed about the West. A question on the hostage-takers brought a little smile, perhaps a hint of satisfaction on his face. 'Why was the whole world interested in those two? Why has the kidnapping of a few foreigners in Lebanon shocked the world's conscience? The killing of women and children, the bombing of their homes and the illegal detention of tens of thousands of Palestinians and hundreds of Lebanese has not affected Israel's image in the West. It certainly hasn't shaken the conscience of the West.' He knew, of course, the answer to his first question. Hizbollah kidnapped Westerners precisely to display its power to the outside world.

After September 11th, Nasrallah thanked Syria and Iran for rejecting the US and European Union list of 'foreign terrorist organizations', which included Hizbollah and Palestinian groups not involved in the attacks. He praised Iran and Syria for insisting on a distinction between 'terrorist networks' such as al-Qa'eda and groups fighting Israeli occupation of Arab lands. Hizbollah had no particular liking for al-Qa'eda. The strict Wahhabi tradition that bin Laden and his Saudi supporters adhered to promotes a virulent hatred of Shi'ism, which it considers a deviant, unbelieving faith.

The American invasion of Iraq has again brought out the rhetoric of Islamic violence, despite Iran's quiet pleasure at the overthrow of Saddam. 'This is the war of a despotic, arrogant and cruel country against the nations of the world. We view America as an enemy of the Islamic nation yet we have not engaged it directly in a military act as of yet,' Nasrallah warned. He also praised suicide bombers as effective tools of resistance to American occupation. 'The Islamic nation has resumed the use of suicide attacks, without the act of suicide the struggle is meaningless . . . We must act in order to spread the concept of death in order to protect our land.'

While I dined in Tehran with the *bassiji* twins, Mehdi and Hamed, and their parents, another subject arose that highlighted the differing priorities and language of a divided world. I was asked how America could claim to be a civilized country and shoot down an Iranian airliner killing 290 passengers. In July 1988, a missile fired from an American warship, the USS *Vincennes*, struck Iran Air flight 655. The Iranian Airbus was flying within its approved commercial airline course in broad daylight over international waters. 'It was an accident,' I said and it was clear that the family didn't believe me. They scoffed in a most polite way and then said that the West should understand why people blow up American planes such as the Pan Am flight over Lockerbie. I asked them whether Iran had anything to do with that. 'I don't know,' the father replied, 'but perhaps Allah's justice works in mysterious ways.'

The downing of Iran Air 655 caused anger and shock in Iran but was generally passed off as an unfortunate accident in the Western media. A Libyan intelligence officer has since been convicted of the Lockerbie bombing and no official Iranian involvement was ever established. The conversation with the twins' father reminded me of a trip I'd made to the Beka'a valley in 1989 to meet Ahmed Jebril, the leader of the Popular Front for the Liberation of Palestine–General Command. At the time, he was one of the primary suspects in the Lockerbie bombing. He controlled some Palestinian camps in the region, where forty years of exile still burnt like a fuse. Jebril had split from Yasser Arafat's PLO and decamped to Damascus, where his movement became an instrument of the Syrian government.

I met Ahmed Jebril in Damascus and he took me to his headquarters in the Beka'a Valley across the border in Lebanon. The partnership between Iran and Syria, with Saddam Hussein's Iraq as one of many common enemies, allowed secular Palestinian groups like the PFLP–GC to operate alongside Hizbollah forces. Jebril had a squat frame and a Gallic nose that he peered down, giving him a smug demeanour. He appeared to enjoy entertaining journalists from the BBC and lectured me on the Balfour Declaration and Britain's role in the creation of Israel. 'One day, Britain will pay for it,' he warned. He led me from one location to another and left me in a room with bead curtains and brown walls. Ahmed Jebril's organization had been using bombs triggered by barometric pressure devices, similar to that hidden in a Toshiba radio-cassette recorder that brought down Pan Am 103 over Scotland. Lengthy police inquiries found no link between Jebril and the bombing but the role of Iranian, Libyan and Syrian intelligence services and their links with militant organizations was never penetrated by Western investigators.

A comment that Jebril made was repeated, uncannily closely, by the *bassiji* Hamed several years later. 'The Americans shot down one airliner. Someone else brings down an American airliner. Both are tragedies but America was responsible for the first act of terrorism,' Jebril told us when we spoke about the downing of the Iranian airbus. Seven years later I munched on grilled chicken when Hamed reflected on the Lockerbie disaster. 'Our airliner was shot down. Yours was also bombed. Two tragedies. But who started the aggression?'

12 / DEATH OF THE FREEDOM FIGHTER

'One man's terrorist is everyone's terrorist.'
Brian M. Jenkins, Senior Adviser on Terrorism, RAND Corporation

They swarmed over the wooded hillside shouting with their hands in the air. Most of the men and boys wore jeans, some had check shirts. It was almost like a herd of football supporters descending on a rival town. In this case, they were demanding the independence of their country. They were Kashmiris who had fled from Indian forces and crossed into Pakistani-controlled Kashmir.

It was 1990. The hundreds of young men belonged to the Jammu and Kashmir Liberation Front (JKLF), a political organization that campaigned for the independence of the former British Indian state of Jammu and Kashmir, generally known as Kashmir, which is divided between Indian and Pakistani rule.

The JKLF militants were known in Indian-controlled Kashmir affectionately as 'the boys', but since 1988, their activities had become increasingly violent. They were fleeing the Indian police. 'The CRPF beat us up,' said one. He looked no more than fifteen and displayed a red gash under his eye like a battle trophy. The Central Reserve Police Force was a paramilitary outfit sent from the Indian capital, Delhi, to quell rioting or combat separatist groups when the situation was too serious for the state police. They looked like soldiers, wearing army-style helmets and khaki fatigues. 'They mistreated his sister,' someone said. 'Whose sister?' I asked, trying to scribble names in my notebook as the crowd jostled around me in a friendly but irritating way. 'His sister. His sister. All our sisters,' said Malik, a serious man in his twenties. 'Every Kashmiri is terrorized by Indian forces. They shoot people in the street. They insult our mothers. One man was killed five minutes before curfew. The CRPF wallah just said his watch must have been wrong.'

Their accounts of abuse and discrimination were impossible to verify because the Indians had prevented foreign journalists from travelling into their segment of Kashmir. Later, when I looked back at my notes and the television reports, I realized that there was no mention of Islam, which was at the heart of the dispute in Kashmir. Yet Islam was not driving the confrontation in 1990; instead it was *azadi* (freedom).

A few years earlier, India had blatantly rigged state elections to prevent a secessionist alliance, the Muslim United Front (MUF), from gaining power. Two weeks before the vote, six hundred MUF workers were arrested, ballot boxes went missing and the police threw MUF counting agents from polling stations. The Delhi-based political magazine *India Today* said: 'These events . . . have only served to produce a deeper feeling of alienation among the youth who have flocked to the opposition – even the MUF – in search of an alternative power structure in Kashmir.'

The JKLF launched its first violent attack a few months later, on the motorcade of the Chief Minister of Jammu and Kashmir, Farooq Abdullah. No one was seriously hurt. In September 1988, after a month of small-scale rioting, the police killed a JKLF militant, Ajaz Dar; the movement had its first 'martyr'. The JKLF was growing into a powerful underground organization that could bring Srinagar, the summer capital of Kashmir, to its knees by ordering businesses to shut for a day. At one musical performance at a bandstand in the city, four masked men suddenly appeared on stage, and raised AK-47s above their heads. According to one onlooker, 'the entire crowd fell into an electrified silence for a few moments. And then it exploded like a wave, the resounding cries of *azadi* or freedom.' The four men were from the JKLF. The 'boys' were becoming more influential than the pro-Delhi government of Farooq Abdullah, which had lost its popular credibility.

The crisis in Kashmir was to be propelled into a newer, dramatic phase that captured the attention of the world's media in December 1989. Six days after her father became India's Home Minister, members of the JKLF kidnapped a twenty-three-year-old student, Rubaiya Sayeed. The movement demanded the release of its jailed activists. The government in Delhi capitulated and agreed to free five militants in return for Rubaiya, including the JKLF leader, Hamid Sheikh. As soon as the news of the five men's release filtered through Srinagar, the streets filled with crowds that danced in celebration. According to the Indian journalist Tavleen Singh, 'by the time Rubaiya Sayeed was kidnapped, ordinary Kashmiris were convinced that *azadi* was barely weeks away.'

After Rubaiya had been safely returned, her father, Mufti Sayeed, who was directly in charge of India's internal security, packed the Kashmiri Valley with police and paramilitary forces. An undeclared civil war began and the flood of young men that I saw crossing into Pakistan were fleeing arrest or seeking to regroup before returning, better armed and better trained, to confront the Indian forces. The young men who had congregated around me asked where I was from and whether I played cricket. They were mostly teenagers and were inquisitive and friendly towards Western journalists. Not many reporters described them as terrorists. Nor were they Islamists. The JKLF 'boys' were Muslim, and in common with other South Asians of the faith they dropped 'inshallah', or 'God willing', regularly into the conversation, but the JKLF was a secular organization, which sought independence for Kashmir, had a popular support base and held legitimate grievances against the Indian government.

Kashmir is a victim of the disputed division of British India during the transfer of colonial power in 1947. A border was created on religious lines, and states with a Muslim majority formed the newly created Pakistan alongside a predominantly Hindu India. When India and Pakistan became independent, it was generally assumed that Jammu and Kashmir, with its 80 per cent Muslim population, would accede to Pakistan, but Kashmir was one of 565 princely states whose rulers had given their loyalty to Britain but preserved their royal titles. The partition plan, negotiated by the last viceroy, Lord Mountbatten, excluded these princely states, which were granted independence (albeit without the power to express it). Of the 565 princely states, 552 agreed to become part of India but the remainder posed problems: Hyderabad and Junagadh had Muslim rulers but Hindu majorities and were surrounded by Indian territory. Indian troops occupied the states and overthrew the Muslim rulers. In Kashmir a Hindu nobleman, Sir Hari Singh, was the maharaja, or governor. Two months after the independence of India and Pakistan, he was still unable to make up his mind.

Opposition to the autocratic rule of the maharaja had emerged before the Second World War and his prevarication now triggered an armed revolt by farmers in the south of the Kashmir Valley. Many Muslims were deserting the state forces and the crisis was complete when thousands of tribesmen from Pakistan's North-West Frontier Province, armed with modern weaponry, invaded Kashmir and reached thirty miles from Srinagar. The maharaja despatched a hurried letter to Lord Mountbatten, who had remained in India after independence. 'I have no option but to ask for help from the Indian Dominion,' he wrote. 'Naturally they cannot send the help asked for by me without my state acceding to India. I have accordingly decided to do so . . .'

The formal accession of Kashmir to India was announced on 27 October 1947. Indian troops were airlifted to Srinagar airport to support the maharaja's forces and waged a successful defence of the capital. The invading Pashtun fighters were driven out of the Kashmir Valley and into the surrounding mountains. Within three months of their independence, Pakistan and India were at war. The United Nations eventually brokered a peace deal, which left Kashmir with an arbitrary ceasefire line curling through its territory and divided between the Indian- and Pakistani-controlled segments. A UN Resolution was passed on 5 January 1948 that agreed the accession of Kashmir to India or Pakistan should be decided through a free impartial plebiscite. But this was not forthcoming.

'We picked up the gun because it is our basic right, which has been taken from us. It is contained in the UN resolution,' Abdullah told me, jabbing his finger. He wore a black scarf over his face to conceal his identity but otherwise wore camouflage fatigues. He had been labelled a terrorist by the United States and Europe and several Kashmiri militants have been linked with al-Qa'eda. He was battle-ready; his AK-47 had been cleaned and was by his side. He said India had repeatedly denied Kashmiri people a meaningful democratic voice. 'At the time of partition of the Indo-Pak subcontinent,' he told me, sighing heavily, 'it was decided that the Muslim-majority areas would be asked which country they wanted to join. But even after the lapse of fifty years this right has not been given to Kashmiris, whether they wish to affiliate themselves with India or Pakistan, or to remain independent.' Abdullah said the West applied double standards; it was willing to support UN resolutions that attacked Muslim countries 'in the interests of peace' and yet was unwilling to implement those that defended

Muslim land. 'UN resolutions about Kashmir, just as those on Palestine, are ignored,' he complained.

It was autumn 1998, more than eight years since I'd seen the jubilant groups of 'boys' cross into Pakistan, naive and unsure of their fate, but eager to do something to rectify the injustice they saw around them. Abdullah had been one of those boys. He fled to Pakistan after the Indian government rigged the 1987 state elections in Kashmir and detained members of his party, the Muslim United Front. 'I was from Kupwara and training to be a medical technician. I spent two years in jail. After the kidnapping of the Home Minister's daughter, the Indian forces targeted my family. I crossed into *azad* ['Free', or Pakistani-controlled] Kashmir.' Later that year, but now armed and trained, he crossed back as a 'Kashmiri freedom fighter'.

Abdullah had made the journey across rugged, mountainous terrain, in both directions, on three separate occasions since 1990. He followed a route that kept him under the cover of thick forest to prevent Indian helicopters or spotters finding him. 'We travel in small groups, four to six fighters,' he told me. 'Sometimes I stay there for a few months at a time.'

I met Abdullah in Muzaffarabad, the capital of the part of Kashmir held by Pakistan. The main street ran alongside a dramatic ravine cut by the merging of the Jhelum and Neelam rivers, which flowed from the mountains on the Indian side of this divided state. Houses and hotels perched on the edge of a cliff face, hundreds of feet above the river. Muzaffarabad was only about eighty miles from Pakistan's capital city, Islamabad, but the drive, along winding roads that hugged the picturesque, forested mountains of the Murree Hills, took over four hours. Muzaffarabad was the staging post for the insurrection and was surrounded by training camps for militants. It was said to be teeming with men from Pakistan's military intelligence agency, the ISI. There were also refugee camps; about twenty thousand Kashmiris from the Indian side had been living there since the early 1990s. It was a town where 'freedom-fighters' were bred, schooled and armed.

Abdullah was packing his bags for another journey across the border. His mission was to attack Indian posts and kill members of their security forces. He proudly showed me his kit. 'This is a Kalashnikov, this is our weapon of choice,' he said, holding up a freshly polished and shining assault rifle. 'We use it to strike our targets. It's also for our defence if the enemy attacks us.' Before loading it, he took aim and pulled the trigger to make the point. 'This is my pistol,' he said and placed a black Chinese-made 9mm handgun into his backpack. 'This is useful for a close target, especially if I need to hide the gun.' He then packed his Yaesu radio handset, supplied by the ISI. 'We use it twenty-four hours a day. It's essential when we carry out an operation or arrange for our group to meet up.' He also put six magazines of ammunition into the backpack along with some food. He offered me some pickle and sweet fruit jam as he made his 'lunch box'. He rolled the pickle in some rather gritty chapattis. 'Dates and dried fruit are also useful,' he told me, 'if we are in the forest and we find that there is nothing to eat.' Abdullah then smiled, unable to resist making a political point, raising his thick eyebrows to form a 'V' above his nose. 'If there is a real need for food, we go to villages and people there feed us. They fully support us.'

Abdullah told a chilling story, which I couldn't verify, of the methods used by the Indian security forces to persuade a militant to turn himself in. He said that two of his family's houses were blown up when he refused to surrender. Then members of his family were killed, one by one, leading finally to the murder of his wife. 'You cannot believe the atrocities that are being inflicted on us,' he said. 'Seven members of my family were killed to make me surrender. But we will not give in.'

Abdullah believed that the support enjoyed by his militants from a significant part of the Kashmiri population meant that he could never be considered a terrorist. 'Our movement is alive because it has the support of the people of Kashmir. The movement is continuing inside,' he said as he thumped his chest. 'Whenever I went to Kupwara or elsewhere in Kashmir, people welcomed us, housed us and sacrificed their homes, even their lives and their children for us.' He signed heavily. 'With the help of God, India will leave Kashmir very soon.'

I'd visited Abdullah's hometown in the tense frontier district of Kupwara a few weeks earlier. It felt like a city at war; the roads were deserted long before nightfall. At dawn, dozens of Indian troops scoured the main street, searching for bombs using metal detectors. Many shops, with shutters drawn, never opened. There were very few young men; just the very old, and women and children. In this dirty war with no front line, Pakistan and India faced each through the people of Kashmir. At least thirty thousand, perhaps as many as fifty thousand, have perished since 1990.

Neeraj Bali was the local Indian commander; his expertise was counter-insurgency warfare. He was a jovial, intelligent, slightly portly colonel with a wily military mind. I later recalled something Abdullah told me, that his task was to kill a senior officer in the Indian security forces. 'We want a high-ranking officer like a colonel. If we find one we will kill him.' Bali enjoyed his cat-and-mouse game with militants like Abdullah and such a threat would have only entertained him. He had a relish for battle as if he was one of the Three Musketeers.

Colonel Bali led a unit of the Rashtriya Rifles, a force established primarily to quell the uprising in Kashmir. 'Our mandate is to carry out counter-insurgency operations, to make sure the areas are sanitized and the militants either fall into our bag by way of surrenders or are eliminated.' He gave a mischievous smile and a South Asian sideways bob of the head. 'We've eliminated . . .' he paused, 'and by that I mean killed, approximately thirty-five militants during the last year.'

Colonel Bali had an appealing arrogance. His round face would break into a smile even during the most serious discussion. 'The scales have tipped against these young boys,' he said as he sipped a brandy with me in the mess hall. 'They are badly trained and inexperienced. They need to learn a few new tricks,' he said. 'We've got them cornered. They have trepidation in their hearts. They really don't stand a chance.'

I later told Abdullah about Colonel Bali's assessment. His face visibly reddened. 'The Rashtriya Rifles are rogues and thugs, people who bear malice against Muslims . . .' He paused and pointed his finger at me. 'You ask him: if we cannot fight them, could he tell us about the three major generals that have been killed to date? In addition to this nearly two hundred others killed, including colonels, majors and brigadiers?' I felt I was in the middle of a schoolyard brawl, rather than 'the war on terror'. 'God willing,' Abdullah sniffed, 'India will surrender very soon and she will run from Kashmir and the colonel will not even look back.'

Colonel Bali allowed us to join his unit during a raid in a village just outside Kupwara. An informant had told Bali that a group of militants was holed up in a house in the village. Local people had little love for India and even less for its army but were weary after nearly a decade of war. The Rashtriya Rifles were quick to exploit the disillusioned. 'People are fed up with the militancy so there are more and more people informing us.' Their counter-insurgency tactics had been repeatedly criticized by human-rights groups but Bali scoffed at outsiders' opinion. He believed the deliberate display of force had been a successful tool of psychological warfare. 'Locals gravitate toward the stronger force,' he said. 'If we were not able to dominate the militants, then we would not have so many people informing for us.' He smiled and bobbed his head from side to side.

Colonel Bali was a Hollywood-style performer for our television cameras. Before the raid, he summoned the head of the village mosque for a meeting. 'Whatever the Almighty will do it will be righteous,' the Hindu commander told the Muslim leader. 'You may go. Tell the children to sit with comfort, not to worry.' The village elders around the Imam looked at each other with a combination of bemusement and fear. They only broke into an ironic smile when Bali added, 'Relax. This is your army, not the Pakistani army.'

Suddenly, shots rang out. The militants had opened fire. For half an hour, the two sides exchanged a hail of bullets. We had to run about twenty yards across an area that was in the line of fire. The Rashtriya Rifles provided cover as we fled. My heart was pounding as we burst into someone's house; the occupants and their children were huddled under a table, their faces frozen in an expression of primal fear.

As darkness fell, the gunfire subsided and the father of one of militants signalled that the men wanted to surrender. He asked Colonel Bali to spare his son's life. Bali stood up and marched without a helmet or bulletproof vest toward the house where the gunmen were hiding. In the midst of the crisis, he even turned to our camera to provide a commentary. 'He's saying there are two. He said they are piddling . . . Bastards. Piddling out of fear. He said he'd get them out.' Shortly afterwards there was movement in the darkness and the militants walked out and laid down their arms.

It later emerged that the two men had crossed the border from Muzaffarabad just three days earlier. According to Colonel Bali, the men had been trained and were given a simple order by the ISI. 'They were told, now that you've been trained, go and fight the [Indian] army.' Bali showed me their AK-47 rifles; they were shiny, similar to Abdullah's. 'Brand new, by the look of it,' he commented.

During the week that I spent with Colonel Bali, he never once described his adversaries as terrorists. He even joked once that they were *not* terrorists because they 'frightened no one'; they were just 'young boys'. He meant, of course, that his men, the militants' chief target, were not intimidated. He was open about the support that militants had from many civilians. His job was to separate the militant from those who housed and fed him. Bali was a clever military tactician who was well versed in psychological warfare; I think he would have considered a 'war on terror' a phrase that may have meant something to politicians but had little value for soldiers.

There is another reason that accusations of 'terrorism' had been rarely exchanged. Pakistan and India have technically been at war for over half a century in a low-level conflict, where each nation's intelligence agency has covertly armed and trained guerrilla groups as proxy armies. Instead of waging a lengthy, conventional military confrontation, such as Iraq's seven-year bloodbath with Iran, each nation has preferred to sponsor guerrilla groups in order to harass and weaken its adversary. While they have fought three fully-fledged wars, each was short and escalated from cross-border insurgency.

The involvement of Indian and Pakistani intelligence agencies is widely assumed to extend to random bombings, which have killed hundreds of civilians on both sides while mystery surrounds the carnage. No group ever admits planting the bombs, rarely is anyone caught and rumours of conspiracy and intrigue circulate. In August 2003, two coordinated blasts rocked Bombay within minutes of each other. The first was at the stone arch of the Gateway of India, the second in a crowded jewellery bazaar. At least fifty people died and more than a hundred were injured. The Indian police said that local Muslim militants had planted the bombs with the support of Pakistan's ISI. There was speculation that the attacks were in retaliation for riots in the neighbouring state of Gujarat, which had left more than two thousand people dead, mostly Muslims. Railways have been easy targets of this covert conflict, apparently chosen randomly in a bloody tit-for-tat exchange.

Following one such attack in Lahore, I visited the city's Bomb Disposal Laboratory, where the debris from the explosions was analysed. The explosives expert was Commander Mushtaq Hussein, a man in a baggy white salwar kameez who was always smiling. He enjoyed talking about bombs and explosives, as well as the devastation they cause. Did he have conclusive evidence of the involvement of Indian intelligence? 'When the bomb explodes, no evidence is left,' he pointed out, rather pompously. 'But we can tell where it has originated by its weight and power. Who else would do this deed? They attack us, we must strike back.' He chuckled and his head bobbed sideways. While no firm evidence was discovered, Commander Hussein claimed that the large number of unexploded bombs proved the existence of a broader campaign and a hidden hand. 'Everything is clearly marked,' he said. ' "Made in India". No other evidence is needed. After all, they are our enemies.' At times, Commander Hussein seemed a part of this gruesome, murderous game, played out by the powerful using the lives of the innocent.

It was a murky, opaque war fought by anonymous men. Yet while Commander Hussein repeatedly spoke of India's nefarious role in planting bombs in Pakistan, he never once accused India of terrorism. As both countries conducted their covert war, they maintained a political dialogue. They did not condemn their rival's actions as 'evil terrorism' because both sides used similar tactics. It was a strategic matter rather than a moral crusade and self-righteous terms such as a 'war on terror' would have seemed inappropriate.

The bloodiest act of political violence that I have witnessed in immediate aftermath was in the northern Indian state of Punjab in June 1991. In the 1970s, Sikhs, who form a majority in the state, began complaining about unfair treatment from the central government in Delhi. The Sikh religious party, the Akali Dal, demanded greater autonomy for the state and, with money from Sikh migrants in Britain, Canada and the United States, the idea of reviving an independent, nineteenth-century Sikh kingdom gained popular support. A holy man, or *sant*, Jarnail Singh Bhindranwale, became the focus of the demand for a separate Sikh homeland called Khalistan, or 'Land of the Pure'.

It went very wrong. Bhindranwale began to assassinate opponents and harassed the large Hindu minority in the Punjab, hoping to expel them from the state. His supporters gathered in the complex surrounding the Golden Temple in Amritsar, the Sikh Vatican. Bhindranwale's men fortified the holy site and turned it into a base for an armed rebellion. In June 1984, the Prime Minister, Indira Gandhi, launched Operation Blue Star, in which infantry, tanks and artillery were used against the armed Sikh militants inside the Golden Temple. Bhindranwale and his 250 disciples were eventually flushed out and many killed but the Golden Temple complex resembled a war zone; bullet holes pock-marked the site and the Akal Takht, the shrine that symbolizes the temporal power of God and where the Sikh holy scriptures are solemnly laid to rest every night, had been burnt and turned into rubble by a bombardment of tank shells. In outrage, there were mutinies in several army battalions and prominent Sikh politicians resigned. As chaos hung over India, Indira Gandhi was assassinated by a policeman guarding her home.

Just over three years later the Golden Temple had again been turned into an armed fortress run by militants seeking independence. I walked around the Sarowar, the Holy Pool in the middle of the complex, and dozens of young men wearing white robes and saffron turbans (the colour of martyrdom) milled around carrying rifles and Sten guns. One boy was barely twelve years old, carrying an AK-47 that was as large as he was. I asked why he had a gun. 'I am defending my faith,' he replied instantly and then smiled. 'Where are you from?' he asked, quickly dropping the guise of adulthood.

After Indira Gandhi died, enraged Hindus massacred thousands of Sikhs in Delhi, often with the complicity of the police. Bhindranwale and his followers had become martyrs for many Sikhs and an armed uprising evolved in the state. By 1988, around twenty people were killed each day, either by the militants or at the hands of the police, who routinely executed suspects and claimed the incident had been an 'encounter'. As so often in any counter-insurgency, the army had taken many more lives than the militants.

The second attack on the Golden Temple, codenamed Operation Black Thunder, was run by India's new counter-terrorism force, the National Security Guard Commandos, or 'Black Cats'. While Black Thunder was conducted with more precision and the casualties and damage were much smaller, the assault continued to feed Sikh anger and fuel the rebellion. 'Terrorism' began to be used more frequently to describe the activities of the militants, especially after they threatened newspaper editors and murdered newspaper vendors. The attempt to intimidate the media seemed a literal attempt to terrorize, rather than conduct, an insurgency. While the *Times of India* maintained 'militants' as its preferred description in its news reporting, the *Sunday Observer* in Delhi reported in 1990 that 'Punjab Press Succumbs to Terrorism' after newspapers in the state printed statements issued by the militants. Newspaper editors were warned of 'dire consequences' if they did not comply with the directive to publish the statements in full.

Many Indians regarded the Sikh demand for secession as a family betrayal; Sikhism had emerged as a monotheistic offshoot of the Hindu faith and the two had existed within the same culture and traditions. 'Terrorism' was used more frequently by Indians to describe the insurrection in Punjab than the violence in Kashmir; it was because the Kashmir problem was directly tied to relations between India and Pakistan and was considered part of that war. Despite routine claims of Pakistani assistance to the Khalistan rebels, the violence in Punjab was less comprehensible to Indians and 'terrorist' made more sense than 'insurgent'.

Another interesting understanding of 'terrorism' emerged from a policeman one day in June 1991, when Sikh militants gunned down eighty-two passengers on two different trains near Ludhiana, in Punjab. A group of four or five gunmen had told Sikhs to leave the train and then fired bullets indiscriminately at the remaining Hindu passengers.

'What kind of people would do this?' I asked an attending policeman.

'The killers are just young boys. They don't know what they are doing. They are not terrorists,' he replied. For some in India's security forces, terrorism gave a status and purpose to the killing. Instead, they argued, the Sikh militants were angry boys who had no serious political agenda.

Any hesitation over the use of 'terrorism' by the Indian establishment disappeared after 2001. In the 1990s, the Hindu nationalist government was already seeking international support for its conflict against insurgents in Kashmir by playing on the anti-terrorist sensibilities of the West. After September 11th, the conflict in Kashmir was presented in the national media as India's contribution to the 'war on terror'. The prolific writer and journalist Asghar Ali Engineer was concerned by this new vocabulary. 'We have had violence from across the border since the 1990s but never used "terrorist violence" for it. We called it either extremism or militancy. But now, we call it "cross-border terrorism" after 9/11. Thus, American rulers and American media set the term for us to be used. America devises terms to reflect its own interests . . .'* The Kashmiri independence fighters had already been defined as terrorists and it served Indian interests well to associate Kashmiri independence with Osama bin Laden. Intriguingly, one of the additions to the US list of terrorist organizations in 2003 was a

---

* *Tribune of India*, 5 January 2003.

Sikh independence party, even though the rebellion inside the Punjab had fizzled out in the early 1990s.

Nine days after the attacks on America, Bush made his defining speech on the 'war on terror'. 'Our "war on terror" begins with al-Qa'eda, but it does not end there. It will not end until every terrorist group of global reach has been found, stopped and defeated.' The implications of this statement were phenomenal and although the administration initially targeted al-Qa'eda, governments across the world lost little time in using the failure to define a terrorist to their advantage. The global 'war on terror' became an excuse for some countries to crack down on internal opposition.

The Israeli Prime Minister, Ariel Sharon, called Yasser Arafat 'our bin Laden' and threatened to assassinate him. Russia condemned Muslim rebels in Chechnya as 'terrorists' and justified its army's brutality. How could the West criticize President Vladimir Putin for human-rights abuses when he was fighting the same war as America and Europe? And it worked. Western countries began to downplay their criticism as Moscow joined the coalition. The autocratic regime in Uzbekistan justified as part of a global 'war on terror' its crackdown on opposition politicians and Muslims who practised their religion peacefully. Muslim separatists from the Uigher minority in western China became 'terrorists' as Beijing's media repeatedly linked Uigher militants to al-Qa'eda. A prominent Chinese pro-democracy activist was given a life sentence after a secret trial convicted him of 'terrorist activities'. Jordan introduced anti-terrorism laws that allowed the government to imprison anyone who wrote articles deemed to undermine the king or the royal family. Even Zimbabwe's President, Robert Mugabe, justified a crackdown on independent journalists as part of a global fight against the 'supporters of terrorism'.

President Bush played into bin Laden's hands. In the mid-1990s, Islamic militancy was at a crossroads; most Islamists were fighting for religious, social and political rights within their own countries but were failing to dislodge their secular, authoritarian governments. Most Islamists, including Hamas and Islamic Jihad in the Palestinian Territories, Hizbollah in Lebanon and sections of the armed groups in Algeria and Egypt, believed that a broad, utopian international campaign against the West was pointless. The Taliban movement, which had taken over in Afghanistan in 1996, found the idea quixotic and impractical. They harboured Osama bin Laden because of his largesse and his impeccable credentials as a dedicated Muslim. At that time, few Islamists put any credence in the theory of a 'distant war' that bin Laden and his deputy, Ayman Zawahri, would shortly declare on America.

On the other hand, bin Laden was becoming a figure of awe and fascination while the Islamic revival triggered by the Iranian Revolution and the expulsion of the Soviets from Afghanistan was foundering. The authoritarian regimes in Egypt and Algeria were gaining the upper hand in their conflicts using brutal methods. Muslims were being slaughtered in Bosnia and women systematically raped. Whole towns and villages in Chechnya were razed and thousands of civilians killed by Russian planes and artillery. Rather than enjoying the benefits of democracy and freedom after the collapse of communism, Islamists in the former Soviet republics in Central Asia were facing even harsher abuses and restrictions on the practice of their faith. There were massacres in Sri Lanka as worshippers prayed in their mosques. Human-rights violations in Indian-controlled Kashmir continued as the outside world looked away. The prospects of peace in the Palestinian territories receded sharply with the murder of Yitzhak Rabin in 1995 and the gradual collapse of the Oslo accords.

Islamists began to ask why their fellow Muslims were suffering. I remember armed rebels in Algeria in 1994 telling me how well Muslims were treated in Britain and America. One told me that the Islamic republic they were hoping to create in Algeria would become a close ally of Britain. 'Come back and visit us then,' he told me. 'You will be a guest of honour.' France alone was their enemy, blamed for supporting the military coup that ended the prospect of an elected Islamic government. The Gama'a Islamiyah fighters that I met in 1992 pleaded for Western countries, who they believed were concerned with human-rights abuses, to prevent the torture and mistreatment of Islamists in Egypt. I met a Tunisian Islamist, living in exile in London, who believed that the ending of the cold war would usher an era of openness and democracy to the Middle East. He argued that superpower rivalry had created client states in the region and propped up the despots and tyrants who governed them; that would be no longer necessary.

The Islamists' understanding of openness and democracy was, of course, rooted in the Qur'ān. While it differed from Western models of democracy, it was in keeping with the lifestyle and values of most within those nations. The Western media showed little interest in understanding Islamic notions of consultation (*shura*) or public interest (*al-maslaha*), or describing the aspirations of Islamists for an egalitarian and spiritual society, free from exploitation and corruption. Instead, it focused on local cultural practices found in villages in Sudan or Afghanistan, such as female genital mutilation, the stoning of adulterers or amputating limbs of those convicted of theft. In the American and European media, obscure and primitive practices, usually in remote areas, are elevated to represent Islamic values. I have had numerous debates with well-educated Islamists and these activities were mostly condemned and were certainly not the defining features of an Islamic society. I attended a class in Iran where women were taught about birth control. It was a controversial issue in Islam and yet the Iranian government had launched a campaign to educate women about family planning that would be frowned upon in some Catholic countries. The teacher, wearing a flowing black chador, asked me whether the West was bringing up its children well when both parents worked and divorce rates were soaring. 'Women are equal but different in Islam,' she told me. 'As a mother and as a human being, it is my duty to bring up my family. I don't feel inferior to my husband because of that.' Many in the West may disagree with the teacher's view but she presented an intelligent argument.

A prominent member of the Muslim Brotherhood in Egypt expressed a common mood amongst Islamists in 1997. Abou Elela Mady was always immaculately dressed with a well-trimmed beard and a commanding presence. While we discussed the arrest of many of his colleagues on trumped-up charges, I dropped in the subject of the genital mutilation of women in Egypt, which had recently had extensive coverage in the international media. 'It's wrong,' he said. 'It's not an Islamic practice. Many Islamic countries are still poor and their people lack education. Why do we always have to defend our faith because of that? Christians introduced slavery. Hitler was a Christian. Christians dropped nuclear bombs on Japan. But we don't associate these things with Christianity.' I sensed that Islamists who rejected violence, such as Abou Elela Mady, were increasingly on the defensive. Another prominent Islamist complained that the only question the Western media asked of him was to condemn Islamist terrorism, rather than examine the conditions that created it.

Two particular events occurred in the 1990s to accelerate the circumstances that led to the globalization of Islamic militancy. The first was the Gulf War, following the Iraqi invasion of Kuwait. The kings and princes of the royal families of the Gulf states were detested by large numbers of Arabs for their privileges, ostentatious displays of wealth and, very often, hypocrisy. I spent several weeks in Baghdad during that conflict and found the Iraqi people warm and friendly, representing a rich culture but suffering terribly under the rule of a cruel despot. In Saudi Arabia, I met Muslims working in the kingdom from Bangladesh, the Philippines and Pakistan, as well as Palestinians, and when I grabbed a private, whispered conversation, they spoke of hatred and fear of their Saudi masters. I entered Kuwait City and heard stories of rape and beatings. Yet when the supply of oil was under threat, a vast American-led army was sent to the Arabian desert to restore the Kuwaiti royal family and secure the defence of Saudi Arabia and the other Gulf states.

The United States had been criticized by Islamists in the past for propping up undemocratic, corrupt and un-Islamic leaders, whom they dubbed the 'Eunuchs'. The British had placed the House of Saud in power in the 1920s and after the Second World War the United States became its primary foreign patron. The US had leased an air base in Dhahran since the 1950s but the sight of women GIs driving through Riyadh and the conspicuous display of American power on Saudi soil brought to public attention an uncomfortable truth: the Saudi king, the Custodian of the Two Holy Places of Mecca and Medina, was propped up by the US. The spectre of Islam's holiest shrines depending on Western protection was an insult for many Islamists. It particularly shaped one man's world view and convinced him that the survival of Islam was in jeopardy. He was Osama bin Laden.

The second development of the 1990s that made Islamists feel insecure about a partnership with the West was globalization. It was transforming the planet and the relative economic weakness of Muslim nations made them especially vulnerable to the encroachment of Western culture. The communications revolution brought satellite television, including MTV with its diet of sexual innuendo and scantily clad dancers, into Muslim homes that had raised their children to believe in the sanctity of marriage and modesty in dress. On the other hand, America was outraged when the pop singer Janet Jackson revealed a breast during half-time entertainment at the 2004 NFL

Super Bowl, America's most important sporting occasion. It shocked the nation and the story dragged on for days; many commentators wrote that the fabric of family life had been seriously eroded. If an Islamic nation tries (and inevitably fails) to ban satellite dishes, it is regarded in the Western media as censorship and the mark of a dictatorship unwilling to become part of the global community.

Globalization also meant that the plight of Muslims in the world was no longer being perceived as the result of local or national factors. Satellites brought pictures of Bosnian Muslims being killed by Christian Serbs to television screens in Egypt, Malaysia and Indonesia. The Israeli treatment of Palestinians reinforced a common theme; Muslims were victims of something beyond their control. I was travelling through Eastern Java in 1990 and after I said I was a journalist, a kindly taxi driver asked me about Israeli policy during the first intifada. He didn't seem angry, just bemused. 'The Jews have guns,' he said, 'the Muslims only have stones. It's not fair. Why don't Muslims have guns too?'

Twelve years later I was in Indonesia once more, milling with crowds leaving the Istiqlal Mosque in Jakarta after Friday prayers. The atmosphere was relaxed and friendly. At a nearby market I met a man selling kitchen utensils. He was in his late thirties and had a cheery, round face and a small clipped moustache. He wore a baseball cap with Osama bin Laden's stern face glowering from its centre. I asked what he thought about bin Laden. 'He's protecting Muslims. He's a good man.' He smiled at me as if his view wasn't particularly controversial.

'What about the attacks on the World Trade Center?'

'Sorry, sorry,' he replied, as if September 11th was an unfortunate necessity. 'But bin Laden is a strong man. He's defending Muslims.'

It was in 1996 that Osama bin Laden emerged in the wider Islamic world with a theory that attempted to make sense of the suffering of Muslims. He declared that the Crusaders and Jews were to blame and the faith was in a state of crisis. His war on America began in earnest with the attacks on the US Embassies in Nairobi and Dar es Salaam in 1998. Here was a man who was able to give America a bloody nose and many non-violent Muslims that I've met, while grieving for the families of the victims, felt that America had it coming. The 'Eunuch' leaders, endless Arab summits, even the United Nations when it passed resolutions in favour of Muslim nations, were powerless to challenge America. Now this lanky billionaire cave-dweller in Afghanistan was taking on a superpower.

Thousands of Islamic radicals who had fought for specific national objectives, from Malaysia to Morocco and Bangladesh to Indonesia, found al-Qa'eda ideologists joining them at conferences and they began discussing the idea of a common goal. Many of these groups spurned al-Qa'eda's global ambitions as irrelevant to their local fight but they often maintained informal links.

America's 'war on terror' allowed bin Laden's vision to materialize. The US and Europe branded as terrorists and confiscated funds from scores of Islamist organizations, including regional insurgents, educational organizations and charities. Many organizations had no quarrel and no desire to target the United States but found themselves in its sights. For many Islamist militants around the world, Bush had pushed them into a corner. They were forced to choose between surrender or bin Laden. Most chose the latter.

Bush's 'crusade' against terror, which he declared but later retracted because of its historical connotations, fulfilled the vision held by Islamist militants who had read Sayyid Qutb and conjured up an inevitable clash between Islam and the West. Al-Qa'eda's programme became easy to export because it was a simple idea without the complications of a movement rooted in specific, local grievances. Immediately after September 11th, Palestinian militant organizations, including Hamas, roundly condemned the attacks on America and distanced themselves from bin Laden. More than three years later, following the assassination of its leader, Sheik Ahmed Yassin, Hamas' rhetoric changed. In the past, the movement had declared its mission was simply to expel Israel from Palestinian lands. Sheikh Yassin's successor, Dr Abdel Aziz Rantisi, now announced: 'President Bush is the enemy of God, the enemy of Islam and Muslims. America declared war against God . . . and God declared war against America and Bush.' Dr Rantisi was assassinated by the Israelis shortly afterwards. The American President had picked up the gauntlet that al-Qa'eda had thrown down. Osama bin Laden had declared a global war; it was a global war that he would now have.

Before the bombing of Afghanistan, Bush's first action was to pass legislation that froze the funds of foreign terrorist groups. The definition of a terrorist now included any person or organization that raised

THE BASQUE COUNTRY

26. *Top, right.* Jesús Maria Pedrosa (right), with his Popular Party colleague Juanjo Gaztañazatorre, at a Durango council meeting shortly before his murder.

27. *Centre, right.* Portraits of Urko and Aranba, hanging in an *herriko taberna*, or 'popular bar', in Durango. The two men were driving along a street in Bilbao late at night in August 1999 when the bomb they were carrying exploded.

28. *Bottom, left.* Nekane (left) and Ainhoa, activists in Haika, the Basque separatist Rise Up movement.

29. *Bottom, right.* Barricades set up by Haika supporters during a riot in Bayonne, in the Basque Country in south-west France.

LEBANON

30. *Left.* Sara and her children in their house in Ba'albek, Lebanon. Sara's husband gave his life as a suicide bomber for Hizbollah. The movement now supports her.

31. *Below.* A Hizbollah fighter, close up.

32. *Bottom.* Hizbollah fighters at a military parade.

33. *Above.* Hizbollah's rulers watch a parade. Their leader, Hasan Nasrallah, seated on the right, later addressed the crowd, declaring that 'We live in a world of bullying, which is led by the Great Satan, the United States of America.'

34. *Below.* People living in homes on the Green Line, which divided Christian from Muslim Beirut (1994).

IRAN

35. *Top.* Hamed, a member of the Bassij, the Mobilized Resistance Force of the Oppressed, teaches a twelve-year-old member of the group the skills of loading an AK-47. Recruits are taught to 'love death'.

36. *Centre.* The twin brothers Hamed and Mehdi visit the grave of their brother, Mohammed, who died on a suicide mission. Half a million Iranians are buried at the War Martyrs' Cemetery in Behesht Zahra, south of Tehran.

37. *Bottom, left.* Maryam, a Tehran fashion designer. She confided that in private women in Tehran wear short skirts and high heels under their chador.

38. *Bottom, right.* In the West there would be an advertising hoarding; in Tehran it is a portrait of Ayatollah Khomeini.

INDIA AND PAKISTAN

39. *Top right.* A member of India's security forces prepares for an attack on the Sikh holy temple in Amritsar, in 1988.

40. *Centre right.* A twelve-year-old Sikh militant says he's prepared to fight to the death with his Kalashnikov rifle.

41. *Below, left.* The gung-ho Colonel Bali of India's Rashtriya Rifles. 'We've eliminated, and by that I mean killed, approximately thirty-five militants during the last year'.

42. *Below, right.* The author with Abdullah, a Kashmiri militant from the JKLF, just before his journey into Indian-controlled Kashmir in 1998. Kashmir is an example of a secular struggle for nationhood that has been tagged onto the wider Islamic movement.

FRANCE

43. *Above, left.* A police photograph of a young French Algerian, Khaled Kelkal, which was released as a wanted poster. He was later shot dead by police, causing outrage in the French Algerian community.

44. *Above, right.* Nabila Kourrad, who was born in France but believes that her headscarf leads people to classify her as a terrorist. 'People stare, and I see fear and anger in their eyes.'

45. *Left.* Faouzia Ouadou holds a picture of her husband, Kamel, a chemist at Lyon University. Kamel spent sixteen months in a high-security jail on suspicion of being a bomb-maker before being released without charge.

USA

46. *Left.* Ramee Mohammed (left) and Amin trying to convert locals in Southside Chicago to Islam. Mike, in the wheelchair, was a gang member: he was paralysed when gunned down by a rival.

47. *Opposite, top.* Muslim converts at Cooke County Jail, Chicago. Nearly one in three black inmates in US prisons has turned to Islam.

SRI LANKA

48. Armed JVP guerrillas at a secret rendezvous in Sri Lanka. They were called terrorists and yet the regime killed many more innocent civilians.

MONTENEGRO

49. *Above.* A paramilitary group trained i
Montenegro by Western intelligence, includ
Britain's SAS, to combat President Milošovi
Yugoslav army. What made them any differe
to a terrorist organization?

BURMA

50 & 51. The Karen insurgents in Burma
are never called terrorists because the
West despises the regime they are fightin
in Rangoon. The Karen army includes man
child soldiers, some as young as twelve.
The Karen's armed resistance is generally
backed by the West despite the use of
child soldiers.

© Fred Scott

money for listed organizations. The US realized that the opening of economic markets, the freedom of movement and the growth of global communication, which had brought it great wealth, could not continue unchecked: globalization could create a major threat to America's security.

Al-Qa'eda's transglobal complexion had roots in a phenomenon that began taking shape after the Arab–Israeli war in October 1973. Syria and Egypt launched a surprise attack on Israel in an attempt to regain territory and prestige lost during the Six Day War in 1967. In order to prevent an Israeli counter-offensive, Arab oil-exporting nations declared an embargo on oil destined for Israel's Western allies. Oil prices soared and Israel, under American pressure, signed a peace treaty that allowed Arab leaders to declare a victory to their people. Saudi Arabia was the primary beneficiary of the war and its rulers gathered hundreds of billions of dollars from 'Allah's gift' beneath the desert sand.

Members of the royal family, the House of Saud, became instant billionaires and bought their luxury cars, yachts and mansions in London. Other less conspicuous events were quietly taking shape in a country sharply divided by regional and religious rivalries. Deals were made between merchants, religious leaders, tribal chieftains and public officials so that the money could satisfy competing interests and maintain stability within the state. One of these agreements was between the House of Saud and powerful clerics who followed a creed founded by Muhammad Ibn Abd al-Wahhab, a puritanical religious reformer, in the eighteenth century. His followers call themselves 'Unitarians'; non-Muslims and opponents generally use the term Wahhabi. Abd al-Wahhab's aim had much in common with later Salafists: to purge Islam of the idol-worshipping and to oppose all *bid'ah*, or innovations introduced by clergy to the holy texts. He held a fanatical dislike of Shi'ism, which he considered heretical. His supporters destroyed domes and intricate Islamic architecture; I was once told that a Wahhabi desires his mosque to possess the 'charm of a hospital ward'.

At that time, Muhammad Ibn Saud was one of many tribal rulers battling for control of the largely lawless deserts of central Arabia and he struck a tactical bargain with Abd al-Wahhab. Nearly two centuries later, the deal allowed the Saudi royal family to govern the country while Wahhabi clerics controlled religious and cultural standards, including the religious police, the *muttawas*. This management of the Ministry for Religious Affairs allowed them to collect vast sums of money to export their interpretation of Islam throughout the world. A new phenomenon was evolving; the globalization of Sunni Islam. In the 1960s Salafist radicals made their first serious contact with Wahhabism when members of the Egyptian and later Syrian Muslim Brotherhood fled persecution in their own countries and Saudi Arabia became a refuge for Salafist dissidents.

Once the flood of petrodollars poured into Saudi Arabia, hundreds of charities, ad hoc associations and foundations were set up to build mosques, train clerics and distribute cassettes and literature. While many of these Islamic associations required the approval of the World Muslim League (founded in 1962 and linked to the Saudi Ministry of Religious Affairs) there was often a carnival atmosphere to the spending, and even if the Saudi government had wished otherwise, it became impossible to prevent funds being diverted to militant groups, which began with the 1979 'holy war' in Afghanistan.

After September 11th, President Bush repeatedly asked the Saudi government to seize the assets of organizations funding militant Islam. Apart from the personal wealth of bin Laden, al-Qa'eda was suspected of receiving substantial donations from sympathizers inside Saudi Arabia. The problem for the House of Saud was the links between businessmen, charities, Wahhabi clerics and members of its own royal family. They were so intertwined that to discover the supporters of al-Qa'eda would require redrawing the country's economic and political landscape and possibly implicate people who, if challenged, could threaten the survival of the regime.

After the withdrawal of the Soviets from Afghanistan, the next step on the evolution of militant Islam into a globalized phenomenon was Kashmir, an easy move for demobilized international brigades eager to find a new jihad. While the primary sources of funds for the war against the Soviet Union were petrodollars from Saudi Arabia and money from the CIA, it was Pakistan's ISI that had the most direct control over the mujahedin. The ISI and the Wahhabi sect in Saudi Arabia had forged a partnership in Afghanistan that would be difficult to split later.

Pakistan had been ruled since 1977 by General Zia ul-Haq, the chief of the staff of the army, who had gained power by overthrowing and later hanging the Prime Minister, Zulfikar Ali Bhutto. Pakistani nationalism had suffered badly after the defeat by India and the amputation of East Pakistan (Bangladesh) in 1971. General Zia steered Pakistan toward greater Islamization, seeking in religion a principle of unity that would define its nationhood. He was a great admirer of the Salafist writer Maulana Maududi, the leader of Pakistan's main Islamist party, Jama'at-i Islami. Maududi had read Rashid Rida's magazine, *al-Manar* (the Minaret), in the 1930s and later became a major influence on Qutb. This cross-fertilization of ideas and the war in neighbouring Afghanistan placed Pakistan at the centre of the global jihad.

I was in Pakistani-controlled Kashmir in 1990, with the indefatigable cameraman Rory Peck, searching for camps in Pakistan where Kashmiri militants received training. Their existence was known but since the military coaching was conducted by the ISI, it was officially a secret. Rory telephoned a few days later to say that he'd had permission to film at a camp for members of the Jammu and Kashmir Liberation Front (JKLF). Young men holding AK-47s were crawling beneath barbed wire a few feet above the ground. We also discovered an arms cache, which included rocket-propelled-grenade launchers. It was remarkable access because the Pakistani government was denying that it had any such camps and yet the ISI allowed us to walk in and film. When the report was aired, the recently elected Pakistani Prime Minister, Benazir Bhutto, made a formal complaint: 'Pakistan does not exercise influence over freedom fighters. All such reports are totally baseless,' a government spokesman announced. It made me realize that the ISI was more powerful than the Prime Minister and I suspected that our access was a deliberate attempt to embarrass her. When I saw Abdullah in 1998, I faced a reverse situation. The ISI did not, on that occasion, want its role given publicity and our rendezvous had to be carefully planned. We were constantly and obviously under surveillance. Abdullah was from the JKLF and detested the way that the ISI had hijacked the Kashmiri demands for independence and placed them in the context of a global jihad.

Our meeting was in a safe house where he had already brought his supplies and arms much earlier in the day. It was, perhaps, slightly staged, but Abdullah was keen to get his message out on the BBC before his perilous trip into Indian-controlled territory despite what his masters wanted. The JKLF demand for independence didn't fit with the ISI's desires; the agency wanted to absorb the state into Pakistan.

Using money from Saudi Arabia and weapons, the ISI bought the loyalty of sections of the JKLF and neutered those who refused. The intelligence agency attracted fighters intent on continuing a global jihad from Afghanistan, and within a few years it had elevated the pro-Pakistan Hizb-ul-Mujahideen into the prominent militant group. The JKLF was marginalized, and six months before we met him the ISI attempted to forcibly shut down Abdullah's training camp.

'After two or three years,' he told me privately, 'the JKLF was hijacked by religious extremists. Pakistan tried to destroy the movement.' Abdullah took a deep breath as he recalled bitterly: 'In those years, nobody cared about Kashmiris. The independence movement was taken over by intelligence officers and people who were bought off by money from foreign countries. Kashmir just became a staging post for a worldwide jihad.'

Between 1990 and 1998 the genuine grievances of Kashmiris had become overshadowed by a global battle between Islam and its enemies. The first stage of the fanning of the Afghan war into a global conflict was conducted not by America's professed enemies, such as Iran, Libya or Iraq, but by its staunchest allies, Pakistan and Saudi Arabia.

Shortly afterwards, Abdullah finished packing his belongings and was battle ready. We shook hands. He grabbed his AK-47 and wandered, somewhat resentfully, into the clear night air.

13 / WAR OF TERROR

'We used terrorist methods to attack terrorism
even before it had appeared.'
Mohammed Samraoui, former officer in the
Algerian secret service

When I feel anxious about my safety, I usually feel a knot developing
in my lower intestines. It makes its presence felt at five or six in the
morning, before I wake up. It is during that period, in stressful times,
that nightmares and consciousness merge and my worst fears spin
around in my head. In Algeria, the stories of disembowelment and
decapitation that I had repeatedly heard began to haunt my sleeping
hours. When I finally awoke and showered, the panic melted in the
dawn sunshine. I rationalized my thoughts and continued planning the
next stage of the elaborate plot to visit Algeria's Islamic guerrillas. All
that remained was the knot, a dull, vague discomfort that accompanied
my stay in Algeria.

Before breakfast, I would often stroll through the botanical gardens
of the El-Djazair Hotel and pause at a small veranda. I breathed in the
sweet scents of Mediterranean flowers; that moment of serenity helped
me face the ordeals that would follow once I left the sanctuary of the
hotel. I was surprised to see, in a largely disused section of the hotel
grounds, a hole in the perimeter fence, easily large enough for a person
to slip through. I quickly reassured myself that while an assassin might
be able to wander into the hotel, he would soon be confronted by an
array of government agents. From the hotel's location in the gentle
hills above Algiers, I could look north toward the Casbah, the heaving

and cluttered ancient Turkish quarter with its cramped housing and overhanging laundry, and beyond to the district of Bab el Oued, where Algeria's Islamist movement had been launched five years earlier. These were called *quartiers populaires*; the term was usually translated as working-class neighbourhoods but it had become a euphemistic cliché that meant 'hotbeds of Islamist militancy'. One day, an elderly lady on the hotel staff grabbed my hand and told me to be careful. 'Do not go to the *quartiers populaires*,' she whispered as she poured my morning coffee. 'They're full of terrorists.' From her expression, she thought I was clearly mad to be in Algeria in the first place.

It had been a year since Islamist militants warned foreigners to leave the country or risk being killed. Over fifty had already been murdered, as well as twenty local journalists. A few months before I arrived, an Australian television producer, Scott White, and his French cameraman, Olivier Quemener, were attacked shortly after arriving in Algiers.

'We talked in great detail about what we should do and the risks we faced,' Scott told me many years later in a London restaurant. 'Of course we were scared. We'd have been mad not to be.'

Olivier was married to an Algerian woman from Kabylia, and some of her relatives lived in the Casbah. Their main objective had been to show the plight of the dwindling numbers of foreigners who remained in Algeria. Their local assistant, known as a 'fixer', had arranged an interview at the Casbah with a woman about her everyday life in a volatile district at the heart of a rebellion. When they entered the Casbah they found themselves in an open area. They stopped to film some general shots. Suddenly, there was a loud crack of gunfire.

Scott still cocks his head as he listens; he lost his hearing in one ear and has had problems with vertigo but otherwise recovered fully. Thirty-four-year-old Olivier died. Five bullets from a low-calibre handgun were fired into his chest. The bullet that hit Scott entered his brain. 'The eardrum bone is the hardest in the body,' Scott told me in a matter-of-fact manner as he fingered the right side of his head. 'The bullet smashed the bone but stayed in my brain.' Scott praised the French-trained surgeons at the Military Hospital in Algiers. 'I couldn't have been shot in a better place,' he said without a smile.

A screwdriver had been used to remove the video from the camera, just in case the murderer had been captured on tape. The Algerian authorities never contacted Scott again. Nor did the fixer, of whose fate he had no knowledge. He didn't say so directly but it was clear that he had pondered whether their fixer had set them up. Nobody else knew they were travelling to the Casbah. The shooting seemed too quick and precise to be random. 'We didn't know him very well,' Scott recollected, 'and a good fixer is more valuable than gold.'

The deep sadness he feels for Olivier and his widow is mixed with a spark of gratitude. 'I was extraordinarily fortunate. Many others were killed after having their balls cut off and shoved in their mouth. This method allowed room for error; enough for me to survive.' Scott remains doleful and bemused about the events that Monday morning in 1994. As with most of the other hundred and twenty thousand or more killings in this cruel conflict, Olivier's death remains mysterious and unresolved, his murderer unknown.

No one really knows how many died, let alone who did the killing during that diabolical decade that ripped the soul from the Algerian nation. In 1999, the regime announced the ballpark figure of a hundred thousand. Others have suggested that a hundred and fifty thousand perished; some Algerian NGOs estimate two hundred thousand. Most observers compromise on an arbitrary figure of a hundred and twenty to a hundred and fifty thousand. Algeria ranks alongside Rwanda and Yugoslavia as one of the slaughterhouses of the 1990s, yet unlike those nations, the country was rarely in the news and there is no United Nations War Crimes Tribunal to punish the guilty. In fact, few outsiders know what really happened. The war adopted surreal, hallu-cinogenic traits. The brutality seemed inexplicable and motiveless.

One of my first goals was to grasp the true scale of the conflict; at that time in 1994 there were no credible figures for the number of casualties. Colleagues at Amnesty International had suggested that official statistics were suspect, believing that the regime was deliber-ately playing down the magnitude of the crisis. It seemed absurd in a decade when communications began linking the world that in a relatively well-developed nation a few miles from Europe, a civil war was taking place but no one knew how many were dying. My first task did not seem that arduous: to find out for myself.

I was keen to meet the man who led the 'official' state-funded human-rights organization, the Observatoire National des Droits de l'Homme, to see if he could help. Kamel Rezzag Bera had a Poirot-style moustache and a beaming smile. He wore a black suit with sharp creases and a heavily starched white shirt. He parroted the official numbers and said that the conflict had, by 1994, claimed three and a half thousand casualties.

'Don't the security forces accurately list their own dead?' I enquired.

'Oh no, no, no,' he said. 'That's a state secret. Giving that away would be helping the terrorists.' He warned that foreigners were exaggerating the numbers of dead in order to discredit Algeria. He did accept that the FIS, the banned political party that promoted Islamic values, had legitimacy and a popular base. I sympathized with Rezzag Bera after a while; he had a tough job as a government-appointed human-rights inspector in a nation where the regime itself was often accused of being the chief violator of human rights.

It was also the first occasion that I heard the argument that the military was the defender of Algeria's democracy. Rezzag Bera told me that the conflict was 'between democratic forces and those who don't want democracy'. This confused me; the crisis had begun when the FIS was outlawed to prevent it becoming the first avowedly Islamist movement to win a democratic election in the Arab world. With France's support, the Algerian army cancelled the second phase of the elections and took power instead. Supporters of the FIS fled to the hills and began a rebellion. Did Rezzag Bera mean that the 'terrorists' were the defenders of democracy while the military opposed it? Of course, he meant it the other way round. The military had repeatedly insisted that it took power to safeguard democracy. The regime argued that if the FIS had formed a government, it would have cancelled all future elections. 'How can a terrorist respect democracy?' he asked, nodding and smiling, believing that he had finally cornered me with the logic of his argument.

Within a few days of my meeting with Rezzag Bera the regime suddenly announced that the number of dead was ten thousand. All of a sudden, another six thousand or so corpses had been discovered. The figure emerged from the Ministry of the Interior and was fed to the media without any breakdown or explanation. How could such loss of life simply be accounted for by plucking a number from the air?

My next step was to ask local journalists and human-rights lawyers. After some discussion, they pointed me toward an unlikely politician, the leader of the Front de Libération Nationale (FLN), the former guerrilla organization that brought independence to Algeria and governed for a quarter of a century. Its rule resembled much of the current regime with its tight grip on power and its heavy-handed military.

As with any one-party state, the FLN had contained several factions and some of the most aggressive proponents of change had come from within the movement. In the early 1990s the party's general secretary was Abdelhamid Mehri, an avuncular, genial man in his fifties. He believed that the tsunami of democracy that flooded Eastern Europe after the fall of the Soviet Union would send tremors to North Africa and transform his nation. While the party continued to use the language of Leninism, with its politburo, central committee and general secretary, Mehri was committed to openness and freedom. He bitterly opposed the army coup in 1991 and the banning of the FIS. 'We need dialogue between the government and the Islamist groups,' he told me. 'You can't defeat terrorism with more terrorism. We need to form a ruling coalition that includes all parties in Algeria, including the Islamists.' It was a curious spectacle to see the leader of the FLN condemning le Pouvoir, or 'the power', the term Algerians use to describe the obscure military-financial elite that is commonly said to govern this nation from the shadows. Until a few years earlier, it had seemed that the FLN was le Pouvoir.

The FLN did retain one important advantage: it was one of the few organizations in Algeria that had a functioning nationwide structure. Mehri had also been keen to know what was really going on in his country. 'Our party members are able to gather accurate information because, unlike the government, they are present throughout Algeria. Our figures are more comprehensive.' He was referring to the swathes of territory that apparently had no government presence and where Islamist rebels were able to roam freely. He also implied that the government was deliberately lying about the extent of the uprising. 'The official figure must be doubled. And I think, personally, we are looking at as many as twenty-five thousand dead.' A few weeks earlier, most reporters were saying that three and a half thousand had perished. Now I discovered the true figure might be seven times as large. Mehri uncovered another sobering statistic. 'The number of civilians is increasing as a percentage of the total. Those not directly involved in the conflict are suffering as both sides overstep the mark. Remember that a large section of the population is helping the armed groups and they are paying the price.'

'Do you mean that the security forces are massacring civilians?' I asked.

He smiled. 'The circumstances of some of these massacres raise questions as to the identity of the perpetrators. Algerians want answers and they are not receiving them.' He went on to suggest that the war was not simply two sides fighting each other. 'The violence is practised by several groups and some of these groups do not have a recognized identity or aim.'

What did that mean? 'It is more than likely that some parties would like to see the Algerian crisis continue with no solution, even if this means committing more massacres,' Mehri said.

'Who? Le Pouvoir?' I asked.

'Those who refuse a democratic political solution.' It was a much-repeated rumour in the coffee shops of Algiers that a twisted symbiosis had developed between the Islamic militants and the regime; each was said to benefit financially from the unaccountable political terrain created by war.

'Do you have any evidence?' I asked.

'I *know*,' he answered, 'I don't need evidence.' Sadly, I did.

Following the cancelled election, the army announced a state of emergency and forced President Chadli Benjedid, the man who had started the process of reform more than three years earlier, to resign. Muhammad Boudiaf, one of the founders of the FLN who was highly respected for his integrity and honesty, replaced him. Boudiaf had only recently returned to Algeria after twenty-seven years in political exile, and his power base within the army was not strong. In June 1992, he was assassinated by one of his bodyguards. Initially, most reports accepted the official view that the FIS ordered the murder. Gradually, suspicion moved on to the regime, as it became clear that the assassination could not have been executed without inside assistance. But the army had by now regained control of the important levers of power in Algiers and a military council ruled the country. In 1995 General Liamine Zeroual was elected to a five-year term in a carefully managed election that excluded the FIS.

During my first visit to Algiers, I asked journalists, lawyers, officials and intellectuals I met who they thought was responsible for Boudiaf's death. About two-thirds believed that factions within the regime had killed him but had no evidence. Others said that speculation was pointless; the only people who accepted the official narrative that Islamists had murdered the President worked directly for the government.

One national newspaper reported on the day after Boudiaf's death that he had been killed by the politico-financial elite within le Pouvoir.

El Watan speculated that a 'mafia' inside the regime had murdered him because the President was trying to curtail corruption. *El Watan*'s editor, Omar Belhouchet, was a small, sprightly man with a well-manicured, slightly greying moustache. 'Boudiaf was extremely popular,' he told me as he adjusted his large brown-rimmed glasses. 'In just six months he succeeded in attracting young people with simple messages. He was hoping to build a credible government and put an end to corruption. Some people were not prepared to let him do that.'

Belhouchet had a cheery, amusing expression and a playful smile even when he talked about the most nefarious subjects. 'There are men who rule this country who don't appear in the media,' he continued. 'These people are behind the scenes and, at times, it's them who make the most important decisions that shape the future of this country.'

'Such as murdering the President?'

'Absolutely.'

'Do you know who they are?'

'I know some of them, but I cannot be sure. They are far away from the limelight. The population at large doesn't know them. I may know who they are but I cannot name them.'

A year earlier, Belhouchet had spent fifteen days in jail for disobeying requests from the Ministry of Information. 'We are between two firing squads,' he sighed. The Islamic guerrillas had already tried to kill him; two men shot at his car as he drove to work one morning. In his office in the Maison de la Presse he had a large file, stuffed full with death threats from the Islamists. A letter was postmarked in a nearby district in Algiers: 'It has been decided', it declared, 'that you shall die today. Or tomorrow. Or the day after tomorrow. That means that even if they have to wait for months or years, one day they will carry out this death sentence.'

Belhouchet sent his two children to live with a relative in France. His wife, devastated by the daily threats to her husband's life, died of a heart attack. I marvelled at his ability to carry on living in this wretched habitat of hatred and bloodletting. I found meetings with men like Belhouchet unsettling. I envied and respected his bravery but when I considered my own plans, I became agitated and unsure of myself. In such a paranoid world of mirrors, the advice of my fixer, Hamid, was rock solid. The suspicions that the journalist Scott White raised about his fixer made me aware of how important Hamid was to my project. I trusted him completely.

When I arrived in the *maquis*, the French word that literally means scrubland but usually refers to areas controlled by rebels, the guerrillas seemed genuinely surprised that I was not panic-stricken. I don't know whether they thought I was unbalanced or simply staggered that I distrusted the media clamour that the militants had a pathological need to murder all foreigners. Before coming, I had tried to analyse the situation logically while placing my fear to one side. I jotted in my notebook three groups that the militants wanted to kill.

— Foreigners who worked for companies that had government contracts. They killed them in order to isolate Algeria economically and weaken the regime.
— French citizens. France was blamed for supporting the 1991 military coup. A French journalist would not have been welcomed by the guerrillas, such was the mistrust of the former colonial power and the anger over the coverage of Algeria in its media.
— Local journalists, killed because they would not or were not allowed to write stories that criticized the regime.

I concluded that I didn't fall into any of these categories. There were times, of course, when doubts crept in; when I read the newspapers or listened to accounts of throat slitting, or *l'egorgement spectaculaire*, as it's theatrically described in Algeria.

I also tried to push to the back of my mind the senseless shootings of Scott White and Olivier Quemener. One of the rumours circulating was that maybe the Islamists were not responsible. The regime knew where the two journalists were going because they paid fixers and taxi drivers to inform them. According to some whispers, the ubiquitous Sécurité Militaire wanted to kill a foreign journalist in order to allow the security services to commit atrocities out of sight of the world's media. It was hoped that most reporters would then be too fearful to investigate the massacres. In addition, the regime could control the movements of journalists by insisting on providing 'protection'. Rumours and conspiracies multiplied like a noxious plague.

We met Oussama, the guerrilla leader who resembled Peter Sellers, in a small village inside guerrilla territory. It was a beautiful, peaceful scene. The arid, rocky slabs of the Atlas Mountains were cast in a warm orange glow by the morning sun. Clutches of small green shrubs peppered the desolate terrain, which now stood against the backdrop of a cloudless, blue sky. The altitude provided a hint of a cooling wind.

We were taken to a blue Toyota Landcruiser, which had been stolen from the police a few weeks earlier. The driver, Djaffar, was young, perhaps nineteen or twenty and clean-shaven, with a flashing smile. He seemed to enjoy the prospect of escorting a Western visitor where none had been for at least five years. Spears of light emerged through bullet holes in the door alongside me. Djaffar noticed my hand touching the sharp edges of the pierced metal; he told me that three policemen had been killed during the ambush that garnered the vehicle, but not the driver. 'Not the driver,' he repeated.

As we climbed higher into the barren hills, it seemed that Djaffar wanted me to ask about the policeman who had been driving the jeep. After a pause of several minutes, I took my cue. 'What happened to the driver?' Djaffar beamed. He said the driver had been captured alive, but was later despatched. 'I slit his throat,' Djaffar blurted before adding purposefully, 'but I let him pray and drink water before he died. They would never have let one of us do that.' Djaffar slapped me on the knee and smiled. He apparently believed that allowing the man to pray before his crude execution would persuade me of his kindness.

We drove into a flat clearing where there were three or four mud-built huts with brown tents alongside. A group of about thirty men were squatting in a circle and repeating the most important verses in Islam. '*La-ilaha-illallah*,' they proclaimed, 'There is no deity except God,' '*Ashhadu-anna-muhammadur-rasoolullah*,' 'We bear witness that Mohammed is God's messenger.' The chanting was led by a small man with an unsmiling round face and well-trimmed moustache. He was probably about twenty and wore a striped robe over his military fatigues. He held a small, slightly tattered Qur'ān aloft in his right hand; in his left hand he gripped a short-barrelled machine gun. He'd had a clerical education and one man referred to him as a mullah, a term more commonly used in Farsi-speaking Iran and parts of Afghanistan. Most of the men wore trousers and shirts and at least half were armed only with ageing shotguns; the remainder had automatic weapons of differing origins. As the group repeated the verses after the mullah, they raised their guns in the air. One man in the circle rotated a cleaver, its blade glinting in the sun. I then noticed that every man carried a long knife in a sheath attached to his belt. Several also wore the *kolas*, the mujahedin's woollen cap. When I enquired whether any had joined the jihad in Afghanistan, no one raised their hands. It didn't seem to me that many had fought there; most were young, local people and former students whose politics was honed in the protests of 1992. But however many jihadists there were, they were clearly held in high esteem and the war in Afghanistan provided the role model for the armed revolt in Algeria.

Oussama led our team from place to place and I was under the impression that he was in charge of a company of perhaps eighty or a hundred men. He said that he was a member of the Consultative Council of the AIS and represented the Western Region; the command structure was apparently divided unto three geographical divisions spanning northern Algeria. It was hard to determine their precise military organization and Oussama wasn't too forthcoming about details.

We ran into a group of eight militants travelling in the back of a small Mazda pickup truck; one fighter rested a large machine gun on top of the driver's cabin. He gave a friendly wave. It was then that I noticed a light flashing from the hilltop above. A man in a lookout post holding a mirror signalled that the road ahead was clear. It became evident that Oussama had planned a tour and our first stop was at a field hospital run by a doctor who had qualified in France. There were three beds, a comprehensive supply of sterilized surgical tools, bowls, first-aid packs and shelves packed with drugs brought from Algiers. One man had been shot in the leg some time ago and the doctor was checking his blood pressure.

In a nearby house, a large man was hunched over an old Singer sewing machine making bandoliers. A strip of leather was looped and attached to an adjoining cloth in order to create the housing for the shotgun cartridges. The bullet belts hung from the ceilings alongside new olive-green uniforms; it resembled a clothing stall in a Bombay or Bangkok market. The guerrillas wanted to demonstrate that they were a self-sufficient army and were not supported by foreign nations, as the Algerian government had alleged. Their uniforms were made by hand; their guns and ammunition were mostly stolen from the police.

Each small building that I entered was covered by mud that matched the terrain. The plain, square structures had a few small windows and a door painted white or brown; small flocks of sheep roamed nearby and sometimes clothes billowed from a makeshift washing line. From a distance they appeared like the homes of shepherds and their families.

Amongst the fighters that trailed around with us was a well-built, slightly awkward man in his late forties with receding hair. He wore a scruffy red anorak over a plaid lumberjack shirt and ill-fitting trousers. At one point, Oussama said, we must interview the emir, the word the guerrillas used to refer to their leader. 'Fine,' I said, 'if he's here, we'll talk to him now.' I assumed the emir was in one of the nearby buildings. Instead, the balding man in the red anorak stepped in front of the camera and began to address us.

'I am the Deputy Emir of the Army of Islamic Salvation, the army of the FIS. My name is Aouad Abu Abdallah and the name of our fighting unit is Nour Eddine, in the Western Military Division,' he proclaimed. Aouad was a dour man but on closer inspection exuded an authority and calm that I hadn't noticed before. He had the presence of a deeply religious man. In the AIS, the title of emir suggests religious as well as military leadership.

'In our area, the mujahedin move wherever they like with the utmost ease, on foot, by car, by all means of transport. The forces of this corrupt regime do not really come into our area ... only in exceptional circumstances,' he added. 'They might pass by quickly but they never stay long. They cannot hold any position in our area.'

The emir rarely looked at me, instead staring into the distance, speaking quietly and answering my questions slowly. Our experience with the guerrillas supported his claim that large swathes of admittedly sparsely populated territory were effectively under their control. We travelled for over a hundred miles without seeing any policemen or government soldiers.

I wanted to pin down the emir on the killing of foreigners but his answers were elusive. 'The killings are only carried out against the men of the regime and its helpers,' he said. 'Whoever supports this regime is against us. Whoever is not with this regime are our brothers in Islam and have nothing to fear.'

'Have you killed any foreigners?' I asked.

'No,' he said, 'we have always respected Islamic law.'

'Does Islamic law allow for the killing of foreigners?'

'Islamic law allows Muslims to defend the faith against enemies who are trying to destroy it. If these assassinations are carried out by the regime this doesn't concern us. If they are carried out by our brothers then we have nothing to say and we accept the consequences of our deeds.'

Oussama stepped in when he saw that I had scrunched up my face, as if to say, 'What on earth does that mean?' There were already disagreements emerging between the GIA and the AIS but I was not aware of them at the time. The AIS did not support the random killing of foreigners but Oussama was not interested in talking about divisions in the Islamist movement.

'There were communiqués and warnings telling these foreigners not to help this regime. It would have been better if these countries had called back their nationals instead of selling arms to our regime so it can repress our people.' Oussama's voice was suddenly raised. His playful manner, running around like a goofy Peter Sellers, had been replaced by a more assertive, wide-eyed cast. Angering a man with a gun is never a good idea. I had wanted to ask another question but, perhaps wrongly, remained silent. I had wanted to know how they could believe that killing a priest or a nun, or Olivier, was justified under Islamic law. Instead I nodded, as if in agreement.

Oussama carried on blaming the West for their plight. 'Western countries help our regime, which everyone knows is a dictatorship which has denied free choice to our people. It should be the other way round; we should receive help from Western countries as the democratic rulers of Algeria. The whole world ought to be helping us but it is against us. Why?' There was a brief pause and I shrugged. I didn't want the group to become fired up with the belief that Westerners were their enemy.

'Your people preach about democracy. But if Western governments stopped supporting this regime it would collapse in two weeks.' After a pause, he smiled again and looked toward the emir, who was listening quietly.

'And no one really knows who is behind the massacres,' I added, trying to stay on the subject without being accusatory. The emir picked up the baton. 'We are fighting a war and all wars have tactics and strategies. Each side has an organization, supply lines and communications. Wars are similar in nature. What differentiates us from other armies is that our jihad is carried out in accordance to the sharia [Islamic law] and the Sunna [the traditions of the Prophet]. Sometimes we hear that the secret police have committed unspeakable deeds against human dignity. Our mujahedin would never do that because they do not go beyond the bounds of Islamic law.'

I didn't believe him; it was nearly a decade before I discovered that he was mostly speaking the truth. All I could do then was add a senior commander in the Islamic Salvation Army to the list of men and women who believed the Sécurité Militaire was chiefly responsible for the massacre of the innocent. I was also struck by the genuine outrage amongst these fighters that the West had taken sides in their dispute and apparently betrayed their trust in its much-vaunted commitment to democratic values. At the time, it was something that I hadn't considered much, but the growth of this anger culminated in the formation of al-Qa'eda and bin Laden's declaration of a holy war on Western nations four years later.

Oussama told me that he had been the FIS mayor of a town near Blida, south of Algiers, in the 'Triangle of Death'. When the army took over, his cousin had been killed and the police came looking for his brother. 'They broke into the offices of the FIS and took all the files that gave the names and addresses of its members. I had to flee,' he said. 'I had no choice but to pick this up.' He held up his AK-47. 'It was our duty to defend our lives and fight the regime. Our stand is lawful according to Islamic law.'

Shortly afterwards, a large beaten-up blue truck passed by with about a dozen men standing or sitting in the back. Oussama told us not to film until he had arranged permission. As it passed, Oussama suddenly waved his hands; 'Go ahead!' he shouted. The men in the truck responded by shouting, '*Allahu Akbar!*', 'God is Great!' while smiling and waving their guns. Oussama then whispered, 'GIA,' and gave me a big smile.

I was repeatedly told that in these hills, guerrillas from the GIA, which was led by hardened veterans of the war in Afghanistan, mingled with the AIS fighters. The GIA had been blamed for killing civilians using heinous methods and was considered a more brutal organization but it was impossible for me to tell the two groups apart. 'We cooperate fully on the ground,' Oussama said. 'They may have different structures and methods, but we all want the same thing, an Islamic state.' To prove the point, he took me to a room filled with over a dozen GIA fighters, who looked much the same as the AIS. The common understanding amongst journalists, usually gained from briefings with Western diplomats, was that the two groups had a tense, uneasy relationship. While this was soon to become the case, in the autumn of 1994 it did not appear to be true.

My experience appeared to confirm how little solid evidence emerged from 'intelligence briefings' on Islamist groups. Where had this information come from? The regime, perhaps? Newspaper reports on Algeria regularly recorded comments concerning the armed groups, which were attributed to 'Western diplomats'. In Algiers, American and French diplomats were not allowed to leave their compounds, so had scant opportunity to gather meaningful intelligence.

One of the other houses I visited with Oussama was the Nour Eddine unit's command centre. It was a similar building in style as the others but it was larger with a much higher ceiling. Three men were sitting at a large table covered by a blue cloth. On the wall above them were half a dozen maps of Algeria with red markings. There was a fax machine, an electric typewriter, a large communications radio and a relatively up-to-date computer on the desk. The fax machine was used to send death threats to 'enemies of Islam', which were described by Oussama as 'warnings'.

When we left the command centre, the sun was weakening and reddening as it beckoned nightfall. The evening was drawing in and we had to arrive in Algiers before curfew at eleven o'clock. We said our goodbyes with hugs and kisses as the camouflage netting was removed from Malek's taxi. We hid the four videotapes in a concealed compartment at the back of the station wagon. I asked Malek if he was OK and he replied with a nod. 'It's been very interesting,' he understated with a grin. As we loaded our gear and prepared to leave, Oussama was smiling but warned me: 'Just show the truth.'

Whatever I thought about the methods or religious goals of these men, they all proved to be men who abided by their word. They had responded to orders from a political leadership with whom I had trusted my life. My impression was that these men were rational; perhaps brutal and driven by a profound religious conviction, but part of a fairly well-organized insurgency where military commanders remained under the general stewardship of their 'political wing'. It did not resemble the conflict that I had read about in press reports, where anonymous, sadistic 'terrorists' roamed the countryside murdering for no apparent reason. I had to remind myself that it was the *regime*, rather than the militants, that had closed off the country and choreographed this paranoid tableau, devoid of independently established facts. Why, I repeatedly wondered, was the government so fearful of independent reportage if the 'terrorists' were truly responsible for the daily horrors that littered Algeria's landscape?

As we gingerly approached Chlef, I concocted an excuse to explain our unauthorized absence from the hotel. The announcement on the car radio of the murder of Cheb Hasni, Algeria's leading *rai* vocalist, provided the ultimate ruse. Shortly before Algiers, Malek pulled over to the hard shoulder and we all got out. We rubbed our hands against the tyres to make it appear that a puncture had delayed our return.

That was 1994. The slow, lumbering moves toward normality began with the election of a civilian, Abdelaziz Bouteflika, as President in 1999. He had been a foreign minister in the 1960s and 70s and his relaxed, Western style was liked by visiting politicians from Europe and America. Algeria has benefited greatly from the 'war on terror', becoming a close ally of the US and an important economic partner.

In the late 1990s, the military gained the upper hand in the conflict and the AIS became a demoralized, if not defeated force. Soon after Abdelaziz Bouteflika was elected, he persuaded AIS guerrillas to lay down their weapons in return for an amnesty and a release of prisoners. The AIS had observed a unilateral ceasefire since October 1997, in part to distance itself from massacres of civilians blamed by the authorities on the GIA. The GIA dismissed the truce as a sell-out and vowed to continue its jihad.

In the summer of 2003, the two senior leaders of the FIS were released from custody after serving their twelve-year sentences. Shortly after their release, the Algerian authorities announced that they were banned from all political activity. The party's leader, Abassi Madani, signed a statement agreeing not to take part in any political, social or religious activities. His deputy, Ali Belhadj, refused to sign. When the two men were freed, the Algerian authorities told all foreign correspondents to leave the country to prevent international coverage of the event.

There remained small pockets of resistance and the occasional bombing or massacre, but by 2004 the rate of killing dropped to perhaps a few dozen a month. In 2003, a small force called the Salafist Group for Preaching and Combat (GSPC) kidnapped a party of thirty-one European tourists. The group did not provide a meaningful political challenge to the state and remained little more than a gang that blended politics with smuggling and kidnapping. The GSPC was listed as a 'terrorist group' in 2002 and was said to have links to al-Qa'eda but little evidence has emerged to substantiate that. The GIA continued to formally exist but it became too weak to conduct regular operations.

Does this mean that William Burns, the US Assistant Secretary of State for Near Eastern Affairs, was correct to assert that 'Washington has much to learn from Algeria on ways to fight terrorism'? Perhaps he should listen to the great French novelist Honoré de Balzac. 'There are two "Histories",' Balzac wrote, 'the official History, full of lies, which is taught to us, and the secret History where rests the true causes of the events, a shameful History.'

In February 2001, Habib Souaïdia, a former officer in Algeria's special forces, published *La Sale Guerre*, 'The Dirty War', a searing account relating how his colleagues roamed the countryside, killing at will, raping and torturing prisoners. He confirms that the secret police had infiltrated the GIA and that some of its actions were conducted under orders that originated within the regime. After eight years in the special forces, Souaïdia wrote: 'I have seen colleagues set fire to a boy of fifteen, who burned like a living torch. I have seen soldiers slaughtering civilians and blaming "the terrorists". I have seen colonels kill mere suspects in cold blood. I have seen officers torture fundamentalists to death. I have seen too many things and so many attacks on human dignity that I am unable to keep quiet.'

La Sale Guerre infuriated the Algerian regime and one of the men accused of involvement in the dirty war, the former Defence Minister, General Khaled Nezzar, sued the author in the French courts. In launching a libel case, Nezzar inadvertently provided a public forum for dissidents, human-rights workers and former agents who were called before the court to corroborate Souaïdia's allegations. An ex-colonel in the Sécurité Militaire (DRS), Mohammed Samraoui, testified that 'the Algerian army used every available means to attack the Islamic rebellion: blackmail, corruption, threats, killings. We used terrorist methods to attack terrorism even before it had appeared.'

Still more former secret service officers were coming forward; most were outraged by the atrocities committed by their agency. Abdelkader Tigha was a brigadier in the DRS from 1993 to 1997, when 'terrorists' claiming to belong to the GIA murdered hundreds of people, including 117 foreigners. He spoke to France's *Libération* newspaper about the murder of seven Trappist monks and confirmed that the army controlled the GIA guerrillas involved. He added that Djamel Zitouni, the head of the GIA at the time of the kidnapping, was a member of the Sécurité Militaire. This was corroborated by other exiled agents.

The Sécurité Militaire infiltrated the GIA in order to sow confusion and discredit the Islamist movement by attributing to it unspeakable barbarism. Although some of its fighters may not have known it, at some point the GIA effectively became a counter-terrorist operation, integrated into the military strategy of the regime.

The FIS leadership in exile appeared disorientated as the Western media concentrated its reports on atrocities attributed to the GIA. When the FIS proposed a 'platform for a political and peaceful solution to the Algerian crisis', it seemed that its leaders abroad were either out of touch with the killers at home or simply lying to cover for the bloodlust they had unleashed. The mass slaughter committed in the name of the GIA fatally eroded the credibility of the FIS in the minds of Western governments. The FIS insisted that the GIA was acting on the orders of the regime but the Western media did not believe it. While the AIS had claimed legitimacy as a guerrilla movement in a struggle to regain democratic rights, the GIA had none. The word 'terrorism' could have been invented for the group; even sceptical journalists, who normally hesitated before using the term, accepted that these men were the 'real thing'. The GIA (under the control of the Sécurité Militaire) killed civilians in such grotesque ways that it even sickened many AIS guerrillas, who lost the will to fight.

While the Sécurité Militaire was manipulating the GIA, the regime needed to control the flow of information emerging from Algeria. The regime attributed the slaughter to the GIA and the Algerian media created a narrative using a simple lexicon, 'terrorists' versus 'democrats'. The French media also upheld the regime's version of events and encouraged support of the military government. The Algerian–French media axis went to great lengths to persuade Europeans that Algeria was fighting for shared values of freedom and democracy, while resisting terrorism and zealotry. The common enemy was Islamist terrorism.

Shortly after the transmission of my documentary, *Algeria's Hidden War*, the region where I had travelled with the guerrillas was bombed for three days by the Algerian air force. I thought of the fate of Oussama and the Nour Eddine Military Unit. I was reminded of Oussama's assertion that the West had let the armed Islamists down, depriving them of the democracy that it had claimed to advocate for the Arab world. The 'war on terror' announced by George W. Bush was fought along battle lines drawn up during the 1990s when the West had to choose its allies and its enemies. One of the earliest and most important decisions was made over the fate of Algeria. A decade after that insurgency began, *Jane's Defence Weekly* reported that 2,800 Algerians had passed through al-Qa'eda's camps in Afghanistan, making that country the third biggest supplier of manpower and the main source of militants willing to take al-Qa'eda's war into Europe. A year after the destruction of the World Trade Center, an Algerian community worker in Britain said that there were '200 known terrorists' seeking asylum in the country. The discovery of a plot involving the poison ricin in Birmingham later that year was the first sign that the UK might be threatened by Islamists whose anger and hatred stemmed from an injustice, more than a decade earlier, which swelled during a brutal, unreported and largely ignored civil war.

I wondered what lessons for America's 'war on terror' Assistant Secretary of State William Burns had carried back to Washington. During the 1990s, the West allied itself with repressive Arab leaderships rather than allowing the government to open to wider, albeit Islamic, strands of society; for it is usually Islamist groups that benefit most from the ballot box. Before the invasion of Iraq, Brent Scowcroft, the National Security Adviser to the first President Bush, asked the obvious question: 'What's going to happen the first time we hold an election in Iraq and it turns out the radicals win? We're surely not going to let them take over.' 'Terrorism' only began in Algeria because le Pouvoir would not surrender control of Algeria to the victors in largely free elections. It continued in the most bloodthirsty manner because factions within the Algerian state conducted it. Who, William Burns, were the real 'terrorists' in Algeria?

14 / 'TERROR' ON THE NILE

'The ruling to kill the Americans and their allies – civilians and
military – is an individual duty for every Muslim . . .'
Osama bin Laden, February 1998

We were told to stay close to our military escort as we drove along the
two-lane highway that hugs the waters of the Nile. In front of us was
a blue pickup truck; behind the cab, a khaki tarpaulin was mounted
over a makeshift frame. Huddled inside, six soldiers were scouring the
lush scenery of the Nile valley, their rifles with long bayonets protruding
from the flapping canvas. The route passed fields of grain and cotton
lined with arching palm trees, where solitary farmers with large spiralling
turbans were hunched over their crops. There were mud-built villages
set just off the road; children stacked hay onto donkey-carts. Occasionally, a forest of green shrubs, sugar cane and banana palms crowded
into the road. We were heading toward Asyut, the largest city in Upper
Egypt and the administrative capital of the region. It was here that the
'Che' Guevara of Islamist militancy, Sayyid Qutb, was born. It was also
the birthplace of the Gama'a Islamiyah, the Islamic Association, an
armed movement that had taken control of several mosques in the city.

We had just left Dairut, a mid-sized town where tourist buses
sometimes stopped for lunch on their journey south. There wasn't
much in Dairut; after leaving Cairo in the morning it was a convenient
stopover before heading toward the ancient city of Luxor. It would be
another three or four hours before tourists reached their journey's end;
perhaps the archaeological treasures at Karnak, the Valley of the Kings
or the vast hillside monument dedicated to Pharaoh Hatshepsut.

I was following the route that a twenty-eight-year-old British nurse had travelled a month earlier in October 1992. She was in a tour bus with eight other British holidaymakers, heading towards the ancient sites at Luxor. As the van passed one village, a boy no older than twelve stood near a bend. He whistled a signal and a few seconds later the minibus was sprayed with bullets; gunmen on either side of the road fired automatic weapons at the passengers. There was screaming: the windows blew out and glass covered everyone as they ducked behind seats. The driver floored the accelerator but was forced to slow down after one of the tyres burst. The attackers fled into a patch of dense undergrowth. Three of the tourists had been hit, including Sharon Hill, who died a few hours later at a nearby hospital.

Three weeks earlier the Gama'a Islamiyah had warned tourists not to visit Upper Egypt. After Sharon's death the movement sent a hand-written statement to a local reporter in Asyut declaring: 'Tourism is our second target after high-level politicians in our effort to implement sharia in Egypt.'

Sharon was the first tourist to die in the Gama'a Islamiyah's struggle for an Islamic state; many more would follow. The impact of Sharon's death was immediate and dramatic. Within a week, nearly forty charter flights to Egypt had been cancelled. Western embassies warned their nationals to avoid travelling to parts of Upper Egypt. An embarrassed government in Cairo decided to crush the organization using whatever means necessary: tourism was Egypt's main source of foreign income, worth about $3 billion a year. A few months earlier, the regime had introduced wide-ranging amendments to the penal code for 'terrorist' offences, including the death penalty and expanding the police's power to detain suspects. On the day that we followed Sharon's tracks toward Asyut, Egypt's *al-Ahram* newspaper trumpeted with a bold headline that a military court had sentenced eight 'terrorists' to death. The suspected members of Gama'a Islamiyah were convicted of plotting the violent overthrow of the regime. The news wasn't as much of a triumph for the government as it initially appeared; seven of the men remained at large and were found guilty in absentia.

The Nile had become a stately river by the time it flowed unhurried past Asyut on its path toward Cairo and beyond to the Mediterranean. Egypt's past and present merged in its waters. The Nile provides a fertile strip of land through the barren Sahara that has kept Egypt's population tied to its banks since ancient times. At dusk, the Nile in

Upper Egypt casts its idyllic charm on visitors with an orange blanket of tranquillity. By the autumn of 1992, however, the river was providing portents of disorder.

Three weeks earlier, several gunmen fired at a cruise ship carrying more than a hundred German holidaymakers as it passed Asyut. Three Egyptian crewmen were struck but each survived. Many cruisers were now moored in their docks at what should have been the height of the tourist season. Local people had complained that some ships had become 'floating brothels'. The liners usually have pools and bars, where Egyptian laws are ignored; alcohol flows freely and topless women walk the decks. 'Unmarried men and women share rooms,' one elderly man told me.

Young men from Asyut University took binoculars and waited along the shores of the Nile. As a cruise ship passed by, the men scoured the decks checking on the dress code of women on poolside loungers. I laughed at first, but soon realized that these men were motivated by anger rather than titillation. The clash of cultures over sexual mores leads to remarkable misunderstandings; I recall reading an article in an Egyptian newspaper in which a columnist warned his readers to turn down advances from Western women. They have ravenous sexual desires, claimed the middle-aged writer; Arab men must do their utmost to resist. My experience in Egypt is of a reverse phenomenon: Western women have regularly complained that local men harass them.

Many of the more pious students at Asyut University had received instructions by videotape from a former teacher at a local theological college who was now preaching in the United States. Sheikh Omar Abdel Rahman, who was blind since contracting diabetes as an infant, was considered the 'spiritual leader' and founder of the Gama'a Islamiyah. When a Muslim militant plans to plant a bomb or assassinate someone, he needs the approval from a man of learning in order to establish that an otherwise criminal act would be considered morally justified in the eyes of God. Sheikh Omar, with his doctorate from al-Azhar University and his immaculate knowledge of the Qur'ān, had been accused of issuing the religious decree that authorized the killing of the former President, Anwar Sadat. In 1984, an Egyptian court cleared the sheikh of involvement in the assassination despite his association with the killers. Travelling to Peshawar in Pakistan, he met up with an old colleague from al-Azhar, Sheikh Abdullah Azzam, who'd set up the 'Office of Services' for the international brigades of Muslim combatants. After the Soviets were driven out from Afghanistan, Omar Abdel Rahman obtained a visa and later a green card to live in the United States, where he married an African-American woman. The remarkable ease by which the sheikh obtained his visa remains a source of controversy; the most plausible explanation is that the CIA arranged it through the US Embassy in Sudan as payback for his formidable success in recruiting foreign mujahedin for the war in Afghanistan.

Sheikh Omar agreed to meet us in January 1993 at al-Salam (Peace) Mosque in Jersey City, just across the Hudson River from New York. Masjid al-Salam is easy to miss; it is above a shop in a congested street. The sheikh was a rotund man, now with a flowing white beard that rested on his chest. His left eye was closed but for a crack, a dark hole from which water was dripping like tears. His right eye was wide open and bulbous, covered by a milky-white membrane that shook as he spoke; underneath, his eyeball moved from side to side when his anger rose.

'We warned tourists not to visit this area,' he said, referring to the region surrounding Asyut and Luxor. 'It's not safe there. But they ignored our warnings.' His most recent videotape circulating amongst Islamists in Egypt had been filmed in al-Salam Mosque. In the video, he issued the fatwa that tourism was evil. 'Tourism should not be about drinking, women and music,' he implored. 'Tourists who go to Egypt spread immorality and sexual diseases like Aids. They bring gambling, adultery and alcohol. We cannot accept that.'

So it was OK to murder tourists? 'They didn't listen to my words, so I was not responsible for what happened,' he replied. Soon after our meeting a bomb exploded under the twin towers of the World Trade Center. Sheikh Omar Abdel Rahman was indicted for masterminding the attack, which left six dead. The sheikh was later sentenced to life imprisonment for plotting a 'war of urban terrorism against the United States'.

The sheikh had a remarkable publicity machine operating in Egypt: scratchy audio and fuzzy videotapes of his pronouncements blared from mosques and street vendors wherever the Gama'a Islamiyah had a presence. In one of the tapes, he proudly announced that the movement he 'led' as spiritual guide had indeed been involved in killing Anwar Sadat, who was 'an apostate' for making peace with Israel.

After Gamel Abdel Nasser's death in 1970, Sadat deliberately developed a pious image and, like several other Muslim leaders in the decades that followed, encouraged the growth of Islamist movements as bulwarks against a perceived threat from leftists. While Nasser had sided with the Soviet Union, Sadat looked to the West for financial support and believed that Islamists would be suitable allies. The largest was the Gama'a Islamiyah, which at its outset was a peaceful movement.

President Sadat had given his blessing to the Gama'a Islamiyah and was styling himself as the 'Believing President'; in return for its political support, he allowed cultural and religious freedom. This arrangement lasted until November 1977, when the President visited Jerusalem in preparation for the Camp David Accord the following year. The shock waves reverberated through the middle classes of Cairo and up the Nile valley to the student unions of Upper Egypt. How could a president who was leading a national Islamic revival make peace with the Jewish state? Such an act could never receive religious sanction; it was described as 'a shameful peace' and 'treachery' in Islamist newspapers. Sadat replied by initially preventing candidates from the Gama'a Islamiyah standing in student elections and finally disbanding the Egyptian Students' Union. All political meetings were banned at universities and summer camps were closed down.

Moderate elements, especially in Cairo and Alexandria, joined with the Muslim Brotherhood to embrace a programme of gradual Islamization while rejecting armed confrontation with the regime. But in the face of government harassment, as often occurs in these circumstances, a section of the Islamist movement gravitated toward violence.

In Upper Egypt, at strongholds such as Asyut University, the Gama'a Islamiyah adopted a more clandestine structure and a revolutionary creed. Sayyid Qutb, whose publications had been widely distributed during the previous decade, had laid the foundation for rebellion. His final treatise, *Milestones*, once again became relevant to a generation that felt betrayed. It placed the Gama'a Islamiyah on a trajectory that would ultimately lead to violence. A small group from the Gama'a formed an avowedly militant and secret organization called Jihad, whose mufti (religious adviser) was the blind sheikh. At that time, Jihad believed that the critical battle for Muslims was to fight 'infidels and hypocrites' within Muslim nations and replace their leaders with an Islamic order, rather than launch a global war with the West.

The city of Asyut, a strategic gateway to Upper Egypt, often stood as a challenge to rulers more than two hundred miles to the north in Cairo. It was said that 'whoever governs Asyut, governs Upper Egypt'. The region also has a large Christian population; about one third of Egypt's Coptic minority live in the provinces of Asyut, and Minya, which lies to the north. 'Coptic' simply meant 'Egyptian' in the language spoken before the Arab Muslim conquest. There are only estimates of numbers, which are often disputed, but at least one in ten Egyptians is a Copt. The Copts in Upper Egypt had lived in relative peace with Muslims for a thousand years.

When Sheikh Omar Abdel Rahman arrived to teach at al-Azhar's theology college in Asyut in 1973, he began to apply Qutb's absolutist theories to the local Christian population. The Copts were *jahili*, or barbaric, and should pay *jizya* (protection tax), he preached. Some young Islamists followed the sheikhs' guidance and set up mafia-style racketeering operations. Sheikh Omar later issued a fatwa that formally permitted the plunder of Coptic-owned goldsmiths and jewellery stores and, if necessary, the murder of the shopkeepers. His theological justification for killing Christians was based on Qutb's judgement that a technical state of war exists between Muslims and non-Muslims; the gold was needed to finance the jihad so it constituted the 'spoils of war' rather than stolen goods.

The Gama'a Islamiyah was growing in influence at Asyut University during the 1980s and their attacks on Copts became more frequent. I visited a nearby farming village, Manshiet Nasser, where tensions between the two communities had been rising for the past two years, A few months before my visit, the lush fields of fodder, vegetables and wheat surrounding the village had become graveyards.

The Copts are proud of their history, which is mostly defined by their churches and monasteries. Every evening, the blue chapel in Manshiet Nasser is packed to the brim and thrums to the liturgical rhythms of Coptic hymns. The priest, who came from the nearby town of Dairut, led the singing with a strident, lung-opening rendition. He insisted on conducting services in Manshiet Nasser despite needing a police escort to make the half-hour journey from his home. 'We cannot be intimidated by these criminals,' he insisted. 'Copts have lived in Egypt for over five thousand years. We will not become foreigners in our own land.'

The priest called the Gama'a Islamiyah cell 'criminals' because most of the local Copts believed the dispute was over money, rather than religious doctrine. The majority of the grievances related to demands for money. The police told me they began over the sale of a house, which escalated into a gun fight between police and militants. The Gama'a Islamiyah responded with a chilling statement from its commanders in Dairut; it promised to murder four Copts, who were named, in retaliation for the death of its fighter. The communiqué warned all Christian men in Manshiet Nasser to remain indoors. Anyone who ventured out would be killed

In almost every Coptic home I visited, the men sat idly around while their wives and children were out attending to the fields. In one house, three Coptic men in their forties and fifties were sipping tea around a table, unsure what to do with their lives. 'We cannot go out or work in the fields!' they shouted. 'Our livelihood has been lost. If we leave our homes, our lives will be at risk.' One of the men wore a small white cloth wrapped tightly around his head and had a pencil moustache under a dominating nose. 'They are always spying on us. These young boys have been told they can get money from Christians because they are too lazy to work. They are thieves.'

The border between political and criminal violence is often blurred but it was interesting that an atrocity that was perceived internationally as religiously motivated violence or 'terrorism' was mostly seen in the village as gangland thuggery. Each side knew each other; they had grown up together and questions concerning a broader, ideological confrontation between Christianity and Islam elicited mystified expressions.

The Gama'a Islamiyah succeeded in fulfilling the pledge in their communiqué. Early one morning, a four-man unit from the Gama'a moved like a scythe through the fields surrounding Manshiet Nasser. The targets were any male Coptic farmers who had ignored their threats. A car stopped at the edge of a field of millet; the gunmen got out, took a few steps into the grass and sprayed their victims with automatic weapons. Six members of one family perished, along with five other Christians and two Muslims.

While both perpetrators and victims were from Manshiet Nasser, the causes of the communal violence seemed alien to the rhythms and customs of life in the village. Did the Muslim murderers really believe they were 'soldiers' in a 'war' against Christians?

Sheikh Omar Abdel Rahman claimed from his lair in New York that Copts and Muslims were not necessarily at war. 'We are at war with Mubarak,' he growled. 'Christians must respect Islam; if they do, they are not our enemies. They can live peacefully in an Islamic state.' He refused to be drawn on the communal killings. 'Copts can live alongside Muslims without discrimination,' he said. Whether to believe him is another matter but his venom on this occasion was directed at the Egyptian President. 'Hosni Mubarak cannot convince people that he should remain in power. He is a corrupt oppressor. We all know what happened to Ceauşescu in Romania,' he said. 'Mubarak is worse than Ceauşescu,' the sheikh concluded in his high-pitched, melodic delivery.

The prospect of an Islamic state is nevertheless a perplexing prospect for non-Muslims. Educated Copts, who were well represented in the professional and business classes, repeatedly voiced concerns about creeping Islamization and feared they would become second-class citizens. I have often wondered whether an authentic, modern Islamic state can coexist alongside a Western liberal democracy. It is a debate that is central to relations between Islam and the West but it is hard to reach a conclusion. The West does make significant demands on other cultures that it confronts; I had a debate with an Algerian-born French television journalist, who told me that an Islamic state should be treated in a similar manner to the former apartheid regime in South Africa. It must be opposed because it would not preserve the universal rights of man and in particular would prevent women gaining equality. 'Hitler came to power through democracy,' she warned.

On the other hand, the 'young generation' of the Muslim Brotherhood (they are called this despite being in their forties and fifties) told me that an Islamic state would, for example, fully safeguard the freedom of Copts in Egypt without imposing the punitive *jizya* 'tax' or preventing them reaching positions of authority in society. Of course, an Islamic state would seek its authority from within the holy texts rather than through Western political philosophy. My experience is that Islamists are very egalitarian in spirit. Over the centuries, Islamic cultures have shown greater concern for racial equality than their Christian counterparts. I have also met countless Muslim women from

Tehran to Atlanta, Georgia, who believe that Western liberalism misunderstands the freedoms that women enjoy within Islam. Peaceful Salafists such as the Muslim Brotherhood seek to construct a modern society rooted in the culture and civilization of their region, which is mostly Islamic. Most Egyptians do not view an Islamic state as a threatening prospect. For more than a thousand years, Islam has been the sole compass that has guided their lives. For the typical Egyptian, the adoption of a secular, Western-inspired system of government fifty years ago has not ushered in an era of glorious rewards.

The events in Manshiet Nasser, while committed in the name of an Islamic state, were rooted not in Qur'ānic thought but modern strategies of political revolution. Sayyid Qutb contributed to Salafism what Lenin, Mao and 'Che' Guevara did to Marxism. The objective of murdering thirteen Copts in Manshiet Nasser was to instigate instability, provoke greater repression from the authorities and trigger a wider conflict with the state. The target was the Egyptian regime. I reached this conclusion after a lengthy conversation late one night with a lawyer, Sayyid, who was closely linked to the Gama'a Islamiyah in Asyut.

Sayyid was a small man of slight frame with a wispy beard. He wore a Western-style white shirt and dark baggy slacks with sandals. His office was down a dusty, poorly lit road in an area of Asyut that was congested with small square houses, often built on top of one another at random angles. The sparse white room had a wooden desk and a few stools. Bare strip lights buzzed overhead. Sayyid was worried about his own future as he rubbed his hands and fumbled with his fingers. 'Anyone could be picked up at any moment,' he said. He was typical of the men who sympathized with Islamist movements; these men are well educated, usually in science or law. They are from a traditional background and are probably the first generation to graduate from university. They believe that their government is both corrupt and weak and has had to turn to the West, cap in hand, for support. They are a generation numbed by a succession of ideologies founded on Marxism, pan-Arabism and state nationalism that have failed to provide a secure, let alone proud identity. When all that is scraped away, who are they? These young men have found certainty and pride in Islam; not the corpulent, tainted faith that is nominally followed by their leaders, but a genuine, unblemished and for them empowering Salafist belief.

Al-Rahme Mosque was a dour concrete structure that had been built to commemorate Egypt's meagre but much-vaunted 'victory' over Israel in October 1973. A month earlier, 200 anti-terrorist police had sealed off the mosque and 70 worshippers had been arrested as suspected members of the Gama'a Islamiyah.

The police had erected barriers at either end of the road; dozens of armed officers stood at street corners and in positions outside the mosque. Several plainclothes police, in this case wearing the traditional djellaba robes, held large walkie-talkies and monitored those who entered the mosque. A vet called Dr Mahmoud led the sermon. A speaker mounted on the side of the minaret broadcast the proceedings to the police outside. 'You are surrounding God's house,' announced Dr Mahmoud, who was wrapped in a Palestinian black-and-white *kuffiyeh*. 'You are arresting those who bring the people to God and who believe in God's calling. Stop arresting the faithful who want to pray in God's house. Why are you doing this?' he appealed across the evening air.

The regime adopted a policy of 'nationalizing' the twenty thousand state-controlled mosques. The problem was the forty thousand or so 'independent' mosques that had sprung up as centres of anti-government activity. The political field had become so reduced in Egypt that these mosques were the only rallying point for opposition, which gelled around the faith; many of these mosques were now under the control of the Gama'a Islamiyah.

After prayers, we were ushered into a walled area that was within the warren-like complex of al-Rahme Mosque. A young man in his mid-twenties walked in and introduced himself as 'Ahmed'; he was a gunman in the Gama'a Islamiyah. He had studied agricultural science at Asyut University and combined a youthful nervousness with the calm determination of a man who believes his day is about to come. He was polite and almost excessively courteous. He was sorry but he had to cover his face in a white woollen scarf. Did I mind, he asked. If he didn't hide his identity, he'd be arrested immediately the film was transmitted, he told me apologetically. It was the first time a member of the Gama'a Islamiyah had given a television interview.

'We are marching to God's calling,' Ahmed announced once the camera was turning. 'The more the government attacks the Gama'a Islamiyah, the stronger we become. Every time the regime confronts us we win the sympathy and the support of the people.'

'What can justify killing a young Western tourist?' I asked.

'Everybody's patience has a limit. We are being forced to use weapons. Tourists should not come here. There is a war taking place and it is dangerous on the battlefield. This is our war. Tourists are not welcome here.'

Ahmed possessed both the confidence and the innocence of those who have discovered certainty. He spoke about taking power within the next few years. 'The system of government in Egypt has failed,' he concluded. 'We will replace it with an Islamic government that will provide justice for everyone.' Whenever I questioned his right to take human life he repeatedly portrayed 'terrorism' as a defensive measure. 'We have to carry guns to defend ourselves. All we do is call on people to follow God. What should we do when someone shoots at us? We must use violence to repel violence.' It was a deceitful argument in the sense that the Gama'a Islamiyah used unprovoked violence against Copts and tourists to weaken and undermine the regime. In the broader sense, the rise of Islamic militancy in Muslim countries has usually been a reaction to state suppression. When the corpses are counted in the Middle East, state-sanctioned 'anti-terrorist' violence has killed more people than Islamist 'terrorism'. The authorities in Asyut had rounded up a number of young men on suspicion of membership of the Gama'a Islamiyah. Cafes were full of stories of missing sons and brothers. There was also evidence of systematic torture.

At al-Rahme Mosque, several men came forward claiming they'd been tortured either at the Asyut office of the domestic intelligence agency, the General Directorate of State Security Investigations (Mabahith Amn al-Dawla), or at the Central Security Forces' military camp outside the city. Abdul Moeti was a teacher at a local secondary school. He was plump, in his early forties, with a dark beard but greying hair. He had thick glasses and wore an ill-fitting loose sweater. At midnight a few months earlier, agents from the SSI went to his house. He was arrested and blindfolded. He was taken to a jail where he said the beatings began. 'I was punched and slapped and then they threw cold water over me. They put electric cables on my stomach. My muscles were ripped open.' Abdul lifted his baggy sweater to show damaged scar tissue, about four inches long and half an inch wide, where the electricity had lacerated his skin.

Ahmad Thabet was seventeen years old when the SSI arrested him. When he was taken to its offices, he was doused with water and electrocuted before he was even questioned. He said he was later suspended by his hands for hours on end and beaten on the soles of the feet. He denied any involvement with the Gama'a Islamiyah. Tarek was also a student, just a few years older than Ahmad Thabet. During an interrogation, police officers asked him about a named suspect they were hunting. 'I said I didn't know where he was,' he recalled. 'I knew him but had no idea where he'd gone. So they put electric wires into my ears. Then they increased the voltage. I was screaming. I just didn't know where to find this man.' That was not the end of Tarek's ordeal. He was stripped and doused with freezing water and suspended by his arms. After a while the police realized that he didn't know the whereabouts of their suspect, so they released him.

People were lining up to speak to me in the mosque, eager to give their stories of torture in front of the BBC's cameras. It was clear that a large section of the community had been affected by the crackdown, which had been brutal and indiscriminate. In Asyut, the regime wanted to show the Islamists just who was in charge. Ahmed, the militant with the Gama'a Islamiyah, vowed to continue to fight 'oppression' using guns and bombs. He said that if the regime continued its crackdown on the movement, 'Mubarak will not survive the consequences.'

When the documentary was transmitted in February 1993, the Egyptian government wrote to the Director General of the BBC complaining that the film had totally misrepresented the scale of the problem. The Gama'a Islamiyah was just a 'small bunch of criminals', the letter insisted. It was interesting that while the regime regularly referred to the Gama'a as 'terrorists' in Egypt, the letter referred to them as 'criminals' in an attempt to deprive them of the status of a movement with political goals. It reminded me of a much later comment by Charles Kennedy, leader of the Liberal Democrat Party. He rejected the rhetoric of the 'war on terror' because it granted al-Qa'eda nobility that they didn't deserve. 'They are murderers and criminals, not warriors,' he declared. The Gama'a and al-Qa'eda were certainly murderers but to call these groups 'criminal' is unhelpful; they do not kill for personal gain.

History has not proved kind to the Egyptian government's complaint; the documentary recorded the beginning of a six-year insurgency that claimed nearly fifteen hundred lives and resulted in up to fifty thousand people detained under emergency powers. By the time the angry letter reached me for a reply a few weeks after transmission, a bomb had killed two tourists and an Egyptian at a crowded Cairo coffee shop; dozens were injured. The attacks on tourists continued month after month.

During the 1990s, Egypt became more 'Islamized'. More women dressed in Islamic garments. The Islamic content of school curricula and media programming increased. Alcoholic beverages were banned in a majority of Egypt's provinces. During a UN Population Conference in Cairo in 1994, while Mubarak tried to showcase Egypt as a modern, sophisticated nation, the Grand Sheikh of al-Azhar issued a fatwa that female circumcision was 'a noble practice that honours women'.

A turning point in Mubarak's battle with the Gama'a Islamiyah occurred in November 1997 outside the mortuary temple built by Queen Hatshepsut, the only woman to have ruled as a pharaoh of ancient Egypt. It is one of the world's most popular tourist destinations, set on the northern side of the Valley of the Kings, across the Nile from Luxor's hotels and Karnak's temples. Six Egyptian men ambushed the site, murdering fifty-eight tourists. Most of the victims were shot at close range. Some tourists hid behind the pillars of the colonnade and watched as Gama'a Islamiyah militants pulled out daggers and slit the throats of the injured when their ammunition ran out. The killings proved to be the final convulsion of the Gama'a Islamiyah.

Adel Abdel Bary was a roly-poly man with a thick neck who seemed to take life at a gentle pace. I used to watch him amble down Dowland Street in London's Kilburn district usually wearing a brown djellaba with an anorak over the top. We had a procedure; when I arrived at the printing press he ran above a shop on the corner of Dart Street, I'd give him a call. He and his family lived in an apartment block down the road and once he knew I was there, he'd set off. I'd wave as I saw him approach and he would wave back but his pace remained constant. Nothing could speed him up and nothing much seemed to excite him, apart from telephone calls from his old friend, Ayman Zawahri.

Adel was wanted in Egypt for his involvement with the Islamist movement and had been sentenced to death in absentia a few years earlier for a plot to blow up Cairo's historic Khan El-Khalili bazaar. He had been granted asylum in the UK and operated an organization called the International Office for the Defence of the Egyptian People, which I knew was a mouthpiece for the Jihad movement, led by Dr Zawahri. Adel knew the doctor from his activities in Cairo. 'He is a good Muslim,' he told me softly of the man who became bin Laden's deputy in al-Qa'eda, 'He's been working hard for Islam.'

Dr Zawahri came from a distinguished medical dynasty: his father was a professor of pharmacology at Ain Shams University in Cairo; his brother was a highly regarded dermatologist. The next generation produced thirty-one doctors, chemists or pharmacists, as well as an ambassador, a judge and a member of parliament. Zawahri followed in the family tradition and became a surgeon. He was always secretive about his politics, rarely discussing them with those around him. The biggest influence on his life was Sayyid Qutb, whose torture and suffering in Egypt's jails had become a modern-day passion play that was inspiring a generation of Islamists. Zawahri was arrested for membership of the Muslim Brotherhood in 1966, the same year Qutb was executed. Zawahri was fifteen years old when he created a cell in his secondary school to overthrow the government and was then tortured in an Egyptian jail. In a detailed profile in 2002, Lawrence Wright wrote in the *New Yorker* magazine: 'One line of thinking proposes that America's tragedy on September 11th was born in the prisons of Egypt [where] torture created an appetite for revenge . . . They held the West responsible for corrupting and humiliating Islamic society . . . humiliation, which is the essence of torture, is important to understanding the Islamists' rage against the West.'

After the assassination of Anwar Sadat, Zawahri was again arrested along with hundreds of other militants. He established himself as a forceful theorist who had numerous debates about tactics and strategies with the blind sheikh, Omar Abdel Rahman. The latter believed in developing a populist, mass movement from the ranks of the disenchanted, much like the Gama'a Islamiyah of the 1990s. In contrast, Zawahri followed Qutb's model and advocated a Leninist-style vanguard, which would operate in stealth. A lawyer who later represented dozens of members of the Gama'a Islamiyah was imprisoned alongside the two men. 'Zawahri wanted to infiltrate the army,' Montasser Zayat told me as he munched cake in a Cairo hotel. 'He thought that a guerrilla war could never be won in Egypt. The geography is all wrong.' Zayat said that the two men argued ceaselessly. Zawahri was by then the effective leader of the Jihad movement, which consisted of a small group of plotters who were waiting for the right moment to strike and seize power.

'He's a quiet man, a very polite man,' Adel told me in the office of his 'human rights' organization in west London. I was working on this story with an energetic young producer, Charlie Clay. It was the winter of 1997 and our meetings continued with their low-key rituals. He lumbered up the outside stairs and told us to sit on either a stool or a worn-out upholstered chair. In deference to age Charlie would usually allow me to slump in the chair. We'd wait in silence while Adel lit a small stove heater and put the kettle on for a cup of tea. 'It's cold outside,' he'd say as if it was a surprise. The room was the rather modest headquarters for the grandly named International Office for the Defence of the Egyptian People. It was full of discarded Arabic leaflets, newspapers and unused newsprint. Discussion, like the room, took a while to warm up. I had wanted to find out what contacts Adel could provide in Egypt that could tell me about the Luxor killers and the Gama'a Islamiyah's strategy. He was not very forthcoming. 'I don't know,' he said. I wasn't clear about the relationship between the Gama'a and the Jihad and Adel was again unhelpful. 'How close are the two movements?' I asked. 'I'm not sure,' came the reply. Then Adel told us, 'You should go to Afghanistan. It's very interesting what's happening there. It's better to go there than Egypt.' Charlie and I looked at each other.

'I can help you go to Afghanistan,' Adel said. 'Ayman will treat you as his guests.' Then he threw in a question that neither of us expected. 'Can you take me with you?' Once more Charlie and I looked at each other. 'Let us think about it,' was our joint reply. In retrospect, I believe that Adel knew that some significant changes in the international Islamist movement were about to take place in Afghanistan. His problem was that he didn't have a United Nations travel document as a recognized refugee. Asylum-seekers must hand over the passports of their country of origin and wait until a UN 'passport' is issued. Adel wanted me to write to the Home Office to speed up the procedure, which I did, but received no reply.

I suspect the Home Office passed the request over to Special Branch or MI5. They had no intention of providing Adel any travel documents because they wanted him just where he was, so that he could be watched and monitored. Adel already suspected that he might be under surveillance and asked if he could be given a phone to make plans for our trip to Afghanistan. 'The calls are very expensive,' he told us, 'I dial a satellite phone.'

Increasingly Charlie and I believed that access to the training camps of the Gama'a in Afghanistan would lead to a very good story. There was also this mysterious Saudi billionaire called Osama bin Laden who we would probably meet.

Charlie and I drew up a list of filming requests:

— Access to life in the Camps
— Prayers and sermons
— Military training
— Interviews with the Gama'a leader, Refai Ahmed Taha
— Interview with Ayman Zawahri
— Interview with Mr bin Laden

Adel nodded when he read it. Then he mumbled into thin air, as he often did, that there would be an important announcement. 'Soon,' he said. 'About what?' I enquired. 'I don't know,' he replied, 'maybe about war with America, or something like that.' He spoke as if it was an everyday occurrence that a group of Islamists would declare war on the United States. Unfortunately his downbeat tone made it seem farcical. My notes contain exclamation marks – 'Al Z. (Zawahri) to declare war on West!!' – as if they were the quixotic thoughts of a harmless lunatic.

Zawahri had visited Afghanistan for the first time in the summer of 1980, shortly after the Soviet invasion. He was working at a Muslim Brotherhood clinic in Cairo when its director asked if he would like to accompany him to Pakistan to tend to refugees who had fled Afghanistan. He spent four months in Pakistan, working for the Red Crescent Society. After his release from jail in 1984, his interest in Afghanistan grew and two years later he returned but this time with a greater interest in jihad. It was then he built up his close relationship with bin Laden.

'Ayman says hello,' Adel told us once as he offered some digestive biscuits and tea in stained mugs. Zawahri had called him while he was driving on the M25 near Gatwick Airport. He had read out our filming requests and apparently received approval for most of the items. 'Most things should be fine. Some things may be difficult and we will have to be careful in Afghanistan,' he told us. 'Ayman will take care,' he assured us in his unassuming manner.

The documentary that Charlie and I were trying to make still required filming in Egypt, which we considered more important than the goings-on in Afghanistan. The journalistic consensus at the time decreed that the important story in Afghanistan was the Taliban, their absurdities and in particular their attitude toward women. Interest was not focused on the thousand or so Egyptian guerrillas and their Saudi paymaster in the eastern hills. The killing of tourists in Luxor, on the other hand, affected British holiday plans.

We decided to visit Egypt on tourist visas, without telling the authorities, in order to assess the situation. I had not travelled there for four years and I wanted to test the water as well as make contacts with militants while the authorities were not aware of our presence. I had been told that the General Directorate of State Security Investigations has a department that monitors the output and activities of foreign journalists based in Cairo or visiting Egypt. This includes electronic surveillance and sometimes gathering information from Egyptians who work alongside the foreign teams. I wanted our team to be 'off-radar' while we assessed a longer-term strategy. Our team included Hamid, the assistant I worked alongside in Algeria who had been forced to seek asylum in the UK because of the repercussions of the documentary we had made together. I felt a debt to a man whose life had been turned upside down because he had worked for me.

We had been influenced by an article written by a US journalist, Jack Kelley, who was later shortlisted for a Pulitzer Prize. He had apparently infiltrated the Gama'a Islamiyah in Asyut a month earlier and we wanted to follow his path. In Kelley's encounter, the gunmen pointed toward a picture of Yasser al-Sirri, an Islamist in exile in London, and described him as a 'good man, like Jesus'.

Yasser al-Sirri had feline, almost feminine mannerisms. He was small and gaunt with a wispy beard that he regularly tugged and shaped. He fidgeted and never maintained eye contact. I never trusted him and felt that he talked up his role in the Egyptian Islamist movement. I recalled that someone in London's Islamist community had remarked that Yasser was 'a pipsqueak' and his militant movement, the Vanguards of Conquest, was little more than him and a few friends drinking coffee while reading Qutb's *Milestones*. On the other hand, he had been sentenced to death in Egypt for attempting to kill a former prime minister and had a reckless streak in his personality. Kelley had seemingly discovered clear evidence that al-Sirri had influence in Asyut.

Al-Sirri was from Suez, in eastern Egypt, and I was surprised to read that he had such a following in the south. At the time we didn't realize that Kelley had made the whole dramatic article up. That and about twenty other groundbreaking pieces.

Hamid and I met Yasser several times for tea and cakes, either at the Hyde Park Hilton or a coffee shop in a hotel opposite Marble Arch. He was spindly but gobbled sweet cakes and syrupy desserts with ease. He was an energetic campaigner, and was about to have an 'important international press conference' in Bayswater where he would expose as 'a lie' reports of dialogue between the regime and the Gama'a Islamiyah after the Luxor carnage. The second item to be discussed, according to the press release, would be 'the Egyptian government's accusations that Britain is harbouring terrorists!' 'The Egyptian government thinks you are a "terrorist",' I told him. He giggled.

Hamid gathered information from al-Sirri, who promised the type of access that Kelley had apparently achieved. He seemed rather pleased that Kelley had quoted guerrillas who compared him to Jesus. He did not voice suspicions that it might not be true. He loved intrigue and just smiled when I asked if these were his men. Nevertheless, Hamid thought that al-Sirri's contacts were highly valued.

Because of the sensitivity of the subject, we decided to work covertly on our arrival. The first problem began when we followed up on al-Sirri's contacts. Hamid had arranged with him that we would visit al-Shuhada Mosque in Suez, the town where the shipping canal opens into the Red Sea. We were told to call al-Sirri's brother, Mohammed, and had been given distinct instructions and codes in order to arrange a meeting. It didn't take long for alarm bells to start ringing once we arrived in Suez. I told Hamid that we shouldn't visit the house belonging to the brother of one of Egypt's most wanted men. It turned out to be a mistake. We arrived at a small white-fronted property, where we met Mohammed. He seemed as excitable as his brother but bemused as to why we had come. 'The Gama'a Islamiyah aren't around these parts,' he smiled. We drank tea and ate some dates and fruit. I then saw Hamid give Mohammed an envelope that Yasser al-Sirri had asked to pass on to his brother. Mohammed opened it, and I cannot be sure, but it looked as if it contained money. I was both outraged and suddenly uneasy. 'Let's go,' I told Hamid. I had noticed a man outside, a thin man in his fifties in a blue djellaba. When we left, he followed us. We had been set up by al-Sirri. The whole exercise had been organized by him, in my view, simply so that we could act as couriers. We had been manipulated and our cover had been blown.

In October 2001, Yasser al-Sirri was arrested in London in connection with the murder of the anti-Taliban leader, Ahmad Shah Massoud, in northern Afghanistan on 9 September. I must admit that I smiled when I heard that he'd been arrested. It looked like a stitch-up to me; but then, it is often said 'what goes around comes around'. I think he was set up because people close to al-Qa'eda, such as Adel, would not have trusted him to take part in such an operation. The suicide bombers who killed Massoud had used a supporting letter from al-Sirri to obtain the interview. They even carried al-Sirri's mobile phone number on them. I wondered if they had also agreed a lexicon of secret code words.

I later had several meetings with senior politicians including Nabil Osman, the always suave but approachable Director of State Information and a former adviser to Mubarak. I discussed my meetings with Adel and Yasser and raised the vexed question of militants convicted in an Egyptian court seeking asylum in the UK. Osman felt we should raise it as a matter of the utmost concern in the film. 'Terrorists linked to the Luxor slaughter have found safe haven in London,' he said and shrugged his shoulders. 'Are British people happy with that?' There was no secret that these men were in London. Mubarak repeatedly raised it when he met British politicians and diplomats. The Egyptian government had placed a 'Wanted' poster on the Internet. Yasser al-Sirri was in the middle on the top row, alongside Ayman Zawahri. Adel Abdel Bary's mugshot was at the bottom, next to the brother of the man who assassinated Anwar Sadat.

While Montasser Zayat had been in jail with Ayman Zawahri and Sheikh Omar Abdel Rahman after the murder of Anwar Sadat, his recent role had been as a defence lawyer in the military courts. He was also the main source of information about the militants in both the Egyptian and the Western press. Charlie christened him 'Tweedledum', which became our jocular code for meetings with him because of his generous girth and unhurried manner. It followed Charlie's earlier description of Adel as west London's 'Tweedledee'. Zayat and our team met several times in coffee shops around central Cairo. We discussed human rights and the state of the Gama'a Islamiyah after Luxor. 'The Afghan leadership were responsible for this attack,' he told me, 'the movement is split in two.' He loved cakes and knew which hotel coffee shops stocked his favourites. When he sat, his head was perched back because of his significant waistline. Crumbs would inevitably fall on to his beard and sometimes stain his tie. I asked him whether he was being watched. He lifted his eyebrows and put his finger to his mouth. 'You cannot be too careful,' he said and then let out a hearty horse laugh.

What did that mean? I did not know what relationship, if any, Zayat had with the security services. He was either under surveillance or had some arrangement with the SSI. He certainly loved conspiracies and enjoyed talking about them to Western journalists. I gently raised the question of the Gama'a Islamiyah. Did he think it was possible to meet one of their leaders? He took another bite of cake and mulled over the question for an excessive time. 'Maybe,' he said dramatically, 'we'll see.' We met on several occasions and each time the response was the same. Zayat was entertaining; however, nothing ever emerged apart from a huge cake tab. On one occasion, he ordered a box to take home for a family birthday and left it on my bill. I meekly accepted paying for the desserts, as I was still hopeful that 'Tweedledum' had something up his sleeve. My exasperation was reflected in my notes. The reference to our final rendezvous read: '13.00 – Fat man. Meridien (hotel) cake shop.'

It was not long before I realized that I was being followed. My first hint was when I saw a man in a restaurant in the prosperous Cairo suburb of Heliopolis. I had seen him in the reception of my hotel earlier in the evening. He was paunchy and wore a brown leather jacket and read from a pile of newspapers. The Chantilly Restaurant was a fashionable eatery, full of laughing couples and well-dressed businessmen, and he seemed a little out of place. He also seemed lonely and melancholy and I felt sorry for him. It wasn't until I lay in bed that night that I realized that he probably worked for the secret police.

Men wearing similar jackets and moustaches followed us day and night. When I sent a fax from my small hotel in Zamalek, one of Cairo's wealthiest districts, the man at the business centre refused to return it. We almost had a fistfight, as I grabbed the paper and he tugged it back, tearing it in half. I left with my half; unfortunately the bulk of the message was scrunched up in his hand. After a while I thought 'fine'; I had nothing to hide, so if the SSI wanted to follow me, I let them.

My ire at the secret police had been aroused by the early departure of Hamid, who had been poisoned in his hotel. I was convinced the perpetrators were the SSI. Once my visa expired, I was told that I must leave Egypt. I was not formally expelled; that would damage Egypt's reputation as a free and democratic nation. I was just told that my journalist's visa would not be extended by the Press Department. The press attaché, Zaki Ghazi, held out an apologetic hand. 'I'm sorry it didn't work out.' Then he smiled insincerely and added, 'You are always welcome here as a tourist.' With nothing left to lose, I returned his duplicitous smile. 'I'm sorry,' I said, 'I hear Egypt's a little dangerous for tourists these days.'

The massacre at the Valley of the Kings was more or less the end of the Gama'a Islamiyah. Its ranks had already been depleted by the security services; members of its ruling Majlis al-Shura (consultative council) were either in jail or abroad, in Afghanistan. Egypt was very different to Algeria, where rugged mountains had provided ideal terrain for insurrection. In Egypt the militants had no cover and nowhere to run. By 1998, about twenty thousand Gama'a members were in prison; at least five hundred had been killed in shootouts with the police. Fifty-five had been hanged and two shot by firing squad. A further thirty-three were on death row. But more importantly, most Egyptians found the massacre repugnant and sickening; any sympathy was seemingly lost. The leadership in Afghanistan claimed it had not ordered the attack and was 'shocked' by this 'unacceptable incident' while the seven Majlis al-Shura members in jail called for a truce. It took another year for the Gama'a to formerly renounce violence but the movement was broken as an insurgency within Egypt. It had moved on to Afghanistan and a formal merger with another organization, al-Qa'eda.

In the immediate aftermath of September 11th, Mubarak stood shoulder to shoulder with George W. Bush as allies in the 'war on terror'. They share an enemy; if al-Qa'eda drew up a 'top 10' most-wanted-dead list, I suspect they would occupy the first two spots, jostling only with members of the Saudi royal family. Mubarak continued to rule using an iron fist, and despite criticizing US foreign policy he has remained loyal. Indeed, Washington pays the regime $2 billion annually in aid.

With the death of the incumbent Grand Sheikh of al-Azhar in 1996, Mubarak appointed a loyalist, Sayyid Tantawi, as his replacement. The President became more comfortable with pronouncements made within the ancient mosque. In times of crisis, Sheikh Tantawi has read soothing sermons. 'God help Muslims everywhere, and God help their presidents and kings,' he once intoned. 'God help our President.' The state has also succeeded in reducing al-Azhar's control over education and has 'nationalized' tens of thousands more mosques. It has imposed strict training requirements for those who wish to serve as imams, preventing the holy sites being 'taken over' by groups such as the Gama'a Islamiyah. Despite Mubarak's success in controlling the power of faith in his country, he has been unable to prevent Sheikh Tantawi tying himself in knots over his fatwas on 'terrorism'. The sheikh remained the highest spiritual authority for a billion Sunni Muslims but was unable to clearly define the difference between terrorism and jihad. At one time, he condemned suicide bombings against Israeli civilians as 'terrorism' but later said it was a Muslim's duty to wage jihad to defend Palestinian land. While his fatwa opposing attacks on Israeli civilians was still considered valid, he also demanded that the Palestinian people 'intensify the martyrdom operations [suicide bombings] against the Zionist enemy. Young people executing them have sold Allah the most precious thing of all,' he pronounced.

President Mubarak must be totally bemused by the Bush administration's policies. He must be asking himself whether President Bush is actually working for al-Qa'eda. Mubarak would certainly be forgiven if he thought the Bush administration secretly wanted to see him overthrown by Islamist radicals. Bush's policies in the Holy Lands and the invasion of Iraq sparked overwhelming popular anger in Egypt and have made Mubarak's pro-American posture difficult to maintain. When Mubarak complained, Bush added an extra $300 million in aid for 2004.

To add to the surreal nature of the Bush–Mubarak financial contract, a former director of the CIA and close friend of the President, James Woolsey, announced that authoritarian rulers in the Arab world, such as President Mubarak, needed to mend their ways. 'We want you nervous,' Woolsey said in a comment directed at Mubarak. 'We want you to realize now, for the fourth time in a hundred years, that this country and its allies are on the march, and that we are on the side of those you most fear: we're on the side of your own people.' President George W. Bush announced a moral crusade to transform the Arab world into a region that held the same values as the United States. He asked Mubarak to become the first Arab despot to allow free elections, just as Egypt had been the first Arab nation to make peace with Israel. 'The great and proud nation of Egypt has shown the way toward peace in the Middle East,' he declared, 'and now should show the way toward democracy in the Middle East.'

Mubarak must have thought that Bush had gone mad. After years of warning the US about Islamist 'terrorism', which went unheeded, Washington still didn't get it. I can picture the ageing autocrat foaming with rage and then screaming to one of his advisers. 'What planet is Bush on? Doesn't he realize that if there were free and fair elections in Egypt, the largest party would be the Muslim Brotherhood? Should I let these nut cases from the Gama'a out of jail just because I tortured them to get confessions? Get real, Dubya. We may have used the odd electric wire but at least we didn't sexually humiliate our prisoners in front of women!'

The rage generated in Egypt by the American-led invasion of Iraq forced the regime to allow the Muslim Brotherhood to stage a 'rally', even though, officially, three people in a room constituted an illegal political meeting. Opinion polls have been banned in Egypt, but most people would expect the Muslim Brotherhood to emerge as the single largest party if an election were genuinely free. Curiously, Mubarak has allowed Egypt to become a more pious society while imprisoning the political proponents of this shift, including the prominent doctor Essam El-Erian. 'We're still a long way from achieving our aim of an Islamic state,' he said after emerging from five years in jail, 'but we have succeeded to a large extent in changing the fabric of society toward religious piety except for a minority that's still hung up on Western values.'

During my first weekend back in London, a crisis unfolded in Kosovo. I cancelled our proposed trip to meet the Islamist fighters in Afghanistan. I went for a final meeting with Adel Abdel Bary in his small print shop in Kilburn.

I told him the news. 'Shame,' he replied, 'there was a very important fatwa issued last week. There will be a war with America,' he said as he handed over a cup of tea. He offered me a stale digestive. Before I left I told him to thank Zawahri. 'Tell Ayman that I would like to see him next time.' I added cheerfully, 'Let's give him a call in a few months.' We said our goodbyes; we hugged and exchanged the greeting '*Asalamalikum*', which literally means 'Peace be upon you'.

While I was in Egypt, the 'World Islamic Front' had been formed.

A fatwa had been issued and the top three signatories were Osama bin Laden, Ayman Zawahri and Refai Ahmed Taha, the leader of the Gama'a Islamiyah. It looked like the interview list we had given Adel. The fatwa proved to be highly significant in establishing al-Qa'eda's strategy. It formally overthrew the traditional notion of a 'just war' within radical Islamic thinking. It was written using the logic and language of conventional Sunni jurisprudence and included quotes from several learned scholars. It argued that America had declared 'war on Allah, his messenger, and Muslims', by stationing its troops in Saudi Arabia, imposing sanctions on Iraq that had killed a million of its people and adopting policies that serve 'the Jews' petty state'.

Traditionally, the precedents in sharia reasoning on 'legitimate targets' reflected the teaching of the Prophet when he said, 'Do not mutilate or kill women, children or old men.' It was a ban on what some consider 'terrorism'; it was assumed to be wrong for Muslims to intentionally target non-combatants. Now, an edict declared that Christians and Jews were legitimate targets instead of the protected 'People of the Book', as the Qur'ān usually described them. The authors of the fatwa called for a violation of sharia tradition because the United States was destroying Muslim countries and threatening the survival of the faith. During such an extreme emergency, there is sufficient reason, they claimed, to override the Qur'ānic directive against the deliberate murder of civilians.

Many in the West consider these decrees as irrelevant to the motivation of militants prepared to kill themselves in the name of their God. They should not. When established Muslim leaders, such as Sayyid Tantawi, the Grand Sheikh of al-Azhar, became discredited as rubber stamps for corrupt regimes, a vacuum emerged in the spiritual leadership of the Muslim world. It sucked in men with little or no religious training, such as Osama bin Laden and Ayman Zawahri. It provided the voiceless with a rebel mouthpiece, fearlessly speaking truth to power. Most devout Muslims rejected it. Some did not.

Shortly afterwards, bin Laden gave his definition of 'terrorism'. Using arguments from Muslim jurisprudence, he distinguished between 'commendable' and 'reprehensible' terrorism. He appeared to define 'terrorism' in terms of non-standard military tactics, which by themselves were neither right nor wrong – what mattered was whether the action was just in the first place.

'There is no doubt that every state and every civilization and culture has had to resort to terrorism under certain circumstances for the purpose of abolishing tyranny and corruption ... The terrorism we practise is of the commendable kind for it is directed at the tyrants, the traitors who commit acts of treason against their own countries and against their own faith and their own prophet and their own nation. Terrorising those are necessary measures to straighten things and make them right.'

I never saw Adel Abdel Bary again. He was charged with involvement in the bombings of the US embassies in east Africa, in which 224 people died. He and another London-based man were accused of conspiring to murder American citizens abroad. The US authorities claimed Adel sent direct instructions to the cell that carried out the attacks. He was facing extradition to the United States.

Without Adel, I was never able to call Ayman Zawahri. After September 11th, the deputy leader of al-Qa'eda had a bounty of $25 million on his head and no longer met journalists. It would have been interesting to interview the man who has had so much influence on bin Laden. Zawahri is the architect of the theory of the 'distant enemy', or *al'adou al-ba'id*. He created an 'army' that declared war on a superpower and yet remained outside the reach of its military. During an era when governments have satellite surveillance, communications monitoring and other sophisticated technology, Zawahri has taken strategies of insurgency to a new level, well beyond those envisaged by 'Che' Guevara.

I also wished I had met Osama bin Laden. I was privileged to witness history unfold from the mid-1980s onwards: amongst it, the fall of communism in Europe, the Tiananmen Square massacre, the Gulf War, the break-up of Yugoslavia. I have seen violence used by nations and rebels, each in the name of righteousness. Whether or not bin Laden was evil would not have been my starting point. I wanted to know what made him tick. Why had he become the man he was? Why were young Muslim men willing to join him in battle and die for their faith? What was his endgame? Did he want to turn the West into a Muslim caliphate or just expel US troops from Islamic lands? Could Islam and the West live side by side in peace and mutual respect? Could there be, from his side anyway, a negotiated end to the 'war'? I regret that missed opportunity. The film I made in Kosovo won numerous awards, but I would happily trade them for a plate of lamb and a cup of tea with Osama bin Laden.

15 / A WORLD AT WAR

'You slam your fist into it and it suddenly bursts into
a hundred small pieces.'
Bob Graham, US Senator, comparing al-Qa'eda to a blob of mercury

On a typical Saturday night in the Indonesian holiday island of Bali,
Jalan Legian filled up with revellers. The long, straight road, adjacent
to Kuta Beach, was lined with shops, cheap hostels, bars and restaurants. There were modern stores selling surfing and diving equipment as well as boutiques trading in wooden Balinese masks and batik,
the dyed cloth where the design is made by covering parts of the
material with wax. The road attracted predominantly young, independent travellers rather than package tourists. It sprung into life at night
when the beach emptied and the festivities began. A branch of the
Hard Rock Café was just around the corner. Some bars on the road
were open-fronted, often draped with flags from Western countries.
Jalan Legian was known as a favourite haunt for Australian backpack-
ers but attracted tourists from Europe as well. Very few Americans
were there in 2002 because the US government had warned its citizens
not to travel to Indonesia. The Sari Club was a slightly downmarket
destination for the often drunk holidaymakers who wanted to stretch
the night into the next morning. A few locals sold hash and offered
heavily cut cocaine to customers. It was loud and brash, and free-
lancing prostitutes from Jakarta and beyond were usually available. In
September of that year, a group of Muslim militants had placed the
club under surveillance and made a fateful decision. At their trial, one
of the men described how they sat in a parked car on Jalan Legian. 'I

saw lots of whiteys dancing and lots of whiteys drinking there. That place . . . especially Paddy's Bar and the Sari Club was a meeting place for US terrorists and their allies.' It seemed that militants in Indonesia considered a Westerner who brought his culture and customs to a Muslim country as a terrorist.

At around eleven o'clock, a man wearing a vest packed with explosives walked into the much smaller Paddy's Bar opposite the Sari Club. He blew himself up. It was the first known suicide bombing in Indonesian history. That explosion was intended to draw people onto the street from nearby bars. A white Mitsubishi van had been parked outside the Sari Club. It was crammed with a ton of ammonium chlorate. This volatile chemical is commonly used as a fertilizer but when combined with other explosives it becomes a lethal concoction. When the bomb in the van was detonated, the blast was devastating. Large gas canisters supplying the Sari Club's kitchen also ignited, magnifying the scale of the explosion. Over two hundred died in the inferno and around a thousand were injured. The Balinese are a polite, spiritual people. They are also Hindu. The global 'war on terror' seemed part of a different planet. Shortly after the attack, shops in the area sold T-shirts blazoned with 'Fuck Terrorist, Bali Black October 12th 2002'. The Balinese who marketed the shirts may not have realized that the language offended some in the West; they had probably heard the word commonly used in the bars of Jalan Legian.

The man who owned the Mitsubishi van and filled it with explosives was Amrozi bin Nurhasyim. According to the police, after two days of questioning, he admitted his role in the bombing and said he'd been a 'naughty person'. At the police station in the Balinese capital, Denpassar, Amrozi caught the eye of my cameraman and producer, Darren Conway, and flashed a smiled with perfectly formed white teeth. We watched through a window as Amrozi seemed to enjoy his first court appearance in front of the cameras. The Australian media called him 'the smiling bomber' amid outrage from relatives of the victims. Amrozi looked younger than his forty years; he was handsome and his relaxed manner didn't suggest anger, poverty or deprivation, the assumed handmaidens of terrorism. He gave us a thumbs up as he left the hearing.

General Made Pastika led the multinational team investigating the bombings and was interrogating Amrozi. 'He's showing no regret at all. He believes he was doing his duty to God,' the sprightly, balding

Balinese policeman told me. 'He's very calm, very cool. He is proud of his activities.' After Amrozi had parked his van outside the Sari Club, he took the ferry from Bali to the port city of Surabaya, on the nearby island of Java. His home village of Tenggulun was about an hour's taxi ride from Surabaya. He slept well and the next morning he turned on the news. 'He was very happy when he listened on the radio that the explosion was very big and successful,' Pastika told me. 'He was pleased and surprised that so many had died.'

Amrozi and the rest of the men involved in the bombing had agreed that their mission was to target American interests in Indonesia. He thought that the Sari Club would be full of US citizens. 'He actually believed he was going to kill Americans,' Pastika said. The final death toll for the bombings was 202 people, mainly foreign tourists: eighty-eight were Australian, the remainder from twenty countries. Seventeen were British and only seven of the dead were Americans. Pastika was not surprised by this lack of international knowledge. 'Many Indonesians can't distinguish between American, English or Australian. Even I can't before they speak,' he joked, inappropriately I thought. It seemed the enemy of the faith was perceived simply as a 'whitey'; to Amrozi and the other foot soldiers of global war, the details of nationhood were irrelevant.

I later drove to Amrozi's village, Tenggulun. It was an unrémarkable hamlet. It wasn't a poor *kampong* (farming village), though many worked in the fields surrounding it. Most of the houses were brick and some were large: money had apparently come to the village from those who'd worked abroad in Malaysia. Amrozi lived with his wife in a comfortable though modest house. He looked after his elderly parents; his father was disabled. Alongside the house was the small garage where he had worked as a mechanic. He was often seen in the village riding his red motorcycle, which was still parked in the garage. He was known as a good-natured, normal man. Amrozi bought the white van with money given to him by one of the bombing team. The main vehicle identification number on the engine had been filed smooth but another number, stamped to the chassis, survived the blast and police traced the van's ownership immediately to him.

By unravelling Amrozi's life, prosecutors were led to thirty other men involved in the attacks, as well as information concerning a shadowy militant group known as Jemaah Islamiah, the Islamic Association, which allegedly had links to al-Qa'eda. Following others in

Tenggulun, Amrozi left for Malaysia in the late 1980s in search of work; according to a neighbour who lived opposite, he returned after a few years with more devout Islamic beliefs. While in Malaysia, he joined his elder brother, Mukhlas, a deeply religious man, at an Islamic school near the southern city of Johor Bahru. Amrozi was one of thirteen children and described Mukhlas as his 'inspiration'. Mukhlas and another of Amrozi's brothers, Ali Imron, were also convicted of involvement in the Bali bombing.

Mukhlas admitted in court that he was the 'operations chief' of Jemaah Islamiah. His involvement in militancy began when he became a teacher at a *pesantren*, an Islamic boarding school, near Solo, in central Java. He travelled to Pakistan in 1987 and later joined Arab mujahedin fighters involved in a gun battle with Russian troops at Joji, in Afghanistan. He was asked in court whether he knew Osama bin Laden. 'Yes,' Mukhlas replied, 'I know him very well. The leader of the mujahedin at Joji, and also the camp commander, was Osama bin Laden.' Mukhlas denied that bin Laden knew about or played any part in the Bali attacks. 'We received no help from Osama bin Laden,' he said. Prosecutors believe Mukhlas attended a meeting in Bangkok in February 2002, when a decision was taken to bomb 'soft' targets in South-East Asia following a message from al-Qa'eda's deputy leader, Ayman Zawahri. That was the last time anyone directly linked to al-Qa'eda was apparently involved. Mukhlas then chaired the meetings that planned the attacks and channelled funds to finance them. He was found guilty of being the overall coordinator of the bombings and was given the maximum sentence of death by firing squad. Mukhlas was willing to describe himself as a terrorist but only when it was also used to describe his enemies. He was a 'small-fry terrorist', he told the court, compared to 'big-fish terrorists' such as President Bush, Ariel Sharon and Tony Blair. According to his lawyer, Mukhlas portrayed the Bali bombings as 'an act of vengeance for America's tyranny against Muslims in the Middle East'.

When Mukhlas returned to Tenggulun from Malaysia, he became involved in the village's own *pesantren*, Al-Islam boarding school, which had been founded by another of Amrozi's brothers. Religious schools were a growing feature of Indonesian life following donations from Saudi charities. Al-Islam was a collection of wooden rooms and a large brick structure, located near the entrance to Tenggulun. The school, which had a reputation for discipline and hard work, had over a hundred pupils: parents sent their children from nearby villages. The school promoted the Wahhabi tradition of rote learning and literal adherence to the Qur'ān, rather than the more liberal, Indonesian interpretation. I was told that there had been arguments in the village when Mukhlas and other teachers at the school criticized some local Islamic practices, which they judged as heretical.

The media attention following Amrozi's arrest had forced the school to close down temporarily. There were rumours that portraits of bin Laden had been hurriedly removed and most of the children were sent home. When I arrived, a few students remained and walked around the grounds in dark baggy shirts and trousers. The principal was called Zakaria; he sat at the gates and watched the steady trickle of foreign journalists approach the school. He had the smile of the Cheshire cat and seemed to enjoy the attention. He showed no regret at the carnage in Bali or surprise that members of his village were involved. He said Amrozi was no different to many others growing up in the village, sharing a common resentment of the United States. 'Amrozi is just like any other person. There's nothing special about him.' He shrugged his shoulders before adding, 'I think America should learn and listen more, in order to understand why Muslims always suffer.' The school had no links to the men who bombed Bali but many who taught and studied there spoke about the plight of Muslims around the world. As I left the school and walked down the main street, children played with water pistols in the midday heat. I was gleaning a disturbing picture of why a child growing up in a remote village such as Tenggulun can later become a man proud to kill in the name of his God.

As well as his brother Mukhlas, the other man that had influenced Amrozi was a cleric in his sixties, Abu Bakar Ba'asyir. The tall, thinly framed Ba'asyir wore white robes and a plain white *kopiah*, the Malay-style rimless cap. Amrozi met him on several occasions, and attended religious lessons he ran in Malaysia in the early 1990s. After the preacher's return to Indonesia in 1998 he was invited to speak at Al-Islam school. General Pastika told me that Amrozi's eyes lit up when he spoke about Abu Bakar Ba'asyir. 'He's the idol of Amrozi, so maybe he accepted all his teachings as his belief too. We don't have significant evidence . . .' he paused, 'not yet, linking Ba'asyir to the attacks.'

Abu Bakar Ba'asyir had become an inspiration to thousands of young Muslims in Indonesia as the head of the Ngruki Islamic boarding school in Solo, where Mukhlas had also taught. Ba'asyir had become notorious in the Indonesian media for his praise of Osama bin Laden as 'a true Islamic warrior' and his description of the United States as 'a terrorist nation'. As a result of suspected pressure from the US, Ba'asyir was arrested shortly after the Bali bombings but on separate charges relating to attacks on churches in Indonesia two years earlier. General Pastika never discovered any evidence that linked the cleric to the slaughter on Jalan Legian. 'My only weapon is teaching,' the cleric had told his prosecutors.

Indonesia's intelligence service had developed a brutal reputation during the autocratic rule of Suharto, which ended in 1998 after more than two decades. The national intelligence agency, now known as BIN, the Bahasa Indonesian acronym for the State Intelligence Board, tried to improve its image by appointing a public-relations man to speak to the media. Muchyar Yara invited me to his palatial house in central Jakarta. 'All of Indonesia's problems go back to the class of Afghanistan,' he told me, puffing on a cigar and gazing at the large chandelier above. 'There were 272 Indonesians who fought in Afghanistan. Most are members of the Jemaah Islamiah but their actions are not automatically known by the JI as an organization.' He tried to explain the group popularly assumed to be Asia's version of al-Qa'eda. 'The Jemaah Islamiah is very broad. It's not like a Western organization with an official structure. It is more like a brotherhood. In the Bali bombing, members of JI may have been involved but Jemaah Islamiah as an organization had no relation to it.'

Muchyar Yara had an appealingly slippery demeanour. He seemed to enjoy the power of holding information and every statement was carefully nuanced. Nothing was *exactly* what it seemed in the world that Yara inhabited. 'Members of the JI may be involved in Bali but that doesn't mean that it leads to Abu Bakar Ba'asyir,' he added. When I then asked whether that meant Ba'asyir was not involved, his reply was, 'I can't give you any comment on that, you'd better ask the police.' He smiled from cheek to cheek. I understood the message to be that the cleric had no role in the bombings.

Abu Bakar Ba'asyir was generally assumed to be the founder and spiritual leader of Jemaah Islamiah, whatever its precise nature as an organization. He was a symbol of Islamic rebellion during the rule of the American-backed dictator, Suharto, and emerged from a tradition of Islamic militancy that had its roots in the colonial struggle. In circumstances not dissimilar to those of the Muslim Brotherhood in Egypt, Islamists helped secular nationalists overthrow Indonesia's colonial rulers but were sidelined when the nation gained independence. An Islamist leader, Sekarmadji Kartosuwirjo, fought Dutch colonial rule during the 1940s and refused to become part of a secular Indonesian Republic. In 1949, he proclaimed the 'Islamic State of Indonesia' in the areas of West Java that he controlled and spent the next thirteen years fighting the newly independent government. The areas under his control were known as Darul Islam, or the 'Abode of Islam'. Kartosuwirjo was finally captured in 1962.

Again, in a pattern that was also followed in Egypt, the Suharto regime exploited and attempted to manipulate Islam for its own advantages. More than seven million Indonesians were descendants of Yemeni Arab traders and many retained their culture and links to families in the Arabian Peninsula. They tended to be more radical and a group of Yemenis from the Darul Islam movement was revitalized in the 1970s by Indonesian intelligence in order to discredit communists and divide the legal Islamic movement. After fostering their support, the regime later arrested the militants when they had no more use for them. The government imprisoned 185 people whom it accused of being involved in an unknown organization called Komando Jihad, which prosecutors later called Jemaah Islamiah. By this time, Abu Bakar Ba'asyir and a colleague had started their own Islamic radio station. It was soon closed down and he was arrested and charged with agitating for an Islamic state, a crime under Indonesia's subversion law. While in jail, he met some of the men arrested earlier. By 1979, it was difficult to tell whether Jemaah Islamiah was a construct of the regime, a revival of the Darul Islam movement or simply a loose association of like-minded Muslims. It was probably a little bit of each.

The operation set in motion by Indonesian intelligence to establish Jemaah Islamiah had unintended consequences. It renewed bonds between Muslim radicals in different parts of Indonesia and tapped into intellectual ferment in university-based mosques. An undercover movement became energized by ideas from the Iranian revolution. Cassettes and translations of writings on militant Islam, provided by Wahhabi charities from Saudi Arabia, also became increasingly available in mosques.

Many of the leaders of this loose Islamic association were forced into exile, including Abu Bakar Ba'asyir, who fled to Malaysia. He taught at an Islamic school in Johor Bahru, on the border with Singapore, where Mukhlas later became a teacher. In the 1980s, it suited Malaysia's Prime Minister, Mahathir Mohamad, to shore up his credentials as an Islamic ruler in order to champion the interests of the Malay majority in his country, who were Muslim. He accepted largesse from Saudi Arabia and allowed Islamic universities and banks to flourish. Most of the men involved in the Bali bombing had attended lessons led by Ba'asyir. The school at Johor Bahru became a place for disgruntled Indonesian exiles to gather. In the mid-1990s, a group that included Ba'asyir met members of the Gama'a Islamiyah from Egypt. The Gama'a was responsible for the Luxor massacre in 1997 and their leader was one of bin Laden's closest lieutenants. As a result of their new affiliations, Ba'asyir's ideology shifted. He moved beyond a commitment to an Islamic state within Indonesian boundaries and promoted the notion of an Islamic caliphate in South-East Asia, extending from Thailand to the southern islands of the Philippines.

Some members of the Jemaah Islamiah were said to have maintained relations with al-Qa'eda, particularly Mukhlas' predecessor as 'operations chief', a man known as Hambali. The overwhelming majority of Islamists had no sense of an international organization in their midst, beyond that of their local group occasionally receiving help from larger, better-funded organizations from the Middle East. One movement that was repeatedly linked to the Jemaah Islamiah was the Council of Mujahedin for Islamic Law Enforcement, which was formed in 2000 as an umbrella group for those wishing to turn Indonesia into an Islamic state. Before his arrest, Abu Bakar Ba'asyir was the council's emir, which literally means commander. The office of the Mujahedin Council is a low-slung building in Yogyakarta, not far from the Ngruki boarding school in nearby Solo. It was the holy month of Ramadan, when Muslims fast during daylight. As dusk fell, about thirty young men congregated at the council. At the entrance there was a shop that sold T-shirts and key rings with emblems of the movement, as well as tapes and DVDs glorifying Islamist causes. As soon as prayers were completed, the men were given glasses of preserved sweet fruit, in order to provide a burst of energy after fasting. The council had a small kitchen and curries and rice were heated. I joined the group for their buffet-style dinner and we talked about politics in the aftermath of the Bali attack. Everyone was courteous towards my Australian producer, Darren Conway, and me. We were offered the Indonesian staple of *nasi goreng*, fried rice with egg, onion and chillies. There was a beef curry with carrots and *laksa* prawns, an orange-coloured dish from Malaysia. The food was good and they insisted we had extra portions. The young men, most of whom were under twenty-five, were finally regaining their energy after the day's fast.

'Are you here because of Bali?' one of them asked. 'Yes,' I replied. 'We want to find out why it happened.' 'America,' he answered. 'America, that's why.' I asked whether he approved of the bombing. 'It happened,' he said quietly and turned away.

The Mujahedin Council was run by Irfan Awas, a man with a wispy moustache and a red *kopiah*. He was fresh-faced, and appeared too young to have spent nine years in Suharto's jails. 'Since the Mujahedin Council was formed we have been facing an international power that is trying to damage Islam. Why is that?' he asked, as he edged in, preventing me speaking for too long to the younger activists. 'It's understandable that one of the men who bombed Bali expressed his hatred towards the United States, Australia and their allies,' he announced. 'It's understandable that he committed such action. America has to learn the true meaning of peace. America is the biggest contributor to a violent world.'

Irfan Awas spoke in a gentle tone, as most Indonesians do. He seemed analytical, not angry. 'The US has to change its attitude toward Islam. It must learn not to use democracy or human rights as a tool to maintain its imperialism.' He denied that an organization called Jemaah Islamiah existed. 'It is a name which has been engineered by the US to justify their ambition to control Indonesia and South-East Asia.' We sat in a plain room without pictures under a fluorescent light. Awas believed America had abused the usage of 'terrorism'. 'We don't recognize the word "terrorist". It's a word used only by Western countries because they have all the sophisticated weapons. Islam never had a weapon so when it defends itself, it is called "terrorism". In the US, "terrorism" means opposing Western civilization, wishing to establish an Islamic state or having Osama bin Laden as an idol.' He smiled. 'That means there are millions of terrorists in Indonesia.'

As I listened to Irfan Awas speak about the attacks on Bali and Manhattan, I realized that he felt proud that Muslims had drawn Western blood. It was an emotion that millions of other Muslims experienced, in varying degrees, around the world. He condemned the Bali bombings but found satisfaction in a consequence of the carnage; the attacks struck at a force, call it perhaps Westernization, that seemingly could not be challenged by any other means. 'If Osama bin Laden has the ability to destroy the World Trade Center or Amrozi to kill two hundred people on Jalan Legian in Kuta, then America has to consider that maybe they are not too powerful or advanced in their technology.' We discussed America's military power, the weakness of the Arab world and the onward march of Western-driven globalization. The future would have looked bleak for Irfan Awas if he had not been able to console himself with one possibility. 'If America and its allies continue to dominate Islam,' he threatened, 'there will be a new generation of Muslims who will fight the crimes which have been committed by America, and with God's help, this generation will be able to do something much more spectacular than what happened in Bali.'

The turmoil of Indonesia's recent history contributed to a sudden upsurge in violence in the vast archipelago that sweeps across South-East Asia. In the fifteenth century, Arab traders brought Islam to its furthermost eastern margins, the islands of Indonesia and the southern Philippines. Islam did not conquer by the sword of the Mogul or Ottoman Empires but seeped in, mingling with Hindu–Buddhist cultures and drawing men to the worship of one God. It was testimony to the capacity of Islam to adapt to different cultural circumstances and express itself in forms more varied than existed in Arabic lands. During the Suharto years, the faith had been cynically manipulated, and when he was deposed a cauldron of discontent was brewing in parts of Indonesia. The combination of sudden liberty, traditional rivalries and meddling politicians boiled over onto the streets of one city, Ambon, the capital of the Moluccan Islands. The violence had its origin in the Suharto regime's policy of transmigration, in which Javanese Muslims were transported to outlying regions in order to encourage a greater sense of national identity, which usually meant imposing on others a Javanese Muslim culture.

The Moluccan Islands traditionally had a Christian majority but the transmigration policy moved more than a hundred thousand Muslims to the islands, and as the Islamic population grew it became increasingly aware of its exclusion from institutional life. There had been a recent policy of intentionally recruiting Muslims into the civil service, but that sparked resentment in the Christian community. As the authoritarian rule of Jakarta slackened, groups vented their frustrations more openly. In December 1998, tensions finally exploded into open armed conflict. A Muslim militia was pitted against its Christian counterpart and thousands died in three years of street fighting. Many parts of Ambon were religiously 'cleansed' as both sides attempted to create religiously contiguous areas. Amongst Javanese Muslims, the conflict heightened a determination to defend the faithful against onslaughts by the West, and militant groups in Jakarta orchestrated much of the conflict. The faithful in Java could simply pick up a gun and join the jihad there. The civil war also became a magnet for Muslim fighters from abroad. Ambon became for a new generation what Afghanistan had been for an older one.

The fighting in Ambon was captured on videodiscs and sold at Islamic institutions such as the Mujahedin Council, as well as market stalls and mosques throughout Muslim regions of Indonesia. Sidney Jones was the director of the Indonesian office of the International Crisis Group, a think tank based in Brussels. She had been a researcher with Human Rights Watch and three months before the attacks had written a remarkable dossier on the group later convicted of the Bali bombings. Her research became essential reading for journalists reporting on the aftermath of the attacks. The gently spoken American wore round glasses and an academic demeanour. 'The videos are used as a recruiting tool,' she told me as she placed one of the discs into her computer. 'This one is "Live purely or die like a martyr".' The footage was grisly and bloody. It was an endless collection of pictures of martyrs, with their brains or intestines dragging on the floor as they were carried to hospital. Groups of young men symbolically brandished their Islamic swords as they searched for the Christians responsible for the killing of their Muslim brothers. The message was not subtle. On one disc, Irfan Awas's brother, Abu Jibril, held aloft an AK-47 and the Qur'ān. 'The Qur'ān is to build our people. The gun is to destroy the obstacles that stand in our way,' he declared to a cheering crowd. 'We cannot separate them.'

Sidney gave me a typical example of how the videodiscs were used to encourage young fighters to take up arms for their faith. 'Somebody would go to usually a religious school and get a group of men together and show one of these tapes. People would be angry at the brutality they see, the gore, people being killed, bodies.' She paused as we saw a dead child soldier, barely older than twelve.

'It's one image after another that's drilled into the minds of the viewers,' she told me. 'Afterwards they have a discussion about jihad and ask what needs to be done to resist this oppression of Muslims. That often leads to an invitation to take part in some kind of quasi-military training and after that it would lead to someone going to the Moluccan Islands to fight.'

It seemed simple. On the other hand, it needed a receptive, angry audience to believe the messages of such unsophisticated propaganda. According to Sidney, America's 'war on terror' has helped to solidify the opinion of Indonesia's young Muslims. 'Everything that has happened since September 11th has reinforced the notion of Muslims under siege. You get the reports here of Indonesian students in America being interviewed by the FBI because they are between ages eighteen and forty and come from a Muslim country. All that reinforces perceptions that the "war on terror" is a war against Islam and that the West has an agenda and that agenda is to get rid of Islam.'

In June 2004, Sidney Jones was ordered to leave Indonesia by the authorities, accused of visa violations. In reality, BIN, Indonesia's intelligence agency, was behind her expulsion because it considered reports published by her group, including detailed studies of the separatist conflicts in Aceh and Papua provinces, to be subversive. Her expulsion was criticized by the US State Department, which said it threatened freedom of expression in Indonesia.

Sidney had told me that that the media's symbol of Islamism in Indonesia, the cleric Abu Bakar Ba'asyir, was unlikely to be part of an active militant cell. 'After all, he's well into his sixties,' she told me. One of the men convicted of the Bali bombings said that Ba'asyir had no significant role amongst his circle of jihadists. 'He bored us,' he said. 'We wanted to wage war. I respect him but his lectures sent me to sleep.'

Most of the case against Abu Bakar Ba'asyir had been based on statements made by a Kuwaiti man, Omar al-Faruq, who was arrested in Indonesia in June 2002. According to reports leaked to the US media, al-Faruq admitted under interrogation that he was responsible for plotting to blow up US embassies in South-East Asia. A CIA report also described him as the 'mastermind behind all the Christmas 2000 bombings in Indonesia', which left eighteen dead and scores injured. He apparently said that Ba'asyir and Jemaah Islamiah were involved in these incidents.

We drove in the dead of night to Cijeruk, in western Java, just over an hour from Jakarta. It was raining as we reached the hamlet, which was little more than one street lined with a row of well-kept houses. Near the village mosque, a driveway led to a metal gate and a small concrete house. It was about 4 a.m., but the lights were already on. Omar al-Faruq had moved there a year earlier with his wife, Mira Agustina, the twenty-three-year-old daughter of an Islamic radical who led one of the Muslim militias that fought in Ambon. Mira was cooking breakfast for herself and her two children; she was deep frying *roti isi*, bread filled with coconut root. It was Ramadan and at dawn the family would begin its day-long fast.

A few months earlier, at a mosque in a nearby town, ten men from Indonesia's intelligence service arrested Omar al-Faruq. He was handed over to the CIA for interrogation and three days later was flown from Indonesia to the US military base at Bagram, in Afghanistan, without any legal process. Mira said she knew nothing of her husband's involvement in al-Qa'eda. She knew him only as Mahmoud and believed that he was from Ambon, rather than Kuwait. Mira wore a black niqab that covered her face and her small, plump body. It was impossible to tell if she was lying but her story seemed unlikely. According to information leaked by the CIA, al-Faruq told his interrogators that Mira kept the accounts for al-Qa'eda's money and translated notes of meetings into Arabic.

Mira hadn't heard any news of her husband and didn't know if she would ever see him again. 'He never had a chance to appear in court or defend himself,' she said bitterly. 'What right has America got to just snatch him away?' When she became angry about the plight of her husband, she began to link her circumstances to a wider conflict. 'Now I can share what women in Bosnia and women in Palestine feel. My children lost their father, I lost my husband. I feel just like them.'

When I asked her about the Bali bombing, she brought up events half a world away, in Jerusalem, the West Bank, the Gaza Strip. 'How can anyone blame the suicide bombers?' she asked me. 'They get so angry when they see their brothers shot and killed in Palestine. They are resisting, so I don't blame them.'

All of the world's conflicts appeared to merge in Mira's mind into one essential narrative, America versus Muslims. 'The US has to look at itself and solve the Palestine conflict peacefully. Like everywhere else, the bombings are a reflection of the anger felt towards America.' She paused and sighed. 'Talking about America is rather risky for me. I don't know what they might do to me. I might already be on their list . . .' She gave an embarrassed laugh. 'I don't want to say any more.'

Omar al-Faruq remained in US custody without trial at an unknown location and with no contact with his family. While his accounts seemingly linked Abu Bakar Ba'asyir with violence, Indonesian anti-terrorism officials have criticized the United States for not offering enough assistance during attempts to convict the cleric. In 2003, prosecutors failed to prove Ba'asyir's involvement in the spate of Christmas bombings. He was, however, sentenced to prison for immigration offences and forging documents. A year later, the authorities again tried to link Ba'asyir to the Bali bombing. Prosecutors claimed that Amrozi had confessed to asking the cleric to sanction the attack under Islamic law. Ba'asyir was also charged with ordering the bombing of the Marriot Hotel in Jakarta in August 2003, which killed twelve, despite being in jail at the time of the attack.

Abu Bakar Ba'asyir was initially arrested alongside another militant cleric, Habib Rizieq, following international pressure in the aftermath of the carnage at Bali. Neither was immediately charged with involvement in the bombing. It seemed like a round-up of 'the usual suspects' and Rizieq was released after three weeks. I visited him while he was under house arrest shortly afterwards. I followed a narrow alleyway into a courtyard outside his house. He was a small, energetic man and was known to be a firebrand, unlike the quietly spoken Ba'asyir. The families of both men were immigrants from the Yemen at the beginning of the last century; Rizieq frequently claimed that he was a direct descendant of the prophet. Rizieq's young daughters played on swings in the courtyard beneath a stern picture of Osama bin Laden. The bombings at Jalan Legian did not come as a surprise to him. 'What's happening now is a globalized resistance,' he told me. 'After the build-up of disappointment and anger, Muslims are acting against attempts by America to rule the world.'

Rizieq sat cross-legged on the floor and spoke quite happily about his support for bin Laden. 'We see Osama bin Laden as a symbol of Muslim resistance against the tyranny and the arrogance of the US. We are united behind him in a war with America,' he announced matter-of-factly. He had a cheery circular face, and tufts of wispy hair formed a goatee. He seemed to be smiling even when he discussed global conflict. He spoke about bin Laden as if he possessed a magical power to galvanize radical Muslims the world over. As his image peered down at me, Rizieq recalled the reaction of those around him in Jakarta when bin Laden declared his war on America. 'Osama bin Laden announced his oath, which was broadcast internationally. It said: "In the name of Allah, who created this universe, the people who live in America will never have a peaceful life until those who live in Palestine or other Muslim countries will have one too." ' He looked at me as if the rest was obvious. 'Then that oath inspired and motivated young Muslims to fight against the US. What Amrozi did is a reaction to American brutality. Whether it is right or wrong, we have to solve the root of the problem to prevent these things happening.'

Dinner was brought into the courtyard where we were sitting. I wasn't hungry and refused the main course of chicken curry and rice. I accepted some dessert, fried banana in an avocado and chocolate sauce – it sounded too irresistible. I told him to congratulate the chef. His wife had made it especially for the BBC, he fawned.

Habib Rizieq led a band of militants called the Islamic Defenders' Front. The movement campaigned for the introduction of an Islamic legal code in Indonesia, including a ban on the sale of alcohol. His followers often travelled in the back of one of their trucks and attacked bars or nightclubs that sold drink. Armed with clubs and metal rods, they smashed signs advertising beer and forced the premises to close. Only a minority of Indonesians wanted the introduction of Islamic law but millions of others were resentful that Western values were creeping into Indonesian life and sympathized with the closure of nightclubs.

Indonesia has the largest Muslim population on earth, and within it a small but significant minority believed that Osama bin Laden provided an overarching theory that explained the suffering of Muslims in Bosnia, the Palestinian territories, Iraq and elsewhere. The logic was simple: if Muslims share a common identity, then they must also share a common enemy. Rizieq quoted a parable from the prophet. 'The relationship between Muslims is like that of one body. If one part of the body is hurt, it affects the whole body. You simply can't sleep or it might cause a fever. When we see our brothers in Palestine or Chechnya hurt, we feel the pain. When we see our brother in Xinjiang being oppressed, we feel the suffering too. This is a Muslim brother-

hood which crosses the world's zones and regions.' His speeches had
dramatic pauses as every phrase was given due pomp and weight.
While he was eating, he added, in a tone that suggested he was talking
rather than lecturing, 'I used to like McDonald's, but a Muslim who
cares shouldn't eat there now.'

Only a tiny number of Indonesians have had contact with al-
Qa'eda. But there was a popular sentiment that the man who personi-
fied evil in the West was on the side of righteousness. Islamic identity
has increased as many young Islamists have pledged affinity with
Palestinians and Iraqis. In some of the Saudi-financed boarding
schools, children have learned Arabic and performed plays that eulo-
gized those who volunteered to become suicide bombers. Until the Bali
bombings, the broad-based Jemaah Islamiah had confined its attacks
to sectarian disputes within Indonesia. As I listened to supporters of
the Mujahedin Council and the Islamic Defenders' Front, their once
parochial identities had given way to a vision of a global jihad.

Al-Qa'eda made its most successful inroads into Indonesian militant
groups during the conflict on the Moluccan Islands. Camps were built
around Ambon, and money provided by Saudi charities financed the
arming and training of the militias. These private armies also had links
to powerful politicians and sections of the Indonesian security services.
Habib Rizieq's movement, the Islamic Defenders' Front, was often said
to be activated or folded depending on the wishes of groups within
Indonesia's establishment. As so often happens when politicians or
security services attempt to manipulate Islamist organizations for their
own gain, the groups soon adopt a life of their own.

By loosely grafting itself onto local disputes, al-Qa'eda evolved into
an idea rather than an organization with a tightly knit structure like
a Western insurgency group. A former director of the CIA, George
Tenet, told the Senate Select Committee on Intelligence in February
2004, 'What I want to say to you now may be the most important
thing I tell you today. The steady growth of Osama bin Laden's anti-
US sentiment through the wider Sunni extremist movement, and the
broad dissemination of al-Qa'eda's destructive expertise, ensure that a
serious threat will remain for the foreseeable future, with or without
al-Qa'eda in the picture.'

The notion of a 'global intifada' is so much more disturbing for the
security of the West because of the ability and willingness of trans-
national groups to use weapons of mass destruction such as anthrax,

smallpox, sarin gas, blood and choking agents and so forth. The traditional theories of national defence, based on threats from nation states, have largely been jettisoned by the world's only superpower. Yet the United States' insistence on waging a 'war on terror' against an ill-defined foe is allowing radical Muslims to validate their prediction of a global conflict between Islam and the West.

There are not many Indonesians who share the views of Amrozi, the man who parked the van outside the Sari Club in Jalan Legian. A week before a court sentenced him to death for his part in the bombing, he appeared before journalists and offered them a rendition of his favourite song. ' "Continue the holy struggle, get rid of Zionists, get rid of the Christian filth. God is great, this is my song." ' He smiled broadly from behind prison bars. The United States knows, however, that the security of the West is threatened if only a few hundred men share his views in a country of more than two hundred million.

'Tomorrow, a thousand Osama bin Ladens will be born in Indonesia,' Habib Rizieq warned me with a glint in his eye. 'If the government doesn't want to produce any more of the people who bombed Bali, it should act firmly against American influence in Indonesia.' Perhaps Rizieq's threat should not simply be dismissed as the ranting of a zealot.

16 / GOD OF REBELLION

'Some Westerners . . . have argued that the West does not
have problems with Islam but only with violent Islamist extremists.
Fourteen hundred years of history demonstrates otherwise.'
Professor Samuel P. Huntington, *The Clash of Civilizations*

One Sunday afternoon in the late autumn, I parked just off the main road running through the sprawling housing estates of Vaulx-en-Velin, outside Lyon. Vaulx is typical of the suburbs that have grown up around large French cities. A large part of the town is row upon row of tower blocks and drab open spaces, with rusty swings and shops with metal shutters. I passed the disembowelled carcass of a car, its tyres, seats and even the engine removed. Despite its run-down air, Vaulx-en-Velin did not resemble the wastelands of America's decaying inner cities. The authorities had freshened the dull colours of concrete with orange and pink paint on the walls. There were even lawns with a smattering of newly planted trees. But it remained a soulless, bleak place. My impressions were not helped by the weather; it was colder than it should be for October and a hint of drizzle hung in the air. The wintry light from a milky white sky seemed to suck any colour from the landscape.

On the hillside overlooking the high-rise estates stood a large church, a reminder of older France. The road sign on the route into Vaulx pointed left to the Centre Ville. In the town centre, a sculpture of a cockerel was atop a well-kept memorial to the fallen from the two world wars. There were *charcuteries*, *boulangeries* and a *fromagerie*. Nearly everyone I saw was of European ancestry. The road sign at the edge of town also had an arrow pointing to the right but the destination had been sprayed over with paint. Instead, the graffiti artist had written CASBAH, the Arabic word for a fortress or citadel. It also means for North Africans a place of refuge or a city within a city.

This is home for Vaulx's large immigrant population. Eighty per cent of those living in the estates are non-white. There are significant numbers of Africans and West Indians but the majority are Muslim Arabs from Algeria, Morocco and Tunisia. Most families arrived in the early 1960s, when the economy was expanding quickly and workers were needed to fill the gleaming new factories on the outskirts of France's main cities. The government financed the construction of new housing estates for what was then an ethnically mixed workforce. Gradually, the jobs dried up and the white families moved to the countryside. The children of the immigrants, who are known as *beurs* in the local slang, found France a less welcoming nation than their parents. Despite French citizenship and education, young North Africans grew up in the now decaying estates with too few jobs and too meagre opportunities to integrate. A combustible cocktail of unemployment and despair, prejudice and lack of identity was fuelling a generation of young *beurs*. The word *banlieue* translates simply as 'suburbs' but it has taken on a new meaning in France: ghettos where Muslims live and danger lurks.

The streets of Vaulx's 'Casbah' were mostly deserted, even though it was a Sunday afternoon. A woman wrapped in shawls and head-scarves wheeled a pushchair while dragging older children on foot. An elderly white man with a flat cap sat on a small wall, a rolled-up newspaper in one hand, watching us. I was there to investigate the emergence of a common worldwide Islamic identity; there was a growing belief that Muslims from dissimilar cultures nevertheless shared, in some ways, a common destiny. It was 1996; the Internet had only recently become commonplace and the world was said to be transforming into a 'global village'.

I was aware of the deep anger that many *beurs* felt towards their lighter-skinned fellow Frenchmen. My Algerian-born assistant, Sadia, had warned us not to go into the estates after dark; Vaulx-en-Velin was notorious in France for occasionally bursting into flames at night. Amongst the graffiti, there was a painting of a *beur* holding a pistol and shooting at policemen. On several occasions, praise for Saddam Hussein was scrawled on the high-rise apartments. 'Saddam is a hero for the Arabs', proclaimed one message. It was left over from the First Gulf War, five years earlier. At that time, the young men here had not yet found a new hero, an Arab willing to stand up and confront the West.

I had watched the visceral film by Mathieu Kassovitz entitled *La Heine*, or Hate, a short time earlier and was aware of the regular confrontations between young people and the police. The film was shot entirely in black and white and chronicled a day in the lives of three men from the *banlieue* who survive by selling drugs and thieving. Its portrayal of an alienated youth caged in a world without hope startled French public opinion. The Prime Minister, Alain Juppé, was so alarmed that he arranged a special screening of the film for his cabinet.

Despite hearing talk of an intifada in the *banlieue*, I was shocked when the first stone was thrown. A man shouted from a nearby shop, 'We are all criminals here. Go away!' Another man moved his hand across his throat threateningly.

Then, as if from nowhere, about a dozen young men surrounded us, jumping up and down, showing their fists as if shadow boxing. 'We hate journalists,' screamed one. 'Are you Jews?' asked another man with a cigarette in his mouth and his face distorted by disdain. 'We will burn the camera,' said another. 'We'll burn you too,' added another man. All of them looked to be in their late teens and early twenties. Sadia said we'd better leave. One man claimed we'd been spying on local people. Another wanted us to hand over the tape. By now, we were climbing back into our minivan and began to drive away. I heard stones land in the street around us and one hit the roof of our vehicle.

We stopped a mile further on. As we got out, two cars sped toward us and screeched to a halt on either side of our minivan. Now we were trapped. One man had a handgun tucked in his trouser pocket; he pulled out just enough for me to see his finger wrapped around the trigger. He was older and I didn't recall seeing him with the earlier group. The gunman was thickset with a receding hairline. He had a black leather jacket, fashioned like a suit rather than a biker's jacket. 'You must leave Vaulx-en-Velin,' he said. 'Do not come back.'

As we piled back into the minivan, the men glowered and one shouted, 'Kelkal is not a terrorist, he is a martyr.' He was referring to Khaled Kelkal, a twenty-four-year-old Algerian immigrant who grew up in one of the tower blocks in Vaulx. A few months earlier, he had been France's most wanted man. A mugshot of his rounded, pug-nosed face was posted at public buildings throughout the country, along with 'Wanted for Terrorism'. His fingerprints had been found on an unexploded bomb. Shortly afterwards, he was spotted waiting at a bus stop in the nearby suburb of Vaugneray. When the special gendarmes arrived in their military-style fatigues, Kelkal pulled out a 7.65mm pistol and opened fire. Police marksmen then cut him down. Video of the shooting, which included one of the gendarmes kicking the corpse, was repeatedly broadcast on French television and hailed as a victory over 'Islamic terrorism'.

'Kelkal is a hero,' the group chanted as we started the engine. It was only after a tense minute or two's wait that one of their vehicles reversed to allow us room to leave. I thought Sadia had been exaggerating the difficulties of the *banlieue*. It was easier to work in a war zone, I told her. We were in the heart of Europe, yet I felt I was in enemy territory.

At this time, France felt under attack from its former colony to the south, Algeria. Paris was enjoying a warm, sunny day at the end of July 1995. At the cafe Départ Saint Michel, in the heart of the Latin quarter, tourists rubbed shoulders with Parisians planning their August holidays. In shade under red and white canopies, patrons of the cafe sipped their coffees and beers. It was about 4.30 in the afternoon. A loud crash shook the floor and smoke rose from the stairs leading to the Saint Michel–Notre Dame Métro station. A nail bomb had exploded on the platform below, killing eight people and injuring over a hundred.

The attack was the first in a two-month bombing campaign that set all of France on edge. An explosion in a rubbish bin near the Arc de Triomphe wounded seventeen people. Another bomb went off in a busy market near the Place de la Bastille. The last explosion was at the Maison Blanche Métro station in the south of Paris, injuring twelve. The police said the attack was intended to coincide with the funeral of Khaled Kelkal.

The bombing came to an end that October as suddenly as it started, and in the same mysterious manner. No one declared responsibility for the attacks but the GIA was assumed to be the perpetrator. Two Algerian men were sentenced to life imprisonment in 2002 for their role in the bombings; both had already been convicted of membership of the GIA. A third man who lived in London was accused of financing the operation by sending a money transfer for £3,635 from a Western Union office in Wembley.

The established consensus amongst the growing field of 'terrorologists' is that the bombings in France provided Western investigators with their first evidence of the loosely knit cell structure of Islamist groups, as well as their organizational and recruiting methods. It was commonly said by law-enforcement agencies that al-Qa'eda copied the GIA's strategy and structure.

A less popular understanding emerged from the confessions of former members of Algeria's Sécurité Militaire. A man claiming to be one such, using the pseudonym Hakim, contacted *Le Monde* to say the Algerian government orchestrated at least two of the Métro bombings. Additionally, a former colonel in the Direction des Renseignements de Securité and intelligence operative in Europe, Mohammed Samraoui, made a staggering claim. It was known by Western intelligence that Ali Touchent was the head of the GIA's operations in Europe and was believed to have set up cells in Paris, Lyon and Lille. His recruits included Khaled Kelkal and the two men convicted of the Métro bombings. 'Ali Touchent est un agent des services,' Samraoui announced in front of a stunned courtroom. One of Algeria's most senior spies in Europe at that time had declared under oath that Touchent had been following orders from the Algerian military secret service. It seemed unbelievable and few journalists credited his claims.

The Islamic Salvation Front had spokesmen in Germany and the United States who operated relatively freely, but in France, many of those associated with the FIS were rounded up during 'anti-terrorist' raids. A year after the Paris bombings, two hundred suspects languished in French jails but no one had been charged. The state of alert called Vigipirate was still in force; it had brought troops onto the streets of Paris and authorized random stopping and searching.

The most senior FIS representative in France headed a front organization called the Fraternité Algérienne en France (FAF); the FIS, unlike other Algerian political parties, had been prevented from setting up offices in Paris. The leader of the FAF, Moussa Kraouche, had been arrested in one of the first swoops on suspected militants in November 1993 and for the past two years had been under house arrest. Several FIS members had been forcibly flown to Burkina Faso, the former French colony in central Africa, in a bizarre act of expulsion. The

FAF's offices were raided and it was prevented from organizing rallies or press conferences.

Moussa Kraouche had an upright gait and a formal, precise manner. He was charged with 'criminal association with a terrorist group' but insisted that the Sécurité Militaire framed him by placing documents purporting to come from the GIA in his apartment. 'They watch my apartment,' he warned, 'and they think that anyone who contacts me is a terrorist.' The courts eventually accepted that the evidence linking him with the GIA was false but he remained under 'judicial custody'. 'The French authorities will do anything to deprive us of a voice,' he explained. The group tried on three occasions to print a newsletter but were prevented under 'anti-terrorism' legislation. 'All I can do now is release communiqués on the Internet.'

The newsletters, with titles such as *The Criterion* and *Resistance*, argued that violence was the only language that the unelected Algerian regime understood. The French government insisted that the magazines were supporting 'terrorism'. Kraouche remained in favour of the armed uprising: 'The regime gave us no choice,' he said. But he condemned attacks on innocent civilians, whether in Algeria or abroad.

He poured tea into small china cups and spoke without emotion. We hadn't had lunch and the camera team munched the biscuits that he neatly laid out on the plate. 'Of course it was the Algerian government who planted the bombs in the Paris Métro,' he continued. 'Why should we open a second front and provoke war with the French government when we are struggling to confront the regime in Algiers?' I obviously looked puzzled and Kraouche shook his head. 'The French media doesn't believe us either,' he said. I asked what evidence he had.

'Do you know that the Algerian newspaper, the *Tribune*, wrote an article fifteen days before the death of Sheikh Abdelbaki? It stated that five "terrorists" had penetrated French territory in order to carry out acts of sabotage, plant bombs and kill people.' Kraouche was referring to the murder of Sheikh Abdelbaki Sahraoui, a founding member of the FIS, in July 1995. The eighty-five-year-old theologian was shot dead by a group of men in the prayer room of a popular mosque in Rue Myrha, in the Barbes quarter of Paris. Onlookers had just finished evening prayers. The murder weapon was found in Khaled Kelkal's backpack, though he was not believed to be one of the killers.

'Amazing, isn't it? The Algerian government plant this story in the papers and then, two weeks later, the Sheikh is assassinated and the bombings begin. *Voilà!*' he added sarcastically before continuing in a lower tone. 'We have information from very reliable quarters that Algeria was doing everything it could to ensure that France became directly involved in the war in Algeria.'

As we left his apartment, he wagged his finger and asked me to keep in mind who benefited from the bombings. 'Just think about it and it all makes sense.'

The bombings in France proved to be a turning point in the history of Islamic militancy and its relations with the West. It solidified a general belief that conflicts born in Arab lands had come west. Islamic militancy had been internationalized in the first sustained attacks on Western interests on its own soil. Until the Paris bombings, the United States' policy on Algeria was neglectful and unsure. The US had also allowed the leader of the FIS parliamentary delegation in exile, Anwar Haddam, to operate from the offices of the American Muslim Council in Washington. But that suddenly changed. Haddam found himself jailed for an irregularity concerning his residence permit. Devout Muslims who wanted an Islamic society but only within a democratic and tolerant framework had become undermined, outflanked and marginalized by murderous extremists. The middle ground was swallowed up and many hard-line Islamists felt the choice was either the logic of the GIA and 'terrorism', or defeat. The link between committed Muslims and 'terrorism' had been cast. The attacks on the Paris Métro proved to be the first shots in the global conflict that continued with al-Qa'eda. Is it not one of the bitterest ironies of the 'war on terror' that the logic of taking Algeria's civil war to Europe was probably driven by the Algerian government and not Islamic radicals?

Yves Bonnet was a straight-talking man. He had pale blue eyes that seemed to search my soul as we discussed Islamist violence, which he readily categorized as 'terrorism'. In the 1980s, Bonnet was head of France's counter-espionage and internal intelligence agency, the Direction de la Surveillance du Territoire (DST). 'Rubbish,' he said to the claims of Algerian security services' involvement. 'It's their fantasy.' Bonnet's demeanour hinted of arrogance; his head was cocked back as he spoke and his words were finely honed. When he had finished his point, his head gave a theatrical bow. I was not encouraged to interrupt him before he had completed his answer. 'The problem with terrorism is that it is perpetrated from within,' he said. 'The terrorists in Algeria used Muslims in France to do their deeds.'

The retired Bonnet maintained an ill-defined, semi-official role in dealings between France and the regime in Algeria. He had preserved close links with the Algerian military and security services. He advised the French government as early as 1993 that the country was facing an enemy within. Bonnet believed Algerian militants had covertly infiltrated suburbs to recruit disillusioned French Muslims. 'The methods used by the Islamists here are the same as in Algeria,' he told me. 'In depressed areas the Islamists have been able to exert their authority. They sorted out problems and became credible in the eyes of the people. Local Muslims accepted their meddling.' He paused slightly and hardened his stare. 'They developed a networks of sympathizers. It gave them a structure. After that, the circle of friends became secret cells. After that a terrorist organization.'

'Are you worried that militants operate in no-go areas in the *banlieue*?'

'There are about a million people who live in areas where there is no law. These no-go areas do exist. But we must reconquer them.'

Since 2001, Western intelligence organizations have said the knowledge built up by their French counterparts dealing with Algerian militants proved invaluable. Most British diplomats and agents would, I suspect, find Bonnet an immensely charismatic and competent spy. There was, however, a difference in character and motivation between him and his British colleagues. Yves Bonnet was a man of conviction. He believed in *Liberté, Egalité, Fraternité*. He believed in French culture, its righteousness and, probably, its superiority.

'The French have strong principles concerning secularity. Religion should not interfere with daily life,' Bonnet announced as if he were a soldier issuing orders. 'This is a key part of our democracy. A Muslim who wishes to practise every tenet of his faith, even prayer, which is five times a day, cannot do so in France. People must behave according to the customs of the country in which they live. People should express their religion privately and anonymously.' He leant forward as if he had decided to let me in on a secret. 'The republican, secular state is an issue that will never be open to debate in France. No French citizen is willing to forsake the principle of a secular nation, even for the price of peace with Muslims. On this issue there is unanimity in the political classes.' He paused. 'No way!' He sat back and smiled proudly.

Bonnet told me that his department began dealing with the 'terrorist' threat in the 1980s. It started with the Iranian revolution, which had its proxy battles amongst Iranian exiles in Paris. 'The mosques were kept under surveillance as well as the peripatetic imams, who travel from one mosque to another instilling revolutionary ideas. These men are highly dangerous.' I asked whether the French security services had succeeded in infiltrating the radical Islamic groups. 'This is a classic services operation,' he told me, waving his hand, nonchalant and dismissive. 'We have a large number of citizens of Maghreb origin. It is a standard recruiting operation, targeting the right personnel. It's easy.'

The default theme of Bonnet's interview was of a clash of cultures between Islam and the West, which was about to become a bloody battlefield. Bonnet did not say it directly, but he was suggesting that the West should brace itself because an enemy in a Trojan horse had entered the gates of Europe. Bonnet believed the Métro bombings were a prototype of the conflict to come.

He invited me to a function at a meeting room in France's National Assembly building. Saïda was a senior diplomat in her thirties and was typical of the Algerian women who represent the regime in France. She was, of course, Muslim by heritage but I doubt she obeyed the injunction to pray five times a day. She did not wear Islamic clothing and her faith was anonymous and private, as the French ruling classes wanted it to be. She was culturally more Western than Islamic. She travelled around Europe on behalf of the Algerian regime; her mission was to draw Europe into its war against Muslim radicals. 'In Brussels,' she said, 'I saw a notice outside a Moroccan bookshop: "We are collecting money for the Holy War in Algeria". The terrorists receive money from Europe and then buy guns to kill innocent Algerians. Propaganda sheets calling for murder, rape and theft are issued from London. I called on Mrs Clinton and told her, "Why are you harbouring the terrorist Anwar Haddam in Washington? Moussa Kraouche is here in Paris with other terrorists. Why?"'

France has five million Muslims, more than any other European nation. Paris is as much a racial melting pot as London or New York. A French intellectual will waste no time during a political discussion with an Anglo-Saxon in explaining that the French, including most of the far right, are not racist. 'We do not have ghettos here for immigrants, like you do in London or Detroit,' an old friend told me over dinner. Pascal worked for the French civil service as an economist. He and I had studied together at Oxford University and he later went to the École Nationale d'Administration, the production line for France's political caste. 'Look, we have Le Pen [the leader of the far-right National Front party] but only a small section of the population follows him. In general, Americans and British are more racist than the French because here, everybody integrates,' he told me. Then he added after taking a bite, 'They *have* to in France.' His last words didn't sound ominous or threatening, just matter-of-fact. But what if they didn't *want* to integrate?

'Universalists' often claim to be apolitical when their views adopt a specific set of political values. Pascal reminded me that his country invented the modern idea of human rights. 'I'm not political,' he told me. 'But neither is Amnesty International. Nor is the UN. Some things are not debatable, they are human values. We need international bodies to protect the rights of people where they can't protect them themselves.' He beckoned me to lean closer. 'France must accept blame for what happened in Rwanda. We should have gone there sooner to prevent the bloodshed. That's the way it's going to be in the future.' In the 1990s, those who saw international institutions as a newly invigorated force in the post-cold war world welcomed intervention in foreign countries. After September 11th, intervention was reinterpreted by the Bush administration as 'pre-emptive action'. Pascal sent me an email after the Anglo-American invasion of Iraq. 'How can you just invade another country like this?' He was appalled. 'It's unbelievable, like the Wild West.' Pascal is unmistakably French; he scrutinizes wine lists, scoffs at fast food and fakes a *franglais* dialect in order to charm British women. While he has travelled extensively and is fluent in several languages, his essential 'Frenchness' has remained intact. Yet he is partly Jewish. His mother's maiden name was Polish. His grandfather fled from Ukraine during Stalin's murderous rule.

Paris has been a lifeboat for Europe's castaways for generations. One in four French people is either an immigrant, the child of immigrants, or, in Pascal's case, a grandchild. It is difficult to rank nations according to the extent of racism in their society; most cultures include some forms of racial stereotyping and France is no different. I attended the annual 'Fête des Bleu-blanc-rouge' of the Front National, France's right-wing, anti-immigration party. The party's President, Jean-Marie Le Pen, told the audience, 'Yes, I believe in the inequality of the races,' before offering evidence from biologists that racial differences existed. Le Pen's speeches are portraits of a sentimentalized 'lost France', where the ruddy-cheeked enjoy carafes of rough wine, with bread and foie gras on red-checked tablecloths. He is giving voice to the 'common man', who has been silenced by France's privileged political class. During the day's festivities, a small group of blacks, including one from Martinique, another from Senegal, were announced as 'model French men and women'. Le Pen glowed with pride and pinned a *Bleu-blanc-rouge* badge on the breast of each immigrant. Each shook hands and bowed courteously with the towering party leader, who flashed a caring, avuncular smile. The crowd clapped and a hint of the 'Marseillaise' percolated as background from the loudspeakers. I looked around; the audience was an amalgam of beer-drinking, shirtless skinheads, elderly men who looked like old soldiers and young housewives with babies, but no people of colour. While this strange ceremony may have been no more than a cruel and cynical gesture, it reflected a distinction between skin colour and culture that crosses the political spectrum in France.

'The French political class believes its culture is superior to Islamic culture,' said Dr Ali Merad, a professor of Arabic literature and civilization at the University of Lyon. 'The impact of this is, in effect, to create another form of racism.' His words flowed at a gentle pace but his comments carried a force. 'If a woman wears a short skirt and drinks wine, Frenchmen don't care about her skin colour. But when she wears a headscarf, France becomes neurotic.' Dr Merad accepted that the republican values of France are anti-racist but believed the system did not know how to react when it was challenged by another culture. He spoke about the 'ideologization' of Islam in France, meaning that the faith had been transformed into a political ideology. Muslims who felt excluded from French society asked why they were being discriminated against: 'They concluded that it was primarily their faith rather than their skin colour.' A generation ago, such people might have joined radical socialist movements; they have since disappeared. To convert to Islam today is a way for a rebel to find a cause.

When Islam and Western cultures collide, the issue that rouses the greatest passion is gender politics, and in particular women's clothing. The picturesque town of Albertville lies in a valley carved from the western foothills of the Alps. Its high street is lined with cafes and bijou shops, including delicatessens specializing in the distinctive cheeses from the Savoie region. When I visited, two slender young girls were walking along the high street wearing *khimars*, the Islamic headscarf that is pinned around the chin and covers the neck and temples but not the remainder of the face. It fell over their shoulders and upper body, like a short baggy shirt. It was autumn and the girls, who were sisters, wore light raincoats: from afar, each could have been wearing a scarf wrapped tightly around her head like a 1960s starlet in an open-topped car. In Albertville, however, the square metre of white cloth that covered their hair was snagging at the foundations of the French Republic.

'They give you nasty looks, as if you're from another planet,' said Hind, who was nineteen years old. She was born in Morocco but had lived in France since she was four months old. 'I was carrying a bag once and I saw that two women were staring at me. They spoke loudly and I could hear them saying, "Look at that girl's bag. It must be a bomb." People link the headscarf to terrorism.'

Nabila Kourrad is a year younger than her sister and was born in France. They were fair-skinned Arabs and could easily have passed as European French. 'Before I started wearing a headscarf, I went around unnoticed. Now people stare at me. I look back and see fear and anger in their eyes.' The sisters said they wear the headscarf because their faith requires a woman to dress modestly. 'It's a religious duty,' said Nabila. Two years earlier, the Kourrad girls had been expelled from school because they refused to remove their headscarves in class.

The row over Muslim girls and their headwear began in 1989 in a school in Creil, north of Paris. Two sisters and their cousin were expelled by a head teacher who applied a government guideline that prevents pupils wearing 'ostentatious' religious symbols in the classroom. The French education system is aggressively secular. After the revolution, the state became suspicious of the irrational power of religion which was associated with the Ancien Régime, and in 1905, France codified the separation of Church and state in the law of *laïcité*, or secularism. It banned religious practices in state schools, including the conspicuous display of religious belief.

The law never defined what constituted an 'ostentatious' religious symbol and pupils regularly wore crosses on their necklaces without arousing a problem. Until 1989, many Muslim girls also wore headscarves while most head teachers gave a wide interpretation to the guidelines issued by the Education Ministry. The expulsion of the three girls at Creil unleashed a confrontation that until then had been sidestepped. Islamic groups staged demonstrations; television crews invaded the town and even the King of Morocco became involved, suggesting that the girls take off their headscarves in class. After a series of legal appeals, the girls were allowed to return to school wearing their scarves.

In 1994, the government tried to clarify the rules and advised head teachers that religious symbols in school were permitted unless they constituted 'an act of provocation, proselytism or propaganda'. The government circular had intended to allow girls to wear the scarf unless it was disrupting classroom activities. In the same year, a new head teacher took charge of Albertville's Lycée Jean Moulin, named after the French Resistance leader who was captured and executed by the Nazis in 1943. Jean-Pierre Taguel interpreted the guidelines strictly and viewed the head covering as a direct challenge to France's principles of equality and liberty. 'The headscarf is a symbol of a woman's inferior status,' he told me as he banged the desk with his finger. 'The headscarf was not accepted by our pupils, because it denigrates women. It was then that the scarf was denounced in our school.' M. Taguel believed in his culture. He was in his fifties with a full head of white hair. He wore a brown-checked jacket and suede shoes. He cared for his pupils and was well liked by them. He saw no need to respect the culture of others who had chosen to live in his community. It was a peculiarly aggressive stance for a man who otherwise seemed sympathetic and kindly. 'These girls should make the effort to blend in with our society. They should respect the secular values in our schools. If they do that, I will welcome them to return to class.'

I met the sisters one day when they walked to the school gates in the morning to meet friends. They chatted and laughed until the bell sounded. Their friends went inside while they remained outside the gates. The deputy head teacher, François Doche, then arrived for work. He was a small precise man wearing a striped jacket and an oleaginous smile. He told the girls, 'We've always said you can come back if you don't wear the veil in class. We've agreed that you can wear it up to the classroom door. We have made a great effort to accept this.'

The deputy head ended the discussion by announcing it was time for class. 'If they wanted to integrate they wouldn't wear the veil. They are turning their back on French society. Most girls belonging to the Islamic community come to class wearing European dress. This is just a case of an extremist family. Goodbye.' Doche shut the school gates behind him.

Nabila and Hind remained outside, forlorn and tearful. 'They've asked us to chose between our education and our religion. It's not fair. For me, the headscarf is part of my life, like my faith is.' Nabila told me that she was unsure of her identity. 'I have discovered that they do not treat me as a French national and they do not treat me as a Moroccan. I am both, French and Moroccan. I haven't lived in Morocco. I do not know how people live there. I know life in France.' She placed her fist under her chin and sniffed in defiance. 'What I definitely know is that wherever I happen to be or whatever they do to me, I'll always be Muslim. This is the main thing.'

The girls challenged the teachers' ban in court and won an initial victory. The teachers appealed and the legal process dragged on until the girls were too old to attend school. In 2004, the French parliament finally clarified the law, specifically banning the headscarf worn by Muslim girls in state schools. The ban was passed by 494 votes to 36. The French President said the principle of *laicité* was 'non-negotiable'.

After I left the Kourrad sisters in Albertville, I popped into a bar in the nearby town of Ugine. A large bulbous Kronenbourg sign projected an eerie red glow above the doorway. It was a bar for locals, about twenty drinkers who all appeared to know each other. I brought up the subject of the Islamic headscarf and the bar erupted. One man with an earring and short-cropped black hair stood on a chair like a stand-up comic. 'OK. I am Italian. So I take my gun to school like a Mafioso!' His hands gestured as if he were holding a machine gun, mowing down the drinkers. Everyone laughed and he took another sip of his drink. 'It's not done to wear a veil,' he concluded. 'We are in France, we must live like the French.' The bar burst into applause.

A girl with a blonde bob and a cross on her necklace was about the same age as the Kourrad sisters. 'For me it's all right if they put on a veil, but they must take it off in class. If a boy has a cap he is obliged to take it off before entering the classroom. It's a sign of respect for the teacher. It's just being polite.' The girl added that she would not support the National Front of Jean-Marie Le Pen. 'He would lead the country straight into civil war.' The intoxicated comedian manqué jumped in: 'When I see a mosque I become mad. We give too much freedom in France. These veiled girls must obey French law because they are in France. If we go to Algeria we get killed. If these girls don't comply with French values we should put them on a boat and expel them.'

The conversation turned to the Muslim suburbs of the big cities. The young in this bar saw a divided France with an alien culture in their midst. A thin, finely boned man with blond hair and black bomber jacket said that everyone there feared entering a Muslim-dominated district. 'They are so numerous,' he exclaimed, waving his hands in the air, making circles of smoke with his cigarette. 'We've reached the point where the police do nothing. The Muslims make their own law and do as they please. The poor old Frenchman who has lived there fifty years shuts his mouth because he is helpless.' The comedian raised his voice. 'If you go there after 8 p.m., fifteen people will surround you and . . .' He paused and passed his flat hand theatrically across his throat. The bar burst out in laughter.

The Picasso Estate was the type of the district that the beer-swilling joker would fear. It comprised half a dozen tower blocks, some soaring thirty floors, separated by concrete paths and grass mounds. An overwhelming majority of the residents were immigrants or their children. The towers were roughly circular but had a lumpy, undulating facade. They were decorated in a military camouflage design, using dollops of olive green, browns and blues. The estate is in the *banlieue* of Nanterre, north-west of Paris.

According to police, young Muslims in the estate have become more fervent. 'Nanterre has three mosques and they have never been so full,' Officer Lamarre told me as we toured the *banlieue* in a blue and white Peugeot squad car. He was in his late twenties with high cheekbones and a focused stare. Officer Patoux, with a handlebar moustache and devil-may-care glint in his eyes, was behind the wheel. He licked his lips when the call came to 'blue-light' to a suspected stolen car on the Picasso Estate.

Lamarre had no fear of the *banlieue*. 'We've had special training,' he told me. 'The authorities are forecasting an explosion in the housing estates. You need specially trained people to deal with street battles.' France had recently passed new laws to provide the police with additional powers to stop and search suspected 'terrorists'. In practice, it meant stopping and questioning North African youths. 'It really is war with them,' Lamarre said without irony. I asked if there were any policemen from North African backgrounds who worked alongside Muslim community leaders. Both men burst out laughing. 'If we had North African policemen, it would just mean that the criminals had somebody on the inside,' Officer Patoux said as he flashed a wide smile.

We found a group of about a dozen young men who looked of North African descent surrounding a car. A few were sitting inside. They were smoking and chatting and didn't seem at all surprised to see two police cars arrive with sirens screaming and lights flashing. Officer Patoux checked the men's identity papers. The car had apparently been borrowed from someone's brother. I never found out why the police suspected that the car had been stolen. It proved to be properly licensed and the police left after searching the men.

The police officers took me back to the station and later that night I returned to the Picasso Estate to meet the suspects, who were prowling like wild animals and glaring at passing cars. 'If you're white, you get respect. If you've got dark skin, the police insult you,' spat a twenty-year-old whose father had brought him to Nanterre from Algeria as an infant. 'They'll handcuff you and beat you up for nothing.' Another man, with bandages over his broken nose from a previous confrontation, was more explicit. 'The cops are bastards. I'd like to fuck their mothers! If we had guns, we'd use them!'

Many young Muslims who never used to attend the mosque now saw Islam as part of their battle with the state. The sons of North African immigrants believed their identity was marked not by their origins but by their religion. 'The Moroccan, the Algerian, the Tunisian realizes that the link that unites us is Islam. So we have put forward Islam in our fight for recognition,' said a thoughtful man who had just given me a heroic account of a battle with skinheads. 'The police know that Islam is the symbol of our union, and they are trying to destroy this symbol in order to destroy us.'

As another police car drove by, the man with the broken nose gloated. 'They don't understand Islam. They are frightened of it. Islam unites us and gives us strength. There are Muslims all over the world. If they want to destroy us they will have a lot to do!' Another man in a jean jacket with a frayed collar questioned the doctrine of assimilation. 'They want us to integrate. What is integration? To eat pork and drink wine? For them, if you're a Muslim, you can't integrate.' Broken-nose stepped in again. 'We are Muslims, they must respect our religion. If they do not respect it, there'll be war!' The man in the jean jacket dragged on a cigarette and stood aside from the group, staring at the tower blocks of the Picasso Estate. 'It's like the Intifada. Give us a Kalashnikov. We'll use it.'

France's police were instructed to search out Islamist militants.

Officers Patoux and Lamarre drew a cartoon image of suspects in France's 'war on terror'. 'There's always a bearded man behind them. These "bearded men" are the Muslim Brotherhood,' declared Patoux with certainty. The police had constructed a theory that Islamists linked to the uprising in Algeria were conspiring to spark a revolt on the estates of the *banlieue*. 'They take the worst ones and make them their agents,' according to Officer Lamarre. 'The young are easy prey.' Officer Patoux explained the mechanics of the Islamic challenge as he saw it, orchestrated by groups of bearded men wearing robes. 'They go out to the housing estates and preach to young people. They have a very convincing discourse to entrap these young men so forcefully. The youth give up their old ways. It transforms them into devout extremists. The goal of the bearded men is one word: Islam.' Officer Lamarre chipped in with the assumed association of religious devotion to terrorism. 'The war against the Algerian regime needs money and weapons. These Islamists raise money in France to buy arms for the war in Algeria. They try to recruit terrorists like Khaled Kelkal.'

The name of Khaled Kelkal had become the shibboleth that was bisecting France. The non-Muslim French were mostly jubilant when they watched on television the gunning down of a young man who was described as a terrorist. But five million French Muslims refused to celebrate. Even those representing the state-supported 'official' Islam were horrified. Kamel Kebtane was the head of a large mosque in Lyon that had been opened by the Minister of the Interior. He wore a shirt and tie and was clean-shaven. He believed that Islam could adapt to the character and traditions of France. But since Kelkal's death even he had become alarmed that the government saw Islam largely in terms of state security. 'Our youth feel the impact of the bullets that hit Kelkal in their own flesh and blood. It was an execution. For us, most people believed he had nothing to do with the bombings. He is dead. Alas, the truth will never be known.'

Most French are horrified that the Muslim community can see Khaled Kelkal as a victim. Kamel Kebtane explained that by creating an enemy called 'Islamist terrorism', France was failing to understand why young Muslims had turned their back on society. 'Khaled Kelkal is the product of French society. Those two veiled girls, the Kourrad sisters, they are also the product of French society. They were brought up with French culture and education and they rejected this society and its customs, in which they had placed great faith.'

Abdelkarim was born in France but dressed as if he was living in the Arabian desert in the seventh century. He wore a white djellaba and a crocheted skullcap. His hair was cropped short and his beard was untrimmed but sparse and dangling, the facial growth of a teenager. 'Khaled Kelkal is my brother in Islam. For us he is a martyr. For the Muslim Brothers, it was a joy, because he died a beautiful death as a martyr.' Abdelkarim prayed in a large concrete bunker-like mosque in the Lyon suburb of Les Minguettes. A green light in the entrance hall beckoned worshippers and mostly young men in their late teens and twenties gathered in a warren of rooms with white walls and no furniture. The imam was a thin, alert man in his sixties with beady eyes. He'd watched the situation deteriorate since Kelkal's death. 'From what I've seen, France is a police state,' he told me without emotion. 'The police frame people in order to intimidate the youth. Young people have been arrested and some tortured. This may be the country of human rights but as far as Muslims are concerned they have no rights.'

The anger was heaving like a bound animal struggling for freedom. Since I was not French, the congregation felt sympathetic. At that time, Britain was believed to be more tolerant towards Islamist ideas than the French Republic. Several men wanted to give their accounts of abuse and discrimination. Abdelkarim was born into a Christian family. He'd converted to Islam three years earlier. 'Before I was a delinquent who used to steal and do forbidden things. When I became a Muslim my whole life changed.' His parents warned him that it was dangerous to dress in robes in France. 'I shall live according to the Sunnah. I will obey the laws of the Prophet, not the laws of Pasqua [France's hard-line Interior Minister].' Abdelkarim was sinewy but small and gentle in his manner. Shortly after Kelkal's death, the police stopped him on the Métro and accused him of plotting terrorism. 'They handcuffed me and took me to the police station. They started calling me a fundamentalist and an Islamist terrorist. Then they got violent. I was slapped and kicked in the stomach.' He was put in a cell for six hours. 'They insulted me again and rummaged through my bag. They found books about Islam and a small Qur'ān.' Throughout the interrogation the police offered no evidence suggesting that he had any links to bombings. Two other policemen then entered the room. 'They took my arms and held me down. One shoved the Qur'ān into my mouth. They said, "You are a pure one, a total Muslim. You have the beard, the robe and the books. You're the same as Khaled Kelkal. You're going to end up like him." '

Many left-wing politicians who campaign tirelessly against racism are struck dumb when the state is accused of infringing the rights of Muslims. The left in France is uncomfortable with Islamism, which it primarily views negatively through issues such as women's rights or artistic freedoms. France had been shaken by the Métro bombings and the mention of terrorism made many in the French left nervous. The government insisted that 'national interest' was at stake, overriding concerns about human rights.

Amongst those arrested were Kamel and Faouzia Ouadou, a young Algerian couple who lived in the Lyon suburb of Duchère. Faouzia wore a light brown *khimar* and dark brown robe beneath. 'He liked a good laugh,' she reflected as she held a picture of her husband, an attractive clean-shaven man who was smiling in all the photographs. 'He wanted to enjoy himself. He was always joking.' Kamel Ouadou was a chemist at a local university. He was accused of making bombs as a member of what the police called a 'scientific cell'. 'They rushed in and threw my husband on the floor. They handcuffed me. My husband was saying, "She's pregnant, leave her alone." They wouldn't listen. They asked me crazy questions about armed Islamic groups in Algeria. They said, "If you don't answer, your baby will be born in prison." '

Faouzia had a genial temperament and when she finished her sentence her face opened into a generous smile. Although I was a stranger, she chatted and confided in me over a cup of tea as if we were old friends. She was released after one night but her husband was still in jail; he'd been charged with 'conspiracy to commit acts of terrorism' and was awaiting trial.

Faouzia regularly went to see her husband's lawyer in Paris. Jean-Louis Pelletier was a distinguished barrister with an office on the Quai de Montebello on the left bank of the Seine. Unlike many left-leaning Frenchmen, he was angered by the breadth of the anti-terrorist laws. 'It goes on and on,' he groaned. 'We're always back to what the judge first told me: Kamel Ouadou is part of an Islamist secret cell. End of story. I feel so powerless and hopeless.'

Pelletier was in his fifties, with a broad, chubby face. It hardened as he recounted Kamel's story. 'For over a year he's been treated as a guilty man yet I can assure you that his file does not contain one shred of evidence against him. The only crime he has committed is to sympathize with Islamist ideas. But freedom of opinion is one of the main articles of the French constitution.' A few months later, Kamel Ouadou was released from prison without charge. He had spent sixteen months in a high-security jail, suspected of being a bomb-maker. When he was freed, he was not told why he'd been arrested; the only evidence against him was his qualifications as a chemist.

Following the end of the cold war, American political scientists contemplated the 'new world order' and whether there would be any post-communist challenges to American-led market capitalism. One concept possessed an elegant symmetry and was easy for the mass media to grasp: replace the Soviet threat with the Islamist threat. It drew parallels with the Crusades and latched on to popular images of fanatical Muslims, which at that time were most closely associated with Iran and its Shi'ite allies in Lebanon. Tracts such as Samuel Huntington's *The Clash of Civilizations* received international acclaim. Journalists condensed these ideas to fit into a simplified, bipolar world where the bad guys were no longer communists, but Muslims. In his follow-up book, Huntington documented a propensity for violence in Muslim societies in a section entitled 'Islam's Bloody Borders'. He pointed out that 'a concept of non-violence is absent from Muslim doctrine and practice' and that, unlike Christ or Buddha, the Prophet Mohammed is celebrated as a brave warrior and skilful military commander. Despite his search for a bellicose core to the Islamic faith and his intellectual commitment to an impending conflict, he accepted that the cause of the violence is the expansion of Western culture. 'The problem for Islam is . . . the West, a different civilization whose people are convinced of the universality of their culture and . . . an obligation to extend that culture throughout the world.'

Bin Laden apparently ordered the attacks of September 11th because American troops were stationed in Saudi Arabia, one million Iraqis had died because of international sanctions initiated by the US, and Washington had given Israel, year after year, ample funds to allow its military to do as it pleased with the Palestinians. Terrorism trails American foreign policy like a loyal sheepdog. One could conclude that the best way to prevent terrorism in the West is to allow Muslim civilization to live according to its traditions and customs.

The 'war on terror' is serving to continue the peculiar, corrupted meaning of 'war' that became established during the stand-off over the

Iron Curtain: the cold war was an ideological not a military confrontation. There was no 'ceasefire' to establish peace. The 'war on terror' once again places the West in conflict with an inhuman enemy in a chronic confrontation that freezes, perhaps for generations, abstract hatreds.

Khaled Kelkal became the symbol of the enemy within. He was brought up in France but turned his back on the society that his parents had migrated to join. He was so soured by his world that he was prepared to bomb the country he lived in. A German sociologist, Dietmar Loch, published an interview he'd conducted with Kelkal three years before his death. Kelkal was in jail at the time for stealing cars. Using the title, 'Moi, Khaled Kelkal', the notes of their meeting became a reference manual for sociologists studying the alienation of youth in the *banlieue*. Kelkal was a bright child, but in his mid-teens he started playing truant from school and soon turned to crime. Before prison, he'd had no interest in religion. 'I was in the same cell as a Muslim. I learnt Arabic as well as my religion, Islam. It opened up new horizons. Everything was thrown aside and replaced. My life became . . . more coherent.'

Islam was his parents' religion, which had meant little to him. By associating with it, he discovered dignity and a sense of belonging that was denied him in the country in which the family had settled. 'I had the power to succeed but I was an outsider. When you go looking for a job and say you are from Vaulx-en-Velin, they won't even ask your name,' he complained.

Second-generation European Muslims were attracted to a transnational form of Islam, rather than the faith as it was practised in the country of their parents' origin. As Kelkal dramatically declared to the sociologist, 'I am neither Arab nor French. I am a Muslim!' This led to a search for a Salafist, pure faith that transcended national borders. An international community of Muslims, an Ummah, emerged, which developed largely on the back of the Internet. The French political scientist Olivier Roy has defined this phenomenon as 'Neo-fundamentalism', which addresses 'the universalist yearning of Muslims who cannot identify with any specific place or nation'. Roy argues that the second generation of al-Qa'eda militants in Europe (those recruited after 1992) was characterized by men who had broken their ties with the 'real' Muslim world they claim to represent. This applied to most of the September 11th hijackers. They were cultural outcasts both in their countries of origin and in their host countries. Most were trained in technical or scientific fields and spoke a Western language.

Khaled Kelkal assessed a Muslim's life in France thus: 'Integration is impossible,' he told the German sociologist in 1992. 'Erase my culture? Eat pork? I cannot.' From his grave, he forecast a looming confrontation. 'Now is only the beginning. It'll get hotter and hotter until it's too late.'

Kelkal's account of his transition from small-time criminal to devout Muslim revealed the influence that Malcolm X, the American black-power leader, had on his life. He saw Malcolm X as a role model. The Spike Lee film based on *The Autobiography of Malcolm X* was popular amongst young *beurs* in the suburbs and many Islamic associations distributed it freely to worshippers. A phenomenon was developing in Europe that had been taking place amongst the African-American people for generations; Islam was becoming the voice of urban rebellion.

Cooke County Jail in Chicago, with its rolled walls of razor wire and marksmen peering from watchtowers, seemed an unlikely crucible for the expansion of a faith. Inside one of the prison buildings, guards armed with shotguns ushered about a hundred men from the high-security unit into a large hall. All were black and wore the brown prison uniforms with a large M, L or XL emblazoned on their chest. A black Muslim cleric stood behind a pulpit and greeted the prisoners with '*Asalamalikum*' ('Peace be upon you'). The imam, who had the frame of a wrestler, was a former convict himself. 'There is only one truth. There is no God but Allah,' he announced. 'If a man is not serving Allah, he is serving Satan. There is no other way than Islam, period.' Black prisoners were listening to a new voice of authority, a practice that was repeated throughout the toughest jails in America. Thousands of hardened criminals converted to Islam each year.

In a manner similar to Khaled Kelkal's adoption of a born-again faith, many blacks, ungodly and Christian alike, discovered that Islam provided answers to the problems that had led to their life of crime. In America's inner cities, more black men go to jail than to college. One nineteen-year-old inmate had been a gang member who had sold drugs since he was thirteen. Islam had provided a blueprint for a life without drugs or alcohol. He said that many black teenagers in the slums of Chicago were chasing a false dream. 'We've been brought up and seen the drug dealers, the big cars, the fancy cars, the pimps and players and hustlers. I'm not chasing that dream any more; I'm dealing with reality.'

Imam Ramee Muhammed, a former US Marine, taught himself Arabic and converted to Islam while working as a prison guard. Ramee opened the Masjid al-Qadir, a converted shop that once sold office equipment but had been empty for years. The mosque is on 75th Street, in the heart of Southside, a run-down district of decaying buildings a half-hour drive from the glittering skyscrapers of central Chicago and the shores of Lake Michigan. The area is known locally as 'Terrortown' because of the number of drive-by shootings. Behind the mosque's battered shop front, about twenty young black men began prayers. Ramee recited the prayers in Arabic. Amongst the faithful were several former gang members, including Amin.

Ramee and Amin had a daily ritual, walking the streets of Southside on a mission to 'clean up' the area. They wanted to shut down the shops that sold alcohol and persuade drug dealers to start another trade. On one day, I followed the two men into a liquor store. They warned the owners that the 'wrath of Allah' would befall them if they didn't close their shop. The threats are direct: 'We're going to close your shop, your mouth, your heart, your lungs. You will be punished for what you are doing.' When I asked about his belief in direct action, Ramee quoted Malcolm X. 'You got to talk to our people in the language they understand. The language of a .38 is a .45,' he told me.

Wearing their Arab robes with weapons tucked under their belts, Ramee and Amin were an unusual sight in the ghetto. Yet they had the broad support of the community. I bumped into one man who'd sold drugs for five years, and now, still standing on the street corner, sold bottles of scent. The gang that claimed to control this part of Chicago was even known as El Rukns, an Arabic term meaning a military unit. The gang was said to have Muslim leanings. El Rukns used Islamic terminology and apparently tried to spread the word of the Qur'ān in the ghetto, even though they still dealt in drugs.

Ramee had the support of El Rukns' leadership. 'They want to be good Muslims but they ask: "How can we support our families?"' Ramee also described the gang as the only family that some young black men know. 'Whole communities are based on narcotics sales,' he said. 'You've got to create jobs in these neighbourhoods. The gang members would then become Muslim overnight.' It was a strange, occult world, where prison, the gangs and the mosque intermingled.

'It's a conflict,' Amin told me, 'but eventually, many go all the way and become true Muslims.'

There are around two million African-American followers of orthodox Islam. One in three black inmates in America's jails professes an interest in the faith. One of the attractions of Islam for black Americans is that it has nothing to do with white America.

A former Black Panther activist, Ahmad Abdur Rahman (formerly Ron Irwin), argued that the faith empowered black Americans and offered a culture distinct from the otherwise dominant white Christian culture. Countless African-American women across the nation told me that Islam had a liberating rather than an oppressive role in their lives. Amira Wazeer believed that the faith offered black women more dignity than they were usually granted by white society. 'When a woman wears a veil, men know to treat her with respect,' she told me. 'Men think that a woman in minis or spandex is sexually loose and has no morals. A veiled woman can hold her head high and men don't cat-call or molest her.' Amira was a confident, forceful woman who has no sense of being inferior to men after her conversion to Islam. 'We are different and Allah has given us different roles.' She accepted that some traditional cultures had not provided women the rights or dignity they should. 'In those cases it is because of the history of those places,' she said, 'not Islam.' She continued: 'Many girls in America grow up believing they should be stick-thin. Women are trapped by the consumer industry into having to spend money and behave in a certain way. Islam cuts those chains. We've been economic slaves, we've been mental slaves. When I discovered Islam, I found out that, by submitting to Allah, I no longer cared about the standards of America, I only cared about the standards that Allah set.'

Six years later I met Ramee in Britain. He'd left America because of concerns for his safety after September 11th – many Salafist believers had been arrested or harassed – and he was seeking asylum in the UK. He lived with one of his two wives and eight children in Nelson, a suburb of Manchester named after the English military hero, Lord Nelson. The town has a large Pakistani population and a vibrant Islamic community.

The imam believed the 'war on terror' was an excuse to 'clean up' anyone the United States didn't like. 'It's one big lie,' he told me. 'It should be "war on my enemy".' The 'war on terror' 'has placed the clash of civilizations in a military context. Islam must defend itself when it is under attack,' he warned. Perched on his head was a crimson fez. He said the cap was a symbol of the blood of the Moors, the Muslim civilization that ruled Spain for seven hundred years.

Ramee Muhammed spent his time in Britain lecturing at mosques and urging young people to ignore the temptations of drugs and alcohol. An Islamic newspaper advertised one of his tours: 'Ex-gangster from the streets of Chicago embraced Islam and is now a learned scholar fighting against corruption. Will be talking about controlling your desires and the role of Muslim Youth today.' The local press had a different angle on his activities in this corner of Lancashire. 'Muslim Students Spark Terror Scare' screamed the *Birmingham Post* after students from the United States were barred entry to the UK for a course he had organized. 'Al-Qa'eda Recruiting in Nelson' exclaimed another regional paper, quoting sources that people from 'outside the community' were preaching to young Muslims.

Ramee had arranged for six American students, aged between sixteen and eighteen, to study at an Islamic college in Birmingham. When they landed they were detained and interrogated. 'They asked me about Osama bin Laden, do I think he's a good Muslim or a bad Muslim and do I feel sorry for the people who died at the World Trade Center,' according to Ramee's stepson, who was one of the six. They asked whether he would fight for America or for the Taliban. 'I told them that I'm just going to fight for my religion,' he answered. The Home Office said it was not satisfied that the students had a genuine intention to study. When they returned to the States, the American police said the students had a 'terrorist profile'. Imam Ramee believed that many in the White House consider Islam as the enemy. He said that life in America had become intolerable for Muslims like him, who refused to integrate into the world of predominantly Christian white America. In April 2004, while his asylum process was being processed, the tabloid newspapers reported his case. An article on the front page of the *Sunday Express*, headlined 'Maddest asylum plea yet', claimed Ramee had taught Richard Reid, the so-called 'shoe bomber', and had links with the radical preacher Abu Hamza. Other newspapers followed up his story. The *Daily Mail* reported: 'A Muslim cleric living in Britain is claiming asylum – from our closest ally America. US born Imam Ramee Abdul Rahman Muhammed, who preached to suicide bombers and wants the UK to become an Islamic state, says he will be persecuted if he is sent home. He is now receiving £1,400 a month from the taxpayer to look after his pregnant wife and eight children while his application is considered.'

When Ramee attended an immigration appointment a few days later he was detained; he believes his arrest followed the allegations in the newspapers. Two weeks later he was released without charge.

The US government believed that the end of the cold war liberated Eastern European people from the oppression of communism. A decade later, George W. Bush portrayed the new global conflict as a battle between 'freedom' and 'terrorism'. But unlike Eastern Europe, the Muslims of Iraq and elsewhere, including millions within America itself, do not want to accept principles enshrined in the American constitution. The values that underwrote the revolutions of 1776 and 1789, based on the writings of Thomas Paine and others, emphasized equality and civil rights and became enshrined in the French and American constitutions. Islam is challenging the universal acceptance of this political ideal, and even within those countries, millions believe that these values have failed them. Many believe Islam liberates them from the oppression they have experienced. The former Black Panther activist Ahmad Abdul Rahman positions Islam as a liberation ideology. 'The growth of Islam has something to do with the failures of the civil-rights movement and it not just failing but having reached a peak where it can't achieve any more.' Another former activist, Haneef Abdul Rahman, added, 'Islam historically has been accepted by the dispossessed very readily. After a while, you know, if people keep telling you, "You're not in, you're not in," pretty soon you'll say, "OK, you go your way and I'll go mine." '

In the *New Statesman* in August 1997, I wrote that there were ten million Muslims in Europe and more than seven million in the United States and they were not leaving. 'The need to reject the "clash of civilizations" notion is urgent. If we continue to define Islam in terms of terrorism or intolerance, we will reap the effects directly.'

CONCLUSION – THE CLASH OF DEFINITIONS

'A definition of terrorism is hopeless . . . terrorism is just
violence that you don't like.'
Professor Richard Rubinstein, the Center for Conflict Analysis and Resolution,
George Mason University, Virginia

The road from Tangalle to Matara in southern Sri Lanka passes
the most enchanting beaches in the world. It was about seven in the
morning, clear and crisp, before the leaden heat of the day descended.
On the winding road a dozen or so people in colourful sarongs had
gathered. A body lay at their feet, shot by a single bullet to the head.
A sign around his neck declared that he was a member of a rebel
Marxist organization that was targeting policemen and government
officials.

I was on my way to visit Chief Inspector Ronnie Gunasinge at
Matara police station. When I said that I'd come across a body, he
reacted like Inspector Clouseau. 'You are reporting a murder! The first
for months in this district.' He picked up the phone and howled to a
deputy, 'Get out the sniffer dogs. Pull out all the stops. We must find
this killer.' The truth was that Gunasinge knew exactly who the killer
was: a fellow member of the security services. He may even have
ordered the killing himself.

This was the first of many cadavers of young men that I saw,
dumped on the roadside during the night, often in piles of half a dozen
or more. Daily life continued as schoolchildren and cyclists passed the
mounds of bodies. During the following night, tyres were placed
around the necks of the dead and set alight. A pile of bones and soot

would be smouldering by morning. Southern Sri Lanka in 1988 was a landscape of slaughter and silence.

Between 1988 and 1990, government-sponsored death squads murdered between forty and sixty thousand people suspected of belonging to the leftist-nationalist JVP (Janatha Vimukthi Pereamuna, or People's Liberation Front), a Singhala nationalist and leftist movement that opposed concessions to Sri Lanka's Tamil minority.

I was later led down a jungle path to a rendezvous with half a dozen members of the JVP who had gathered under a large bo tree. They were all wearing sarongs with no shirts and were armed with home-made guns. Not one looked more than twenty-five. One of them offered me a cup of tea from a thermos. 'We are patriots,' he told me. 'We are fighting the Indians who are occupying our country,' referring to the peacekeeping force sent to arbitrate in another conflict between the government and the Tamil Tigers. 'We are fighting a patriotic war. We are like the fighters who liberated Cuba or Vietnam.'

The media described the young men in the revolutionary movement, responsible for the deaths of a few dozen policemen, as the terrorists. The security services were apparently told by the Prime Minister, Ranasinghe Premadasa, to 'crush their balls' and were given daily financial rewards for killing large numbers of young men. The regime used the term 'terrorism' to vilify the JVP. Ronnie Gunasinge told me that the strategy of the security services was to 'show the atrocities committed by the terrorists in order to separate them from the people'. Often this meant blaming the group for murders committed by the security services. One policeman involved in the anti-JVP suppression made a startling private revelation: 'If we kill a hundred young men and six are terrorists, then that's a successful operation.'

The police terrorized the Singhalese population of southern Sri Lanka and yet the media reported the murders largely using the language of the authorities. The Prime Minister who became President, Ranasinghe Premadasa, knew that 'terrorism' had acquired a talismanic force and he manipulated language ruthlessly in order to strengthen the counter-insurgency. Unless anyone naively believes that governments do not engage in such murderous violence, the one-sided use of 'terrorism' by the media doesn't make sense. The only consistent alternative is for journalists to expand their definition of 'terrorism' to include all organized acts of terror and killing, including those by governments.

It has taken years for the truth to emerge from conflicts such as those in Sri Lanka, Central America and even in Northern Ireland, where sections of the British army colluded in dozens of murders. The role of state agencies in secret political violence only seeps out when journalists, human-rights activists or locals challenge the official, accepted version of events. It has recently been established by enquiries in Guatemala that 90 per cent of the killings in that nation's civil war (1960–96), many attributed to leftist groups at the time, were in fact perpetrated by the government. If actions and tactics alone were to define 'terrorism', then the Sri Lankan security services would be proscribed as a terrorist organization according to today's criteria.

In more recent news coverage, such a standard would require journalists to describe Israeli attacks on Palestinian civilians as 'Israeli terrorism'. The Turkish military have threatened and slaughtered Kurdish civilians and they would be labelled as 'terrorists from the Turkish army'. The technical rather than moral use of the label would also mean affixing it directly on the British or American governments. During the Anglo-American invasion of Iraq, which was considered illegal under international law, missiles and bombs destroyed the lives of thousands of civilians just as innocent as those who died on September 11th.

If 'terrorism' is used even-handedly to include violence by states and agents of states, then it is these, not groups such as al-Qa'eda, that are the most bloodthirsty in the world. The number of civilian casualties in recent conflicts is difficult to assess (the Pentagon does not release estimates) but it remains incontrovertible that the United States and Israel are much bigger killers than their 'terrorist' foes. In the Israeli–Palestinian conflict, between the beginning of the Intifada (1987) and the end of January 2002, Israeli security forces and settlers killed 2,166 Palestinian civilians, while Palestinians killed a total of 454 Israeli civilians. The Israelis claim that many of the Palestinian dead were not civilians but gunmen, but even a reading of the statistics that was sympathetic to the Israelis would conclude that the Israeli forces kill as least three times the number of civilians murdered by Palestinian militants.

In the war between al-Qa'eda and the West, the number of civilians killed during the invasions of Afghanistan and Iraq and the continued strife in both countries is at least fifteen thousand. Some estimates reckon that 100,000 civilians have died in Iraq alone. It is difficult to obtain accurate statistics because the Allied forces try to keep the figures secret. Al-Qa'eda and its affiliated groups are responsible for less than four thousand civilian dead. Counter-insurgency is invariably more brutal than the challenge it seeks to crush. The Mau Mau rebellion in Kenya (1952 to 1959) is remembered in Britain for the savage killing of white farmers by anti-colonialist gunmen. Only 32 European civilians were killed compared to an official estimate of 10,500 rebels, of whom around a thousand were hanged. The Mau Mau were also responsible for the death of nearly two thousand African and Asian civilians; but this figure is still dwarfed by recent evidence that suggests the true tally of those killed because they were suspected of 'terrorism' is more than twenty thousand.

If we don't want to describe America and Britain as terrorist nations, the only principled alternative is to purge the word from the lexicon of journalism. In the Middle East, Bush is repeatedly called a terrorist. The term has simply become an abusive addendum. Many Muslims argue that the 'war on terror' is a crusade, using terror as a euphemism similar to others used by Anglo-American forces during the attack on Iraq. That conflict was described as a war not an invasion, a liberation not an occupation, and cities were secured not captured. In the Arab world, a parallel language was used.

Are there, however, benefits from the 'war on terror' when the funds of a militant organization are confiscated and the group is weakened to such an extent that it ends violence and seeks negotiations? We can remain in the troubled island of Sri Lanka and see how the Liberation Tigers of Tamil Eelam (LTTE) were forced to negotiate their demand for a homeland for the Tamil minority after their ability to raise money and plan operations from Canada and the UK, including the purchase of arms, was effectively curtailed. The Tigers were a ruthless organization whose members carried cyanide capsules to commit suicide rather than surrender. They honed the use of the suicide bomber as effectively as any Muslim organization. They were willing to terrorize and murder in the pursuit of their goal more uncompromisingly than any militant organization that I have known. I recall shaking hands with Seta, a twenty-year-old with a wispy moustache and beard who had recently entered a mosque in eastern Sri Lanka and gunned down thirty-one worshippers. He looked brainwashed and detached from a moral world, staring at me blankly. 'I am fighting a war,' he said. In a similar fashion to the Khmer Rouge in Cambodia, the Tigers believed in taking young children and educating them in the values of revolution and sacrifice. The Tigers killed Tamil rivals and their Singhalese opponents with a moral insouciance.

Surely it must be good to force such a murderous organization to lay down its guns by confiscating its funds? Perhaps. I also think it important that a journalist could visit the Tigers' office in Tavistock Place in central London and discuss politics in a cafe opposite with a senior member of the organization. I did this on many occasions in the 1980s and 90s and was able to gain an insight into the movement's demands and attitudes. After they were proscribed, the Tigers' London office was shut and journalists found access to the group more difficult.

The banning of all insurgents also denies the possibility that some non-state militias should be encouraged and supported if they are fighting tyranny and oppression. In 1991, after the Gulf War, President George Bush Snr. asked Iraqis to rise up and overthrow Saddam Hussein. Later that year, I travelled to Mae Sot in Thailand and crossed illegally into Burma with Karen guerrillas. The Karens often forcibly recruit child soldiers into their movement. In May 2002, two Thai teenagers were killed and fifteen wounded when Karen guerrillas, wearing hoods and military fatigues, opened fire on a school bus near Thailand's border with Burma. The attack was calculated to sow distrust between the Thai and Burmese authorities. Surely this action should be condemned as terrorism? When I visited Manerplaw, it was the isolated headquarters of Burma's opposition movement. I trailed up the Moei River to the headquarters of the All-Burma Students' Democratic Front and an office for the National League for Democracy, which had just been victorious in elections. Beneath pictures of the Nobel Peace Laureate Aung San Suu Kyi, gunmen told me about the need to topple the repressive Burmese military junta in Rangoon. Western journalists including me gave the Karen guerrillas a sympathetic hearing and never labelled them 'terrorists'.

Later that decade I was in Montenegro with masked members of the paramilitary police as they trained for a potential civil war with the Yugoslav army, which remained loyal to the internationally recognized government of Slobodan Milošović. The gunmen wore black fatigues and carried AK-47s. They were jovial and mostly well over six feet tall. They believed the West backed their campaign even though they were a non-state militia planning a conflict with a national army. Officers from Britain's SAS had helped train the rebels a few months before I visited their camps.

The failure to define 'terrorist' means that the 'war on terror' can be used as a cloak to legitimize American military power because it portrays the challenge as a loosely defined threat that will never disappear. By being unable to explain exactly who is a terrorist, the 'war on terror' can mutate into a war against any ideology that challenges America and her allies. Terror can become a code for opponents who question the status quo and a catch-all for ideologies as diverse as Islamic militancy, emerging nationalism or anti-globalization. The world is in danger of accepting the confused idea of an endless conflict against an undefined enemy.

To a Western audience, it seems that Osama bin Laden has no realistic political manifesto beyond a vision, as described by former FBI Director Louis Freeh, 'to overthrow all governments which are not ruled by sharia or conservative Islamic law'. In bin Laden's own constituency, there is a very real vision for Muslims to find a place in the modern world in which they can enjoy genuine political status and hope of meeting their social needs. Bin Laden legitimizes political violence against the West in a fashion that is very comprehensible to his followers. To them, al-Qa'eda has goals similar to traditional insurgency groups rather than a desire to seek a limitless conflict with the West. It demands a space for Muslims to fulfil their faith. Bin Laden also used the Madrid bombing to influence the election result in Spain; he then offered a truce with European nations if they withdrew their forces from Muslim lands. In a message to the US, he said, 'while you are carrying arms on our land, terrorism is a legitimate and morally demanded duty. Your example is like a snake that entered the house of a man and was killed by him. The coward is the one who lets you walk, while carrying arms, freely on his land and provides you with peace and security.'

According to the Prime Minister of Malaysia, Abdullah Badawi, Muslims worldwide believe that a new, colder war is emerging. It appears, he said, 'that the Christian West is, once again, at war with the Muslim world.' The United States makes little attempt to disguise its belief in the superiority of Western Christian civilization. In April 2004, George W. Bush spoke of his vision of a divinely inspired apocalyptic struggle. 'I have this . . . strong belief that freedom is not this country's gift to the world. Freedom is the Almighty's gift to every man and woman in this world. And as the greatest power on the face of the earth we have an obligation to help the spread of freedom.'

The US is under assault by those labelled 'terrorists' not because of what it is but for what it does. Countries such as Holland or Switzerland are no less secular and modern but it is America that has the global reach to undermine traditional societies. A US Department of Defense Report in 1997 recorded: 'Historical data show a strong correlation between US involvement in international situations and an increase in terrorist attacks against the United States.'

The media is finding it increasingly difficult to remain an impartial observer. The *New York Times*, a voice of liberal America, accepted during an internal enquiry that it had reported stories in the run-up to the invasion of Iraq that 'pushed Pentagon assertions so aggressively you could almost sense epaulets on the shoulders of editors'. The BBC suffered a tragedy in Saudi Arabia when a cameraman and correspondent were deliberately shot while filming the house of a suspected al-Qa'eda militant: Simon Cumbers died of his wounds and Frank Gardner was seriously wounded. There was no suggestion that Frank had been individually targeted. His dispatches had, however, reflected the increasing use of 'terrorism' to describe Islamist militancy on the BBC's domestic output. One of his last reports noted that 'anti-Western fanatics' and 'terrorists' remained at large in Saudi Arabia.

In the past, I have made contact with militant groups and been trusted that I would report their version of events fairly and not convey my findings to Western intelligence agencies. Can that now be done with al-Qa'eda? If I were offered the chance, I would be happy to meet al-Qa'eda's leaders. But on my return, would I be arrested and expected to reveal what I saw to Western authorities? Would I be expected to describe the men as 'terrorists'? In Britain, anti-terrorist legislation obliges a reporter to inform the government about 'terrorist activity' anywhere in the world. Such policies are restricting the journalist's role as an impartial observer. The world will become a more dangerous and less understood place if journalism takes sides in the 'war on terror'. Young foreign correspondents who wish to understand the causes of the world's conflicts will no longer have the opportunity of dining with terrorists.

Glossary

Transliteration – Names and unfamiliar words from Arabic and other scripts have been transliterated into the Latin alphabet using spellings as they were given to me in different countries. For example, I was given the name of a Hizbollah commander as Shaykh Muhammad; I maintained faithful to the way it was written in my notebook, though another cleric with the same Arabic name could spell it as Sheihk Mohammed.

AIS – the Armée Islamique du Salut or Islamic Salvation Army, the military wing of Algeria's banned religious party, the Islamic Salvation Front (FIS).

ANC – African National Congress.

ansar-e Hizbollah – Companions of the Party of God, a movement of Islamic vigilantes in Iran used by the clerical leadership to intimidate opponents.

al-Aqsa Martyrs' Brigades – a secretive and avowedly militant movement that has used suicide bombers. Formed in 2000 from within the broader Fatah faction of the PLO.

ashna – 'beloved one' in Pashto. It usually describes young male lovers taken on by wealthier, older men in Afghanistan.

AUC – Autodefensas Unidas de Colombia (United Self-Defence Forces of Colombia), an alliance of paramilitary groups formed in 1997 under the leadership of Carlos Castaño.

Aum Shinrikyo – Japanese religious sect whose name means 'Supreme Truth'; it hoped to hasten Armageddon by releasing Sarin nerve gas on the Tokyo underground in 1995.

ayatollah – literally the 'sign of God' but used as a title of senior clerics within Shi'a Islam.

azad Kashmir – free Kashmir. Used by pro-Pakistani groups to describe the sector of Kashmir under Pakistan's control.

banlieue – French for 'suburb'; now usually used in France to refer to areas with large immigrant populations.

batzoki – Basque social and political club.

Bassij – a volunteer militia in Iran that enforces Islamic law. The *bassijis* are loyal to religious leaders rather than the president or parliament.

Batasuna – roughly translated as 'Unity', the name of the outlawed Basque separatist party that is considered the political wing of ETA.

beurs – French slang: the children of immigrants from North Africa.

bid'ah – Arabic for 'innovation'. It applies to religious judgements not sourced in the Qur'ān or Sunnah and can be considered either an attempt to 'modernize' the faith or a deviation from Islamic tradition.

BIN – the Bahasa Indonesian acronym for Badan Intelijen Nasional, the country's intelligence agency.

Black Panther Party – a radical leftist group that emerged from the black-power movement in the US in the 1960s. It advocated armed confrontation with the police but was seen as a communist threat rather than a terrorist group.

burka – a head-to-toe shawl that covers a woman's body as well as her face, allowing vision only through a mesh screen.

burnous – an Arab robe, now worn mostly in Morocco and Tunisia, similar to the djellaba/gallabiyeh but traditionally white and including a hood.

caliph – for Sunnis, the ruler appointed to lead the worldwide Islamic community.

campesinos – the peasant farmers of South and Central America who, like the industrial proletariat in Europe, were considered the cornerstone of leftist revolutions in the region.

chador – a traditional Iranian robe that covers a woman from head to toe but not her face and conceals the contours of her body.

Contras – counter-revolutionaries trained and supported by the United States from bases in Honduras to destabilize the leftist Sandinista regime in neighbouring Nicaragua.

Council of Guardians – a body of twelve clerics and jurists in Iran with the authority to veto candidates or legislation that it considers un-Islamic. It is dominated by religious hardliners.

CRPF – Central Reserve Police Force; a paramilitary force responsible for maintaining internal security, often against secessionist movements.

da'wah – a 'call to Islam'. Missionary work that encourages Muslims to be more pious.

Deobandism – an austere Salafist tradition that developed from a school in Deoband, near Delhi, and influenced radical Muslims in South Asia.

departamento – administrative unit in Colombia.

djellaba or **gallabiyeh** – the traditional floor-length Arab robe.

DRS – Direction des Renseignements de Securité. The Office of Research and Security, also known as Sécurité Militaire, the popular name for Algeria's military secret service. The intelligence agency was accused of manipulating the GIA and being responsible for mass killings.

l'egorgement – slitting the throat. A method of murder favoured by Islamist groups in Algeria. It is intended to humiliate because the victim bleeds like an animal slaughtered for halal meat.

ELN – Ejercito de Liberación Nacional (National Liberation Army), the smaller of Colombia's two leftist guerrilla groups, with around three thousand fighters.

emir – 'leader' or 'commander'. Often used for the head of an Islamist militant group.

éradicateurs – members of the Algerian secret police and military that refused to negotiate with the FIS and were accused of orchestrating extrajudicial killings.

ETA – the Basque-language acronym for Euzkadi ta Azkatasuna, or Basque Homeland and Freedom.

FAF – Fraternité Algérienne en France (Algerian Brotherhood in France), a front organization based in Paris for the outlawed Algerian Islamist party, the Islamic Salvation Front.

FARC – Fuerzas Armadas Revolucionarias de Colombia (Revolutionary Armed Forces of Colombia), the nation's largest guerrilla group, with an estimated eighteen thousand soldiers.

Farclandia – a Marxist mini-state, twice the size of Wales, controlled by the FARC. It was established with the agreement of the Colombian government in 1999 in order to bring the guerrillas into negotiations. Government troops retook its capital and ended the agreement in 2002.

Fatah – the largest faction within the PLO under the control of Yasser Arafat. Fatah also controls the Palestinian National Authority.

fatwa – a formal religious edict made by an Islamic cleric.

FIS – Front Islamique du Salut (Islamic Salvation Front), the Islamist political party that was posed to win elections in Algeria in 1992. The military took over instead.

FLN – Front de Libération Nationale (National Liberation Front), the anti-colonialist movement in Algeria that fought the French from 1954 to 1962.

Front National – France's right-wing, anti-immigration party.

GIA – Groupe Islamique Armé (Armed Islamic Group), a radical Algerian guerrilla movement that was infiltrated by the security services.

Gama'a Islamiyah – Islamic Association. It formed as a loose-knit group of students in the 1970s but in the 1990s became a militant organization with its strongholds in Upper Egypt.

GSPC – the French acronym for the Salafist Group for Preaching and Combat, a tiny militant force that emerged in Algeria as the main Islamist opposition disbanded.

gudariak – a Basque word used to describe soldiers who defended their homeland from invaders during past centuries and now used by sympathizers for gunmen in ETA. The Spanish government calls them terrorists.

gusle – in Serbia, a single-stringed lute that sounds discordant to outsiders.

hadiths – a collection of the sayings attributed to the prophet, used by religious scholars to expand on aspects of Islamic law revealed in the Qur'ān.

Haika – 'Rise up'. Pro-independence Basque youth movement often involved in street confrontations with police.

halal – a Qur'ānic term which means allowed or lawful. Usually applied to halal foods, which are permitted for consumption by Allah. Halal meat requires the blood drained from the dying animal.

Hamas – Harakat al-Muqawama al-Islamiya (Islamic Resistance Movement). It is also an Arabic word meaning zeal or bravery. Formed in late 1987 in Gaza as an outgrowth of the Palestinian branch of the Muslim Brotherhood.

haram – a Qur'ānic term which means prohibited or unlawful.

al-Haram ash Shareef – the Noble Sanctuary, the Arabic name for the site of the Dome of the Rock and al-Aqsa Mosque in Jerusalem. Jews refer to it as the Temple Mount.

hijab, hejab or **hedjab** – a general term for modest Islamic dress for women but often used to refer to a scarf or head covering rather than the more severe chador or niqab (or nikab).

Hizbollah – the Party of God. Refers to a Lebanese Shi'ite movement formed with the help of Iranian Revolutionary Guards in 1982.

al-Ikhwan al-Muslimun – the Muslim Brotherhood.

Imam – meaning 'leader', in Shi'ism it refers to the twelve men who succeeded the prophet along the lineage of Ali, the first Imam. Ayatollah Khomeini was known as Imam because of his respected position but he was not formally considered one.

Inshallah – 'God willing'. Used regularly by Muslims in South Asia at the end of sentences.

intégriste – a term used in Europe in the past to describe Roman Catholics who believed that their faith should be the state religion. Now applied in French-speaking countries to Muslims who want to install governments that rule according to Islamic law.

intifada – uprising.

IRA – Irish Republican Army.

Irgun Zvai Le'umi – National Military Organization, the Jewish militant movement that declared a revolt against British rule in Palestine in 1944.

Islamic Jihad – a name used by a Palestinian militant movement that modelled itself on Hizbollah. The name was also used for a shadowy group under the auspices of Hizbollah, which was suspected of involvement in the kidnapping of Western hostages in Lebanon.

Islamist – a person who believes that Islam should guide political and social life.

jahiliyyah – a period of ignorance and barbarity prior to the rise of Islam, now used by Muslim radicals to refer to un-Islamic society.

Jamaat-i-Islami – the largest of Pakistan's religious parties. It was founded in 1941 by the writer Maulana Maududi to promote Islamic values in British India.

Jemaah Islamiah – the Islamic Association. A loose and secretive association of Islamic radicals in South-East Asia which allegedly had links to al-Qa'eda.

jihad – the striving to follow Islam, which could involve personal improvement or armed struggle in a holy war.

Jihad – a militant group responsible for the murder of Egyptian President Anwar Sadat. Advocated operating as small, secretive cells. It was later led by bin Laden's deputy, Ayman Zawahri.

jizya – a tax that early Islamic rulers demanded from Jews and Christians.

JKLF – Jammu and Kashmir Liberation Front, a movement campaigning for the independence of Kashmir. It began a violent insurgency in Indian-controlled Kashmir in 1988 but in the following years divided into factions and became overshadowed by overtly Islamist fighters.

JVP – Janatha Vimukthi Pereamuna (People's Liberation Front), a Marxist as well as nationalist movement that claimed to defend the rights of Sri Lanka's Singhala majority.

kafir – unbeliever.

kampong – a village or hamlet in Malaysia or Indonesia.

Khmer Rouge – also Red Khmers, the term used by outsiders to describe the Communist Party of Kampuchea, which governed Cambodia from 1975 to 1979.

khimar – an Islamic headscarf pinned around the chin to cover the neck and temples but not the remainder of the face.

kippah – the small skullcap worn by Jews during prayer and attached to the head by clips. Many Jews wear it at all times as a statement of being Jewish.

KLA – Kosovo Liberation Army.

kolas – a flat, circular woollen cap that became the trademark of the mujahedin during their war with the Soviet Union.

kopiah – a rimless cap similar to a fez, worn by Muslims in South-East Asia.

kos – often translated from Serbian as blackbird but actually a type of brown-speckled thrush.

Kosovar – the name given to Albanians who lived in the Serb province called 'Kosovo and Metohija'.

kuffiyeh – an Arabic headscarf.

laicité – the French word for secularism. It has political significance following a 1905 law, which guarantees the separation of Church and state in France.

maharaja – the princely governor or ruler of a state in British India.

Maktab al-Khadimat – the 'Office of Services' for mujahedin from around the world arriving in Peshawar in the 1980s to fight in Afghanistan. It was run by Sheik Abdullah Azzam, a Palestinian religious scholar.

maquis – to take to the *maquis* means to go underground in Francophone countries.

maulvi – a learned man or specialist in Islamic law.

Mau Mau – the Kenyan independence movement that launched an uprising against British colonial rule from 1952 to 1959.

mostaz'afan – the oppressed or disinherited. The Iranian Revolution was made in its name, though the poor have not benefited noticeably in the years following.

muezzin – the mosque official who calls the faithful to pray five times a day. Traditionally, the call to prayer was made from a minaret.

MUF – Muslim United Front, an alliance of Islamic and secessionist parties in Indian-controlled Kashmir that was prevented from winning state elections in 1987.

muhabarat – general name used for the secret police in some Arab countries.

mujahedin – soldier of God.

mullah – a general word for a cleric used in Iran and parts of South Asia.

muttawas – the religious police in Saudi Arabia, from the government's Committee for the Promotion of Virtue and Prevention of Vice.

niqab or **nikab** – a robe, usually black, worn by women that covers the head, face and body with a slit for the eyes.

Northern Alliance – the Tajik-dominated opposition group in Afghanistan that fought the Taliban and after September 11th became an ally of the United States in its 'war on terror'.

Pashtunwali – traditional civil code providing a set of obligations regulating honour, hospitality and revenge for Pashtuns in Pakistan and Afghanistan. It draws from Islam but its interpretation of Islamic law arises from centuries of tribal customs.

Pasdarans – the Iranian Revolutionary Guards.

Patriotic Front (Rhodesia) – a movement that fought a guerrilla war against the white minority government. Its members were often described as terrorists in the Western media. The leader of one of its factions, Robert Mugabe, was elected president in 1980.

pattu – the woollen cloak worn over salwar kameez by Afghans. It is used as a blanket, and protects from the sun and dust.

pesantren – an Islamic boarding school in Indonesia.

PFLP-GC – Popular Front for the Liberation of Palestine–General Command. A movement, now mostly inactive, led by Ahmed Jebril and supported by Syria. Jebril was at one time suspected of involvement in the Lockerbie bombing.

pieds-noirs – the name given to French settlers in Algeria, possibly because they wore black leather shoes.

PKK – the Kurdish acronym for the Kurdistan Workers' Party, a militant group fighting for the creation of an independent Kurdish state in southern Turkey and northern Iraq.

PLO – Palestine Liberation Organization.

polje – Serbian word for 'plain', which forms the geographical centre of Kosovo.

pouvoir – French word for 'power'; Algerians use the term 'le Pouvoir' to describe shadowy groups that exercise real power from behind the scenes.

al-Qa'eda – the base, or alternatively the guide or method.

qeleshe – a white conical hat, usually made of wool, now only worn by elderly Albanian men.

RAFD – Rassemblement Algérien des Femmes Démocrates (Assembly of Democratic Women of Algeria). A women's group with links to military leaders that was implacably opposed to a religious government in Algeria.

rakija – a clear, very strong fruit brandy drunk in Serbia.

Red Army Faction – the most active left-wing militant group in Europe in the 1970s, based in West Germany.

Salafist – a follower of the pious ancestors (*salaf*), the first three generations of Muslims. Their faith is considered pure and unblemished because of their proximity to the prophet.

sarong – cloth wrapped around like a skirt and worn by men in southern India and Sri Lanka.

SAVAK – the Shah of Iran's secret police.

salwar kameez – pyjama-like long shirt and baggy trousers worn in South Asia.

sant – a Sikh holy man. Literally, 'one who knows the truth'.

shaheed – a martyr, or a witness to true Islam.

shallvare – traditional baggy trousers worn by Albanian women.

sharia – literally meaning 'path', it refers to Islamic law derived from the Qur'ān.

Shi'ites – those Muslims who believe that Mohammed designated Ali and his descendants as the rightful leaders of the Muslim community.

Sinn Fein – 'We ourselves', the political arm of the IRA (despite its denials).

SSI – General Directorate of State Security Investigations, Egypt's internal intelligence agency.

Stern Gang – Avraham Stern formed his Fighters for the Freedom of Israel movement during the Second World War. Yitzhak Shamir was the group's operations commander.

Sunna – the recorded traditions and practices of the prophet. The Sunna is the second source of Islamic jurisprudence, the first being the Qur'ān.

Sunnis – the majority branch of Islam, who believe the Caliphs were the true heirs of Prophet Mohammed.

takfir – the proclamation by a Muslim that a fellow believer is an infidel.

Tamil Tigers – officially known as as the LTTE, or Liberation Tigers of Tamil Eelam, a group demanding an independent Tamil state in the north and east of Sri Lanka.

UCK – Albanian acronym for National Liberation Army, known in English as the Kosovo Liberation Army or KLA.

ulema – literally 'those with knowledge'. It applies to the body of religious scholars.

ummah – the worldwide community of Muslims.

Wahhabi – a follower of a movement founded by Abd al-Wahhab, a puritanical religious reformer in the Arabian Peninsula two hundred years ago. The movement adheres to a strict interpretation of the Qur'ān and is followed by Osama bin Laden.

World Islamic Front – the name used in 1998 by the group in Afghanistan that became known in the West as al-Qa'eda.

zakat – charity; an Islamic tax levied on the wealthy and distributed to the poor through mosques.

Further Reading

One of the best overall compendiums on terrorism is the tightly written *Inside Terrorism* by Bruce Hoffman (Columbia University Press). A thorough chronicle of the history and workings of al-Qa'eda can be found in *The Base* by Jane Corbin (Pocket Books). The source and development of Islamic militancy is described with great authority in *Jihad* by Gilles Keppel (Harvard University Press) and *The Age of Sacred Terror* by Daniel Benjamin and Steven Simon (Random House). John Esposito's *Unholy War* (Oxford University Press) is a readable and informed guide to political Islam. Samuel Huntington's *The Clash of Civilizations* (Simon & Schuster) is a seminal and thought-provoking work. *Rogue State* by William Blum (Zed Books) and *The Great Terror War* by Richard Falk (Arris Books) are admirable critiques of American foreign policy. One of the best history books on any subject is Alistair Horne's *A Savage War of Peace* (Macmillan) on the Algerian civil war. *The Battlefield, Algeria 1988–2002* (Verso) by Hugh Roberts is a highly informed collection of essays on the more recent conflict. *Reaping the Whirlwind* (Pluto Press) by Michael Griffin reveals the author's thorough understanding of Afghanistan, as does *Taliban* by Peter Marsden (Zed Books). Robin Kirk's *More Terrible than Death* (Perseus Books) is a chilling account of the plight of Colombia. *The Question of Palestine* by Edward Said (Vintage Books) is a scholarly and impassioned study of the Arab–Israeli conflict. *The Serbs* by Tim Judah (Yale University Press) provides an insightful analysis into their role in the break-up of Yugoslavia. David Chandler's writings on Cambodia, especially *Brother Number One* (Westview Press) and *Voices from S-21* (Silkworm Books), are superb studies of institutional political violence. *The Basques* by Luis Nuñez Astrain (Welsh Academic Press) is a lean account of ETA's struggle for independence. *Basque Violence* by Joseba Zulaika (University of Nevada Press) is a fascinating examination of a culture that breeds political violence.

A thorough and readable, up-to-date history of the IRA is provided in *Armed Struggle* by Richard English (Macmillan). *Lebanon, Fire and Embers* (Weidenfeld and Nicolson) by Dilip Hiro offers a clear, year-by-year explanation of the Lebanese civil war. *Iran after the Revolution* (I.B. Taurus), edited by Saeed Rahnema and Sohrab Behdad, is an excellent set of essays on the contradictions within the Islamic state. The thorny issues surrounding Kashmir are explored with clarity in *India, Pakistan and the Kashmir Dispute* by Robert Wirsing (Macmillan). *No God but God* by Geneive Abdo (Oxford University Press) is a first-hand study of the Muslim Brotherhood in Egypt. The tentacles of al-Qa'eda in South-east Asia are documented in *Seeds of Terror* by Maria Ressa (The Free Press). Jason Burke's *Al Qa'eda: Casting a Shadow of Terror* (I.B. Taurus) is the most perceptive book on the real significance of the movement. Unlike many others, it is not primarily sourced from information provided by government security agencies but is a true piece of authoritative journalism.

Index